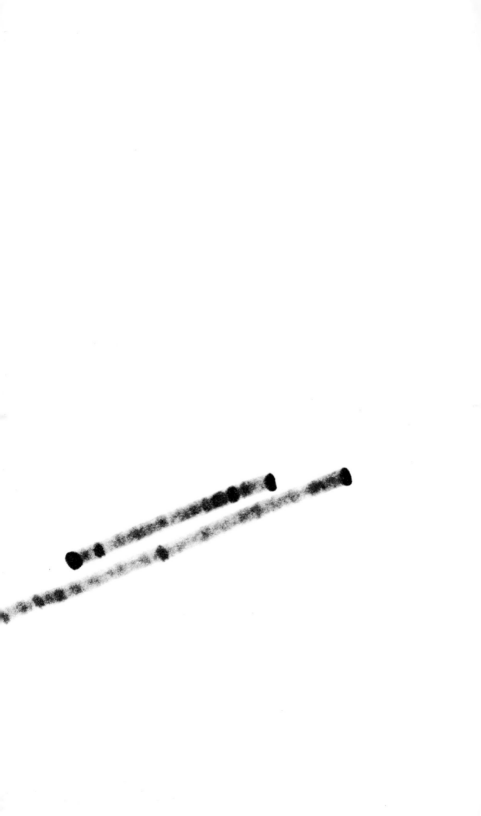

The Comintern

Also by Kevin McDermott

THE CZECH RED UNIONS, 1918–1929

THE COMINTERN

A History of International Communism
from Lenin to Stalin

Kevin McDermott and Jeremy Agnew

St. Martin's Press
New York

THE COMINTERN

St. Martin's Press, Scholarly and Reference Division,
175 Fifth Avenue, New York, N.Y. 10010

First published in the United States of America in 1997

Printed in Hong Kong

ISBN 0–312–16277–4

Library of Congress Cataloging-in-Publication Data
McDermott, Kevin.
The Comintern : a history of international communism from Lenin to
Stalin / Kevin McDermott and Jeremy Agnew.
p.   cm.
Includes bibliographical references (p.   ) and index.
ISBN 0 312–16277–4 (cloth)
1. Communist International—History.   2. World
politics—1900–1945.   I. Agnew, Jeremy, 1950–   .   II. Title.
HX11.I5M38   1997
324.1'75—dc20   96–19746
                                                          CIP

To our parents

Lucy Agnew, 1923–94
William Agnew, 1921–91

and

Vera McDermott, 1923–83
Walter Henry McDermott, 1915–91

Contents

List of Documents

Acknowledgements

We accumulated many debts during the five years this book was in the making. We are most grateful to Dr Michael Weiner, Director of the East Asia Research Centre, University of Sheffield, for contributing Chapter 5 on 'Comintern in East Asia, 1919–39'. Very special thanks go to Monty Johnstone, whose unwavering enthusiasm and trenchant criticisms of the manuscript were invaluable. He also kindly provided much vital source material. Dr Aleksandr Vatlin of the Institute for Human Rights and Democracy, Moscow, gave us the benefit of his impeccable knowledge of the Comintern and its massive archive. Professor Gregor Benton of the University of Leeds reviewed the chapter on East Asia. Professor Aldo Agosti of Turin University, Professor Serge Wolikow of the University of Bourgogne, Dr Brigitte Studer of Lausanne University, Dr Peter Huber, Dr Silvio Pons, Dr Kimmo Rentola and Dr Tauno Saarela generously supplied us with copies of their own work on the international communist movement. This book would have been the poorer without the inspiration, comments and advice of these experts. Needless to say, any mistakes and shortcomings remain our own.

Kevin McDermott would like to thank: the School of Cultural Studies at Sheffield Hallam University and the British Academy for funding research trips to the Comintern Archive in August–September 1991 and April 1992 respectively; the archivists at the Russian Centre for the Preservation and Study of Contemporary Historical Documents, Moscow; the Inter-Library Loan staff of Psalter Lane Library, Sheffield Hallam University; George Matthews and Francis King, formerly of the Library and Archive of the Communist Party of Great Britain; and my colleagues David Mayall, Mike Cronin and

Ian Ramage. My deepest gratitude is to Susan Reid for her constant inspiration and intellectual support.

Jeremy Agnew would like to acknowledge some long-standing debts: to Alan MacDougall and Dr Barry Smart for their friendship and 'wise counsels'; to Harry and Ben — 'a sprig of fine white heather in their future lapels'; finally, to Daryl, 'summa cum gratia'.

We also wish to thank our editors at Macmillan, Simon Winder, Pauline Underwood and Vanessa Graham for their encouragement, patience and guidance.

An earlier version of the section 'Comintern and the Terror' appeared as 'Stalinist Terror in the Comintern: New Perspectives', *Journal of Contemporary History*, vol. 30, no. 1 (1995). The first two sections of chapter 3 were published, slightly amended, under the title 'Stalin and the Comintern during the "Third Period", 1928–33', *European History Quarterly*, vol. 25, no. 3 (1995). Parts of Chapter 4 were published in much condensed form as 'Stalin, the Comintern and European Communism, 1934–39', *Modern History Review*, vol. 7, no. 3 (1996). We thank the publishers for granting permission to reprint them here.

The authors and publishers also wish to thank the following for permission to use copyright material:

Cambridge University Press, for the extracts from J. Haslam 'The Comitern and the Origins of the Popular Front, 1934–1935', *Historical Journal*, 22 (1979);

Frank Cass & Co. Ltd, for the extracts from *The Communist International, 1919–1943*, vols I–III, and ed. J. Degras, copyright © Frank Cass Ltd 1971;

Lawrence & Wishart, for the extracts from G. Dimitrov, *The Working Class against Facism* (1935); and *About Turn: The British Communist Party and the Second World War*, ed. F. King and G. Matthews, (1990) pp. 69–70.

Every effort has been made to trace all the copyright holders, but if any have been inadvertently overlooked the publishers will be pleased to make the necessary arrangement at the first opportunity.

Sheffield   KEVIN MCDERMOTT
                                                                JEREMY AGNEW

List of Abbreviations

CCP	Chinese Communist Party
Cominform	Communist Information Bureau
Comintern	Communist (Third) International
CPGB	Communist Party of Great Britain
CPUSA	Communist Party of the United States of America
ECCI	Executive Committee of the Communist International
ICC	International Control Commission
IFTU	International Federation of Trade Unions ('Amsterdam')
ILP	Independent Labour Party
JCP	Japanese Communist Party
KAPD	German Communist Workers' Party
KCP	Korean Communist Party
KPD	German Communist Party
KPJ	Yugoslav Communist Party
KPP	Polish Communist Party
KSČ	Communist Party of Czechoslovakia
Narkomindel	People's Commissariat of Foreign Affairs
NEP	New Economic Policy
NKVD	People's Commissariat of Internal Affairs
NMM	National Minority Movement
NSDAP	National Socialist German Workers' Party (Nazi)
NUWM	National Unemployed Workers' Movement
OMS	Department of International Communication
PCE	Spanish Communist Party

PCF	French Communist Party
PCI	Italian Communist Party
Politburo	Political Bureau (of the Russian Communist Party)
POUM	Workers' Party of Marxist Unity (Spain)
Profintern	Red International of Labour Unions (RILU)
RCP (or CPSU)	Russian Communist Party (Bolsheviks)
RCPSCHD	Russian Centre for the Preservation and Study of Contemporary Historical Documents (former Central Party Archive)
RGO	Revolutionary Trade Union Opposition (Germany)
RILU	*see* Profintern
SFIO	French Socialist Party
SPD	German Social Democratic Party
USPD	German Independent Social Democratic Party
USSR	Union of Soviet Socialist Republics (Soviet Union)
f.	*fond* (collection)
op.	*opis* (inventory)
d.	*delo* (file)
l.	*list* (folio)

Dates of Comintern Congresses and ECCI Plena

WORLD CONGRESSES

First Congress, Moscow	2–6 March 1919
Second Congress, Petrograd and Moscow	19 July–7 August 1920
Third Congress, Moscow	22 June–12 July 1921
Fourth Congress, Petrograd and Moscow	5 November–5 December 1922
Fifth Congress, Moscow	17 June–8 July 1924
Sixth Congress, Moscow	17 July–1 September 1928
Seventh Congress, Moscow	25 July–21 August 1935

PLENA OF THE EXECUTIVE COMMITTEE OF THE COMMUNIST INTERNATIONAL

First Enlarged Plenum	24 February–4 March 1922
Second Enlarged Plenum	7–11 June 1922
Third Enlarged Plenum	12–23 June 1923
Fourth Enlarged Plenum	12–13 July 1924
Fifth Enlarged Plenum	21 March–6 April 1925
Sixth Enlarged Plenum	17 February–15 March 1926

Seventh Enlarged Plenum	22 November–16 December 1926
Eighth Plenum	18–30 May 1927
Ninth Plenum	9–25 February 1928
Tenth Plenum	3–19 July 1929
Eleventh Plenum	26 March–11 April 1931
Twelfth Plenum	27 August–15 September 1932
Thirteenth Plenum	28 November–12 December 1933

Introduction

In the opinion of almost all observers the collapse of communism in Eastern Europe and the USSR in the late 1980s and early 1990s consigned the Marxist–Leninist ideology to the dustbin of history. If that be the case, the question inevitably arises why we should wish to write a book on the Comintern, an organisation that was explicitly dedicated to the propagation of that self-same failed ideology. There are three very good answers. First, the Comintern was a significant force in inter-war world politics, able to command the loyalty of millions of militants and sympathisers who, rightly or wrongly, regarded the Soviet Union as the beacon of humanity. The growth of international communism alarmed capitalist governments from London to Washington to Tokyo. It may seem strange to readers in the 1990s, but the 'spectre of communism' appeared to be stalking the globe in the 1920s and 1930s.

Secondly, the advent of *glasnost* in the Gorbachev era and the opening of the former Soviet Central Party Archive in Moscow have greatly enlarged the historiographical and documentary base for the study of the Comintern. In the mid-1960s two eminent scholars bemoaned the fact that the bulk of Comintern source material remained secret, submerged like an 'iceberg'.[1] Recently, sizeable chunks of that iceberg have begun to melt and as a result we now know far more about the inner workings of the Comintern than we did even five or six years ago. There is, of course, still much to be done. Reconstructing the history of the Comintern is notoriously difficult, but academics from all over Europe and beyond are avidly engaged in archival research in Russia and in East–West collaborative projects. Already their labours are beginning to bear fruit.[2] In short, it is an exciting time to investigate one of the most controversial aspects of Soviet and world history.

Finally, no readily available one-volume history of the Comintern exists in the English language. Our aim has been to write a general, accessible and up-to-date text, one that attempts to analyse the findings of both Russian and Western experts while simultaneously incorporating elements of original research. The book thus adopts an overtly historiographical approach, introducing students to the main issues in, and interpretations of, Comintern history. These issues are further illuminated by a concise documentary section which draws on old and new sources.[3] The work is directed primarily at an undergraduate audience, but we hope that specialists will find our arguments interesting and challenging.

The Comintern, or Communist International, is also known as the Third International because in many respects it was the direct descendant of the First and Second Internationals. The First was established in 1864 by Karl Marx and a motley amalgam of French and British labour leaders as an agency to coordinate the proletariat in its historic worldwide struggle against capitalism. For Marx and Engels, capital's insatiable hunger for ever-expanding markets broke down national barriers, undermining the bases of nationalism. In this process, modern industrial labour, 'the same in England as in France, in America as in Germany, has stripped him [the worker] of every trace of national character. . . . The working men have no country.'[4] Horizontal *class* allegiance was gradually superseding vertical *national* divisions. In the Marxist schema, international capitalism and the bourgeois state would inevitably be overthrown by national working-class detachments acting under the auspices of the International in the common interests of the exploited proletariat. The effective collapse of the First International in 1872, victim of an acrimonious split between the Marxists and the anarchist Bakuninists, did not prevent the concept of 'proletarian internationalism' from becoming a mainstay of the revolutionary working-class movement: 'workers of the world, unite!' Nevertheless, the tension between national sentiment and internationalist aspiration was never resolved in socialist theory or practice and was to haunt all three Internationals.[5]

The Second International was created in 1889 and, like its predecessor, was from its inception a fractious coalition of reformist and revolutionary tendencies. The principal parties in the International were the German Social Democrats (SPD) and the French Socialists (SFIO). The founders adopted a decentralised organisational structure with no binding disciplinary procedures or programmatic and tactical mandates. This made the International little more than a loose federation of autonomous parties with strictly limited scope for unified action. Ideological schisms also sapped its vitality. The European socialist movement in the period before 1914 comprised 'left', 'right' and 'centrist' factions divided in their attitudes to bourgeois democracy, the national question, the general strike and, most importantly, war. Internally weakened, the Second International foundered in August 1914 on the rock of national chauvinism. In Lenin's eyes, the vote in favour of war credits by German, French and British labour leaders signified a 'sheer betrayal of socialism' and the 'ideological and political bankruptcy of the International'. Already by the autumn of 1914 he had announced as his battlecry: 'The Second International is dead . . . . long live the Third International.'[6] During the war, the minority intransigent revolutionaries gradually coalesced around the Russian Bolsheviks, forming the so-called Zimmerwald Left. Lenin's demand to turn the international war into a revolutionary civil war and his implacable hostility to parliamentary democracy gave rise to fierce debates with the majority socialists.

The October Revolution of 1917 represented for Lenin the first act of a global drama. The Russian working class had fulfilled its historical obligation and European workers would surely follow. However, for the goal of world revolution to become a reality a new International, purged of reformist 'traitors', was deemed an absolute necessity. Accordingly, in March 1919 the Communist International was founded at a congress of revolutionaries in Moscow. Its mission was no less than to build a 'world party' of communists dedicated to the armed overthrow of capitalist private property and its replacement by a system of collective ownership and production. At the time this did not seem utopian. 'Total War' between 1914 and 1918 had, it was believed, irredeemably undermined the nineteenth-century old order. In the opinion of many, and not just on the left, it was doomed. The 'Age of Catastrophe' had begun and the alternative appeared to be socialism.[7] Yet, with the sole exception of Mongolia, the Comintern's mission remained unfulfilled during its lifetime, 1919–43. Rather than becoming a fomentor and organiser of world socialist revolution, the International turned into a compliant instrument of the Soviet state. The core of this book is devoted to unravelling the whole complex of factors behind this unintended outcome.

What are the major issues and controversies in Comintern history? There is no overall consensus on this question, but we can isolate several recurrent themes that have attracted scholars for many decades. First, continuities and discontinuities between the Leninist and Stalinist regimes in the Comintern: was the latter the logical outcome of the former? Secondly, relations between the central Comintern authorities in Moscow and the national communist parties: was the highly centralist Bolshevik model universalised or did the parties retain a measure of autonomy? Thirdly, the relationship between the Comintern and official Soviet foreign policy: was the International merely an instrument of the Soviet state? And, finally, the crucial issue of the attitudes adopted by communists towards the social democrats: how to win over a majority of the organised working class for revolutionary perspectives in an essentially non-revolutionary era? These four themes constitute the basic framework of this text.

However, each broad theme conceals a multitude of more detailed and problematic questions. At what level of analysis should a general history of power relations in the Comintern be focused? There were at least three hierarchical layers of influence in the international communist movement: the Soviet leadership's 'control' over the Comintern's Executive Committee (ECCI) in Moscow; the ECCI's 'control' over the national party leaderships; and the latter's 'control' over the party rank and file. Was this a one-way relationship with all the orders emanating from the central authorities, as most historians have assumed, or was there scope for interaction between the various proactive and reactive elements? A related moot point is whether communist parties faithfully carried out the directives coming from Moscow. As Alexander Dallin wrote over twenty years ago in connection with Soviet internal affairs: 'in general, the concern among Western scholars with decision-making may well have contributed to a neglect of the extent to which a policy can be subverted in the process of its implementation'.[8] To what degree can this dictum be applied to the Comintern? How far were central directives reinterpreted, adapted or subverted to suit local conditions? This line of inquiry necessarily forces us to reconsider the exact nature of the

Comintern. Should it be narrowly defined as the 'headquarters of the world revolution' situated in some shabby offices in Moscow and hence subject to close scrutiny by the Bolsheviks? Or should it be regarded more broadly as an international body operating on a worldwide scale and thus open to all manner of influences outside the direct control of the Russians?

In this unresolved debate between what can be termed history 'from above' and 'from below', we incline to the former. Not only because our focus is on the 'centre' – we are, after all, writing a history of the headquarters of the revolution, not of individual communist parties in all their diversity and complexity – but also because the Comintern and foreign communists *did* succumb to the dictates of the Stalinists, and *did* loyally trumpet the glories of the USSR. Any history of the Comintern cannot but fail to take this fully into account. However, an essential component of our methodology is a recognition that the inter-war communist experience should not be reduced to the crude equation 'communist party = Comintern = agent of Moscow'. Hence, we attempt to integrate into our narrative recent research which places communist activity firmly in its national, as well as international, context and which analyses the *interaction* between centre and periphery.

The periodisation of the Comintern is problematic and still the subject of much debate. The most common model posits five broad, often overlapping, phases:

(i) **1919–23:** a period of abortive revolutionary upheavals, the formation and organisational consolidation of communist parties and the continued isolation of Soviet Russia;

(ii) **1924–8:** years of 'relative capitalist stabilisation', united front tactics and the beginning of the 'Bolshevisation' of the Comintern as Soviet inner-party struggles enter the international field;

(iii) **1928–33:** the so-called 'Third Period' of capitalist crisis, working-class radicalisation, 'ultra-leftist' attacks on social democracy and emergent 'Stalinisation';

(iv) **1934–9**: the Popular Front era of cross-class anti-fascist alliances and limited defence of bourgeois democracy, juxtaposed with the demands of Soviet diplomacy and the onslaught of the Stalinist Terror;

(v) **1939–43:** the ultimate degeneration of the Comintern into an instrument of Soviet foreign policy, epitomised by the Nazi–

Soviet Pact and Stalin's dissolution of the International in May–June 1943.

This periodisation is convenient, but inevitably simplistic in that it ignores variants within each phase. By emphasising Soviet and international factors, it tends to neglect the indigenous conditions which may have influenced the changing tactics of the communist parties. One of our main tasks is to chart and explain the legendary zigzags from 'left' to 'right' in Comintern strategies and tactics. It is our contention that the prime motivation for change came from Moscow, but that national parties, particularly in the 1920s, enjoyed a degree of latitude to adapt the 'line' to suit local conditions. Put simply, strategy was defined in Moscow, but tactics, to a certain extent, could be elaborated on the ground by the parties themselves. This relative autonomy of non-Soviet communists was drastically, though not totally, emasculated in the Stalinist period when rigid ideological conformity, theoretical ossification and bureaucratic centralism became the hallmarks of the international communist movement.

The historiography of the Comintern is diverse and of varying standard. A Dutch expert has recently discerned four main genres: the 'dissident communist' critique; the 'anti-communist' interpretation dominant during the early Cold War; the 'official' communist literature; and the more 'scientific' scholarly studies undertaken since the 1960s.[9] Authors in the first three categories usually had overt political axes to grind, either of an anti- or pro-communist nature, which tended to lessen the value of much of their work. Nevertheless, many of these studies offer important insights into the activities of the International and its constituent national communist parties (known in Comintern parlance as 'sections'). The early account by the German ex-communist Franz Borkenau has survived the test of time and remains a useful volume for students of the Comintern.[10] The Trotskyist critique of the Stalinised International as a bureaucratic caricature of the fundamentally healthy and democratic Leninist Comintern is best conveyed in the work of Lev Davidovich himself,[11] although Isaac Deutscher's thoughts on the Comintern are still well worth consulting.[12] The most recent survey from this perspective is Duncan Hallas's text, a disappointing offering which at times descends into an unsubtle rehearsal of vulgar Trotskyist schemas.[13]

The two most authoritative Western Comintern scholars are arguably E. H. Carr, the renowned British historian, and Fernando Claudin, a former Spanish communist and 'dissident' Marxist. Regrettably, Carr never composed a one-volume history of the Comintern, but this organisation figured prominently in his multi-tome *History of Soviet Russia* (1950–78) and towards the end of his life he penned two specialist books devoted entirely to the subject.[14] Carr's work is daunting, combining massive empirical breadth and detail with precise analytical passages. In the enforced absence of archival material, Carr tended to rely on official Soviet and Comintern sources, which on occasion dented his otherwise scrupulous scholarship. Another criticism of his work is his almost complete reliance on 'history from above'. There is precious little mention of the activity of rank-and-file communists struggling to implement the Moscow 'line'. But in our opinion one of the most positive characteristics of Carr's approach was his unwillingness to submit to the 'totalitarian paradigm' of the Soviet system that was dominant in Western academic circles in the 1950s and beyond. As we shall see in chapters 3 and 4, he challenges the notion that by the mid-1930s Stalin and the Soviet state had imposed a totally monolithic control over the international communist movement. Rather, he adopts a more nuanced understanding which allows for relatively autonomous action on the part of both Comintern leaders in Moscow and communist parties in their national contexts.

Claudin's interpretation is in the Marxist canon. It is forceful and suggestive. His principal argument is that the Bolshevik rulers of the Comintern failed to differentiate sufficiently between the autocratic political culture of Tsarist Russia and the more open parliamentary systems of Western Europe. As a result, the Comintern 'line' too often underestimated the assimilation of the European working class into the national body politic and exaggerated the revolutionary potential of that class. What was required was a strategic and organisational conception more attuned to Western conditions. In this, he is on solid ground. Claudin can be challenged, however, on his categorical insistence that the national sections were *totally* subordinated to the policy of Stalin and the Soviet state. Also, he appears to overestimate the scope for 'social explosions' at specific conjunctures, such as in France during the Popular Front era, while arguably minimising the political constraints on communist parties operating in highly complicated national and international settings. These criticisms notwithstanding, Claudin's work is sophisticated, thought-provoking and without doubt the best one-volume history of international communism in the English language.[15]

Soviet studies of the Comintern can be neatly, if somewhat artificially, divided in two by the year 1985. From the mid-1980s Gorbachev's policy of *glasnost* encouraged scholars to break out of the straitjacket of party orthodoxy which had stunted Soviet historiography since Stalin's time. During the so-called Brezhnevite 'era of stagnation' the official party interpretation of the Comintern had been encapsulated in the handbook *Outline History of the Communist International*, a large tome written under severe ideological controls. It is not a complete whitewash, but glaring omissions, particularly from the Stalinist period, seriously undermine its usefulness.[16] The academic pluralism of the Gorbachev era, combined with the opening of hitherto secret archives, fostered new approaches to the history of the Comintern and we have drawn freely on the work of Russian experts, such as Fridrikh Firsov and Aleksandr Vatlin.

At this point two considerations are in order. The first is the problem of communist terminology. Epithets such as 'left', 'right' and 'centre' connoting real positions on the broad spectrum of leftist politics were appropriated and misused by the various factions in the Soviet power struggles of the 1920s. They were often coupled with terms like 'deviationist', 'sectarian' or 'opportunist' to discredit political opponents who were accused of wavering from the 'party line'. The Stalinists were particularly adept at this name-calling, taking it to absurd lengths during the show trials of the mid-1930s. In the process, the labels 'left' and 'right' tended to lose their meaning. For instance, the designation 'right-wing opportunist' appeared in 1928–9, but in reality there were no anti-party 'rightist' factions in the Comintern at that time. They were artificially constructed by the Stalinists in their campaign against Bukharin and his supporters. Moreover, it was not unheard of for a communist to be vilified as a 'rightist' one year and a 'leftist' the next, as in the case of Trotsky. The second consideration is the need strictly to historicise key moments in the Comintern's evolution. This approach should avoid the pitfalls of a crude teleological rendition of Comintern history, which posits an inevitable straight line progression from 'Leninist authoritarianism' to 'Stalinist totalitarianism'. Links there most certainly were, but we do not believe the Stalinist degeneration of the Comintern was somehow preordained. Only by a close contextual examination of events in all their historical complexity can the student adequately account for this outcome.

But perhaps the greatest difficulty confronting any historian of the Communist International is the daunting one of selectivity. The Comintern was a world organisation operating in all six continents for almost a quarter of a century. A definitive account of the international communist movement would need not only to examine the structures and multifarious activities of the central Comintern bodies and communist parties, but also be sensitive to such pivotal factors as Soviet domestic and foreign policy, the fluctuating state of the inter-war capitalist economy, the diplomatic manoeuvrings of the Great Powers, and the various socio-political national contexts in which communist parties worked. Where appropriate, we have attempted to pay due regard to these phenomena. We have consciously assumed a Eurocentric approach, which we feel is justified in that the Comintern devoted most of its attention to the European continent as the base of the future socialist revolution. In the years 1917–23 Germany was seen as the key not only to the European revolution, but to the fate of Soviet Russia. However, Asia, and in particular China, was a major preoccupation of the Bolshevik guardians of the Comintern. Therefore, Chapter 5 entitled 'Comintern in East Asia, 1919–39', written by Michael Weiner, explores the intricacies of the national and colonial questions.

We acknowledge that many important areas are covered only in outline or neglected altogether: communist attitudes towards the peasantry in Eastern Europe and Latin America, and towards militarism, anarchism and anarcho-syndicalism; cultural policy; the role of women in the Comintern; the 'Negro question'; and the 'front organisations', such as the Red International of Labour Unions (RILU or Profintern) and the Communist Youth International (KIM). It is to be hoped that this slim volume will at least lay the foundations for more detailed research on these significant issues. In the end, the reader must decide whether, given the space constraints, we have been judicious in our selection and interpretation of themes and material.

1. Comintern in the Era of Lenin, 1919–23

For the fifty-one men and women who gathered in Moscow in March 1919 to found the Communist International, world proletarian revolution was no utopian day-dream. Capitalism, if not certified dead and buried, was in its final death throes. Lenin and the Bolsheviks had premised their seizure of power in October 1917 on the inseparability of the Russian and international revolutions. Russia constituted the weakest link in the imperialist chain and the example of Soviet democracy would act as the spark for socialist revolution throughout Europe and subsequently the entire world. With socialism triumphant in the advanced industrialised countries, the survival of the beleaguered Soviet regime would be guaranteed. The Bolsheviks' cast-iron belief in the inevitability of worldwide revolution sprang from two equally important sources. First, Marxist theory provided the 'scientific' prognosis of the collapse of capitalism, an exhausted economic system that generated mass poverty, imperialist conflict and war. Secondly, theory was being borne out by reality. Developments in the European heartland in 1918 appeared to confirm the imminence of revolutionary upheaval. Anti-war agitation, strikes and mutinies; the demise of the old imperial order in Central and Eastern Europe; the creation of the first embryonic communist parties; and above all, the German 'November Revolution' strengthened the Bolsheviks in their unshakeable conviction that history was on their side. International socialism was on the march.

However, the planetary scope of the crisis of capitalism was insufficient of itself to foment proletarian revolution. What was required was nothing less than the establishment of a 'world party' of communists to organise and lead the 'world revolution'. The Comintern was to be this agent of history. Yet the Bolsheviks' millenarian faith in global revolution veiled a number of key questions that were only dimly apparent to the architects of the International. How, in fact, was the monumental task of 'world revolution' to be achieved? What concrete organisational form would the 'world party' take, and what would be the relationship between the 'general staff of the revolution' and the individual communist parties? How to ensure that the Marxist conception of proletarian internationalism would gain ascendancy over 'narrow-minded nationalism', a powerful alternative legitimised by the Western Allies at the Paris Peace conference? Once the revolution had occurred, what should be the political character of the new socialist system? And, most problematically, were conditions in the capitalist countries really ripe for socialist revolution? Such intractable dilemmas were to plague the Comintern throughout its turbulent existence.

The first section of this chapter explores the basic tenets of Leninism, examines the debate between Lenin and Karl Kautsky over the nature of the Bolshevik Revolution and elucidates the foundation of the Comintern. The second part discusses the extent to which the ideological and organisational principles of Bolshevism became 'universalised', mandatory for all foreign communists affiliated to the Comintern. The final section focuses on the origins and outcomes of the united front tactics and the relationship between Comintern policies and Soviet state interests.

DICTATORSHIP OR DEMOCRACY?

The dramatic events of October 1917 elicited fiercely contrasting reactions in the European labour movement. A minority of militant activists viewed the Bolshevik capture of state power as evidence of the superiority of Lenin's revolutionary socialism. For hundreds of thousand of war-weary workers throughout Europe, the infant Soviet republic offered the enticing prospect of peace and social justice. It also issued a fundamental challenge to the discredited leaders of the Second International, the self-proclaimed guardians of Marx's legacy, who had deserted the banner of proletarian internationalism and led their respective working classes into the slaughter of war. According to the socialist leaders, the Bolshevik *coup d'état* was a premature leap into the unknown, a risky departure from the preordained pattern of historical development as laid down by Marx. A socialist revolution in such a backward agrarian country as Russia could only result in a terroristic dictatorship. The October seizure of power and the Bolsheviks' state-building programme thus raised a pivotal issue which drove a wedge between communists and social democrats for many decades. Could socialism be achieved through an essentially repressive 'dictatorship of the proletariat', or could it evolve naturally out of parliamentary democracy? This bitter doctrinal dispute culminated in an irrevocable organisational split in the world labour movement which was to endure beyond the short life of the Comintern.

To understand the roots of this split an examination of the ideas of Vladimir Ilich Lenin is crucial. In the opinion of his many detractors, Lenin was a cynical meglomaniac whose authoritarian policies laid the foundations of the subsequent Stalinist totalitarian monster. To be sure, Lenin was no democrat in the Western sense of the word and distinct lines of continuity can indeed be traced between the Leninist and Stalinist regimes. Yet too often Lenin's pre-revolutionary theories and actions have been misconstrued by Western historians as the inevitable precursors of full-blown Stalinism. Lenin's thought was neither static nor inflexible. His Marxism evolved in response to a rapidly changing world and hence should be placed firmly in the specific historical contexts in which it was shaped. Nor does 'Leninism', an ideology canonised by his successors, represent a totally coherent and consistent body of theory and practice. It displays both anti-democratic and emancipatory elements. As one of Lenin's best biographers has written: 'His mind was pulled between central command and popular initiative; between political will and economic determinism; between massive coercion and mass persuasion; between the intuitive gamble and informed calculation. Tension and change were a touchstone of his thinking.'[1]

Nevertheless, a central core in Lenin's ideas can be identified: his conviction that Marxism was a revolutionary, not reformist, doctrine; his emphasis on the role of the 'vanguard party'; his internationalist perspective on the crisis of capitalism and imperialism; and, after 1914 in particular, his intransigent vilification of European social democracy. Above all, Lenin's was a revolutionary interpretation of Marxism adapted to the repressive conditions of Tsarist Russia. The armed overthrow of the state was an historical imperative. Lenin devoted his entire adult life to the destruction of the Tsarist autocracy, to the conquest of political power by the Russian working class and to the construction of a socialist order based on the 'dictatorship of the proletariat'.

But proletarian revolution was inconceivable without a new organisational form – a highly centralised and disciplined 'vanguard party' of dedicated professional revolutionaries. It was Lenin's advocacy of the vanguard party which in 1903 split the Russian social democrats into two factions, the Bolsheviks and Mensheviks. In his famous treatise on party organisation *What is to be Done?* (1902), Lenin had argued forcibly that leadership was the key to success. The party of a new type would be led by intellectuals equipped with the 'science' of Marxism, but organically linked to the workers and their struggles in the factories. Although this tract was written specifically with Russian conditions in mind, Lenin regarded his prescriptions as having wider applicability. Workers of all countries, he asserted, left to their own devices would develop only a reformist 'trade-union consciousness'. Socialist consciousness could only be brought to the workers from without, by the vanguard party which would act as the historical agent of the proletariat, directing mass spontaneity into revolutionary action.[2] Lenin thus laid great store on the creation of a political organisation that was capable of shaping, rather than merely reacting to, historical events. His controversial views on the party drew sharp criticism from fellow socialists Rosa Luxemburg and Lev Trotsky. The latter warned prophetically that Lenin's predilection for strict centralisation and hierarchical structures would lead to 'substitutionism': 'the party organization at first substitutes itself for the party as a whole; then the Central Committee substitutes itself for the organization; and finally a single "dictator" substitutes himself for the Central Committee'.[3]

Such an outcome was certainly not Lenin's intention. Indeed, his much maligned notion of 'democratic centralism' was originally conceived, and supported by his Menshevik opponents, as a means of making the party leadership more accountable to the membership. First propounded in 1905, the idea was that party offices should be elective and debate on tactics and strategy should be as broad as possible. The voice of the rank and file should be heard at meetings, conferences and congresses. However, once a decision had been reached by the leadership all party members without exception must strictly adhere to it whether they agreed with that decision or not. Therefore, democratic centralism can be summarised as 'freedom of discussion, unity of action' and one could argue that, prior to the infamous ban on factions in March 1921, the emphasis was on the former. To this extent Lenin's views on party organisation did not lead inexorably to the Stalinist monolith. But in the harsh realities of the daily battle, Lenin's democratic aspirations tended to be side-lined in favour of co-option of party officials and control from above. The danger of a slide into 'bureaucratic centralism' was apparent even to pre-revolutionary dissident Bolsheviks.[4]

The third aspect of Lenin's thought to be addressed is his internationalism. Although he concentrated his energies on the Russian labour movement and was influenced by the specific Russian revolutionary tradition, Lenin never lost sight of the world scale of the anti-capitalist struggle. This internationalist perspective was grounded in his analysis of imperialism, 'the highest stage of capital-ism'.[5] Lenin believed that the concentration of production and capital in the hands of a financial oligarchy had created international monopolies which divided the world among the major capitalist powers. Because territorial and economic rivalries among these giants would inevitably end in wars, imperialism represented not only a capitalism in global decline, but one that was positively retrogressive and oppressive. War was the necessary product of this last historical phase of capitalism. Yet, dialectically, finance mono-poly capital through its banks, cartels and trusts had established mechanisms for the social control of production and distribution and had thus laid the objective basis for an advance to socialism. Indeed, for Lenin socialism was the only escape from the barbarism and endemic wars that the imperialists had foisted on the working class.

The outbreak of the Great War in August 1914 was greeted in the capitals of Europe with a mixture of elation and relief. Lenin, a solitary figure in exile in Switzerland, immediately saw it as a watershed. From the war would spring socialist revolution. He insisted, provocatively, on the need to transform the international conflict into a series of national civil wars for socialism, a principle he termed 'revolutionary defeatism'. This aroused alarm even among his staunchest adherents. But it is in Lenin's characterisation of the social democrats as 'traitors' that we see the real significance of the war in his thinking. The fact that the vast majority of European labour leaders voted for their governments' war credits signified, in Lenin's eyes, their desertion from the proletarian camp and the death of the Second International. He wasted no time in pouring invective on their heads. They were 'social patriots' and 'social chauvinists', even 'Kautskyite shitheads'.[6] Crucially, social democrats were now identified as 'agents of the bourgeoisie' in the ranks of the workers. It was this conclusion which, in the autumn of 1914, drove Lenin to demand a new Third, Communist, International purged of 'opportunist dross'.

Before discussing the origins and early activities of this revolutionary International, we must briefly digress to examine the doctrinal polemic between Lenin and the German socialist Karl Kautsky. Before 1914 Kautsky was the pre-eminent theoretician of the Second International, the 'Pope' of Marxism, whom Lenin, a virtual outcast in the European labour movement, esteemed and admired.[7] This admiration quickly turned to antipathy with Kautsky's 'conditional acceptance' of the war credits vote in the Reichstag. Throughout the war Lenin lavished vitriol on Kautsky's 'centrist' position. The gulf between the two men widened still further after the October Revolution with Kautsky's damning assessment of the Bolshevik coup, *The Dictatorship of the Proletariat* (1918). Three components of his critique warrant special attention: the inseparability of socialism and democracy; the premature nature of the revolution and the resultant recourse to dictatorship; and the harm that Bolshevik policies were inflicting on the cause of socialism.

Kautsky began by stating that Bolshevik rule had exposed the clash between 'two fundamentally distinct methods, that of democracy and that of dictatorship.' For him, 'socialism without democracy is unthinkable'. The goal of socialism was the 'abolition of every kind of exploitation and oppression' and this required broad political democracy as well as the 'social organisation of production'. Therefore, the rights of other parties and minorities must be guaranteed. The numerical preponderance of the proletariat combined with universal suffrage would allow a peaceful parliamentary road to socialism. Kautsky inferred that Russia was not 'ripe' for socialism because capitalist industry was retarded, the working class was relatively small and politically immature, and the material conditions necessary for a socialist transformation were lacking. In Kautsky's mechanistic understanding of Marxism, stages of historical development could not be skipped. Furthermore, the mass of the Russian population were small-holding peasants who did not share the 'will for socialism'. In these hostile circumstances, and in the absence of proletarian revolutions abroad, the minority Bolsheviks were compelled to dissolve the Constituent Assembly and establish a dictatorship. But this was not a 'dictatorship of the proletariat', as Lenin claimed, but a dictatorship of one party *over* the proletariat. Kautsky argued that such a method of government 'only too easily compromises the ideas of Socialism itself', impeding rather than assisting the socialist cause.[8] In short, Bolshevik dictatorship threatened the advance of socialism both in Russia and elsewhere.

Kautsky's measured broadside demanded a reply. It came in the form of Lenin's pamphlet *The Proletarian Revolution and the Renegade Kautsky* (1918), a truly acidic diatribe against his former mentor. Lenin excoriated Kautsky as a 'parliamentary cretin', who engaged in 'twaddle' about 'pure democracy'. Did the 'windbag' not realise that parliamentary institutions were no more than a sham, concealing the class rule of the bourgeoisie? Did he really not know that there was only *class* democracy, either bourgeois or proletarian, and that 'proletarian democracy is *a million times* more democratic than any bourgeois democracy'? Why? Because the Soviets, direct organs of the working people themselves, enable the oppressed classes to organise and administer their own state and remove the old bourgeois bureaucracies and privileges. In reply to Kautsky's 'distortion' of Marx's concept of the 'dictatorship of the proletariat', Lenin repeatedly asserted the need for revolutionary violence against the dispossessed bourgeoisie who fight to retain their hegemony. His rallying-cry proclaimed that Bolshevism had become '*world* Bolshevism' by virtue of its revolutionary tactics, theory and programme. By indicating 'the right road of escape from the horrors of war and imperialism. . . . Bolshevism *can serve as a model of tactics for all*'.[9]

What is the significance of this dialogue of the deaf? Above all, it foreshadowed the historic split between the reformist and revolutionary roads to socialism. From now on the Leninists' insistence on the violent dismantling of the capitalist state permanently delineated communists from socialists. To be sure, the animosity between them was not based solely on theoretical wrangles. Concrete acts, such as the murder of Rosa Luxemburg and Karl Liebknecht with the connivance of social democratic ministers, cast a dark cloud over relations as early as January 1919. But the class reductionism of the communists lay at the heart of the matter. Lenin's firm association of social democracy with bourgeois politics meant that the Kautskys of this world were 'objectively' class traitors and thus their influence on the workers had to be eliminated. Temporary tactical co-operation with socialist organisations was not ruled out, but the leaders of those organisations had to be ruthlessly exposed. Once this was achieved the mass of war-weary workers would rally, so it was believed, to the revolutionary call of the communists. The implications for the Comintern were far-reaching indeed. By 1928–9 the reformist bosses were to be dubbed 'social fascists', in many ways more dangerous than the real fascists. In this sense communist theory informed political practice with ruinous consequences.

Moreover, the Leninist identification of parliamentary democracy with bourgeois class rule ignored the commitment of large sections of the European labour movement to constitutionalism and democratic political cultures. Although Lenin acknowledged the 'vast sub-soil of capitalism' in the advanced industrial states, this recognition did not underpin a deeper analysis of the structures of power and consent in the West nor a serious consideration of whether national specificities demanded an alternative approach to the 'frontal' strategy which had been successful in Tsarist Russia. Allied to this was an incomplete understanding of the differentiation of 'the West'. Conditions in rural Spain and southern Italy were hardly the same as in industrialised Britain or America and the idea that the British and German working classes were synonymous with a Russian proletariat that lacked a long political and cultural tradition displayed a crude misconception of the nature of reformism and national diversities. For Lenin, democracy and nationalism were little more than deceptions used by the bourgeoisie to divert the working class from revolution. Lenin's categorical rejection of representative government and his insistence on the universal applicability of the Bolshevik model were to have negative effects on the search for a viable revolutionary strategy in the West.[10]

Underlying the breach between communists and socialists was their divergent view on the prospects of world revolution. For the social democrats, the Bolsheviks were desperate gamblers who were prepared to wage civil war and risk destruction in the hope that European workers would come to their aid. Most socialists feared revolution at a time of economic exhaustion and social flux. The result would be hunger and the slide into terror, as in Soviet Russia.

Therefore, even those socialists who remained committed in principle to revolutionary change balked at the idea of violent class conflict in a dislocated war-ravaged Europe. What the Bolsheviks could not, and did not, accept was that the majority of organised workers, not just the 'labour aristocrats', shared this reasoning. Why endanger hard won political and economic achievements for the sake of an uncertain 'bright future'? The ultimate dilemma of inter-war communism – how to revolutionise an essentially reformist working class – was thus presaged from the very foundation of the Comintern.

The Petrograd coup had created the conditions for the birth of the Third International, but nearly a year and a half was to elapse before its founding congress. This delay is largely explained by the chaotic situation that prevailed throughout 1918. War raged on in Western Europe and hostilities on the Eastern front continued even after the Treaty of Brest-Litovsk in March. In Russia itself a bitter civil war pitting the 'Reds' against the Tsarist 'Whites' broke out in the early summer. At the same time foreign interventionists, including Britain, France and Japan, occupied parts of the former Russian Empire and lent support to the White generals. Moscow found itself almost completely cut off from the rest of Europe and regular contact with sympathisers outside Russia was impossible, a situation that was to last well into 1920. In these unpropitious circumstances concrete steps towards the creation of an international body of revolutionaries remained perforce limited.

The harsh external realities were made agonisingly plain to the Bolsheviks at the time of the Brest-Litovsk negotiations in early 1918. Contrary to all expectations, the workers of Europe had ignored Bolshevik appeals to overthrow the 'imperialist oppressors'. The Soviet Republic stood alone and isolated. The rapid German advance into Russia in February presented the Bolsheviks with an unenviable choice: either sue for peace with the victorious German High Command or launch a revolutionary class war against the Kaiserreich in the hope that German proletarians would unfurl the red flag over Berlin. In the face of massive opposition from the Bolshevik left, Lenin bluntly advocated the former option. Arguing that the very survival of the Soviet state depended on the 'breathing space' afforded by peace, he cajoled and pummelled his adversaries into submission. Sternly realistic, Lenin surmised that the precise timing of revolution abroad was incalculable and warned 'we cannot stake everything on that'.[11] Therefore, a 'shameful' peace was preferable to destruction. Against all their principles, the Bolsheviks were forced to engage in traditional diplomacy with an imperialist power. Foreign Commissar Trotsky had to accept that the issuing of 'a few revolutionary proclamations to the peoples of the world' would not suffice as the basis of Soviet international relations. Under the terms of the draconian Brest-Litovsk Treaty Russia lost vast tracts of territory in the Ukraine, Belorussia and the Baltic. German militarism, temporarily at least, reigned supreme over Russian revolutionary socialism.

More important for our purposes is that in signing the treaty the Bolsheviks tacitly acknowledged that defence of the socialist motherland took priority over proletarian internationalism. Indeed, one Western expert has suggested that Brest-Litovsk ushered in a completely 'new policy . . . which subtly, but decisively, shifted the entire purpose of Bolshevik policy from advancing the case of world revolution to that of preserving the embattled Soviet state'.[12] The primacy of Soviet state interests must be taken seriously, but in our opinion the choice at this time was not quite so stark. Lenin and the Bolsheviks continued to believe fervently that the survival of the Russian revolution and its spread westwards were mutually reinforcing strategies, for if Soviet Russia collapsed, the cause of world revolution would suffer untold damage. With E. H. Carr, we would contend that the outcome of the Brest-Litovsk crisis was a foreign policy:

> designed equally to promote world revolution and the national security of the Soviet republic. . . . [Before 1921] the two facets of Soviet foreign policy – the encouragement of world revolution and the pursuit of national security – were merely different instruments of a single consistent and integrated purpose.[13]

That this dual policy was to have profound ramifications for the relationship between the Soviet state and the Comintern cannot be denied. But at this early stage they were largely unforeseen.

Throughout the fraught months of 1918, appeals to the European proletariat flooded from the pens of leading Bolsheviks and strenuous efforts were made to foster the expansion of revolution abroad. Within a few weeks of the October uprising the People's Commissariat of Foreign Affairs (Narkomindel) was provided with two million roubles for the needs of the world revolutionary movement. For the best part of 1918 and into 1919 Narkomindel was to act as a kind of surrogate International. It soon established a department of international propaganda whose energies were directed primarily at soldiers of the Central Powers, both prisoners of war and troops on the Eastern front. This activity produced encouraging results among Hungarians, Romanians, Czechs, Serbo-Croats and Germans. In May 1918 the Federation of Foreign Groups of the Russian Communist Party was established and in October the Conference of Communist Organisations of the Occupied Territories, known as the 'Little International', convened in Moscow. By the end of 1918 embryonic communist parties had been set up in the Ukraine, the Baltic region, Finland and Poland. All were closely linked to the Bolsheviks and were regarded as bridgeheads to the revolution in the West.[14] Leaders of these foreign communists in Russia, such as the Magyar Béla Kun, were to play a prominent role in the early operations of the Comintern.

The most promising news of late 1918, however, came from Germany. The 'November Revolution' was greeted in Moscow with unalloyed joy and optimism since the Bolsheviks had long viewed the German revolution as the key to their survival. The creation of workers' and soldiers' councils in Germany seemed to confirm the parallels between the European and Russian revolutions. But the German Soviet republic did not materialise. Instead of socialist revolution, events in Berlin remained at the 'bourgeois democratic' stage. The Spartacist uprising in January 1919 was brutally crushed by the *Freikorps* and the murder of Rosa Luxemburg and Karl Liebknecht deprived the German workers' movement of two inspirational leaders. Even so, from the lofty towers of the Kremlin prospects for revolution in Europe looked favourable. The Austro-Hungarian Empire was in a state of collapse; small but tangible communist parties had recently emerged in Hungary, German Austria and Holland; Soviet power had spread to Lithuania, Latvia and parts of the Ukraine; and most importantly the German Communist Party (KPD) had been founded in late December 1918. The Bolsheviks were now more than ever convinced that a permanent mechanism to coordinate the actions of the newly formed communist parties was vital. In addition, Lenin was eager to denounce, and if possible pre-empt, the reconvocation of the Second International whose leaders planned a conference in Berne for early February 1919. Haste was of the essence.

On 24 January 1919 a 'Letter of Invitation to the First Congress of the Communist International' (document 1) was relayed to the world by wireless. The text identified thirty-nine communist parties and revolutionary groups which had broken irrevocably with the pre-1914 socialist International and were therefore eligible to attend. Just six of these organisations were non-European. The meeting was delayed for two weeks because the Allied blockade of Russia made passage to Moscow extremely arduous. The congress finally convened in the Kremlin on the evening of Sunday 2 March 1919 in far from auspicious surroundings. One of the participants later described the 'flimsy chairs at rickety tables obviously borrowed from some café . . . [and] the heaters that blew terrible gusts of frigid air at the delegates'.[15] Only nine of the fifty-one cold guests arrived from abroad; the rest resided in Soviet Russia. The vast majority of them did not carry authorised credentials from the parties and groups for whom they claimed to speak. It was hardly a representative gathering.

The main exception was Hugo Eberlein, the *bona fide* delegate of the German party. He was mandated to oppose any immediate moves to set up a new International. At the congress Eberlein expressed the concerns of the German communists in measured tones. 'We harbor no principled objections to founding' an International, he said; it 'must be founded'. But 'we do not want to proceed . . . just yet' on the grounds that 'real Communist parties exist in only a few countries. . . . Missing is all of western Europe.' He argued that the conference should first elaborate a clear platform of goals and objectives to put before the workers of the world and 'then they will say whether they are ready to found the new International'.[16] Eberlein's public utterances, however, did not reveal the substance of the disquiet felt by the German communists. Shortly before her death, Rosa Luxemburg had intimated that an International prematurely created in Moscow would inevitably succumb to Bolshevik dominance. She evidently warned the KPD leadership that the International would be 'a Russian *Krämerei* [shop] with which we shall be unable to cope. We shall perish with it.'[17]

Regardless of Eberlein's abstention, the congress voted overwhelmingly to establish the Third International. It is commonly assumed that the delegates were swayed by the swashbuckling entrance of Karl Steinhardt, the Austrian representative. Arriving on the second day after a gruelling trip from Vienna, Steinhardt related in glowing terms how the proletariat of Austria was rallying to the communist call.[18] In reality, one suspects that a mixture of Bolshevik charm and backstage arm-twisting had more of an impact on the assembled comrades than Steinhardt's impassioned speech. Whatever the case, on 4 March 1919 the Communist International formally came into being. The ideological split in the world labour movement had been institutionalised.

What else did the founding congress decide? The principal document, Trotsky's 'Manifesto to the Proletariat of the Entire World' (document 2), is noteworthy for its uncharacteristic silence on the role of the party in the forthcoming revolutionary struggles. Indeed, congress did not debate the nature and tasks of the party. With Europe apparently on the eve of revolution and few communist organisations in existence, the concept of highly centralised parties forming 'sections' of a 'world party' was as yet undeveloped. Trotsky emphasised the Soviets, or workers' councils, as the instrument of working-class unity and action. The Russian model of proletarian self-rule was deemed universally applicable. The second major theme was the total dismissal of 'bourgeois democracy'. Lenin reiterated his contempt for those socialists who defended parliamentary forms of rule and he once again insisted on the dictatorship of the proletariat as a necessary and higher form of democracy. On both counts the Bolshevik leaders betrayed a profound misunderstanding of conditions in Central and Western Europe. Workers' and soldiers' councils, shop-steward committees, general strikes, demonstrations and mutinies most certainly reflected the radicalisation of large numbers of war-weary proletarians, but they did not portend revolutionary civil wars as in Russia or express mass disillusionment with democratic political structures. With the benefit of hindsight we can say that the Bolsheviks' 'revolutionary romanticism', understandable as it was in the intoxicating atmosphere of 1919, obscured two realities. First, the bourgeois state and its coercive agencies, even where threatened, remained essentially intact; and, secondly, the majority of workers was not attracted by the notion of a fratricidal social revolution. After four years of international war, Bolshevik rhetoric about an 'era of civil wars' could hardly have been an enticing prospect. Communist revolutions were not on the horizon.

The improvised nature of the founding congress meant that the organisational framework of the new International was rudimentary. No statutes, constitution or rules were adopted, but it was agreed that an Executive Committee of the Communist International (ECCI) should be elected and Grigory Zinoviev, Lenin's trusted confidante, became its first President. He was regularly assisted by Nikolai Bukharin, Karl Radek and, on occasion, Trotsky. Although provision was made for seven communist parties to send one representative each to the ECCI in Moscow, in fact the Bolsheviks predominated. This early Russian hegemony was not the result of some conscious Machiavellian plot. Given the prestige of the Bolsheviks, the weakness of foreign communist parties and the great difficulties of travel to and from Moscow, it was logical that the Russians would assume the day-to-day running of the Comintern. Soon after the congress Lenin, Zinoviev and Trotsky claimed that this would be a temporary hegemony. As the revolutionary wave washed over Europe heralding the 'international Soviet republic', so the headquarters of the Comintern would be transferred from Moscow to Berlin, Paris or some other Western capital. This optimism notwithstanding, it cannot be doubted that the Comintern's dependence on the Soviet regime dated from its birth. Luxemburg's premonitions were to prove all too accurate. Imperceptible to most communists, the long tortuous process of the Bolshevisation of the International had begun.

UNIVERSALISATION OF BOLSHEVISM

Exactly how and why did the Bolshevik organisational model and tactical programme become transposed to the Comintern and its constituent communist parties? To what extent was this process imposed on the international movement by the Russians? Was the 'universalisation of Bolshevism' a deliberate manoeuvre designed to turn the Comintern into an instrument for the defence of Soviet Russia, or was it the result, largely unintended, of objective circumstances – the pressures of civil war and foreign isolation, the failure of revolution in the West and the consequent need to consolidate the communist movement in time of adversity? Historians have grappled with these issues for decades. Their obsession with the directing role of the Bolsheviks is quite understandable. There is ample evidence of the increasing Russian dominance of the Comintern hierarchies, of the tendency to strict centralisation, of Soviet funding of foreign 'sections' and of Moscow's decisive interventions in the affairs of nominally independent parties. Between 1920 and 1922, an organisational structure emerged that undoubtedly facilitated the subsequent bureaucratic degeneration of the Stalinist Comintern.

While recognising these powerful trends, we would claim that the International in Lenin's era also displayed a degree of pluralism and open debate rarely duplicated after his death. 'Communism' and 'Bolshevism' were not yet clearly defined entities. To a certain extent they had to be hammered out in the course of fierce disputes and many European communists retained left social democratic and syndicalist proclivities well into the 1920s. Fully formed Bolsheviks did not appear overnight. Moreover, it is our contention that the universalisation of the Bolshevik model was not simply imposed from above, but had a measure of active support from below. It could also be argued that the emphasis on doctrinal purity and organisational solidity helped to sustain many communist parties in the face of state repression.

Very soon after the First Congress, Soviet republics were established, albeit temporarily, in Hungary, Bavaria and Slovakia. By the summer of 1919 the Italian Socialist Party, Norwegian Labour Party, Swedish Left Social Democrats and Bulgarian Social Democrats (Tesniaki) had affiliated to the Comintern. Later in the year contact was made with major West European socialist organisations, such as the French Socialist Party (SFIO) and the German Independent Social Democratic Party (USPD), founded in April 1917 by socialists dissatisfied with the pro-war policy of the SPD. The 'centrist' USPD far outnumbered the KPD and by the end of the year had a membership of three-quarters of a million with a substantial minority drawn to 'the light from the east'. These developments confirmed for the Bolsheviks that the Comintern was becoming 'fashionable', as Zinoviev boasted at the Second Congress. As a rival to the renascent Second International, the Comintern needed to attract the rank and file of the big socialist parties of Western Europe, many of whom expressed solidarity with the Bolshevik experiment, while excluding those leaders who were suspicious of the Third International's 'eastern' complexion. The dilemma was whether the Comintern should aim for the affiliation of mass parties of the left at the risk of diluting doctrinal purity, or insist on elite parties characterised by ideological orthodoxy and strict centralisation, the hallmarks of the Bolshevik model.

This problem was brought into sharp relief by Lenin's changing perceptions of the revolutionary conjuncture. In the first half of 1919 his views on the question of revolution in the West were distinguished by an inherent ambiguity. On the one hand, aware of the peculiarities of 'backward' Russia, he entertained the possibility that 'West-European revolutions will perhaps proceed more smoothly', producing a 'mosaic reality'.[19] On the other, he never refrained from repeating that the essential features of the Russian Revolution were of general applicability. The Bolsheviks' predisposition to see events through the prism of Russian experience was never far from the surface. A key corollary of this Russocentrism was the Comintern's new found emphasis on the primacy of the vanguard party. In the aftermath of the collapse of Béla Kun's Soviet republic in August 1919, Lenin abandoned the hope that the Hungarian example might give the West a more humane model of revolution. His loss of faith in worker and peasant Soviets as the agents of revolution marked a discernible and permanent shift in the Comintern towards the necessity of a centralised party in the Bolshevik image. The overriding reason for the failure of revolution, it was believed, was the organisational weakness of the working class in Central and Western Europe. World revolution now required that the Comintern and its national sections become a real 'world party' based on those singular organisational principles which had guaranteed the Bolsheviks' success in 1917.

The clearest statement of this universalisation is Lenin's influential pamphlet *Left-Wing Communism: An Infantile Disorder*, written in April 1920 for the forthcoming Second Comintern Congress. He wrote:

We now possess quite considerable international experience, which shows very definitely that certain fundamental features of our revolution have a significance that is not local, or peculiarly national, or Russian alone, but international . . . not merely several but all the primary features of our revolution, and many of its secondary features, are of international significance in the meaning of its effects on all countries. I am speaking of it in the narrowest sense of the word, taking international significance to mean the international validity or the historical inevitability of a repetition, on an international scale, of what has taken place in our country.

The principal lesson was that 'absolute centralisation and rigorous discipline in the proletariat are an essential condition of victory over the bourgeoisie'.[20] These were qualities which distinguished the Bolshevik party from social democratic bodies, but which were still lacking in the emergent communist groupings. It was this triumphalist vindication of Bolshevik tactics and organisational structures which preoccupied the USPD and SFIO delegations as they made their way to Russia in the summer of 1920 for the Second Comintern Congress.

The Second Congress, held in Petrograd and Moscow between 19 July and 7 August, was in many respects the real founding congress of the Comintern. Over two hundred delegates from thirty-seven countries were given an enthusiastic welcome by the Bolsheviks. The festive mood of the participants was reinforced by the Red Army's rapid, though transient, advance on Warsaw. The revolution was spreading westwards! At the same time, the reverses of 1919 had to be explained and lessons drawn. In this contradictory atmosphere very few delegates recognised that the famous 'Twenty-one Conditions' of admission to the Comintern and the organisational statutes, both ratified overwhelmingly by congress, effectively formalised Bolshevik hegemony over the International. In carefully drafting the 'Twenty-one Conditions', there can be little doubt that the Bolsheviks' main purpose was to split the rank and file of the European socialist parties from the influence of their right-wing and centrist leaders who had 'betrayed' the revolution. Zinoviev stated categorically that neither the German Independents nor the French Socialists could be admitted to the Comintern with their incumbent 'vacillating leaders'.

The 'Twenty-one Conditions' (document 5), which gained notoriety almost immediately on adoption and which were readily invoked by Stalin in later years, are essential for an understanding of the 'universalisation of Bolshevism'. The Conditions, drafted primarily by Zinoviev, stated *inter alia* that every organisation seeking to join the Comintern must systematically remove reformists and centrists from all responsible posts in the labour movement and replace them with 'tested communists'; combine legal and illegal activity; break completely and in the shortest possible time with inveterate 'opportunists' such as Kautsky and Ramsay MacDonald; establish cells in trade unions to win workers' organisations over to the communist cause; adhere to the principle of democratic centralism based on iron discipline, fullest powers of the party central leadership and periodical purges of 'petty-bourgeois elements'; unconditionally support every Soviet republic against counter-revolutionary forces; and change its name to 'communist' party (section of the Communist International). Point sixteen is worth quoting: 'All decisions by congresses of the Communist International as well as by its Executive Committee are binding on all parties. . . . The Communist International, working under conditions of most acute civil war, must be organized in a far more centralized way than was the Second International.'[21] This clause, subordinating the national 'sections' to the will of a Bolshevik-dominated Executive Committee, has been seized on by many historians as evidence of the creeping 'Russification' of the Comintern under Lenin's tutelage.

Even if we contextualise the Bolsheviks' urgency in the optimism of the summer of 1920, the intention to form what Claudin has called 'chemically pure' communist parties meant excluding large numbers of workers who were sympathetic to the Russian Revolution, but wary of the Comintern's structures and fissiparous tendencies. For this reason Claudin has termed the 'Twenty-one Conditions' a 'model of sectarianism and bureaucratic method in the history of the working-class movement'.[22] But the Bolsheviks did not wish simply to create tiny sects. The dichotomy was therefore how to establish mass parties on the basis of a rigid discipline that was alien to the majority of European workers. The confidently held belief that once 'Bolshevised' revolutionary parties were constituted, the bulk of socialist party members would flow into them proved unfounded.

The Bolsheviks knew well that the USPD and SFIO delegations would be resistant to their proposals. The four USPD representatives, though divided equally on the question of affiliation to the Comintern, uniformly rejected the Bolsheviks' insistence on expelling socialist leaders, which would amount to splitting the parties 'from above'. The two anti-Comintern delegates, resolutely opposing the premature creation of communist parties, argued that their formation should be an organic process supported by the majority of the working class. On more than one occasion they noted that a genuine dialogue could not take place while those who expressed reservations about the applicability of the Russian model were labelled as 'traitors to socialism'. Even Walter Stoecker, one of the pro-Comintern USPD delegates, affirmed that 'Russian methods cannot be carried over mechanically to western European countries'. Zinoviev retorted angrily that 'a contradiction between "East" and "West" does not exist at all in reality'. For him, the only contradiction was 'between communism and reformism, between social pacifism and communism.' He pilloried 'those who think of the Communist International as a good tavern, where representatives of various countries sing the "Internationale" and pay each other compliments, then go their separate ways and continue the same old practices. That is the damnable custom of the Second International and we will never tolerate it'.[23]

Throughout the congress a range of tactics was employed by the Bolsheviks to achieve their ends: intrigue – unofficial delegates or protégés were used to discredit publicly the official representatives, especially of the SFIO, or mislead them as to the intentions of the Bolsheviks; inquisitional – an extensive campaign on the part of the ECCI in the closed door commissions to force delegates to submit to Bolshevik hegemony; and when this failed, even apparent charm and temporary conciliation.[24] In their contempt for Western socialists, the Bolsheviks were supported by a number of European communists, prominent among them being the Hungarian Mátyás Rákosi, the Swiss Jules Humbert-Droz and the future leader of the Italian Communist Party, Amadeo Bordiga. Their role was most evident in the debates on the key question of the congress, the conditions for admission, where each argued in favour of the most stringent terms.

The Second Congress had placed the creation of communist parties on the immediate agenda. In Germany, where the small KPD was already in existence, the task was to attract the mass of USPD members while excluding the party's 'centrist' leadership. This was largely achieved at the acrimonious Halle Congress in October 1920 at which Zinoviev's mammoth four-hour speech in a foreign language impressed even his adversaries. The result of the ballot on affiliation to the Comintern had been more or less sewn up in advance. Of the 393 delegates, 237 voted to join the Third International and enter into negotiations with the KPD. In December, the United German Communist Party was founded claiming a membership of 350 000, making it for the first time a truly mass party. Similar developments occurred in the French and Italian Socialist Parties, though the outcomes in terms of membership were rather different. Stormy congresses were held at Tours in December 1920 and Livorno in January 1921 from which emerged the French (PCF) and Italian Communist Parties (PCI). The former enjoyed majority support, the latter remained a relatively isolated and internally divided group.

The tiny Communist Party of Great Britain (CPGB) had been constructed in August 1920 from an amalgam of various socialist organisations. Never a serious actor on the national political plane, the party did play an influential role in the trade union movement and industrial sphere. The last major European communist party to be founded was the Czechoslovak (KSČ). Ethnic and ideological tensions prevented the establishment of a united party until autumn 1921 when the 'Marxist Left' faction of the Czechoslovak Social Democratic Party finally merged with the German–Czech communists, much to the relief of the Bolsheviks who had been urging unification for over a year. But, with a few notable exceptions, the communist parties which emerged in 1920–1 were rather weak minority organisations. Even where mass parties were created, as in Germany, France and Czechoslovakia, recruitment figures soon indicated a downturn. Throughout the 1920s and beyond nearly all parties suffered from fluctuating memberships, which seriously hampered their ability to forge stable networks of cadres and activists.

Who *were* the communists? This question is notoriously difficult to answer owing to a lack of verifiable data. The consensus, however, is that the infant communist parties were composed primarily of male industrial workers in their twenties and thirties. Above all, the new communist parties were parties of youth. According to Riddell, approximately two-thirds of the delegates to the Second Comintern Congress were under forty years of age.[25] They represented a younger generation disillusioned with the old staid institutions of labour. In France and Italy, the ideological struggle over affiliation to the Comintern was also a conflict of generations and many of the new leaders – Louis-Oscar Frossard, Antonio Gramsci and Bordiga, for example – were barely thirty years old. The socialist youth movements were symbolic of the post-war mood of radicalism and many of their militants joined the fledgling communist parties. In November 1919 the Communist Youth International was founded with a membership of some two hundred thousand.[26]

Concrete statistics are also hard to come by for the social composition of the parties. It seems, though, that many recruits were unskilled or semi-skilled workers in the newer industries, such as chemicals, and were unschooled in the organisational structures and discipline of pre-war social democracy. Shellshocked by the war and radicalised by post-war material hardships and unemployment, these impatient workers, many of whom retained syndicalist or anarcho-syndicalist leanings, were attracted by the revolutionary 'will to action' of the Bolsheviks. Yet, the picture of early communist parties as 'armies of the dispossessed' is not as clear-cut as it may appear. Some skilled craftsmen in traditional trades – cutlers in the Ruhr, engineers in Paris, Berlin, Turin and on Clydeside – found their way into the parties, and conversely sectors of the unskilled, particularly textile workers in the older industrial regions, remained largely impervious to the appeal of communism.[27] At the same time, some parties incorporated pre-industrial traditions of peasant radicalism. The peasant delegates at the Tours congress, for instance, were the main force in favour of affiliation to the Comintern and a substantial minority of PCF members were small peasants or rural labourers.

The significance of this generational, social and ideological heterogeneity is that the new parties could not be easily assimilated into the evolving bureaucratic structures of the Comintern. They often proved hard to control and direct. Parties composed of young volatile workers led by unruly intellectuals scarcely resembled the standard image of a hierarchical, disciplined Bolshevik organisation. One important method of establishing centralised control was the financing of the international communist movement from the coffers of the Soviet state. 'Moscow gold' has become a controversial, even sensational, issue in the last few years with new information emerging from the former Soviet archives. We now possess quite detailed knowledge of the nature of this funding and its relevance for the relationship between communist parties and the International. A brief summary based on the research of Fridrikh Firsov, the eminent Russian historian, will demonstrate the scale of Moscow's financial involvement in the nurturing of the embryonic parties.

On 13 April 1919 a resolution of the Central Committee of the Russian Communist Party (RCP) transferred the funding of foreign communists from Narkomindel to the Comintern. Firsov lists the valuables that were carried abroad by special couriers in the spring of 1919. They included jewels, diamonds, sapphires, pearls, rings, bracelets, broaches, earrings and other Tsarist treasures worth hundreds of thousands of roubles. Currency transfers between March and August 1919 amounted to 5.2 million roubles. But even this was insufficient and Lenin agreed to a fourfold increase. The figures for autumn 1919 to early 1920 are revealing. In total, millions of roubles, German marks, Swiss francs and other monies were despatched to communist groups in Hungary, Czechoslovakia, Germany, Italy, America, Yugoslavia, Austria, Poland and Holland.[28] As for the British party, it is reported that 'Lenin. . . . secretly provided at least £55,000 – the equivalent of about £1 million today – to help get the Communist Party off the ground'.[29] A meeting of the ECCI Budget Commission on 3 January 1922 noted that an annual subsidy of £24 000 had been supplied to the CPGB, presumably for 1921. The total amount sent to foreign parties in that year represented 10 per cent of the entire Comintern budget.[30]

The body responsible for overseeing the secret financial transactions of the Comintern was the mysterious Department of International Communication (*Otdel mezhdunarodnoi sviazi* – OMS). Created in 1921, the OMS is scarcely mentioned in published Comintern texts and has long been considered the *éminence grise* of the International, its real nervous system. It was headed for many years by Osip Piatnitsky, a staunch Bolshevik stalwart. The Department conducted the clandestine activities of the Comintern abroad, including the distribution of confidential directives and propaganda material, the forging of passports and identity papers for overseas agents and the implementation of espionage operations. Later, under Stalin, the OMS collaborated with the Soviet security and military intelligence organs before falling victim to the Terror in 1937.[31]

The Bolsheviks had no qualms about funding the international communist movement. In March 1919 Zinoviev proudly announced that the Russian party would not stint in its efforts to help foreign sympathisers, saying: 'We shall offer the workers of other countries great financial and material support just as they assisted us under Tsarism.'[32] Lenin too considered Soviet subsidies to be vital, but was concerned by reports of wastefulness and deceit. In a secret letter to the Central Committee of the Russian party dated 9 September 1921, he warned that 'financial assistance from the C[ommunist] I[nternational] to the communist parties of the bourgeois countries, while of course fully legal and necessary, sometimes leads to scandals and disgusting abuses'. The Central Committee must wage a 'merciless struggle against these abuses' and expel from the party all 'thieves and traitors' who try to cover up misdemeanours or use Comintern funds to secure better than average lifestyles.[33]

Regardless of Lenin's well-placed anxieties, the fact that the source of the financial bonanza was the Soviet state treasury, the keys to which were firmly in the hands of the Bolshevik leaders, meant that the Comintern and many of its national sections were economically dependent on the RCP Central Committee and the Soviet state. It is possible that in these early years the Bolsheviks did not intend to use subsidies as a means of bringing recalcitrant sections to heel, but it is undoubtedly the case that certain smaller parties could not have survived without this lifeline. In such unhealthy conditions the authority of the Bolsheviks and their chosen foreign acolytes was bound to grow inordinately.

This trend towards Russian dominance was accentuated by changes in the organisational structure of the Comintern from the Second to the Fourth Congresses. Between 1920 and 1922 the Comintern became increasingly centralised, its organisational framework duplicating the Bolshevik party model.[34] Before 1920 the Comintern had no permanent governing structures or procedures. Therefore, one of the prime tasks of the Second Congress was to ratify the Statutes of the Comintern [document 4]. This important document stipulated that the supreme body of the International was the annual world congress. Congress elected the Executive Committee which was to direct the entire activity of the Comintern between congresses. Point 8 of the Statutes clearly announced that the work of the ECCI 'is performed mainly by the Party of that country where ... the Executive Committee is located', that is Soviet Russia. Furthermore, 'this Party has five representatives with full voting rights on the Executive Committee', whereas the next ten to thirteen most important parties had only one representative. Formally, then, the Russian delegation could be outvoted, but in practice Bolshevik hegemony was virtually ensured. Point 9 empowered the ECCI to expel whole parties as well as 'groups or individuals who violate international discipline'.

The Third Congress in the summer of 1921 sought to reinforce the capabilities of the Executive Committee to intervene in the daily struggles of the communist parties, the goal being to make it a real directing centre of the world movement. One method was to despatch 'authorised representatives' from the ECCI to the national sections to oversee the activities of foreign communists. The sending of 'agents' and 'emissaries' became a common form of Moscow intervention in the affairs of the parties. The Third Congress also ratified mammoth theses on the organisational structure of the communist parties which emphasised the necessity of democratic centralism, the formation of communist 'cells' in factories and trade unions, systematic revolutionary propaganda and direct leadership control over the party press. Although at the Fourth Congress in November 1922 Lenin described these theses as 'too Russian' and 'quite unintelligible to foreigners,'[35] delegates adopted measures which strengthened still further the powers of the Comintern's governing organs. It was decided that national party congresses should convene after, not before, the world congress so that directives could be handed down 'from above to below'.[36] An unstated aim was to prevent parties from sending representatives to Moscow who were formally mandated on contentious issues.

In effect the resolutions of the Third and Fourth Congresses reproduced the Bolshevik organisational model in the Comintern. The creation of the ECCI Presidium, Secretariat, Organisational Bureau and International Control Commission paralleled the Russian party structure and strengthened the tendency to concentrate power in smaller bodies which as a rule were headed by Bolshevik cadres. The drift towards greater bureaucratisation was evident even before Stalin gained ascendancy in the Comintern.

Why were these processes set in train? The idea that the Bolsheviks consciously planned and imposed a form of 'Russian dictatorship' on the Comintern was widely held at the time by social democratic leaders and has since proved attractive to many historians. Lenin and Zinoviev must have realised that the outcome of their resolutions would be a 'Bolshevised' International and that a Comintern moulded in the Russian image would provide a buffer for the defence of the embattled Soviet state. In addition, the Comintern was inevitably influenced by developments in Russia, notably the militarisation of the Bolshevik party during the civil war, the statisation of the Soviets and the infamous ban on factions pushed through by Lenin in March 1921. With the prospect of revolution in Europe ever more distant, the consolidation of the Comintern and its member sections was vital, just as Bolshevik party unity had to be assured at a time of internal and external threat. As the Italian scholar Aldo Agosti has suggested 'from 1921, the "World Party" was no longer the organisational, political and ideological tool to bring about world revolution, but rather the means to stop the communist movement disintegrating, to administer and discipline it while *awaiting* the revolution'.[37]

But factors other than deliberate manipulation and Russocentrism also explain the gradual accretion of Muscovite hegemony. We have already mentioned that from the outset Bolshevik prestige, a product of the only successful socialist revolution, naturally afforded the Russians great political and theoretical authority in the Comintern. Moreover, all communists were convinced that the Second International's loose federal structure was one of the main reasons for its inaction and failure. Revolution on a world scale could only be achieved through a highly centralised and disciplined body in which national interests would be subordinated to international demands. Unity of will and leadership were unquestioned positive attributes. Indeed, the reorganisation of the ECCI at the Fourth Congress was largely the work of the German delegation. When introducing the theses, Eberlein attacked the 'federal spirit' that still existed in the Comintern, maintaining that the International must become 'a really centralised world party'.[38] It was commonly agreed that the best model for this organisational consolidation was the 'monolithic' Bolshevik party. To this extent it is inaccurate to talk unproblematically of 'Russian dictatorship'.

However, despite the fact that public dissent was comparatively rare, cautionary sentiments were expressed privately. In January 1921 the respected German revolutionary Clara Zetkin wrote to Lenin requesting him to use his influence to persuade the Executive Committee to be more 'careful with its letters and declarations [which] are sometimes of a coarse and imperious interventionist character, lacking in genuine knowledge of the actual conditions'. The ECCI, Zetkin continued, 'is cut off' from 'concrete circumstances' in different countries and this 'leads to mistakes' in the practical realisation of the Comintern line.[39] In the same month Steinhardt, the Austrian representative on the ECCI, brusquely asserted that 'the Executive Committee is a mere front [*kulisami*] for the Russian comrades'.[40] More overt opposition was dealt with severely. Paul Levi, the leader of the KPD, was expelled from the party in a storm of controversy after publicly assailing the 'March Action' of 1921 as 'the greatest Bakuninist putsch in history'. Levi berated the 'Turkestani' agents of the Comintern, such as Kun and Rákosi, who had goaded the KPD into this hopeless revolutionary uprising.[41] Expulsions were the ultimate sanction against refractory foreign communists and at this stage were used sparingly by the Bolsheviks.

These discordant voices identified a dangerous proclivity towards imposing the opinions of the centre on the national parties. The thrust towards centralised control was certainly manifest. But execution did not always match intent. The 'binding' resolutions of world congresses on occasion remained confined to the paper on which they were written. Cases of non-implementation of directives, ill discipline among party leaders, poor mutual communication between the ECCI and the national sections and rivalries between opposing party factions perturbed the Bolshevik leaders of the International. The French party was notorious for its endless internal squabbles and relative independence from Moscow. As we shall see below, several parties revolted against the adoption of united front tactics in 1921–2. What is more, in the early years of the Comintern's existence the Bolsheviks could not ride roughshod over renowned European labour leaders. The Germans Zetkin and Levi, the Italians Giancinto Serrati and Bordiga, the Frenchman Frossard, the Czech Bohumír Šmeral and a host of other figures on both the left and right wings of the movement were no docile stooges of the Russians. Their belief that a degree of local autonomy was possible within the framework of a centralised world movement could not be blatantly ignored.

These considerations, together with the plentiful examples of open debate and sharp disputes at the early congresses and ECCI plena, have persuaded some Russian historians that 'communist pluralism' and respect for national specificities epitomised the Comintern of Lenin's era.[42] The frankness of discussion and clash of opinions at the Second, Third and Fourth Congresses do indeed distinguish the Leninist Comintern from the later Stalinist monolith and should not be underestimated. But any pluralism that did exist in the Comintern was not formally institutionalised or guaranteed by the Statutes and Rules of the International. As Firsov has argued, the trend towards centralisation may have been 'partly counterbalanced and neutralised by collective debate' in Lenin's day, but after his death 'it became dominant'.[43]

What we have termed the 'universalisation of Bolshevism' between 1919 and 1923 was a complex process. No one single decision was taken to 'Bolshevise' the Comintern. The slogan of 'Bolshevisation' only became common currency after 1924. Before that date it was more the accumulative effect of a multitude of decisions, many taken in full consciousness of the supposed superiority of the Russian model, others under duress in adverse circumstances, others in the heady flush of expectant triumph when thoughts of 'Russification' were far from the executants' minds. There is evidence to suggest that centralisation was generally welcomed by foreign communists, who believed unity was an essential prerequisite of victory. It is impossible to say for sure whether the Bolsheviks had a long-term design to implant their organisational and tactical principles in the international movement to the exclusion of all other methods. It is quite feasible, but even if such a plan existed, Russian dominance would have been tempered by successful socialist revolutions in Europe. This dichotomy was never openly addressed and the absence of revolution abroad, combined with the survival of the isolated Soviet republic, inevitably strengthened the Bolsheviks' position.

UNITED WORKERS' FRONT

By late 1920 and into 1921 Lenin was reluctantly coming to the realisation that proletarian revolution in Europe was no longer on the immediate agenda. A temporary respite from the all-out assault on the bastions of capitalism was required. The result in the Comintern was the 'united workers' front' policy, which sought to revolutionise workers by indirect means. It was believed that joint defensive struggles with the socialist rank and file against the capitalist offensive would popularise communist methods and expose the hypocrisy of the reformist leaders. In certain conditions the united front could be extended to include temporary alliances with these leaders. These innovations, made in the face of bitter opposition from several communist parties, remained official Comintern practice from December 1921 to 1928.

The adoption of united front tactics had far-reaching implications. It was precisely in the spring and summer of 1921 that the tension between the Comintern's goal of world revolution and Soviet *raison d'état*, a tension which is traced throughout this book, became apparent. For if Soviet reconstruction via the New Economic Policy (NEP) was partly predicated on establishing commercial relations with capitalist nations, then what role for the Comintern, an organi-

sation explicitly designed to overthrow those very bourgeois governments with whom the Bolsheviks were now negotiating and signing
treaties? It was a conflict of interests rarely confronted by the
Russian leaders. But from this time on, the uneasy balance between
Narkomindel's traditional diplomacy and the Comintern's revolutionary mission started to tip unevenly, but steadily, in favour of the
former. The prestige of the 'world proletarian party' was on the
wane and continued to be so throughout the inter-war period.

The roots of the Comintern's united front tactics can be found in
the Bolsheviks' changing perception of the international revolutionary situation in late 1920 and early 1921. The intoxicating optimism
of the Second Congress and the Polish campaign was dissipating.
The following months witnessed a depressing litany of militant, yet
abortive, actions: the factory occupations in Italy, general strikes in
Romania, Czechoslovakia and Yugoslavia, and most disconcertingly
the disastrous revolutionary attempt in Germany, the 'March Action'. It was becoming evident to an increasingly cautious Lenin that
the capitalist order, though progressively decaying, was not on the
verge of collapse. It was also clear that, despite the foundation of
communist parties, the mass of organised workers remained committed to their reformist organisations. The stark conclusion was that
the day of European revolution was no longer imminent and the
communist vanguard was relatively weak and isolated. As Trotsky
admitted at the Third Comintern Congress in June 1921: 'Only now
do we see and feel that we are not immediately close to our final
aim, to the conquest of power on the world scale. . . . We told
ourselves back in 1919 that it was a question of months, but now we
say that it is perhaps a question of several years.'[44]

The first sign of a tactical shift in the Comintern came in January
1921 with the 'Open Letter' from the German party to the SPD,
USPD, the ultra-leftist KAPD and the socialist trade unions. This
appeal, drafted by Levi and Radek, called for common action in
defence of workers' daily interests. It was roundly rejected by the
non-communists, but it did display a more realistic tendency in
Comintern ranks. Lenin later described it as 'a model political step
. . . because it is the first act of a practical method of winning over
the majority of the working class'.[45] Lenin's enthusiasm notwithstanding, the idea of joint action with the reformists aroused a storm
of protest from those on the left of the communist parties. Adherents
of the revolutionary 'theory of the offensive' were strong in the

German, Italian, Hungarian and Austrian parties, but Lenin, despite
his deep antipathy towards the 'diplomats and heroes' of the Second
International, was quick to lambast 'leftist stupidities'.

Deep divisions were also manifest among the Bolsheviks themselves. Bukharin, the architect of the 'theory of the offensive',
Zinoviev and Radek were loth to admit the ebb of the revolutionary
wave and tended to interpret the united front as simply a manoeuvre
to expose the social democrats. Lenin and Trotsky were more
receptive of a broader conception of united actions with non-communists, including when necessary appeals to socialist party and
trade union leaders – the so-called 'united front from above'. This
clash of opinion in the Bolshevik leadership was patched up and
the Russian delegation to the Third Congress presented a draft
thesis on tactics in line with Lenin's thinking. After fierce disagreements and with certain compromises, congress ratified the thesis as
official Comintern policy. The slogan of the congress, 'To the
masses!', epitomised Lenin's desire to win over a majority of workers for revolutionary aims and laid the groundwork for the united
front.

It would be misleading, however, to seek the origins of the new
tactics solely in the internal machinations of the Third International.
The 'turn' in the Comintern was closely interwoven with fundamental changes in the domestic policy of Soviet Russia and in its dealings
with the Western powers. What underlay all three was the unforeseen delay in proletarian revolution. The hopes of a socialist Europe
coming to the aid of a backward Russia were gradually receding.
The failure of the revolutionary left in the industrialised West and
the resultant isolation of Soviet Russia had momentous longer term
consequences for the Comintern. But in early 1921 the Bolsheviks,
victorious at home in the civil war, were faced with the urgent need
to reconstruct the shattered country and appease the long-suffering
peasants and workers. Trade with the capitalist economies was
therefore imperative. As Carr suggests, the Bolsheviks were groping
their way towards:

> a new conception of foreign policy which would emphasize the
> defence of national interests and mark the retreat from a policy
> hostile in principle to all capitalist governments towards a policy
> which was prepared to bargain with capitalist governments indi-
> vidually or collectively on grounds of mutual expediency.[46]

Lenin's conception of international relations was twofold: on the one hand, to direct revolutionary propaganda to the workers of capitalist countries and the subject peoples of the colonies through the Comintern; and on the other, to exacerbate the contradictions and divisions among the imperialists through Narkomindel, the aim being a balance of power which would safeguard the precarious Soviet state. Before 1921 the theory of the revolutionary offensive had been essentially compatible with Soviet national interests, since successful proletarian uprisings in one or more European countries would have greatly reduced the external pressures on the war-ravaged Bolshevik regime. Thereafter, international diplomacy began to take precedence revealing inherent incompatibilities between the aims of the Soviet government and those of foreign communist parties. The Rapallo Treaty of April 1922 signed by the pariahs of Europe, Weimar Germany and Russia, epitomises these incompatibilities. Under the secret provisions of the treaty the German army, severely curtailed by the Versailles peace settlement, was to be rebuilt and modernised on Russian soil in return for military and economic concessions. The KPD was now confronted with the spectacle of a Soviet-sponsored Reichswehr firing on German communists, as indeed occurred in the Comintern-inspired revolution of October 1923. This episode graphically illustrates what Carr terms 'the ineradicable duality of Soviet relations with the outside world'.[47]

If we were to look for a watershed in this process it would be March 1921. Three significant events occurred in that month: the abysmal failure in central Germany of the 'March Action', an ill-planned uprising by the KPD inspired by Zinoviev and Béla Kun, which resulted in thousands of casualties and a mass exodus of party members; the introduction of NEP in Soviet Russia, which permitted semi-capitalist economic relations in town and countryside; and the signing of the Anglo-Soviet trade agreement, the first commercial deal between Moscow and a major capitalist government. It appeared that the Bolsheviks were in retreat on all three fronts, domestic, diplomatic and Comintern. The complementarity is striking. Indeed, the import of the changes for the Comintern was not lost on certain sceptical foreign communists. Dissentient mutterings were heard at the Third Congress and after to the effect that Soviet Russia was 'putting the brake on the revolutionary process' in order to 'do business with the bourgeoisie of the west'.[48] However trenchant these criticisms may have been, they remained isolated and tentative. While accepting that the exigencies of Soviet foreign policy had a major impact on the workings of the International, we have argued that factors other than the national interests of Soviet Russia played a significant part in the 'turn' of 1921. For it seems clear that the united front policy, though undoubtedly elaborated in Moscow, derived at least as much from a rational rethinking of the revolutionary conjuncture as from a conscious and narrow-minded 'Russification' of the Comintern.

Some historians, such as Jane Degras, have inferred that the shift to the united front tactics represented a strategic defeat for the Comintern, 'an implicit admission that the International had been founded on a misconception'.[49] In this view notions of world revolution had proven mythical and thus the Bolsheviks had made a mistake of historic proportions in seizing power in an agrarian country totally ill-suited for socialism. The adoption of united front tactics certainly marked the postponement of Soviet-style revolutions, but the Comintern's fundamental commitment to revolution was undimmed. According to Anthony D'Agostino, 'the turn toward united front tactics was not a turn to the right at all, but really a mobilization of the new Communist parties in industrial and local action'.[50] Hence, the scale of the retreat should be kept in perspective. Comintern leaders continued to stress the *revolutionary nature of the epoch* and envisaged the united front as a roundabout means to the final goal of world revolution: one step back to go two steps forward, to paraphrase Lenin. The problem was that not all foreign communists could comprehend the dialectical logic of the Bolsheviks.

The theses issued by the ECCI on 18 December 1921 formally expounding the united front tactics (document 6) are illustrative of this dilemma. It is noteworthy that the resolution was adopted on the initiative of the Russian Politburo, a striking indication of the Bolsheviks' determinant voice in Comintern affairs. The stated aim of the united front was to mobilise the broadest sections of the working class against capitalist attacks on the achievements won since 1918. In this struggle to defend the workers' daily interests communists were prepared to effect unity of action with socialists, even to approach the reformist leaders in a united front 'from above'. However, it must be borne in mind that the term 'united front' meant *joint action* primarily with socialist workers, not *organisational unity* with their leaders. At this time very few communists seriously contemplated the latter. The organisational gains of the previous two years had to be consolidated. The precondition laid down by the Comintern for any agreement with the socialists was 'the absolute independence of every communist party . . . to put forward its own views and to criticise the opponents of communism.'[15] By forging tighter links with the workers and exposing the 'collaborationist' policies of the reformist bosses, it was believed the mass of social democratic workers would rapidly find their way to the red flag of communism. This was to prove a forlorn hope.

Intense opposition to the united front theses was encountered in many parties, but was most vehement in the French, Italian and Spanish. Some communists, generally on the left, began to challenge the Comintern's authority, doubting the universal applicability of the new line to differing national circumstances. In France, where the PCF enjoyed majority support, the united front appeared completely untenable. In Italy, the PCI accepted it in the trade union sphere, but rejected it in political work. To many communist militants it seemed inconceivable that the 'social chauvinists' of yesterday were now apparently being courted by the Comintern. The awkward question was asked: why did we split socialist organisations in 1920 only to seek united action with them a year later? The mass of rank-and-file communists, so it was vainly argued by the opponents of the united front, would not understand this softening of line towards the social democratic bosses. Some representatives of the left, such as the KPD functionary Ruth Fischer, reluctantly accepted the united front provided that the defence of the daily interests of workers was accompanied by systematic communist propaganda directed towards the seizure of power. The final revolutionary goal should not be subsumed in any kind of unprincipled deal with the reformists.

Even more intractable was the problem of how to forge unity of action with social democrats who knew perfectly well that the ultimate aim was to destroy them. The new tactics presupposed not only communist propaganda activities, but also the creation of clandestine 'cells' in reformist political and trade union organisations, the discovery of which enabled social democratic leaders to expel communists with some justification. More specifically, how were communists to find the 'correct' path to socialist workers between the Scylla of excessive 'rightism' – tendencies to organisational unity 'from above' with reformist bodies – and the Charybdis of excessive 'leftism' – manipulative and hollow appeals 'from below' to the rank and file against their leaders? By never clearly delineating the limits of contact with socialist organisations the authors of the united front tactics prepared the ground for 'deviations' in the communist movement, since the Bolsheviks were the ultimate arbiters of what was the 'correct' path at any given time.

The contradictions inherent in the united front tactics were quickly evident. In April 1922 a conference of the three Internationals[52] took place in Berlin with the modest aim of creating the conditions necessary for common action against the capitalist offensive. Organisational unity was certainly not the order of the day. Nevertheless, the very fact that representatives from the hostile camps sat round a table and discussed the need for united action was of major significance. It was to be the only opportunity, albeit slim, of reconciling the historic split in the labour movement between reformists and revolutionaries. Indeed, the meeting marked the high point of the Comintern's efforts for a united front 'from above'. But the initiative failed. From the start of the proceedings deep mutual suspicions and apprehensions were voiced. Emile Vandervelde, one of the leading delegates of the Second International, described the ECCI's united front directives as 'a strange mixture of ingenuousness and Machiavelianism [sic]' in which 'an appeal is made for union, for the realisation of the united front, but no secret is made of the intention to stifle us and poison us after embracing us'. He insisted that the Comintern should proffer 'guarantees against *noyautage* [cell-building]; against fresh divisions, against attempts to break up the unity of the workers, in such countries as Belgium and England'.[53] The communist threat to social democratic dominance in the trade union movement was particularly worrying to the reformist leaders.

The prime concerns of the Second International delegation, however, were the fate of the arrested Socialist Revolutionaries, who were due to stand trial in Moscow, and Soviet Russia's 'imperialistic' adventures in Georgia, where the Menshevik government had been brutally crushed by the Red Army. The Soviet government's repressive domestic policies did not fit squarely with the Comintern's olive branch to the European non-communist left. The Comintern representatives in Berlin, Radek, Bukharin and Zetkin, made certain concessions on these issues and were severely chastised by Lenin for doing so. Aleksandr Vatlin has concluded that Lenin prioritised Soviet state security interests over Comintern tactics, the important implication being that precedents had been set that were to become standard practice under Stalin.[54]

Social democrats and communists remained as far apart as ever. The frosty negotiations at Berlin had exposed the limits of the 'united front from above', at least on the international level. Yet even on the national plane the Bolsheviks held out little hope for its success throughout the 1920s. It is true that the Fourth Congress in late 1922, meeting in an atmosphere of pessimism and frustration, adopted the slogan of a pre-revolutionary 'workers' government' in which communists would participate with social democrats providing the latter waged a bitter struggle against the bourgeoisie. But the concept was ill-defined, primarily directed at Weimar Germany and tended to be misconstrued as simply a synonym for the 'dictatorship of the proletariat'. Regardless of such united front innovations, the profound mutual animosities between communists and social democrats precluded any meaningful steps towards unity 'from above' until the advent of fascism in the mid-1930s.

Of far more significance was the united front 'from below'. Here, the Comintern's trade union tactics were crucial. Trade unions organised millions of workers and if communist parties were to fulfil the rallying-cry of the Third Congress, 'To the Masses!', they would have to develop clear policies in the industrial field. In the summer of 1921 the Red International of Labour Unions (RILU, commonly known as the Profintern) was created in Moscow as a focal point for the world's revolutionary trade unionists and anarcho-syndicalists. From its origins the Profintern established tight organisational links with the Comintern, its tactics mirroring those of the parent body. Just as the unions in Soviet Russia were subordinate to the Bolshevik party, so the Profintern became little more than an adjunct of the Comintern. The dissident Bolshevik, Aleksandr Lozovsky, served as General Secretary of the RILU from its foundation to its eventual dissolution in 1937.[55]

With the adoption of united front tactics the Profintern acquired a pivotal role in the international communist movement. Yet the concrete application and aims of the united front in the trade union sphere were never properly clarified. Were revolutionary unionists to work *within* the existing reformist organisations to win over the majority of members or should communist minorities withdraw and form independent 'Red' unions? The case of the Czechoslovak trade unions best illustrates this imprecision, and indeed the ultimate failure of the Comintern's trade union policies. The Czech example also reveals the limitations of Moscow's power in the early 1920s to direct the activities of foreign communists.

After World War I trade unions in Czechoslovakia, as elsewhere, experienced a massive growth in membership, despite the fact that the movement was split on political, ethnic and denominational lines. The largest union was the social democratic Czechoslovak Trade Union Association with approximately 820 000 members in 1920. By 1921 a sizeable minority of these workers, radicalised by harsh economic conditions and the conciliatory policies of the union executive, wished to disaffiliate from the reformist International Federation of Trade Unions (IFTU), based in Amsterdam, and adhere to the Profintern. The prolonged battle over 'Moscow or Amsterdam?' became intimately entwined with the Comintern's united front tactics. The official Profintern line was to remain in the reformist union to attract the majority of members to the revolution-ary cause, but most Czechoslovak communist trade unionists ignored Moscow's injunctions and sought to establish independent Red Unions in opposition to the social democrats. In the summer of 1922 pro-Profintern unions and individual activists were expelled by the reformist leadership and in October these revolutionary groups convened the founding congress of the Red Unions. The new organisation claimed some 160 000 members in 1923. A similar outcome occurred in France, the only other industrial country in which the communists formed their own separate union headquar-ters.[56]

Trade union unity had thus been broken in Czechoslovakia and France. The united front tactics, ostensibly aimed at preserving organisational unity and working-class cohesion, in fact made splits almost inevitable. The ideological and power struggle implicit in the tactics could only result in the expulsion of those communist mi-norities who refused to abide by majority decisions. The work entailed in the united front – relentless criticism of social democratic bosses, propagation of revolutionary ideas and methods and the formation of conspiratorial communist 'cells' designed to undermine the authority of union leaders from within – was bound to cause serious friction. Organisational schisms may not have been Moscow's objective, and certainly throughout 1922 Lozovsky insisted, in public at least, on the need for united advance. But they were the logical consequence of the united front 'from below'. Furthermore, Zinoviev deluded himself at the Fourth Comintern Congress when he stated that the Czechoslovak party had 'succeeded in rallying the largest section of the trade unions under the red flag' by 'brilliantly' applying the united front tactics.[57] At no time in the 1920s did membership of the Red Unions approach that of the social democratic union. Ultimately, communists failed to win over the majority of European trade unionists, an important reason for the effective demise of the united front tactics in the late 1920s.

The united front from below was aimed primarily at rank-and-file socialist workers and lower level organisations. But the French occupation of the Ruhr in January 1923 opened up the prospect of a controversial extension of the tactics to include the ultra-nationalist right-wing. This concept, often dubbed 'national Bolshevism', is associated with Radek, who in June delivered his famous 'Schlageter speech' to the Third Enlarged ECCI Plenum. Schlageter was an extreme German nationalist executed by the French for an act of terrorism in the Ruhr. Radek's gambit offered a political and spiritual home to the disoriented far-right nationalist – the 'wanderer into the void' – whose virulent anti-Weimar and anti-Versailles sentiment represented, so it was held, true revolutionary potential. Only the communist party, Radek intimated, could bring salvation and freedom to the entire German people. The 'Schlageter line' was not as radical a departure as it may seem. Radek certainly secured Zinoviev's prior agreement and the intention was to split the 'deluded' proletarian and lower middle-class nationalists from their fascist leaders. It was therefore perceived as fully compatible with the Comintern's campaign against international fascism.

In Germany the new policy was implemented with some gusto, particularly by the left-wing of the KPD who saw the alienated nationalists as more volatile than the sober social democratic workers. For several weeks communist speakers shared platforms with Nazi agitators and on occasion denounced 'the Jewish capitalists'. However, no formal alliance was struck. Indeed, the joint ventures were soon curtailed by the Nazi leadership with little gain to either side.[58] The episode appears relevant to the historian as an unsavoury foretaste of the collaborative actions of communists and Nazis in the years of the Great Depression when the social democrats were attacked by the Comintern as the greater evil. The roots of the Comintern's flirtation with the German fascists can thus be traced to the pre-Stalin era.

The 'Schlageter line' was predicated on a revolutionary scenario in Germany. Although the adoption of united front tactics undoubtedly marked a retreat from the all-out 'theory of the offensive', the Comintern had not lost sight of its prime *raison d'être*. In conducive circumstances, communist uprisings were still very much on the agenda. The 'German October' of 1923 is indicative of the latent revolutionary zeal of the Bolsheviks. The French and Belgian occupation of the Ruhr created what the Russian guardians of the Comintern believed to be a revolutionary situation in Germany. Working-class resistance to the occupiers, runaway inflation and the resultant governmental crisis persuaded both the Bolshevik hierarchy and many KPD activists that the time for action had come. Indeed, not since 1918–19 had the political and social scene in Germany been so tense and potentially explosive.

After the collapse of the Cuno government in August 1923, top-secret meetings between the Russian and German party leaders were held in Moscow. With Lenin terminally ill, the battle for his mantle was just commencing in the RCP. Among the Bolsheviks, Trotsky and Zinoviev were the most enthusiastic advocates of revolution with Radek and Stalin showing rather more caution. The KPD itself was miserably split between an intransigent and vocal left minority who believed revolution was around the corner and a more realistic majority who emphasised the need for systematic united front tactics in the trade unions and other socialist organisations. By September, however, all protagonists, including the KPD leaders Heinrich Brandler and August Thalheimer, were agreed on the need to act. Recent research in the Soviet archives has confirmed beyond all reasonable doubt that 'the plans for a German revolution were discussed and adopted in the Politburo of the RCP(b), while the German Communists were assigned the role of providing information and fulfilling the adopted decisions. The Comintern played the role of a driving gear between Moscow and Berlin.'[59] A five-member commission, including Radek and the Soviet Ambassador to Berlin, Nikolai Krestinsky, was sent clandestinely to Germany. This commission was to direct the political, military and logistical aspects of the revolution and as much as $400 000 were provided by the Russian party for these purposes.

It was decided by the Bolshevik Politburo that the uprising should be based on the districts of Saxony and Thuringia where sympathetic left social democratic administrations were in office. The idea was to enter the regional governments, arm the workers from the provincial arsenal, proclaim a general strike and coordinate a bid for power throughout the industrial areas of the country. However, the German communists failed to secure sufficient munitions. Neither did they win the support of the Saxon social democrats or the mass of workers for the anticipated general strike. Hence, on 25 October Brandler was forced to call off the action. In this he was given the backing of the on-the-spot Soviet advisers. For some unexplained reason the message did not reach Hamburg where local communists under the leadership of Ernst Thälmann fought police and army units for two days. Defeat was inevitable. It was not long before the Comintern and KPD were rocked by recriminations. Who was to blame for the catastrophe?[60] The dénouement of the story will be discussed in the next chapter.

The impotence of the German party to lead the masses to victory revealed three fundamental limitations in Comintern thinking and tactics. First, military preparations for the uprising were woefully inadequate and serious miscalculations as to the political disloyalty of Reichswehr troops appear to have influenced policy-making. Secondly, despite certain successes in the trade union and factory council movements, the inability of the KPD to gain support from social democratic leaders and workers displayed the inconsistencies of the united front tactics. Thirdly, and most importantly, the Bolshevik inspirers of the revolution once again misconceived the political mood of the German workers. Radicalised they were, but when the crunch came the vast majority refused to back an ill-planned coup. The communists' faith in the revolutionary maturity of the European working class suffered a severe shock. Illusions were not shattered immediately, but in the cold light of reflection the debacle convinced many Bolsheviks, most notably Stalin, that European revolution was a distant prospect and defence of the sole socialist bastion was the overriding priority. The abortive German revolution of 1923 thus represented a significant turning-point in the history of the Comintern and Soviet Russia.

In conclusion, we would argue that the Comintern in Lenin's era was characterised by five main contradictions. In the first place was the tension between what has been termed 'communist pluralism' and Bolshevik centralism. The relatively open debates and decision-making procedures of the infant International were gradually superseded by the behind-the-scenes manipulation of the RCP Politburo and its delegation in the ECCI. Secondly, Lenin's apparent willingness to recognise 'national specificities' and the overly 'Russian' nature of some Comintern resolutions clashed with his insistence on the universal applicability of the Bolshevik organisational and ideological model. Thirdly, the task of consolidating united mass communist parties with close links to the working and intermediate classes was undermined by doctrinal disputes and the imposition of strict discipline, which alienated even hardened party members and militated against the creation of mass parties. Fourthly, the attempt to forge united fronts with social democratic workers could not be readily reconciled with the Bolsheviks' profound antipathy towards the 'European Mensheviks'. The belief that rank-and-file socialist workers would flock to the communist banner once their leaders had been exposed as 'betrayers' soon proved illusory. In short, the Bolsheviks underestimated the continuing attraction of social democracy to large numbers of workers. Finally, and most importantly, by 1921 the Comintern's commitment to worldwide revolution was beginning to sit uncomfortably with the national interests of the Soviet state. It was perceived in Moscow that the militant actions of communist parties could endanger relations between Soviet Russia and foreign governments, thus threatening the very survival of the first socialist motherland.

The anti-democratic aspects of Bolshevism, present in Lenin's thinking and actions since *What is to be Done?*, were inevitably accentuated by the exigencies of the Russian Civil War. The dictatorial nature of the Bolshevik regime demonstrated by the dissolution of the Constituent Assembly, the clampdown on the Mensheviks and Socialist Revolutionaries and the statisation of the Soviets, trade unions and factory committees, did not bode well for a 'world party' of equals. Moreover, the delay in the European revolution could only mean that the international communist movement would be increasingly dependent on the resources, both material and moral, of this same dictatorial regime. It is debatable whether this outcome was consciously planned by the Bolsheviks; it was certainly a logical corollary of events. But it must be recognised that the Comintern from its inception was overwhelmingly a Russian invention. Hence, Bolshevik hegemony was always likely. The recourse to strict centralisation, palpable in the 'Twenty-one Conditions' and subsequent Comintern resolutions, was to be strengthened still further by the fierce power struggles in the Soviet party. This trend towards the 'Bolshevisation', and ultimate 'Stalinisation', of the Comintern is the theme of the following chapter.

2. Bolshevising the Comintern, 1924–8

The fiasco of the 'German October', the intensification of the inner-party struggle in Soviet Russia and the first real glimmerings of capitalist stabilisation plunged the Comintern into crisis. Against all expectations the European revolution had failed to materialise. The USSR stood alone and isolated. Factional disputes threatened the orderly functioning of the Comintern and the communist parties. Lenin's untimely demise in January 1924 threw the Bolsheviks into even greater confusion and placed at stake the future direction of the Russian Revolution. The ensuing life and death struggle in the Russian party saw the rise to power of Stalin, a rise accompanied by a process of centralisation and bureaucratisation that was to have a profound and lasting impact on the international communist movement. This process was immensely complex, reflecting the subtle tactical shifts and manoeuvrings of the various protagonists in the battle for Lenin's mantle. Ideological and operational formulas that became commonplace in the RCP found their way almost irresistibly into the Comintern. If the Russian party was to denounce and ultimately be purged of 'oppositionists' and 'deviationists', so too was the Comintern and its member sections. Stalin developed a particular penchant for these activities.

The outcome in tactical terms was that the period from 1924 to 1928 was characterised by ambiguities and waverings from left to right and back to left as the Comintern was forced to adapt not only to the exigencies of the power struggle and Soviet state interests, but also to changing national circumstances. In organisational and theoretical matters communist parties were subject to ever harsher discipline and enforced ideological unanimity, demotions and expulsions of recalcitrants became the norm, and the solid core that remained grew ever more dependent on the Soviet leadership in Moscow. As a result, by the end of 1928 Stalin and his circle were in control of the central Comintern apparatus and his supporters abroad were acquiring key positions in the parties. How was this possible? There is no easy answer, but the 'Bolshevisation' of the communist parties, or more specifically the form in which it came to be implemented, surely lies at the heart of the problem.

Bolshevisation, however, was not simply imposed from above, under pressure from Moscow. Exogenous and indigenous factors often interacted, creating moods and attitudes conducive to the implementation of the 'Russian line'. This chapter will examine the Bolshevisation of the Comintern and communist parties in three sections. The first elucidates the process from the standpoint of the principal protagonists in Moscow. This can be termed 'Bolshevisation from above'. The second assesses the national conditions and circumstances which facilitated, but also limited, this process. We have called this 'Bolshevisation from below'. The final section discusses the origins of the 'Third Period' in Comintern history, a period that was to mark the Stalinisation of the international communist movement.

BOLSHEVISATION FROM ABOVE

We must be clear at the start about definitions. By the term 'Bolshevisation' we mean a trend towards Russian dominance of the Comintern and its member sections, a trend reflected in the 'Russification' of the ideological and organisational structures of the communist parties and the canonisation of the Leninist principles of party unity, discipline and democratic centralism. More specifically, 'Bolshevisation' can be defined as the concentration of power in the hands of the Russian party delegation to the ECCI. This point is pivotal to an understanding of the Comintern's mechanism of functioning. Increasingly in the 1920s, the decisions that mattered emanated from this body, not from the constitutionally empowered broader organs, such as the ECCI and its plena. Foreign communists were called on simply to ratify decisions previously taken by the Russian delegation.[1] On the ideological front, Bolshevik intransigence towards social democracy tapped into a rich vein of 'leftist' communist culture common to all national parties, but most evident in Germany.

Western historians have generally maintained that the Bolshevisation of the Comintern was inherent in the 'Twenty-one Conditions' and was thrust upon reluctant communist parties under the combined weight of the Russian power struggles and the dictates of Soviet foreign policy. The argument that Bolshevisation was imposed from above is a powerful one and certainly cannot be underestimated as an explanation for the degeneration of the international communist movement. It can be summarised as follows: the campaigns in the RCP against 'Trotskyites', then 'Zinovievites' and finally 'Bukharinites' inevitably disfigured the internal regime of the Comintern and national communist parties resulting in bureaucratic centralism, ideological monolithism and a concomitant lack of political independence. To ensure total hegemony Stalin was compelled to defeat his opponents in both the Soviet and international arenas. At the same time, the failure of foreign parties to carry out successful revolutions left the USSR in an isolated and perilous position, surrounded by real or potential enemies. In this situation, the argument continues, Stalin decreed in the late 1920s that the overriding task of the Comintern and foreign communists was to defend the Soviet socialist bastion against imperialist attack. This could only be guaranteed if those parties operated on Bolshevik lines, strictly subordinate to the RCP majority and its current policies. Almost imperceptibly, Soviet state interests took precedence over the Comintern's original mission of world revolution and in the process that organisation became a mere appendage of Stalin's foreign diplomacy.

Such reasoning is no longer confined to mainstream Western historiography. Under the impact of Gorbachev's *glasnost* similar views were expressed by Soviet Comintern experts in what amounted to a sea-change in interpretation. What evidence supports this 'history from above' approach? Quite simply, a lot, and this section of the chapter surveys the existing arguments, both Western and Soviet.

There can be little doubt that in the course of the 1920s the Bolshevik leaders did come to dominate the Comintern Executive, determine its strategies and make and remake party leaderships virtually at will. It appears that almost from the Comintern's inception any major decision concerning tactics or personnel questions was taken in advance by the highest-ranking Bolshevik bodies. The ruling would be communicated to the Russian party delegation at the ECCI which then ensured its passage through the Comintern Executive. This practice evolved under Lenin, was consolidated during the interregnum and became set in stone under Stalin. Firsov writes:

> The most important issues were discussed in the VKP [RCP] Politburo and in its commissions, then the VKP delegation would inform the ECCI of decisions taken and the latter would approve them. The decisions to remove Zinoviev and later Bukharin from the Comintern's leadership were taken at the VKP plenums.[2]

In November 1926 the Italian communist, Palmiro Togliatti, confirmed with unusual frankness the Russians' guiding hand in the Comintern, stating: 'Of course, we have the statutes of the International which guarantee certain rights to certain comrades; but there is something which is not in these statutes, that is the position of the Russian party in the International, its function of leadership. That goes beyond the statutes.'[3] In these conditions the autonomy and competence of Comintern organs became increasingly limited and after 1929 they were virtually emasculated. Communist strategies were elaborated in the Kremlin and disseminated throughout the international movement by the Russian-dominated ECCI. This meant that whoever controlled the Russian party apparatus controlled the Comintern.

To discover the immediate roots of this 'Bolshevisation from above' we must return to the events following the 'German October'. The lessons drawn from the German defeat affected all parties, not just the KPD. In the background loomed the shadow of the inner-party struggle between the 'majority' Zinoviev–Kamenev–Stalin triumvirate and the Trotskyist 'opposition'. For the triumvirate, Trotsky had to be implicated in the Saxon debacle. The way to achieve this was to condemn Radek, his close colleague in the Comintern. At the stormy ECCI Presidium session in January 1924, called to diagnose the German events, Zinoviev attributed the failure of the KPD not to objective conditions, but to the 'opportunism' of

Radek, Brandler and Thalheimer, who had placed too much faith in social democracy and the united front from above. Trotsky, having given qualified support to the accused, was guilty by association. In the terminology of the day the Trotskyist opposition was a 'right deviation' subject to 'petty-bourgeois influences'. The dreaded word 'Trotskyism' made its appearance at this time, soon to be defined as a 'particularly dangerous deviation from Leninism'.

As far as the triumvirate was concerned, the first moral of the 'German October' had been established. In order to overcome 'rightist' errors a turn to the left was essential throughout the Comintern. The second lesson was unstated but no less far-reaching in its consequences. The KPD had failed to make a revolution, very few other parties had even tried and, despite rhetoric to the contrary, it was recognised in Moscow that future prospects were bleak. Inevitably, then, the prestige and dominance of the one party that *had* carried out a revolution, the Russian, was bound to wax. Soviet leaders agreed that if the KPD had acted like the Bolsheviks success would have been guaranteed. Communist parties must continually learn and prosper from the Russian experience. Bolshevik modes of organisation and methods of operation were valid for all. With the Soviet Union's continuing isolation in the 1920s this frame of mind hardened among the leading Bolsheviks and came to shape their attitudes towards the Comintern and member parties.

It was in these circumstances that the slogan of 'Bolshevisation' was first officially proclaimed at the Fifth Comintern Congress in June–July 1924 and later modified at the Fifth Enlarged ECCI Plenum in March–April 1925 (document 8). Ostensibly signifying 'the application of the general principles of Leninism to the concrete situation of the given country',[4] in practice it had the effect of Russifying the communist movement and, what is more, a Russification in an embryonic Stalinist form. The crux of Bolshevisation was the question of the relations of communist parties to the Comintern central bodies and to the Russian party. In conditions of intense internecine dispute, Bolshevisation came to mean above all the creation of strictly centralised, disciplined Leninist organisations fiercely loyal to the RCP majority in its struggle against the 'Trotskyite opposition'. There was to be no room for 'the survivals of traditional social-democratic ideas', the aim being to forge 'a homogeneous bolshevik world party permeated with the ideas of

Leninism'.[5] Bolshevisation was thus an amalgam of Marxist–Leninist ideology and practical political expedience.

The Fifth Congress deemed certain qualities and duties essential in a Bolshevised party: it 'must be a real mass party'; 'its tactics should not be sectarian or dogmatic'; 'it must be revolutionary, Marxist in nature'; and most importantly, 'it must be a centralised party, permitting no fractions, tendencies or groups'.[6] Zinoviev, reporting to congress, made this last duty painfully clear. He intoned, 'we need an iron discipline . . . we must root out all the remains and survivals of social-democratism, federalism, "autonomy"'.[7] In dealing with wayward party leaders, congress empowered ECCI 'to act far more decisively when necessary and not to shrink from the most extreme measures'. These directives did not augur well and when combined with a firm injunction that the 'decisions of the ECCI are binding on all sections and must be carried out by them without delay', made it plain to foreign communist leaders that their positions were dependent on loyalty to the Russian party majority.[8] This was the meaning of Zinoviev's and Stalin's oft-repeated demands for 'iron discipline'. To this extent Bolshevisation of the communist parties and the emerging 'cult of Leninism' in the RCP were two sides of the same coin.

As we have seen, Bolshevisation and the fight against 'Trotskyism' in the Comintern went hand in hand. 'Rightists' were now the main danger to communist orthodoxy and remained so throughout 1924. In that year a series of denunciations and expulsions reverberated through the Comintern. With the consent of the KPD Politburo, Brandler and Thalheimer were removed from the party leadership to be replaced by their bitter leftist antagonists, Arkadi Maslow, Fischer and Thälmann. In the French party Boris Souvarine was condemned as a 'Trotskyite' and expelled, as were Pierre Monatte and Alfred Rosmer. The Polish leaders Warski, Walecki and Wera Kostrzewa, the so-called 'three Ws', had the temerity to question the wisdom of the split in the RCP in a letter to the Politburo of the Russian party. Zinoviev outrageously warned them: 'If you try and move against us, we'll break your bones' and at Stalin's behest they were branded an 'opportunist opposition' harmful to the interests of the Soviet Union. Stripped of their executive functions, they were detained in Moscow.[9] This was Stalin's first sortie into the internal affairs of the communist parties. It was not the last. Precedents were being set that must have sunk deeply into the consciousness of other party leaders. The message was unambiguous: 'purify' your parties and align yourselves with the 'correct' policies of the RCP majority or face demotion, expulsion and marginalisation.

This hardening of attitude towards the 'right' in cadre questions was paralleled in the *Theses on Tactics* adopted at the Fifth Congress (document 7). Drafted by Zinoviev, the resolution betrayed his aim of the moment: to denounce Radek, Brandler and by association Trotsky, who had 'tried to distort completely' the united front tactics, interpreting them as 'an organic coalition with social democracy'. All such alliances and co-operation with 'the treacherous leaders of counter-revolutionary social democracy' had ended in disaster. As a result congress 'categorically rejected' the creation of united fronts solely from above. It was also recognised that the best way to construct truly mass communist parties was through persistent work in the trade unions and other working-class bodies, which were notoriously dominated by the self-same social democrats. Hence, the universal application of the united front from below 'under communist party leadership' was re-emphasised as a means of unmasking the reformist 'bosses' and winning a majority of workers for the revolutionary cause. The theses stated, 'united front tactics were and remain a method of revolution, not of peaceful evolution. They are . . . only a method of agitation and of revolutionary mobilization of the masses.' At the same time, it was rather reluctantly accepted that in countries such as Britain, where social democracy still represented a significant force, both variants – from below and from above – should be employed. Concurrently, 'ultra-left' phenomena also came in for attack, notably the 'extremely dangerous' tendency of communists leaving the trade unions and abandoning united front work. This was evident above all in Germany.[10] Overriding the despairing voices of Zetkin, Togliatti and particularly Radek, who asserted the need for a return to a broader application of the united front, the resolution was carried unanimously.

The significance of the Fifth Congress for the future development of the Comintern cannot be overestimated. On the surface the outcome was obvious. The 'right' had been routed, discipline, centralisation and uniformity had been declared paramount and 'Bolshevisation' had become the watchword for all. Moreover, important personnel changes had been agreed. Radek was removed from the ECCI and Trotsky was demoted to non-voting candidate status to be replaced by Stalin, a distinct sign of the times. Yet both

Carr and Gruber stress the *ambiguous* nature of the resolutions.[11] In effect, congress had failed to resolve the contradiction of implementing a left-wing strategy by right-wing tactics. How to smash social democracy from within? Where was the logic in rejecting contacts with social democratic parties, while simultaneously demanding work within reformist trade unions? United front tactics remained a source of confusion and aroused ongoing dissent from both right and left in the communist parties. From the former, because the united front from below as a 'revolutionary manoeuvre' threatened to reduce the parties to mere sects in the workers' movement; from the latter, because events had proven that social democracy was inherently counter-revolutionary and therefore to agitate within reformist organisations was a waste of time. The response should be withdrawal and the formation of independent 'red' trade unions. These dilemmas of the period 1924–8 were never properly resolved. Consequently, 'zigzags' abounded in Comintern tactics: 1924 marked a shift to the left; 1925–6 saw a tentative and uneven move back to the centre under Bukharin's tutelage, emphasising a broader conception of the united front tactics and a differentiated approach to the transition from capitalism to socialism; and 1927–8 witnessed the beginning of the infamous 'left turn' that was to culminate in the sectarian dogmas of the Third Period.

Carr has put his finger on another closely related problem. The clash between the right and left wings of the communist parties had a powerful impact on the composition of the leaderships of those parties. In conditions of perpetual internal strife, it became vital for the Russian-controlled ECCI to:

> create and keep in being a nucleus of the moderate Left from which the party leadership could be drawn. . . . It was essential that the leaders of the respective parties should be, not men irrevocably committed to a policy, whether of the Left or of the Right, but men on whose unquestioning loyalty the central authorities of Comintern could count.

For this reason the intervention of the Comintern and its agents in the internal life of the parties 'almost always turned on the choice of leaders', irrespective of issues of policy.[12] This was an area in which Stalin took great personal interest.

Stalin's role in the formulation and implementation of the left shift in 1924 is instructive. Before the autumn of 1923 he had scarcely bothered himself with Comintern affairs. The search for allies in the struggle with Trotsky changed all this. According to Soviet accounts based on research in the Comintern Archive, Stalin's star was on the ascendancy from late 1923 onwards. Together with Zinoviev he was instrumental in devising the Bolshevisation campaign and in shifting the united front tactics to the left as a means of exposing both the social democratic 'betrayers' of the German Revolution and by inference their Russian 'Menshevik' counterparts, Trotsky and Radek. Stalin's deep-seated animosity towards social democracy, which he retained throughout the inter-war years, is summed up in his dictum of January 1924: 'no coalition with social democracy, but a mortal struggle with it'.[13] For him, European social democrats had to be defeated if socialist revolution was to take place.

Soviet historians have asserted that the redefinition of the united front tactics and of communist relations with social democracy represented a 'sectarian distortion' of Lenin's more flexible conception of the tactics, isolating the communist movement and laying the theoretical foundations for the subsequent 'social fascist' label of 1929–33. In justifying this interpretation they emphasise Stalin's infamous and deeply flawed conclusion of September 1924 that social democracy was 'objectively the moderate wing of fascism'. The two were 'not antipodes, but twins'. More ominously, Firsov asserts that Stalin's assault on the Polish 'three Ws' as defenders of the Trotskyist opposition in the RCP and as opponents of Soviet power, signalled the beginning of a process that culminated in the epithet 'enemy of the people' and the mass physical violence of the Great Terror.[14] Clearly, Stalin's methods were often crude and injected a decidedly sour note into Comintern deliberations.

Stalin's undoubted role in the left turn of 1924 should, however, be placed in perspective. It can be argued that he did not yet possess the authority or independence of action in the Comintern of a Zinoviev, Trotsky or Bukharin. He was a relative newcomer to the international stage, hardly a cosmopolitan figure. He surely needed to tread carefully, win and re-win allies, undermine rivals, consolidate his own power. To this end, Stalin liked to portray himself as a cautious 'centrist', preferring patient work behind the scenes to loud-mouthed polemics, studied moderation to wilful extremism. By skilfully handling his tactical alliances with first Zinoviev and then Bukharin, by using his dominance in the RCP apparatus and by his occasional, sometimes ruthless, forays into the affairs of individual communist parties, Stalin was able steadily to build up a solid core of support in the ECCI and in the movement as a whole. In the course of the power struggles many top Comintern officials came round to Stalin's way of thinking: Dmitri Manuilsky, Otto Kuusinen, Vilgelm Knorin, Piatnitsky, Kun and Lozovsky to name but a few. We shall come back to Stalin's actual methods later.

The pre-*glasnost* consensus among Western historians tends to confirm this more balanced interpretation of Stalin's position in 1924. Most scholars believe the Comintern at that time was still the domain of its President, Zinoviev. According to Isaac Deutscher, 'Zinoviev had by now complete mastery over the International' and ruled 'with relish, flamboyance, lack of tact and scruple'.[15] However, after the German fiasco and other setbacks in Bulgaria and Poland,[16] the Comintern was in crisis and Zinoviev felt constrained to defend 'his' organisation from critics at home and abroad. It is, then, most probable that Zinoviev was the prime mover of the left turn and the Bolshevisation campaign in a somewhat desperate attempt to discredit his 'rightist' opponents and replace them with loyal acolytes. Hence, the frantic demotions and promotions in the German, French and Polish parties. Yet it is possible that Zinoviev was motivated by ideological as well as opportunist considerations. It was he who provided the theoretical underpinning of the shift to the left by equating social democracy with fascism. Zinoviev, not Stalin, first insisted in early 1924 that social democracy was 'a wing of fascism'. The moral was that the social democratic leaders were now the main enemy and any communist who favoured collaboration with them was no Bolshevik. To the extent that Bolshevisation and 'social fascism' served his goal of political power and, importantly, reflected his ideological convictions, Stalin was quite prepared to follow Zinoviev's lead in Comintern affairs. This is perhaps the most plausible evaluation of the complex developments in the international communist movement in the crucial year of 1924.

That year was crucial in more ways than one. It also saw the birth of the doctrine of 'socialism in one country'. Propounded, tentatively, by Stalin in December, he seems to have drawn and expanded upon Bukharin's earlier notions of 'growing into socialism'. In the mid-1920s the Stalin–Bukharin axis was forged on this theory of 'socialism in one country'. But what did Stalin actually say on the highly problematic subject? He assiduously, though controversially, stressed the authentic Leninist origins of the theory. Lenin's 'law of the uneven, spasmodic, economic and political development of the capitalist countries' signified that 'the victory of socialism in one country, ... while capitalism remains in other countries, ... is quite possible and probable'. However, Stalin could not allow himself to appear overly unorthodox and added: 'it goes without saying that for the *complete* victory of socialism, for a *complete* guarantee against the restoration of the old order, the united efforts of the proletarians of several countries are necessary'.[17] Yet even this formulation did not explicitly recognise the necessity of revolution in other capitalist states. 'United efforts' could cover a whole gamut of activities. Stalin's emphasis was certainly innovative and potentially explosive. The construction of socialism in a single country – the Soviet Union – *was* possible without the need for world revolution.

The immense significance of this doctrine for the international communist movement was not readily apparent, not even, most likely, to Stalin himself. No one at the time took much notice of the General Secretary's rare sally into the dizzy realms of theory. It was only in the changing circumstances of 1925–7 that he felt sufficiently confident to modify and enlarge on his views, spelling out the implications for the Comintern and its member parties. His logic must have seemed impeccable to many Russian and foreign comrades. Starting from the orthodox Leninist premise that world revolution was historically inevitable, he noted that at present the tide of revolutionary upheaval had temporarily ebbed and the immediate prospects were unpromising; the Soviet Union, the only country to have carried out a successful revolution, possessed the capabilities of building a complete socialist society without the preliminary victory of revolution in other countries; as such it was the bulwark of the world socialist revolution and must be safeguarded at all costs from the predatory attacks of international imperialism; in these circumstances the main task of the Comintern and communist parties was to defend the Soviet Union, not to foment premature revolutionary uprisings; indeed, a strengthened socialist USSR would hasten world revolution since it would act as a beacon of inspiration for the international proletariat. The implication was that the revolutionary mission of the Comintern and the communist parties should be subordinated to the interests of the Soviet state and its foreign diplomacy. It is difficult to avoid the conclusion that for Stalin this was the prime aim of Bolshevisation.

Stalin's version of 'socialism in one country' was predicated not only on faith in the socialist capabilities of the USSR, but also on a cautiously realistic evaluation of the contemporary state of industrial capitalism. In 1925 the emerging Bukharin–Stalin duumvirate detected a 'temporary' and 'relative stabilisation of capitalism' in Western Europe and North America. Technological advance, quantitative growth in production and the easing of international tensions as a result of the Dawes Plan and the 'Locarno spirit' meant that capitalism had for the time being consolidated itself, delaying its inevitable demise. But crucially there were *two* stabilisations. In Soviet Russia, the NEP had facilitated the stabilisation of the economy and thus in Stalin's words 'a certain temporary equilibrium' existed between the capitalist and Soviet systems. In these circumstances what the USSR needed was a prolonged and tranquil period of socialist construction, free from the threat of imperialist intervention. Hence, Western governments had to be persuaded of, or pressurised into, 'peaceful coexistence' with the Soviet Union.

This is where Stalin and his followers believed the Comintern and communist parties could combine a commitment to the defence of the Soviet state with the principle of proletarian internationalism. For if the communists could build mass parties by strengthening their influence over the European working class, would not the 'moral support' for the USSR thus engendered be of 'inestimable importance' in helping to prevent Western aggression and stimulate commercial and trading links with Soviet Russia?[18] And would not the 'workers' delegations' from Britain, Germany and elsewhere that toured the USSR in the mid-1920s help to foster pro-Soviet feeling and ensure peaceful coexistence? Yes indeed, as Stalin made clear at the Fourteenth Party Congress in December 1925: 'this pilgrimage of workers to our country' was of great significance for 'if the workers refuse to fight our Republic, if they regard our Republic as their child in whose fate they are closely concerned, then war against our country becomes impossible'.[19]

What effect did these calculations have on Comintern policy? By affirming the notion of 'relative capitalist stabilisation' at the Fifth ECCI Plenum in March–April 1925, the Comintern tacitly recognised the existence of a transitional stage between revolutions. As such, the concept stuck in the throats of many impatient Russian and foreign communists. But a temporary lull in the revolution invariably meant a renewed emphasis on united front tactics. The plenum declared with some urgency that 'a hundred times more attention than before must be devoted' to work in the reformist and other trade unions. This was an 'integral part of Bolshevisation'.[20] For the next two years it was a firm belief in Comintern circles that systematic work in the unions, those 'fortresses' of European labour, and conscientious defence of members' daily interests would serve two inter-related goals: the building of mass communist parties and the consolidation of pro-Soviet sentiments among non-communist workers.

With the same aims in mind, a campaign for national and international trade union unity was launched, the prime example of which was the Anglo-Russian Trade Union Committee formed in April 1925 between the leaders of the British and Soviet central union bodies. According to Stalin, the objective of the Committee was twofold:

> firstly, to strengthen the connections between our trade unions and the trade-union movement of the West and to revolutionise the latter, and, secondly, to wage a struggle against imperialist wars in general, and intervention [against the USSR] in particular.[21]

This last point was paramount for the Soviet leaders. Bukharin, addressing a meeting of the ECCI Presidium in May 1927, asserted that in the event of war the British trade unions 'will not support us, but they will act as ballast around the legs of the British government. And this at least is something'.[22] Evidently the hope in Moscow was that a bloc with the left-inclined British unions would serve as a deterrent to anti-Soviet aggression as well as create a breach in the social democratic trade union movement allowing for international unity on communist terms. In this the Soviet leaders seriously miscalculated and the Committee was dissolved in September 1927 in some acrimony.

The emphasis on the unification of the trade union movement, including the possibility of united fronts from above, the greater subtlety of socio-economic analysis and the tempering, though by no means disavowal, of the endemic Bolshevik hostility towards social democracy suggest the growing influence of Bukharin on Comintern affairs in the period 1925–7. Indeed, by the end of 1925 it appears Bukharin was displacing Zinoviev as the key figure in the ECCI, a position he was to hold until mid-1928.[23] Yet Bukharin's and Stalin's assessment of the domestic and international situation in the 'quiet year' of 1925 and the conclusions they drew from it did not immediately incur the wrath of their opponents. Trotsky spent 1925 in broody silence, Stalin's alliance with Zinoviev and Kamenev teetered on until the autumn. Only then did Zinoviev and, from 1926, Trotsky take up the gauntlet of 'socialism in one country', joining forces in a somewhat ill-assorted bloc against the 'Stalinist apparatus'.

Neither Trotsky nor Zinoviev doubted that the *process* of building a socialist society was ongoing in the Soviet Union, but they could not accept that the *final* or complete victory of socialism was possible without successful revolutions abroad. For Trotsky, the idea of a single socialist economy isolated in an international capitalist market made a mockery of Marxist theory. Hence, the 'narrow national-mindedness' and 'national reformism' inherent in the theory of socialism in one country appalled the nascent United Opposition, as did Stalin's and Bukharin's apparent downgrading of proletarian internationalism and the prospects of world revolution. These were articles of faith for Zinoviev and Trotsky on which the ultimate fate of Soviet Russia depended. As Zinoviev stated in his much interrupted speech to the Fifteenth Party Conference in October 1926: 'The final victory of socialism in one country is impossible. . . . *We are building and will build socialism in the USSR with the aid of the world proletariat*. . . . We will win final victory because revolution in other countries is inevitable'.[24] By then such views found precious few adherents among his unsympathetic listeners.

It would be little exaggeration to say that during 1926 and especially 1927 the increasingly malicious disputes between the Bukharin–Stalin duumvirate and the United Opposition of Zinoviev, Kamenev and Trotsky, accompanied by machiavellian manoeuvrings, tactical alliances and re-alliances, dominated the internal regime of the Comintern and poisoned the atmosphere in the communist parties. The dénouement of the struggle came in stages. In October 1926 Zinoviev was relieved of his post as President of the Comintern and replaced by a 'collective leadership' informally headed by Bukharin. In September 1927 at an acrimonious session of the ECCI Presidium, carefully stage-managed by Bukharin, Stalin and Molotov, Trotsky told a hostile audience, 'I have no doubt that even your verdict is ready.'[25] It was. He was hounded out of the ECCI, out of the Comintern and within sixteen months out of the Soviet Union.

Trotsky and Zinoviev had been vociferous opponents of Comintern tactics on a number of issues: the Anglo-Russian Trade Union Committee, the British General Strike and most vehemently the Chinese revolution. Aspects of their critique were damning, notably the assertion that the Comintern had degenerated into a 'bureaucratic-apparat regime', which, under the pernicious influence of the Stalinists and Bukharinists, had eliminated in theory and practice the goal of world revolution. Even more contentious was the belief that the formation of an 'opportunist' united front from above with the British trade union bosses represented 'collaboration with traitors' and a betrayal of the British working class. Trotsky also assailed the alliance of the Chinese communists with the bourgeois anti-imperialist Guomindang nationalists, an alliance forced on the Chinese party by the ECCI. To be sure, Stalin's and Bukharin's policy in China ended in disaster, but there is no evidence to suggest that when the liaison with the Guomindang was first established in 1922 Trotsky and Zinoviev publicly opposed it. Any misgivings they may have had remained private. But with the benefit of hindsight, Trotsky was to write in the 1930s that the Comintern had suffered a series of 'historic catastrophes which killed the faith of the Soviet masses in world revolution'. Stalin 'looked upon the Communist International as a necessary evil which should be used so far as possible for the purposes of foreign policy'.[26] There was more than a grain of truth in Trotsky's biting analysis, but in the harsh realities of 1927, when revolution in the West seemed an ever more distant prospect, the United Opposition lay open to attacks of 'defeatism', 'splitting the party' and weakening the security of the USSR at a time of imperialist threat. These accusations struck deep chords in party ranks and laid the basis for the rout of the United Opposition in the RCP and Comintern.

The final theme in this section on Bolshevisation from above is a crucial one: the methods used by Soviet leaders to control communist parties and, when necessary, combat 'deviationists'. The subsidising of communist parties remained a vital lever of Soviet influence. The example of the British party illustrates the point. In an unpublished 'confidential manuscript' from 1970, the veteran R. Palme Dutt related how in June 1923 Mikhail Borodin, a leading Bolshevik, asked him, 'How can we count on their [British communists'] loyalty if we do not pay them?' Dutt records his reply, 'You will get the only loyalty worth having if not a penny passes.' Apparently, Dutt's views were 'regarded as a serious departure from the principles of internationalism'.[27] The payments continued. According to party files seized during a police raid, the Comintern allocated £5000 in 1924 and a year later the figure had risen to £16 000.[28] Yet there are indications that by the early 1930s the coffers in Moscow were drying up. On 14 January 1932, the General Secretary, Harry Pollitt, reported to the Political Bureau of the CPGB that 'the whole question of finance' will be raised 'more sharply.... The International is taking up an entirely new attitude ... and they are determined to throw all the parties more and more on their own resources. So far as our Party is concerned, this is long overdue'.[29] It is possible that the funding of other sections followed a similar pattern, though much painstaking research is required to prove this assumption.

Another common method of influencing and pressurising local communists was the practice, begun under Lenin, of despatching agents from Moscow to carry out the bidding of the ECCI. Prominent figures such as Manuilsky, Humbert-Droz and Petrovsky acted as guardians of Comintern orthodoxy in, respectively, the German, Czechoslovak, French and British parties either on a semi-permanent or emergency basis. An unpleasant, and perhaps unintentional, outcome was the impetus given to factional party in-fighting and intrigue. In its campaign to win power, each contending clique would seek the patronage of the ECCI emissary in order to curry Moscow's favour. The result was a strengthening of the bureaucratic and undemocratic tendencies in the parties. In these circumstances outside intervention was not always unwelcome, and indeed was occasionally solicited by embattled party leaders striving to shore up their authority. Moreover, in the course of their activities Comintern agents themselves could fall prey to local attitudes which set them at odds with the ECCI. Influence and control was a two-way game and Moscow did not always have the trump cards.[30]

A third lever open to the ECCI was to detain 'trouble-makers' in the USSR or send them abroad on official Comintern business. This was a useful way of removing discredited communist leaders from the corridors of power in their own countries. The prime example concerned the Germans, Brandler and Thalheimer, who lived and worked in the Soviet Union from 1924 to 1928, largely isolated from the cabals in the KPD. While in the USSR many foreign communists became registered members of the Russian party thus subjecting them to Leninist, and later Stalinist, party discipline. This was yet one more means of control, not to be underestimated.

Soviet scholarship of the *glasnost* period shed light on another fascinating subject. Focusing on Stalin's single-minded quest for personal and absolute power, Soviet historians emphasised his almost paranoic insistence on the 'monolithic party', *vozhdizm* (one-man rule) and his advocacy of 'command-order' solutions to political and cadre questions. One feature in particular stands out: his penchant for *otsechenie*, or 'chopping-off' troublesome comrades. It was a truly chilling term he uttered on more than one occasion. For instance, in March 1925 Stalin informed his audience at the Fifth ECCI Plenum that 'there are times when it is necessary to chop off harmful members from the party in order to safeguard the party organism from chronic diseases'. In a speech a year later he reiterated this theme in starker terms, talking of the need 'to take the surgical knife in hand to cut off certain comrades'. Though Stalin accepted that the 'methods of vivisection' were applicable 'only in extreme cases', his use of such terminology cannot be coincidental.[31] 'Certain comrades' were indeed 'cut off' for their real or alleged associations with the Russian United Opposition – Fischer, Maslow and the 'ultra-left' in the KPD, Bordiga in the Italian party, and Treint and Girault in the French. It is hard to believe that the guiding hand behind such crass moves was not Stalin's.

Nevertheless, two important caveats are required. First, 'cutting off' at this stage did not signify physical destruction, but rather dismissal from executive functions or in extreme cases from the party itself. Secondly, Stalin cannot be held solely responsible for these and other disciplinary measures. Both Zinoviev, while his powers in the Comintern still lasted, and Bukharin were prepared to root out and sacrifice 'harmful elements', thus unwittingly condoning the self-same repressive actions that would soon be turned on them.

How best to evaluate the process of 'Bolshevisation from above'? We have emphasised the decisive role of the Russian party in the development of the Comintern, demonstrating that Bolshevisation was closely linked to the power struggles in the RCP. But another factor deserves consideration. The chaotic faction-ridden state of many parties in the mid-1920s may well have persuaded the Soviet leaders, regardless of their own political ambitions, that order, efficiency and discipline were urgently required. For example, the

French party was being torn asunder by personal vendettas and factional in-fighting long before the 'Russian Question' entered the fray.[32] This 'anarchy', anathema to the Bolsheviks, was paralysing the rational functioning of the PCF. Is it possible, then, that Moscow perceived the Bolshevisation of the PCF more in terms of the positive need for organisational unity and efficiency than the desire to expel French 'Trotskyites' and bring the party under direct Russian tutelage? Was this the main motivation behind the 'Bolshevisation of the parties'? If so, Carr's contention that the increasing centralisation and Russification of the Comintern was 'unconsciously accepted rather than deliberately planned by the Bolshevik leaders' is convincing.[33] Whatever the case, the objective realities combined with subjective predispositions ensured the increasing dominance of the Russians in the international communist movement.

BOLSHEVISATION FROM BELOW

By concentrating on the machinations of the Russian leadership the impression has probably been given that the communist parties were docile, reluctant recipients of directives from on high with no input in the Comintern's decision-making processes. As we have seen, there is solid evidence to support the theory that the sole impetus for Bolshevisation came from Moscow, not Berlin, Paris or Prague. But this interpretation would be an over-simplification. To gain a deeper understanding of the development of the Comintern and communist parties in the mid-1920s we need to examine national conditions and assess whether they were conducive to Bolshevisation, or at least to various aspects of it. We must bear in mind that Bolshevisation was to a certain extent an interactive process with exogenous and indigenous pressures co-mingling to produce subtle variations from country to country. At the same time, we should attempt to delineate between compliance with, and stimulus towards, Bolshevisation on the part of the communist parties, between passive acceptance and pro-active involvement. There are several important factors here: the political and psychological ties that bound communists to the first 'socialist bastion', the USSR; the tendency to bureaucratisation in modern organisations; the expanding role of the State that seemed to confirm the centralist propensities of Marxism–Leninism; and the underlying social, economic and cultural changes that were threatening to fragment and reshape the structure of the European working class. At the same time, we should not neglect the resistance to, and limitations of, Bolshevisation in the communist movement before 1928. Bolshevisation did not yet equal Stalinisation.

Let us take the question of communist loyalty first. Deutscher has argued cogently in his biography of Trotsky that the sincere respect felt by communists for the Bolsheviks could and did lapse into a form of deference. He writes:

> the ebb of revolution in Europe tended to transform the International into an adjunct to the Russian party. The self-assurance of its European sections was weak; and it dwindled from year to year. The defeated parties developed a sense of inferiority; and they came to look to the Bolsheviks, the only successful practitioners of revolution, to tackle their problems, to solve their dilemmas, and to make their decisions for them.[34]

The picture that emerges is one of increasingly subservient party leaders bowing to the will of the Bolsheviks either from conviction, from a sense of disorientation and helplessness or from a resigned awareness that 'our Soviet comrades know best'. The inclination was for parties to await passively directives from the ECCI. But compare this with the following passage also by Deutscher from his volume on Stalin: 'In those years [mid-1920s] the European Communist leaders, though accepting guidance from the successful Bolshevik experts on revolution, still talked to them as equals and took for granted their own right to have a say in Russian affairs.'[35] Evidently the question of submissiveness towards Moscow is far from straightforward. Not all foreign communists lost their self-confidence and critical capabilities. Nevertheless, it is reasonable to conclude that the position of strong-minded leaders became increasingly untenable as the scope for autonomy and open discussion narrowed.

Other historians, such as Eric Hobsbawm, have stressed the more positive dynamic attitudes which galvanised inter-war communists behind the Comintern and the Russian party. These included 'natural enthusiasm' and 'the *certainty*' of socialist revolution; the realisation that, 'while Lenin had succeeded', the social democratic and anarcho-syndicalist alternatives had failed; the 'passionate and total loyalty which individual communists felt to their cause'; and finally a deep commitment to 'internationalism', a corollary of which was 'the immense strength' and sense of identity and cohesion drawn 'from the consciousness of being soldiers in a single international army, operating . . . a single grand strategy of world revolution'. This in turn meant for most party members 'the impossibility of any fundamental or long-term conflict between the interest of a national movement and the International'.[36] Indeed, for persecuted parties, like the Italian and Polish and the relatively weak parties of Central and Eastern Europe, the link with the Comintern provided a sustaining pillar in the face of fascist or neo-fascist repression. Furthermore, the 'feelings of solidarity with the USSR, with the cause of October' were shared by all foreign communists and came to be embodied in Stalin, 'the true pupil of Lenin'.[37] Undoubtedly this deeply felt fidelity, based on the knowledge that the Russians had superior revolutionary experience and held the key to human progress, inclined European communists to accept the 'Moscow line'. How could the Bolsheviks be wrong when they alone had carried through a successful socialist revolution in the face of concerted Western hostility? Such sentiments were widespread and cannot simply be dismissed as 'false consciousness'.

In addition, foreign communists gradually recognised that backing the Soviet party meant logically backing the Stalinist victors in the power struggle. There was little choice if one wished to stay in the communist mainstream. The example of Togliatti, a major figure in the Italian party, illustrates the point. In October 1926 Antonio Gramsci, the General Secretary of the PCI, addressed a letter to the Central Committee of the Russian party in which he expressed concern over the tactics employed by the majority against the United Opposition. Togliatti, PCI representative in Moscow, declined to pass the letter on fearing, correctly, that it would be seen as interference in the affairs of the RCP. He did, however, show it to Bukharin, who apparently warned him that the letter would seriously harm relations between the two parties. Togliatti then sent a curt reply to Gramsci reprimanding him for his 'pessimism', 'incorrect assessment' and his unwillingness to condemn outright the opposition.[38] Togliatti's commitment to the RCP majority was probably sincere, but he also surely realised that the Italian communist movement would suffer if its leaders retained an equivocal attitude to the Trotskyite–Zinovievite opposition. As Hobsbawm argues, 'under the circumstances loyalty to Moscow ceased to depend on approval of the Moscow line, but became an operational necessity'.[39]

These essentially subjectivist explanations for communist adherence to the Russian 'line' can be counter-balanced by more objective factors. Relevant here is the fact that Bolshevisation was *inter alia* a centralising bureaucratising phenomenon. The Twenty-one Conditions of 1920 had laid the basis for a highly centralised organisational structure in the Comintern, but after 1923–4 this structure and mode of administration became increasingly prone to what can be termed 'the logic of bureaucratisation'. As world congresses became less frequent after 1922, so greater power devolved to the Executive Committee and its Presidium. As the demands and variety of work multiplied these two bodies grew top-heavy and hence less and less able to function properly. Membership in them had more than quintupled between 1919 and 1928. This in turn necessitated the establishment of new narrower organs – first the Political Secretariat of the ECCI in 1926, and then the cumbersomely named Political Commission of the Political Secretariat of the ECCI in 1929. These important executive and administrative organs, based in Moscow and staffed disproportionately with Bolsheviks, managed the day-to-day workings of the International and ensured Russian hegemony in the Comintern apparatus.

It has been asserted that this pattern of bureaucratisation, transmitted to the national communist parties, conforms to general trends in organisational life. Again in Hobsbawm's words: 'any effective and lasting organization in modern industrial society tends to be bureaucratised in some degree, including revolutionary parties'.[40] This is no doubt true. Michels's theory of the 'iron law of oligarchy' is certainly applicable to communist parties, but what distinguished the Comintern from the Socialist International was its hyper-centralisation and hyper-bureaucratisation. By the late 1920s the relatively rudimentary organisational structures and the intense debates and disagreements characteristic of the Leninist Comintern had been largely replaced by unanimity, dogmatism and hierarchical control from above. Without idealising the Comintern under Lenin, we can conclude that this process of hyper-bureaucratisation and ossification is one of the main differences between, say, 1920 and 1928.

The expanding role of the capitalist state in socio-economic affairs was a second factor that seemed to confirm the validity of the centralist dispositions of the Bolsheviks. According to the American scholar, Eric D. Weitz, this was especially true of the Weimar Republic, where:

the pronounced statist traditions of the German labor movement, grounded in the daily interaction with an interventionist state, predisposed Germans to the centralized and statist doctrines emanating from Moscow and were recreated in the KPD's support for a dictatorship of the proletariat in its specifically Marxist–Leninist sense.[41]

What is more, the Weimar state was identified by German communists as a social democratic stronghold, and its combination of progressive welfare and labour legislation with repressive police action against revolutionaries created a powerful, but complex synthesis of pro-statist commitments and profound anti-social democratic reactions. This in turn, it has been argued, made the KPD a willing recepticle for the leftward shifts in Comintern tactics in 1924 and 1928. Indeed, some historians have gone further and suggested that the KPD's tactics were conditioned more by internal than external considerations. This theory minimises the role of Moscow in the formulation of the KPD's policies, a view shared it appears by Weitz, who concludes that 'German communist politics had a particular correspondence with essential characteristics of Germany's political economy as it evolved in the Imperial and Weimar periods.' Hence, the Comintern's radical turns in the twenties 'only confirmed the policies that had prevailed in the KPD for most of the decade'.[42]

The final, and arguably most important, factor which underscored for many European communists the basic correctness of Bolshevik hostility to social democracy was the reality of their daily lived experience. Again, most research on this phenomenon has focused on Germany and comparisons with other industrialised countries of Europe need to be treated cautiously. Nevertheless, the thesis is persuasive. From 1923–4 onwards German employers with government support launched an economic rationalisation and mechanisation programme designed to improve labour productivity. In an era of intense international competition, this resulted in structural unemployment and a concomitant process of social fragmentation in the German working class between the employed and unemployed. In terms of party affiliations, the majority of SPD members remained employed workers, while the KPD became increasingly, though not exclusively, a party of the jobless.

These institutional divisions were accentuated by social and cultural fractures at the workplace and in residential areas. Cut off from both the formal and non-formal organisational and friendship networks in the factory – the trade unions, workers' councils, shop-steward meetings, cultural, educational and sporting clubs – unemployed communist workers became isolated with few legal channels to air their grievances. In addition, divergent housing patterns tended to draw a line between the better-off districts inhabited largely by social democratic workers and the rougher dilapidated tenements that were home to the disproportionately communist unemployed. In these conditions it appeared natural for communists to direct their fire against the local social democratic trade union and state 'bureaucrats' who represented the face of authority and law and order.[43] The point is that these social and cultural divides, the reality of life for many German workers, helped to reinforce pre-existing deeply entrenched antagonisms between communists and social democrats even before the Comintern's 'social fascist' line and the onset of the Great Depression.

Despite the direct intervention of Moscow and the auspicious conditions outlined above, the creation of 'Bolshevised parties' and an ideologically and organisationally unified 'world party' steeped in Marxist–Leninist principles was by no means smoothly accomplished. In the years before 1928–9 the Russian leaders often faced an uphill struggle in overcoming the doubts, misconceptions and even open resistance of many foreign communists. Specific examples of such obduracy are well documented and fall into two main categories: first, reaction from both the 'right' and the 'left' against perceived Russian hegemony in the Comintern; and, secondly, widespread indifference to the organisational prescriptions of Bolshevisation. The end result was invariably the browbeating and capitulation of 'doubters' and the expulsion of intransigent 'fractionalists' and 'deviationists'.

The experience of the influential Czechoslovak party provides an interesting case study. At the Fifth Enlarged ECCI Plenum in March 1925 two leading lights, Karl Kreibich and Bohumír Šmeral, delivered speeches that were unusually critical of the high-handed intervention of ECCI representatives in the KSČ. Kreibich upbraided Zinoviev by name and decried the 'commissar methods' of the Comintern, having earlier claimed in an unpublished article that old and trusted party leaders were being cast aside, because they were insufficiently subservient to Moscow only to be replaced by

malleable 'blank sheets'.[44] Šmeral, while recognising the authority of
the ECCI, directed his comments against Manuilsky, whose brus-
que interference on behalf of the Czechoslovak leftists at the
party congress in November 1924 had created 'an atmosphere of
panic . . . a fear in a large section of the party of being expelled'. The
'regular espionage system' installed by the new leftist Central Committee meant that it was 'unable to lead the party even with the
support of the executive [ECCI]'.[45]

Complaints about the imperious behaviour of Bolshevik members
of the ECCI could be relatively easily assuaged. After all it was not
unknown for frustrated party leaders to invite the central Comintern
authorities to sort out the factional mess in their own parties. What
was more worrying for the Russians was the tendency among certain,
generally leftist, European communists to draw a distinction between
an orthodox Marxism, applicable to conditions in the advanced
countries of Western Europe, and a separate Leninism rooted in the
realities of a backward peasant Russia. The doctrine of 'socialism in
one country' and the pro-kulak (richer peasant) orientation of NEP
only confirmed this divergence. In 1925–6 heated debates raged,
especially in the KPD, over the Comintern's broader conception of
united front tactics and trade union work. For the leftists, the
adoption of a 'softer' line towards social democracy signified more
an attempt to establish a bloc to defend the Soviet Union than a
means of prosecuting the European revolution. In fact, the unpalat-
able truth – that the revolution was simply not on the immediate
agenda – rendered redundant the left's essentially anti-united front
and anti-trade union alternative.

Concerns about the predominance of Soviet state interests over the
national revolutionary requirements of the communist parties had
been cautiously raised in Lenin's time, but the universal drive for
Bolshevisation after 1924 lent them a sharper, more critical edge.
Taken to their logical conclusion, these arguments fundamentally
challenged the Russian claim to ideological hegemony in the Comintern. Hence, they were anathema to all Bolsheviks. So too were the
cutting accusations that 'ideological terror' prevailed in the Comintern whereby dissenters were automatically branded 'enemies of the
ECCI' or 'enemies of communism'. In the course of 1926–7
Bukharin, Stalin and their allies lost few opportunities to denounce
such heretical and dangerous ideas. Somewhat exaggerated claims
were made to the effect that an organised 'international ultra-left

opposition' had coalesced around the Germans Fischer, Maslow, Scholem and Urbahns, the prominent Italian Bordiga and representatives of the Polish and French parties. As mentioned above, they were accused of being in league with the United Opposition of Trotsky and Zinoviev and generally suffered the same fate of demotion followed by expulsion.

The resort to 'command-administrative' measures could not hide the fact that some communists were beginning to articulate questions that the Bolshevik leaders strove to keep under lock and key. Were Russian tactics and methods applicable in the different circumstances of Western Europe? Should communists carry out policies emanating from Moscow regardless of their suitability to local conditions? Should the authoritarian ideological and organisational tenets of Russian Bolshevism take precedence over the more democratic traditions and experiences of national labour movements? Were Soviet state interests hindering the aim of world revolution? Few communists were prepared to confront these doubts openly, preferring, as we have seen, to submerge them in a deep commitment to the USSR and revolutionary socialism. But with hindsight the tension between Bolshevik universalism and national specificity must surely be viewed as a central, if not *the* central, dilemma of twentieth-century international communism.

The resistance of the 'ultra-left' to the Russification of the Comintern was damaging and acutely embarrassing for Moscow. It was, though, restricted to individuals or comparatively small groups, at least outside the KPD. More widespread was the reluctance to pursue the specific organisational prescriptions of Bolshevisation. The aim of the Comintern Executive was to make the Bolshevik form of party organisation the model for all communist parties. This extremely important task entailed the substitution of the factory cell for the territorial branch as the basic organisational unit of the parties and the formation of 'fractions', or communist groups, within non-party bodies such as reformist trade unions. The goal was to 'proletarianise' the communist parties and increase their influence over the workers at the place of production. Progress in this field was uneven at best, dilatory at worst.

Again the Czechoslovak example is symptomatic of a general tardiness and lack of enthusiasm. The leaders of the Red Unions in Prague, in flagrant disregard for Comintern and Profintern directives, were extremely wary of forming communist fractions in social democratic unions for several reasons. First, fractions were seen as illogical. Why remain in, and pay dues to, 'enemy' social democratic organisations when the main task was surely to weaken those organisations and strengthen the communist unions? Secondly, fractions were self-defeating. Reformist union leaders considered the creation of fractions evidence of 'Muscovite infiltration' and responded by expelling communists from social democratic bodies *en masse*. Finally, the fraction was viewed as a party-imposed organisational unit, by nature clandestine, conspiratorial and alien to the more open societies of Western and Central Europe.[46] For these reasons the formation of fractions in Czechoslovakia and elsewhere proceeded slowly, a cause of constant anguish in Moscow.

The reorganisation of all party members in factory cells aroused even stronger opposition. Carr's explanation is that 'the Bolshevik conception of the party as an entity composed of workers in factories' diverged sharply from:

> the normal western conception of a party based on local organizations. Territorial organization treated the workers as citizens, and suited the requirements of an electoral machine based on universal suffrage. Organization by factory cells treated the workers as members of the proletariat, and facilitated enrolment and training for revolutionary action.[47]

Although communist parties adopted, with varying degrees of success, the uniform organisational model laid down by the ECCI in January 1925, there is reason to conclude that many members remained distrustful of the factory cell, a specifically Russian form of organisation that clashed with long-held principles. Zápotocký, a luminary in the Czechoslovak party, alluded to these attitudes in his report to the Fifth ECCI Plenum. He asserted that 'the transformation of the party organisation met with great resistance both among the functionaries and the rank and file, which may be explained by the circumstance that in our Party the organisational traditions of social democracy are very strong'.[48] This lack of commitment was also firmly rooted in the immense practical difficulties that hindered the creation of cells. Many communists did not work in factories and those that did were often employed in small or medium-sized enterprises where membership in cells was used as a pretext by vigilant employers to dismiss 'communist trouble-makers' from the shopfloor. Only hardened communist workers were willing to risk their livelihoods in this way.

Predictably, the results were disheartening for Comintern leaders in Moscow. Piatnitsky, responsible for organisational affairs, constantly berated party representatives for their sloth in implementing directives. At the Tenth ECCI Plenum in July 1929 he could record no improvement in cell organisation. On the contrary, in Germany and America the number had actually decreased since 1926–7. In Czechoslovakia the percentage of party members enrolled in cells had likewise dropped from 15 per cent in 1927 to 12 per cent in 1928. The figures for France were better, but still disappointing: 31 per cent in February 1928, only 24 per cent in April 1929.[49] Moreover, a large proportion of cell members performed few duties and many cells existed only on paper. Rapid membership turnover was another major problem afflicting communist parties. They could attract substantial numbers of workers, but could not retain them for long periods. Membership figures for the main parties in the late 1920s were stagnating or even declining.

Bolshevisation 'from below', then, presents a contradictory and conflictual picture. The Comintern's aim to create strictly centralised and disciplined mass communist parties implementing a universally 'correct' Leninist tactical line met with differing responses from foreign communists. Willing acceptance and sincere enthusiasm, resigned acquiescence and passive resistance, veiled dissent and open opposition were all evident in these decisive years. Conditions and attitudes that were conducive to Bolshevisation did exist. But it must be concluded that the prime impulse came from Moscow, not from the leaders of the national parties. They could attempt to influence the Comintern's decision-making process and even delay the introduction of unwelcome measures, but increasingly their main function was to fulfil directives rather than initiate them. The Russian-dominated Executive Committee determined the goals of Bolshevisation and the bitter inner-party power struggles revealed its unspoken essence: communist parties were to display total loyalty to the RCP majority and protect the interests of the Soviet Union against external and internal enemies. As Stalin pointedly announced in August 1927:

an *internationalist* is one who is ready to defend the U.S.S.R. without reservation, without wavering, unconditionally; for the

U.S.S.R. is the base of the world revolutionary movement, and this revolutionary movement cannot be defended and promoted unless the U.S.S.R. is defended. For whoever thinks of defending the world revolutionary movement apart from, or against, the U.S.S.R. goes against the revolution and must inevitably slide into the camp of the enemies of the revolution.[50]

The events of 1928 pushed the Comintern further down this road.

ORIGINS OF THE THIRD PERIOD

The years 1928–33 are known in Comintern parlance as the 'Third Period'. It is one of the most controversial phases in the International's history, one in which socialist revolutions and imperialist wars were placed on the agenda. The reality was the rise of Nazism and the savage repression of the German working-class movement. The origins of the Third Period have been the subject of much debate and mystery. Since the 1930s historians have pondered a series of intriguing questions. Why was the momentous 'turn to the left' undertaken in late 1927 and 1928, and who was responsible? What was the relationship between events in the Comintern and the factional struggles in the RCP? What was the reaction of the communist parties to the new radical tactics? Was the Sixth Comintern Congress a triumph for Stalin or a compromise worked out with Bukharin? Until the 1970s paternity of the term 'Third Period' and of its defining slogans 'class against class' and 'social fascism' was almost exclusively attributed to Stalin. The more militant vocabulary of the Comintern appeared to correlate exactly with the hardline policies he was pursuing in the USSR from early 1928. The battlelines were clear: Stalin the 'leftist' versus Bukharin the 'rightist'. However, such views obscure as much as they elucidate. The origins of the Comintern's Third Period lie in the complex interplay of socio-economic analysis, internal factional struggles in the USSR, Soviet foreign policy concerns and the concrete experiences of the communist parties themselves.

The idea of a Third Period made its debut at the Seventh ECCI Plenum in November–December 1926 and it was not Stalin who first introduced the notion, but Bukharin. The *de facto* head of the Comintern discerned three phases in the development of post-war

Europe. The initial stage was characterised by revolutionary upheaval and bitter conflict between communists and social democrats; the second was the era of relative capitalist stabilisation and the united front; and the third phase, only then opening up, revealed the ever sharper internal contradictions of this stabilisation and a consequent shift to the left among European workers.[51] In Comintern circles it was axiomatic to describe capitalist stabilisation as 'temporary' and 'partial'. The Marxist prognosis of capitalism's inherent crisis and collapse could never be repudiated. The world situation remained objectively revolutionary. Hence, there were few dissenting voices when Bukharin detected the first indications of instability in the advanced capitalist economies of Western Europe and North America despite the unmistakable signs of technological progress, which he himself readily acknowledged.

As a Marxist dialectician, Bukharin based his analysis on the national and international contradictions of capitalist stabilisation. The two were inseparably linked. Stabilisation at the national level rested on rationalisation, which was characterised not only by improved methods of labour organisation, technological innovation and increased productivity, but also, he believed, by structural unemployment, depressed working-class standards of living and a crisis of profitability for capitalism. For Bukharin, the resultant sharpening of class tensions would seriously undermine support for social democracy and lay the basis for the creation of mass communist parties. He recognised that conditions varied from country to country, but he maintained that this differentiated and disproportional rate of development both in national economies and among capitalist states would promote the intensification of international conflict as the pressure to find new markets and bigger profits grew ever fiercer. These inter-state global rivalries would then threaten a new round of imperialist wars and revolutions.[52] With slight modifications this analysis formed the core of Bukharin's thinking from late 1926 to the Sixth Comintern Congress in the summer of 1928. Indeed, throughout that period Bukharin's theory of the contradictions of capitalist stabilisation remained Comintern orthodoxy and underpinned the key resolution of the Sixth Congress (document 10). Stalin, whether from calculation or conviction, deferred to his ally displaying few signs of independent thinking on this issue. In August 1927 he defended Bukharin's thesis against Zinoviev's criticism. There was as yet no sign of disagreement within the duumvirate.

At the Seventh ECCI Plenum Bukharin had struck a more strident note, but he was very careful not to overestimate the pace of capitalist decline. Contradictions there may be, but the process of stabilisation was far from its terminal phase. The plenum resolutions reflected this cautious approach and by no means foreshadowed an immediate and radical break with past policy. Rather they bore witness to a transitional stage in Comintern theory and practice. The broad application of united front tactics and the goal of international trade union unity were re-emphasised, the link with the British trade unions through the Anglo-Russian Committee, though severely tested after the failure of the General Strike, remained operative, and the alliance in China with the Guomindang nationalists was reaffirmed. The term 'Third Period' was not mentioned in the resolutions. At the same time, however, communist parties were instructed to prepare for the 'revolutionary wave' that might come 'fairly soon', and to seek the 'unmasking' of social democracy which was 'finally and everywhere standing . . . on the side of the bourgeois governments'.[53] Despite this ambivalence, the Seventh Plenum could have provided few hints to the foreign delegates of the major tactical and theoretical shifts that were to come in late 1927 and 1928.

The origins of these shifts are manifold. By the spring of 1927 the wary optimism of the Seventh Plenum was rapidly being displaced by grave fears as the international climate veered abruptly against the USSR. A series of setbacks plunged the Soviet and Comintern leaders on the defensive. Two in particular caused great anxiety in Moscow: the catastrophic events in China, described in chapter 5 below, and a sharp worsening in relations with Britain. The 'Chinese Question' became a source of bitter confrontation between the Russian factions. Trotsky's broadside against Stalin's and Bukharin's 'counter-revolutionary' policy, though acutely embarrassing for the duumvirate, found little echo in the corridors of power in the RCP and Comintern. In May the Eighth ECCI Plenum, shorn of Soviet and foreign Opposition delegates, accused Trotsky of 'slandering and discrediting' the Soviet Union and Comintern and officially censured his 'fractional struggle'.[54] However, the Opposition's onslaught was not without impact. It can be plausibly argued that Trotsky's critique of the united front from above in China was sufficiently damaging to impel Bukharin and Stalin to rethink their Comintern strategy. To this extent, it influenced the shift to the left later in the year.

The second setback for the ruling faction in Moscow occurred on the diplomatic front. The duumvirate's 'peaceful coexistence' policy suffered an embarrassing rebuff when in May 1927 the Conservative government in Britain took the drastic step of breaking off relations with the USSR. This action served to confirm the aggressive posture of the British in Eastern Europe and was interpreted in the Kremlin as the preliminary to an imperialist intervention against the Soviet Union, since relations with France were simultaneously deteriorating. These fears, deliberately fanned by the Stalinists, fuelled the 'War Scare' which had been sweeping the country since early 1927 and which was now cynically used to condemn the United Opposition in the Soviet party and their supporters in the Comintern. Trotsky and Zinoviev stood accused of undermining the unity of the party and the country at a time of great danger. According to Stalin, 'something like a united front from Chamberlain to Trotsky' was being formed.[55] Isolated and abused, Trotsky and Zinoviev were formally expelled from the Russian party in December 1927.

The Chinese debacle, the break with Britain and the War Scare 'drove Comintern', in Carr's words, 'automatically and almost unwillingly, into more uncompromising and more revolutionary postures'.[56] Other hopes and fears in the summer and autumn of 1927 acted as a stimulus for the turn. In July Vienna witnessed a spontaneous and ill-fated workers' uprising that Comintern chose to interpret as a sign of a new revolutionary upsurge and radicalisation of the European proletariat. The events also proved 'the treachery of Austrian social-democracy', whose leaders had ignored the communist appeal for a general strike. Two months later the Anglo-Russian Trade Union Committee was dissolved on the initiative of the TUC leaders, another example, so it was held, of the perfidious nature of the social democratic 'bureaucracy'. The noteworthy conclusion drawn in Moscow was that the tactics of the united front 'from above', never pursued with much enthusiasm, lay hopelessly and irrevocably discredited.

Finally, in seeking the roots of the 'turn to the left' we should not overlook indigenous inputs. The domestic experiences of foreign parties, notably the German, did influence the decision-makers in the Comintern hierarchy. Carr has affirmed that 'the branding of social-democracy as social-Fascism had begun in Germany and was inspired by German conditions'.[57] This assertion is not entirely accurate, but there is no denying that the genuine and long-standing hostility between the KPD and SPD reinforced the Bolsheviks' propensity to equate European social democracy with 'counter-revolutionary' Russian Menshevism. More specifically, it has been argued that in 1927–8:

> increasing economic antagonism and the revival of unrest among [German] workers over economic questions led the left wing of the KPD to demand a more aggressive strike strategy against employers, with a more organised communist opposition in the unions; and the repressive reaction of [the social democratic] labour union leaders to the growth in support for the communist opposition convinced many KPD leaders that it should adopt a policy of leading grassroots economic movements. . . . even if this meant confrontation with the labour unions.[58]

It was no accident, then, that German communist leaders, who enjoyed great prestige in the Comintern, were among the first to resurrect the term 'social fascism' in 1928, though encouragement from Moscow cannot be ruled out. The left turn garnered enthusiastic support from many young ambitious 'Bolshevisers' in the communist parties – Barbé and Célor in the French, Gottwald and Slánský in the Czechoslovak, Longo and Secchia in the Italian, Rust and Tapsell in the British. The communist youth leagues generally proved highly receptive to the turn and played a prominent role in undermining those incumbent party leaders who were lukewarm to the Comintern's change of line. Certainly, the process of shifting communist tactics to the left drew on the revolutionary fervour of the more uncompromising elements in the communist parties, particularly in the KPD. Nevertheless, the evidence suggests conclusively that the initial and main impetus came from Moscow.

Uneasily aware of their vulnerability to attack from the United Opposition over the policy failures in Britain and, above all, China, the Comintern leaders throughout 1927 groped towards a new tactical orientation. Change was imperative. It was to come in the form of a renewed offensive against social democracy in the parliamentary and trade union spheres. Already from early 1927 Humbert-Droz, an associate of Bukharin's in the Comintern hierarchy, had begun to reassess the electoral tactics of the French party. It was from these deliberations that the slogan 'class against class' was to emerge and subsequently become a defining characteristic of the

Third Period. The intention of the 'class against class' slogan as it evolved in the course of 1927–8 was to promote the independent identity of the communist party as a distinct and separate entity from the social democrats; indeed, as the *sole* working-class party. The united front had entailed the danger of sliding into reformism, of lagging behind the social democrats. The new tactics inevitably meant open opposition to social democracy, which was allegedly turning into the main pillar of support for the capitalist regime. Hence, from October 1927 French communists, who had customarily voted for Socialist party candidates in the second ballot in order to defeat the right-wing bloc, were instructed to put up their own candidates and effectively split the left vote. The majority of the PCF leadership saw little logic in a policy that could only result in greater victories for the right. As such, the new tactics aroused bitter hostility and were adopted belatedly and under duress.

The same was true of the British party. On 1 October 1927 its executive received a telegram from the Comintern's Political Secretariat recommending the CPGB to step up:

> the fight against the bourgeois leadership of the Labour Party, against parliamentary cretinism in every shape and form and to prepare to fight the forthcoming elections as an independent party with a platform and candidates of its own even in those cases where the C.P. will be opposed by the so-called official candidates of the Labour Party.[59]

Many British communists believed the tactics would merely play into the hands of the Conservatives and thus resistance to the instructions from Moscow was widespread among top party leaders. Any doubts on this score can be laid to rest by consulting the relevant documents in the Comintern and CPGB Archives. The fiery Scot, William Gallacher, had this to say at a meeting of the ECCI Political Secretariat on 18 November 1927: 'The Party will not take the letter seriously. They have decided on their parliamentary policy . . . and then from the International comes a proposal for re-consideration. It is entirely out of the question. . . . I tell you, the Political Bureau [of the CPGB] will not consider the matter as it is. It cannot.'[60] Pollitt, soon to become General Secretary of the party, was in Moscow in October 1927 and three months later described his experiences to the Central Committee. Pollitt recalled that in an interview with 'Joe'

(Stalin) and Bukharin, 'a sharper break with the existing party policy' had been called for. 'At that time I resisted', but subsequently 'I got a hammering from one fellow which lasted 8 hours'. The new tactics were 'the result of the deliberations of the [Comintern's] Small Commission', which had started the discussion 'because we damped it down at home'. At the same meeting John Campbell was equally explicit: 'we are faced from the ECCI with suggestions which in my opinion mean that we ought to change the policy of the Party in a Left direction; it is significant that that demand has not come from the Party itself'.[61] Gallacher's, Pollitt's and Campbell's comments show clearly that the 'class against class' tactics were devised in Moscow, not 'at home' in Britain, and that they were essentially imposed on the British communists in the face of initial opposition. It was not until 1929 that the deep divisions and rancour in the party were overcome and the new tactics finally taken on board.

Bukharin provided the justification for a general leftward shift in tactics in an 'Information Letter' to the communist parties dated 18 September 1927 and marked 'Top Secret'. In it he emphasised the tense international situation, the campaign to form an 'anti-Soviet front' among the Western powers and the preparations for war against the USSR. In this respect, he wrote, 'we must take note of the particularly treacherous and malicious role of social democracy', which had to be 'ruthlessly exposed'. The Soviet leaders were acutely conscious of the fact that the German social democrats had long been staunch defenders of the Western orientation of Weimar foreign policy and far from enthusiastic about the links with the USSR, symbolised by the Rapallo Treaty of 1922. In this sense the SPD was an implacable enemy and the strengthening of the campaign against it would serve Soviet state interests. Having stressed the participation of social democracy in the 'anti-Soviet front', Bukharin went on to discern 'a clear turn to the left' among the 'working masses' as the 'bourgeoisie continues its offensive, sharply intensifying the class struggle. . . . Therefore the *broadest* mobilisation of the masses and the *broadest* unmasking of social democracy must stand at the centre of our work.'[62]

In a second secret memorandum a month later, Bukharin insisted that 'an intensified struggle against reformism' must be conducted 'in the overwhelming majority of cases' via the 'united front FROM BELOW' and not, as before, by 'appeals to the upper strata'.[63] On the thorny issue of electoral tactics, Bukharin reiterated that:

the ECCI regards the policy of supporting a liberal-labour bloc (Lloyd George and MacDonald) in Britain and the Left cartel in France as RADICALLY WRONG. . . . In view of a certain wavering to be observed in its own ranks, THE COMMUNIST PARTY must come forward demonstratively as the only Party of the working class and MORE BOLDLY criticise reformism.[64]

These two documents reveal Bukharin's line of reasoning on the need for a left turn in Comintern tactics: as the contradictory effects of capitalist stabilisation take hold, fiercer class struggles ensue; the social democratic leaders side with the employers and the capitalist state, and, crucially, participate in the international anti-Soviet campaign; therefore, the communist parties must step up the fight against social democracy via the united front from below; that is, split the workers from their 'treacherous' leaders.

We can conclude, then, that it was Bukharin, not Stalin, who initiated the theory and practice of the Comintern's 'turn to the left', the origins of which *preceded* Stalin's hardline domestic policies by several months. Until the end of 1927 Stalin's line was essentially 'Bukharinist'. Stalin seems to have held no firm independent position on such questions as capitalist stabilisation, the radicalisation of the working class and the impending revolutionary upsurge. But with the expulsion of the United Opposition in December 1927, Bukharin became the last obstacle to Stalin's quest for personal power. The main source of dispute between the two hinged on domestic issues, not Comintern tactics. Yet for the Stalinists, Bukharin had to be defeated in both arenas. In crude terms, deviations to the 'right' or 'left' held little intrinsic concern for Stalin. The crucial task was to promote his men into positions of responsibility by isolating, discrediting and ultimately expelling the 'Bukharinites'.

This process began at the Ninth ECCI Plenum in February 1928. At this time and immediately thereafter, the Stalinist faction began patiently to construct a 'right-wing deviation' in the Comintern which was designated as the main danger for the communist parties because of its alleged affinities with social democracy, especially its left-wing. The aim was to identify Bukharin as a 'conciliator' of this 'deviation' by manipulating him into an 'oppositional' stance. This is where the struggle against the 'right' in the Russian party and in the Comintern begins to overlap. In the latter, this required the creation of a second 'Stalinist' version of the turn to the left distinct from, but drawing inspiration from, the initial Bukharinist version. The Stalinist interpretation became associated primarily with two inter-related factors: the theory of 'social fascism' and the idea of a sharper struggle against the 'left' social democrats as the main enemy. Stalin invented neither, and before 1929 was extremely wary in his use of the term 'social fascism', but he was not above appropriating ideas and twisting them to his own advantage. In this the Russian Stalinists enjoyed fervent backing from important foreign communists, some of whom were genuinely convinced of the degeneration of social democracy into a 'fascist workers' party'.

The process of isolating Bukharin and his adherents took many months. Characteristically, Stalin proceeded cautiously, no doubt unsure of his rivals' strength and response. Mikhail Tomsky, a leading ally of Bukharin in the Politburo, graphically described the piecemeal methods used by the Stalinists to discredit their erstwhile colleagues: 'They were gradually refashioning us by means of a special system, every day a little brushstroke – here a dab, there a dab. Aha! . . . as a result of this clever bit of work they have turned us into "right-wingers"'.[65] It was Stalin's great triumph to convince not only the Russian party and the international communist movement, but also, less forgivably, many historians that Bukharin's Comintern policies were conciliatory, 'soft', essentially 'rightist'. This was far from the truth. As Theodore Draper has observed, 'Bukharin was a Bolshevik, before he was a "rightist" or "leftist"'.[66] He was certainly no social democrat. We can no longer assume that Bukharin's comparatively moderate domestic policies were automatically transferred to the Comintern arena. He remained deeply convinced of the revolutionary road to socialism. However, he drew the line at the Stalinists' sectarian inclinations and their recourse to crude over-simplifications in theoretical and organisational matters.

The Sixth Comintern Congress, held in Moscow from 17 July to 1 September 1928, was the scene of a muted, but none the less real, struggle for the future direction of the international communist movement. At the beginning of June Bukharin had written revealingly to Stalin:

Koba, . . . *I do not wish to and will not fight* . . . I ask you now to think over one thing: *give us a chance to hold the congress in peace; do not carry out any superfluous splits; do not create an atmosphere of gossip.* . . . *We'll*

end the congress . . . and I'll be prepared to go wherever you like, without any
scuffles, without any noise and without any struggle.[67]

But Stalin saw the Sixth Congress as an ideal forum to discredit
Bukharin and chip away at his authority, an opportunity not to be
lost. Presumably having planned the campaign well in advance,
Stalin departed for his annual vacation in the Caucasus, content to
let his lieutenants do his bidding. It seems that the German leaders,
Heinz Neumann, Hermann Remmele and Thälmann, carried out
sterling work on behalf of the Stalinists. On the surface unity
reigned, but in the corridors and chambers a veritable parallel
congress was taking place as rumours were spread among the
confused foreign delegates to the effect that Bukharin's days in the
Comintern leadership were numbered and he was the next candidate
for exile to Alma Ata.

In these testing and humiliating circumstances, Bukharin sought to
defend a more nuanced approach to the problems of Comintern
tactics. On the vexed question of whether social democracy was
turning into 'social fascism', a position held by some of the German
and other foreign delegates, he acknowledged that there was a
'tendency' towards this, but hastened to warn that 'it would be a
mistake to lump Social-Democracy and Fascism together'.[68] Togliatti,
while accepting the necessity of a strenuous struggle against social
democracy, categorically stated that 'we think this formulation [social
fascism] is absolutely unacceptable. Our delegation is decisively
opposed to this bending of reality'.[69] The distinction for Togliatti was
in the class basis of fascism and social democracy, the latter having
its roots in the broad working masses whereas the former was a
movement of the petty bourgeoisie dominated by the big bourgeoisie
and landowners.[70] Bukharin's private notes, preserved in the Comintern Archive, show that he agreed with Togliatti's 'pivotal speech',
which upheld 'a correct line'.[71] We must assume that Bukharin did
what he could to limit the impact of the crass notion that social
democracy was simply a form of fascism. In this he was reasonably
successful. The fact that the wording of the congress resolutions was
closer to Bukharin's evaluation than to the German hardliners'
suggests that Stalin was still uncommitted on this issue. As we shall
see in the next chapter, 'social fascism' became a full-blown slogan
only after the final defeat of the Bukharinites in the first half of 1929.

Party discipline was another bone of contention at the Sixth

Congress. Bukharin's original draft *Thesis on the International Situation and the Tasks of the Communist International* spoke of the need for 'amicable work' and 'internal party democracy' as the basis of organisational life. The draft was amended, however, by the Russian delegation a week after the opening of the congress. Now the emphasis was on 'the general tightening up of iron internal discipline, the absolute subordination of the minority to the majority, the absolute subordination of the minor organisations as well as all other Party organisations . . . to the leading Party centres and of all sections of the Comintern to the Executive Committee'.[72] Firsov has concluded that the orientation towards 'iron discipline', combined with a second key amendment placing in the forefront the struggle against 'right-wing deviations' in the Comintern:

> prepared the ground for an offensive against those forces in the communist parties who disagreed with the 'left turn', and created the conditions for the subsequent elimination of Bukharin and his adherents from the leadership of the Comintern and for the transformation of the Comintern apparatus into a strictly centralised organ under the direct control of Stalin.[73]

Herein lies the real significance of the Sixth Congress. Meeting in an atmosphere of intolerance and name-calling (document 9), the congress represented a crucial stage in the undermining of Bukharin's authority. Indeed, in the following months he rarely, if ever, appeared at Comintern headquarters, in effect fulfilling his promise to Stalin to leave 'without a fight'. Unable or unwilling to defend his supporters in the Comintern apparatus and communist parties, Bukharin was denounced as a 'right-wing opportunist' and formally expelled from the ECCI at its Tenth Plenum in July 1929. His place was taken temporarily by Molotov, the General Secretary's murky accomplice who had been co-opted onto the ECCI Political Secretariat at Stalin's express behest in late August 1928 in order to combat 'rightist' tendencies.[74] A new phase in the Comintern's history was about to begin.

Two fundamental and inter-related dilemmas lay at the heart of the Bolshevisation process. First, what should be the future direction of the Russian Revolution after Lenin's premature death? Secondly, what should be the role of the Communist International after the ebbing of the revolutionary tide and the onset of 'relative capitalist stabilisation'? The protracted struggles that ensued over these fateful questions ended in the victory of Stalin's theory of 'socialism in one country'. Tentatively at first, but with growing confidence, Stalin and his adherents embarked on a mighty act of revisionism in theory and practice. By the late 1920s Stalin was in the throes of reversing Lenin's original conception of the relationship between the Russian and international revolutions. In Carr's words:

> the dependence of the Russian revolution on world revolution, persistently asserted by Lenin, was repudiated; and the dependence of world revolution on the building of socialism in the Soviet Union automatically took its place. World revolution became a secondary factor in the formulation of Soviet policy.[75]

This outcome may not have been consciously or deliberately planned at any one time in Stalin's smoke-filled Kremlin office. It evolved from a combination of factors: Stalin's notorious disdain for foreign communists, for the Comintern as a whole (he reportedly referred to it as 'the corner shop' [lavochka]), and for the chances of world revolution; the intractable predicament of avowedly revolutionary parties in an essentially non-revolutionary era; the inability of communism in the industrialised West to strike deep roots among the mass of workers; the foreign parties' awareness of their own fragility and their profound commitment to the defence of the first socialist state; and above all Stalin's firm predilection for Soviet state security in conditions of dangerous isolation and capitalist stabilisation. Under these pressures, the original mission of the Communist International was increasingly likely to be modified and adapted to meet the requirements of the victorious faction in the Russian succession struggles.

What were the effects of Bolshevisation on the Comintern and the communist parties? In what ways had internal party life changed? The main result of Bolshevisation was the transition from democratic centralism to an incipient bureaucratic centralism. From its very birth, strict centralisation and discipline were distinguishing hallmarks of the Comintern. The Bolsheviks' determination to build a united 'world party' on Leninist organisational principles was palpably evident in the 'Twenty-one Conditions'. Regardless of Lenin's fleeting cognisance of the ambiguities and tensions inherent in the juxtaposition of Bolshevik universalism and national specificities, the foundations had been laid for the *eventuality* of a 'Russification' of the international communist movement. In our judgement this outcome was not inevitable. Indeed, it was unforeseen in 1920 when European revolution was still the order of the day. But the failure of this revolution and the intensity of the factional power struggles in the Soviet party turned this eventuality into reality. The inability of foreign parties to carry out their own socialist revolutions shifted the centre of gravity of the international movement ever more perceptibly towards Moscow, and the triumph of Stalin and his faction ensured that uncompromising, undemocratic organisational and operational methods would be transposed to the Comintern. Leninism did not lead with iron logic to Stalinism, but alternative paths of development associated with the more flexible or emancipatory aspects of Bolshevism were eschewed, blocked and ultimately defeated by a complex interplay of subjective and objective factors. The evolution of the victorious 'Stalinist alternative' is the theme of the next chapter.

3. Stalin and the Third Period, 1928–33

In 1928 Comintern theoreticians had detected unmistakable signs of a new revolutionary upsurge, impending imperialist wars and the danger of foreign intervention against the USSR. Capitalism was approaching its final crisis and the historic victory of socialism was at hand. The reality could not have been more devastating or unexpected: the Nazi rise to power, the brutal destruction of the mighty German labour movement and the resultant imbroglio of communist theory and practice. It is no wonder, then, that the 'Third Period' of Comintern history has been the subject of intense debate. Admittedly, there is a near universal consensus that the 'ultra-leftist' tactics of these years proved disastrous, in some cases suicidal. Nowhere was revolutionary rhetoric translated into action; the membership of most communist parties plummeted and only very slowly recovered; communist influence in national working-class organisations declined with the imposition of a sectarian 'united front from below' policy; and inner-party democracy and open debate, already stifled by the attack on the Trotskyite–Zinovievite United Opposition, were all but emasculated as Stalinist 'bureaucratic centralism' took hold.

But many contentious issues remain. What were the consequences for the Comintern apparatus and communist parties of the Stalinists' victory in the Soviet party? Did Stalin personally decree Comintern policy, or did the ECCI and parties manage to carve out a measure of autonomy in the absence of sustained control from above? Indeed,

was the Comintern left to its own devices as Stalin and the other
Soviet leaders concentrated on far more pressing domestic issues?
Was the international communist movement totally 'Stalinised' in
these years, becoming a mere pawn of Soviet state interests? What
was the meaning of the 'social fascist' line and why was it pursued
up to, and even beyond, January 1933? Was this line as senseless and
irrational as most historians have argued? Why did the Comintern
and German communists fail to prevent Hitler's *Machtergreifung*
(seizure of power)? How far did the Comintern's inadequate theoretical formulations distort political practice? This chapter will address
these questions by first examining the defeat of the so-called 'right-
wing deviation', which marked the definitive triumph of the Stalinists
and hence was of signal importance for the future direction of the
International. It will go on to assess the extent to which Stalin and
the Soviet leadership were able to manipulate the Comintern central
bodies and determine the political line of the communist parties in
the years 1929–33. The final section analyses in some depth the
theory and practice of 'social fascism', a concept that informed
communist activity throughout the Third Period. Here, particular
attention will be devoted to the tactics of the German Communist
Party in its struggle against both social democracy and Nazism.

DEFEAT OF THE 'RIGHT-WING DEVIATION'

The adoption by the Sixth Congress in the summer of 1928 of a
strident anti-social democratic platform formalised the 'turn to the
left' which had been in the making since late 1926 and foreshadowed
an onslaught on the 'right-wing deviation' in the international
communist movement. A new orthodoxy had been set, against which
foreign communists could be judged. Events in the Comintern yet
again became intimately entwined with developments in the Russian
party. Throughout 1928 and into 1929 the Stalinist faction was
edging its way towards an all-out campaign for socialist construction
in the USSR. Breakneck industrialisation, forced collectivisation of
agriculture, mass mobilisation and consequent social flux were soon
to become the hallmarks of the Stalinist 'revolution from above'. On
the domestic front, a class war was in train directed primarily at
'bourgeois specialists', the peasantry and the intelligentsia. Bukharin
and other prominent figures in the Russian party, while recognising

the desperate need for modernisation, balked at the imbalanced nature of the Stalinists' economic designs and their willingness to resort to unprecedented levels of coercion. Stalin and his adherents were able to convert this resistance into a full-blown 'right-wing deviation' from the party line. The result in the RCP was the gradual behind-the-scenes undermining of Bukharin, Rykov and Tomsky, culminating in their total defeat by the end of 1929.

For the Stalinists, the international movement could not be spared this assault on the Bukharinists. The fierce campaign against the 'right' in the Comintern complemented the attack on Bukharin in the Russian party. The civil war mentality engendered in Moscow must have affected leading Comintern officials, steeling their determination to overcome the 'renegades' and 'wreckers' in the International. In essence the Stalinist faction conducted a purge of those communists who refused to accept the notion of the imminent collapse of capitalism, the emerging 'social fascist' theory, the imposition of ever stricter bureaucratic controls in inner-party life, and the sectarian tactics in the trade unions which threatened to isolate communist workers. In the past such differences of opinion had been accommodated within shaky and fractious coalition leaderships, but in the intense and intolerant atmosphere of late 1928 and 1929, tight ideological homogeneity was declared paramount. Consequently, a series of denunciations, expulsions and resignations rocked the Comintern. No major party escaped. The worst hit were the German, American, Czechoslovak, Swedish and British, but turmoil also reigned in the French, Italian and Polish parties. Those expelled either rejoined the social democrats, formed splinter groups or drifted out of politics entirely.

The initial clash occurred in the German party. In September 1928 the Stalinist party leader, Thälmann, was accused of concealing a financial scandal involving one of his appointees in Hamburg. His opponents on the centre-right of the party immediately seized on this opportunity to relieve the unpopular Thälmann of his party functions, a move ratified by the KPD Politburo and Central Committee. This was most unwelcome news for the Comintern leadership in Moscow. Stalin hastily sent word to Berlin to halt the attacks on his protégé and in early October the ECCI Presidium effectively reversed the decisions of the KPD, reinstating Thälmann and calling on the party 'to take measures to liquidate all fractional groupings'.[1] This gross intervention in a nominally independent party represented a thinly veiled demand for a drive against the KPD 'rightists' led by the 'renegades' Brandler and Thalheimer.

The 'German question' was deemed central for future developments and therefore was brought before a meeting of the ECCI Presidium in December 1928. The appearance of Stalin and Molotov testified to the crucial significance of the session. Indeed, it was a deciding moment in the Stalinisation of the Comintern. Stalin's pivotal speech to the gathering made it perfectly clear that there was no place for the 'Right faction' in the movement. Invoking the Twenty-one Conditions and the resolution of the Sixth Congress on 'iron inner-party discipline', Stalin accused the German 'rightists' of the ultimate sin: organising within the party 'a new, anti-Leninist party, with its own centre and its own press organs'. This represented a threat to the very existence of the KPD. The 'Rights poison the atmosphere with Social-Democratic ideological rubbish and systematically violate the elementary principles of Party discipline.' Furthermore, they were conducting 'a desperate struggle against the Comintern', aided and abetted by a group of 'conciliators', who refused to combat the 'right'. Stalin reiterated several times in his customary fashion that such ill-discipline 'cannot be tolerated any longer.' The 'rightists' were therefore 'liable to expulsion' and the 'conciliators . . . deserve to be given a most serious warning'.[2]

With Stalin's personal weight thrown into the scales, the signal had been provided for indigenous leftist groups to launch a drive throughout the Comintern against the vilified 'right'. Party leaderships were uprooted, district and local branches were cleansed of real or imaginary oppositionists, and large numbers of party members resigned. Those accused of being 'conciliators' of the right, among them the noted German communists Ernst Meyer and Arthur Ewert, were similarly demoted or forced to capitulate. In their stead emerged the new type of proletarian leader – young, tough, unscrupulous and fiercely loyal to the Comintern, the Soviet Union and Stalin. The purge of the right had its greatest repercussions in Sweden where, in the autumn of 1929, the entire party split in two, the majority following the expelled 'rightists'. In Czechoslovakia not only was the party torn asunder, losing thousands of members, but the Red Trade Unions were similarly convulsed by acrimonious disputes and organisational schisms.

The central Comintern apparatus as well as the communist parties underwent enforced personnel changes. Seven members of the ECCI elected at the Sixth Congress had been expelled from communist ranks by 1930. Bukharin himself was relieved of his duties by the ECCI in July 1929, and his fall from grace was accompanied by a well-orchestrated attack on 'rightists' in the ECCI departments. Between September 1929 and January 1930 a Purge Commission screened 239 communist officials, 201 of whom were 'verified' as loyal party members, thirty-one were handed out various penalties, and seven were expelled from the RCP. This process unleashed a wave of fear and uncertainty among Comintern employees, a grave portent of things to come.[3]

Well before this, however, the Comintern Executive had become the domain of hard-working, but intellectually second-rate Bolsheviks. Figures such as Manuilsky, Piatnitsky, Kuusinen and Lozovsky certainly lacked charisma and initiative, but they were experienced functionaries and staunch Stalinists, convinced of the efficacy of the new line. This loyalty was their prime quality as far as Stalin was concerned. But it did not mean that among them absolute unanimity reigned. Some were to prove themselves slightly more flexible than others. Supervising these lesser lights was Molotov, who operated as the Politburo's watchdog over Comintern affairs from the late 1920s to the early 1930s, but not apparently in a consistent day-to-day capacity. Stalin himself preferred a back-stage seat, content to let his trusted lieutenants run the show. He rarely pronounced publicly on the Comintern after 1929–30 and scarcely bothered to attend its deliberations.

Several influential foreign Comintern officials like Humbert-Droz, the Italian Angelo Tasca and the revered Clara Zetkin tried to minimise the attack on the 'rightists'. They opposed the use of 'organisational measures', that is expulsions, and the suppression of freedom of discussion in the Comintern. At the heated ECCI Presidium session in December 1928, Humbert-Droz and Tasca were subjected to vigorous criticism. Stalin lambasted the former as 'an arrogant journalist', who, together with Tasca, had 'fallen into the swamp of cowardly opportunism', an unforgivable and dangerous sin. Undeterred, Humbert-Droz dismissed as 'simply untrue' Stalin's and Molotov's interpretation of his view on capitalist stabilisation. Stalin's statements had 'the same relation to the truth as to say that two and two make five'.[4] The General Secretary, unused to such daring words, furiously retorted: 'Go to the devil!'[5] Humbert-

Droz survived the ordeal, but was shortly removed from the corridors of power in Moscow to the safer pastures of Latin America.

By late 1928 the atmosphere in the Comintern had degenerated into one of 'labelling' and name-calling in the unprincipled search for opponents. There is much contemporary evidence to substantiate this claim. According to a Trotsky sympathiser, the Catalan Andreu Nin: 'Here, in the Comintern, there is complete disarray. Nothing at all is done. Everybody is awaiting the outcome of the fight between Stalin and the right. Demoralization is complete. The majority of the presidium is, of course, with Stalin, because it's certain that he will come out on top.'[6] In December 1928 Togliatti, at this time a wavering supporter of the new line, confided in similar vein to his friend and PCI colleague Tasca that 'the internal regime of Comintern . . . is bad, and tends to get worse. The struggle of groups and factions increases, and extends to all parties. When the factional struggle is unleashed, inner-party democracy is no more. These phenomena pervert the development of our parties, and also prevent a clear understanding of political issues'.[7]

In the following month, Tasca himself wrote a scathing attack on Stalin in a letter to the Secretariat of the Italian party in which he bluntly declared, 'the Comintern no longer exists'; it is 'under Stalin's fist'. Stalin 'is the "teacher and master", who decides everything'. Yet he is 'a plagiarist', intellectually 'mediocre and sterile', who 'without a twinge of conscience' steals other people's ideas. In Tasca's opinion, 'principles are not important' for Stalin, only 'the monopoly of power'. Inside Russia, he 'is the standard-bearer of counter-revolution . . . destroying . . . the spirit and achievements of the October Revolution. Between Stalin and Lenin lies a gulf. . . . The Russian party and all of us will pay dearly for ignoring Lenin's clear instructions about him'.[8] Tasca's declaration of war on Stalin and the Comintern could only result in his expulsion from the ECCI and the PCI, the latter job undertaken in sordid fashion by his erstwhile friend, Togliatti. In March 1929 Zetkin perhaps best summed up the baleful situation in the International when she noted sourly that the Comintern 'has turned from a living political body into a dead mechanism which on the one hand is capable only of swallowing orders in Russian and on the other of regurgitating them in different languages'.[9] Owing to her old age and personal prestige Zetkin was immune from retaliation, remaining in the KPD as a figurehead until her death in June 1933.

The significance of the Stalinist attack on the 'Bukharinists' should not be underestimated. It silenced, and in some cases eliminated from the Comintern, the most independent-minded communists, who defended three fundamental beliefs now under threat: the commitment to joint action with other working-class organisations; the faith in tactical flexibility based on a relatively sophisticated theoretical understanding of capitalism's differentiated development; and the realisation that some diversity of opinion and freedom of expression were essential for healthily functioning parties. Bukharin, quoting Lenin, had warned at the Sixth Congress that 'if you are going to expel all the not very obedient but clever people, and retain only obedient fools, you will *most assuredly* ruin the Party'.[10] His words were beginning to ring true. The example of the erstwhile 'Bukharinist', Togliatti, is instructive. Though he had attempted to limit the worst excesses of the assault on the 'right', the Italian leader had buckled under the pressure by the summer of 1929, publicly condoning a line he privately doubted. Referring at the Tenth ECCI Plenum to the democratic transitional slogans employed by the PCI in the fight against fascism, he was forced to concede that 'if the Comintern says it isn't correct, we will no longer pose [these problems] . . . each of us will think these things, but will no longer say them'.[11]

Incipient Stalinism in the Comintern thus removed the very concept of 'loyal opposition'. Ominously, the 'renegades', both from the right and left, were accused of objectively serving the interests of social democracy. Within a few years they would be 'enemies of the people' and treated as such. During the Third Period Stalinism in the international communist movement was also characterised by a stultifying tactical and ideological conformity which left precious little room for notions of national specificity. Put crudely, the Stalinist line was valid for all regardless of local circumstances. The centralising tendencies, evident since the Twenty-one Conditions, had by 1929 seemingly reached their apogee.

The refusal to countenance local and national particularities was confirmed with unprecedented clarity by events in the American party. In April–May 1929 a high-level American commission assembled in Moscow to sort out the bitter factional strife in the CPUSA. At this meeting Stalin warned against exaggerating the 'specific features of American capitalism'. These should not be ignored, but the 'general features of capitalism . . . are the same for all countries' and must form 'the foundation of the activities of every Communist Party. . . . It is on this that the internationalism of the Communist Party' is based. The so-called 'theory of American "exceptionalism"' was roundly condemned by the ECCI, which insisted that the crisis of capitalism and the radicalisation of the working class were as evident in the USA as they were in Europe. Furthermore, the 'right' was as much a danger in the CPUSA as elsewhere. This signalled an attack on the 'rightist' leaders of the majority faction, Lovestone, Gitlow, Pepper and Wolfe, who had secured the support of the party's convention in March. But as Stalin correctly and revealingly prophesied:

> You declare you have a certain majority in the American Communist Party and that you will retain that majority under all circumstances. That is untrue, comrades of the American delegation, absolutely untrue. . . . There have been numerous cases in the history of the Comintern when its most popular leaders, who had greater authority than you, found themselves isolated as soon as they raised the banner against the Comintern. Do you think you will fare better than these leaders? A poor hope, comrades! At present you still have a formal majority. But tomorrow you will have no majority and you will find yourselves completely isolated if you attempt to start a fight against the decisions of the Presidium of the Executive Committee of the Comintern. You may be certain of that, dear comrades.

Stalin's cynical, politely barbed admonishments gave way to violent invective once the American delegation did indeed decide to resist the Presidium. According to one of the participants, Stalin shouted: 'Who do you think you are? Trotsky defied me. Where is he? Zinoviev defied me. Where is he? Bukharin defied me. Where is he? And you? When you get back to America, nobody will stay with you except your wives.' It is reported that Stalin even threatened the Americans with the words: 'There is plenty of room in our cemeteries.'[12] With the full weight of the ECCI against them, Lovestone and his supporters were expelled from the CPUSA and the Comintern.

But are we not demonising Stalin, reducing his every action to the need to eliminate rivals in the unprincipled quest for power? Was he not committed to a programmatic vision above and beyond his personal ambitions? It is essential to realise that in both the Soviet party and in the Comintern he was able to harness enthusiastic support behind his favoured policies. Rapid socialist construction in the USSR and a leftist line in the Comintern appealed to impatient and ambitious communist activists who wished to escape from what seemed to them the blind-alleys of the NEP and the united front. What is more, the Wall Street Crash was about to plunge capitalism into the worst economic depression in its history, lending credence to the talk of crisis, wars and revolutions. To the extent that the Stalinists discerned and encouraged these militant strivings and moods, they were arguably more in tune with significant sections of communist rank-and-file opinion than their opponents.[13]

Nevertheless, a distinction can be drawn between Stalin's domestic and Comintern policies. The difference lies in the fact that the drive for state-led industrialisation at home, no matter how ill-planned and coercive, was an absolute political imperative for Stalin in conditions of international isolation and the perceived threat of war against the USSR. The 'revolution from above' combined a lust for personal power with an ideological commitment to a programme of socialist renewal, however grossly distorted. The two appear inseparable. It is hard to see a similar combination at work in regard to the 'revolutionary' line of the Comintern. Stalin almost certainly did not believe in the imminent collapse of capitalism – 'socialism in one country' and headlong industrialisation in the USSR only confirmed this lack of faith in world revolution – or in the ability of foreign communist parties to undertake successful uprisings. Moreover, revolutionary activity in Europe would complicate an already dangerous international situation. Why, then, the Comintern's militant tactics?

Until the Stalin and Politburo archives in Moscow become accessible to researchers the motives for the policies of the period 1929–33 will remain a matter of conjecture. But two inter-related factors stand out. First, the policies were firmly rooted in the continuing power struggle in the RCP. Stalin skilfully used them as a weapon to define and defeat his opponents. Secondly, and more problematically, he reasoned that long-term Soviet security interests would be best served by a monolithic, strictly disciplined international communist movement dedicated to the defence of the USSR. It may be objected here that the ultra-leftist line of the Comintern from 1929 did little to ease Soviet security concerns. This is probably the case, but it must be acknowledged that the revolutionary bombast of official Comintern publications did not necessarily reflect the fundamentally cautious Russocentric aims of the organisation. With the exception of China, no violent uprisings occurred, none were ever planned. Stalin may have been confident that any difficulties arising with foreign governments would be soothed by Soviet diplomacy. In short, Stalin and his immediate entourage can be accused of manipulating the Comintern and abusing the loyalty of hundreds of thousands of communists worldwide who sincerely believed in the revolutionary postulates of the Third Period.

SOVIET DETERMINANTS OF THE THIRD PERIOD

Regardless of Stalin's habitual cynicism, the Comintern line in the dramatic years 1929–33 was not a fixed unchanging entity. To be sure, some key features remained constant, such as the commitment to the defence of the USSR, the belief in capitalism's final crisis and the profound hostility to social democracy, but we must be aware of the subtle variations in tactics, of the altered phrase here, the shift of emphasis there. Before examining the changes that did occur, we should address a question that has exercised the minds of contemporaries and historians ever since the 1930s: how tight was Stalin's grip on the Comintern and its national sections? To what extent did he and his few select companions determine the International's strategies and tactics? The lack of any consensus on this issue is evident from the following two quotations, the first from Franz Borkenau, a German ex-communist writing in 1938, the second from E. H. Carr, the top British expert on the Comintern writing in 1982. Borkenau states categorically that during the Third Period, 'Stalin kept an iron control over all details of Comintern work, and both the policy and the lists of parliamentary candidates of the communist parties were rigidly controlled by Moscow.'[14] Carr begs to differ, arguing that 'Stalin, heavily engaged elsewhere, was not tempted to concern himself with the petty disputes of an institution he had always despised.' Thus, 'it would be misleading to depict Comintern and its component parties in the early nineteen-thirties as a monolithic structure responding blindly to the dictates of a single supreme authority'.[15] It would be hard to imagine a more unequivocal clash of opinion. But which interpretation is closer to reality?

Borkenau's line of reasoning encapsulates, indeed did much to establish, the standard image of Stalin and the Comintern in the 1930s. Since the late 1980s it has been largely resubstantiated by Soviet historians with access to the Comintern Archives in Moscow. It cannot be dismissed lightly. Stalin's pivotal role in Comintern affairs from 1923–4 has been established beyond all doubt. By late 1929 he had become *primus inter pares* in an oligarchical Russian party leadership, a position which gave his words and policies even greater weight. It is at this time too that Stalin's 'cult of personality' began to assume prominence. It would not be long before communists the world over would be paying homage to the 'Great Leader'. More specifically, there can be no question that with the purge of the 'rightists' and 'conciliators', Stalin's hold over the Comintern central apparatus and national party leaderships was immeasurably strengthened. 'His' men were now at the helm and through them he preserved a strict ideological and organisational grip on the international movement. The training of loyal Stalinist cadres became one of the main tasks of the Comintern, and from Moscow's point of view one of its greatest long-term achievements. However, should the 'loyal Stalinist' of today turn out to be the 'heretic' of tomorrow, then ways were found of removing the trouble-maker. The successive campaigns against unruly leaders in the German, French, Czechoslovak and Polish parties in the years 1931–3 are prime examples of Stalin's determination to construct a highly disciplined set of Bolshevik cadres in the national sections.

On the basis of painstaking work in the Comintern Archives, Firsov has confirmed the 'Borkenau line', if we may call it that. He maintains that 'Stalin, personally and through Molotov, Lazar Kaganovich and Andrei Zhdanov, controlled the most important sectors of the Comintern's activities.'[16] As a concrete example, Firsov describes what one suspects was a typical episode in the life of the International. On the eve of the Thirteenth ECCI Plenum, due to open in late November 1933, Piatnitsky became concerned about the theses to be adopted at the meeting. Firsov writes:

On 21 November, Piatnitsky, having found out that Stalin had refused to read the draft theses because 'they are too long', sent him a shortened version with the request 'to read this summary and inform us if the theses' line is correct or if not how it should be reworked. We cannot open the plenum without your instructions on the theses.' On 14 December Piatnitsky sent Stalin, Molotov and Kaganovich the resolutions and theses of the plenum, which were ready to go to press. He asked them to look them over and tell him 'which changes should be introduced into the theses and resolutions'.[17]

It seems that a missive or telephone call sufficed for Stalin and his closest colleagues not only to approve, but formulate the lamentable decisions of the Thirteenth Plenum, which, at a time of ferocious Nazi repression, prophesied 'a new round of revolution and wars', continued to employ the tendentious term 'social fascist', and emphasised the struggle for a 'Soviet government' as the only way out of the capitalist crisis.[18] There was no mention of a broad united front against fascism or transitional democratic demands.

This is not the sole example of Stalin's personal intervention in the framing of Comintern policy. It was he who on several occasions in 1930 and 1931 inserted anti-social democratic diatribes into ECCI resolutions; it was he who in July 1931 insisted on the KPD's participation in the Nazi-sponsored referendum against the Prussian social democratic government; it was his famous 'Letter' to the journal *Proletarskaia revoliutsiia* in October 1931 that served as a sharp reminder of the dangers of flirtations with social democracy; it was he who in the spring of 1933, that is *after* Hitler's accession to power, instructed the ECCI to step up the campaign against the Second International and the German SPD; it was he who as late as July 1934 defended the basic correctness of the 'social fascist' theory. Stalin's burning hostility to social democracy shines through and it was this animosity which, according to Firsov, 'precluded any possibility of establishing contact between communist and social democratic . . . parties for the purpose of creating a united workers' front against the fascist offensive'.[19]

Does this fascination with Stalin mean that Carr's less personalised view is insupportable? Clearly, his assertion that the Comintern was not a monolithic structure is debatable. It was a highly bureaucratised organisation and once Stalin or Molotov had spoken, the ECCI and party leaderships jumped to attention. Where he is on more solid ground is in his depiction of Stalin as 'an absentee director who occasionally turns up unexpectedly and demands that props be removed or the odd actor . . . replaced, and then disappears, leaving others to cope with the mess'.[20] Stalin, weighed down with the massive burdens of the First Five-Year Plan and the ongoing agricultural crisis, had neither the time nor the inclination to indulge in day-to-day supervision of the ECCI. Borkenau's claim that Stalin controlled 'all details' of the Comintern's work is thus an exaggeration. The result, if we believe Carr, was a kind of vacuum at the heart of the Comintern, which encouraged caution, confusion and indecision, but which also gave the leadership a certain leeway in interpreting directives from above. The fact that firm directives were not always forthcoming only added to the vacillation and fostered subtle divisions among the Comintern hierarchy. Piatnitsky, Lozovsky, Kun and Knorin generally adopted more 'hardline' positions, while Manuilsky, Kuusinen and later Dimitrov tended towards greater flexibility. This image of an aloof Stalin, unable or unwilling to exert sustained continuing control, reinforces recent Western research on Soviet domestic history in the 1930s, much of which has challenged the totalitarian paradigm of Stalin's rule.[21]

The picture of the 'absentee director' could profitably be taken further. Is it possible that in 1928–9, Stalin, rather than initiating the 'left turn', actually appropriated and sanctioned the uncompromising positions of others, 'hawks' such as Molotov, Lozovsky, Kun and Thälmann? This appears to be the case with the 'social fascist' slogan, which almost definitely did not originate with Stalin, but which was canonised by him in the course of that year. Perhaps he countenanced the radical rhetoric 'only because he attributed very little practical significance to whatever the Comintern did in those years'?[22] Perhaps, as Sheila Fitzpatrick has argued in relation to the contemporaneous cultural revolution in the USSR, Stalin accepted a predefined and pre-existing hardline platform once he had resolved to move against his Politburo colleagues?[23] Miloš Hájek, a leading Czech Comintern expert, has asserted that the 'class against class' policy 'arose autonomously. . . . Stalin decided to support it only when strong and vital elements in the European communist parties upheld it.'[24]

Like so much in Comintern history, there are no definitive answers to these problems. The received wisdom that Stalin decided everything may need revising. He was a more distant ruler than this interpretation would allow. It is feasible, moreover, that the details of the Third Period line were elaborated by others, both within the Comintern hierarchy and the national parties. But it would be a

brave historian who denied that Stalin maintained a decisive influence over the determination of the general strategies, and, crucially, pronounced them irrevocable and universal. When he decided
to speak, his word was gospel. It is clear that no major policy
innovation was possible without his direct intervention or sanction,
and nor was any change in the composition of communist party
leaderships. The watershed in this process was the Tenth ECCI
Plenum in July 1929. From then on, no public criticism of the 'Stalin
line' was to be tolerated and the suppression of inner-party democracy became a defining characteristic of the Stalinised Comintern.
We do not need to regard the Stalin of 1929–33 as an omnipotent
tyrant to appreciate the extent of his mastery over the Comintern.
Having established this, we must now turn to the broader question
of the Soviet determinants of the new line as it developed during the
early 1930s.

It is axiomatic for most Western historians that the principal
determinant of Comintern policy throughout the 1930s was Soviet
raison d'état. The security of the USSR was paramount for Stalin. The
supreme task was to ensure that the imperialist attack on the Soviet
Union, which all Bolsheviks agreed was inevitable, would be delayed
as long as possible. Time was of the essence if the Soviet economy
and military machine were to be brought up to scratch. Faith in the
notion of world revolution had long since dissipated in the Kremlin
and skilful diplomacy had become the best means of guaranteeing
the peace. What role, then, for the Comintern?

It is commonly argued that in the course of the 1930s the
Comintern became a mere instrument of Soviet foreign policy. It was
kept in existence primarily as a propaganda weapon for the 'first
socialist state', its dual purpose being to trumpet abroad the successes
of the Five-Year Plans and to rally the international working class to
the defence of the Soviet Union. In this the national communist
parties could play a key part. In Borkenau's words, 'Russia laid store
upon having in every country an organization at its orders, an
organization ready to maintain that particular country on the path
desired by Russian foreign policy.'[25] Less readily recognised, but
none the less significant, is the fact that the Comintern served Stalin
on the domestic front in a myth-building capacity. It was portrayed
as a vast 'international army' of proletarians, more powerful than the
bourgeois League of Nations, resolutely supporting the construction
of Soviet socialism. As far as this image of the Comintern gained

currency, it legitimised the policies of the Stalinist Politburo in the eyes of the Soviet worker.

If Soviet *raison d'état* does indeed largely account for the shifts and turns in Comintern policy, and few historians would deny it a prominent place, then some discussion of the uneasy relationship between the International and Narkomindel is necessary. In the early 1920s, personal and ideological ties between the two organisations were close, Soviet diplomats often acting as surrogate revolutionaries in their places of residence. As we have seen, Lenin's foreign policy astutely combined a commitment to international revolution with a diplomacy designed to divide the imperialist camp. Before 1921, the emphasis was on the former. Thereafter, when world revolution became an increasingly unlikely means of protecting the infant Soviet state and when trade with capitalist economies became a priority under NEP, the Bolshevik government was compelled to adopt more traditional channels of interaction with the Western powers. In the search for a peaceful breathing space, Georgii Chicherin, the Commissar of Foreign Affairs, took great pains to distance Narkomindel from the radical agitation of the Comintern, assuring foreign governments that the International had nothing to do with the Soviet state. Few believed him. For the rest of the decade the foreign policy of the USSR was formulated on a dual-track: diplomacy via Narkomindel, revolution via the Comintern. But in an era of 'relative capitalist stabilisation', diplomacy gradually, almost imperceptibly, displaced the original mission of the Comintern, though no Bolshevik, even Stalin, could ever publicly renounce the rhetoric of world revolution. Stalin's theory of 'socialism in one country' implied a temporary improvement of official relations with the West and was thus welcomed by Narkomindel, despite the fact that many Oppositionists served in its offices.[26]

The War Scare of 1927 and the revolutionary bravado of the Third Period complicated the activities of a Narkomindel attempting to soothe relations with the West and maintain the peace. On 20 June 1929 Chicherin wrote prophetically to Stalin that 'the clamour about social fascism is preposterous nonsense' and any action based on this policy 'means leading the Comintern to ruin'. Furthermore, the 'ridiculous talk in the Comintern about the struggle against some imaginary [Western] preparations for war against the USSR only damages and undermines the international position of the USSR'.[27] In Chicherin's analysis, the 'social fascist' line of the Comintern could not but harm the diplomatic aims of the Soviet state. Yet Stalin, at this time still conducting the all-important campaign against the 'rightists', chose to ignore his foreign minister's advice and run the risk of alienating the Narkomindel. Chicherin in any case was ill and about to be replaced by Stalin's protégé, Maxim Litvinov. Under him, it appears that relations between Narkomindel and the Comintern grew increasingly tense. The latter's revolutionary verbiage hampered the intricate business of charting a peaceful path through the dangerous international waters. Its name was strictly taboo in the Foreign Ministry. Carr has concluded that the major Soviet diplomatic moves of the years 1933–4 were prompted by Litvinov, and neither he nor Stalin 'paused to consider their implications for Comintern'.[28] One is left with the impression that the International was a troublesome, if sporadically useful, sideshow for Stalin.

There is plenty of evidence to indicate that the Comintern did adapt to the exigencies of Soviet foreign policy. For instance, in early 1930 a subtle alteration in Comintern phraseology became detectable. The term 'social fascism' remained, but a 'left' danger now reared its head together with the more familiar 'rightist deviation'. The foreign 'leftists' had taken the revolutionary posturings of the Comintern too literally and in so doing had threatened the security of the isolated Soviet Union at a particularly sensitive time. The Politburo must have feared that talk of insurrection in Europe combined with the onset of the Great Depression could provoke a concerted anti-Soviet backlash from the Anglo-French 'imperialists' as a way out of the economic crisis. In 1929–30 relations with France and Britain were at a low ebb. Therefore, Germany was of supreme significance. It was vital for the Soviet leaders to prevent the Weimar Republic from being enticed into the Allied 'anti-Soviet front'. A pro-Western orientation in Berlin would inevitably put at risk the special relationship built up between Weimar and Soviet Russia since 1922, and in particular the close military link between the two countries. Relations with Berlin had to be kept on an even keel and the KPD should be constrained from undue interference in this task.

With these concerns no doubt in mind, a meeting of the ECCI Enlarged Presidium in February 1930 resolved that 'the defence of the Soviet Union against the threat of imperialist attack is more than ever before the most important task of all sections of the Communist International'.[29] In his keynote address, Manuilsky warned that although capitalist stabilisation was collapsing, there was not yet a revolutionary situation. The cautionary tone was repeated in the resolution on the German party which called for a campaign against both 'left' and right 'opportunism', meaning that 'leftist', adventurist tendencies were to be overcome as well as the well-worn 'rightist' deviations.[30] It was probably no coincidence that the resolution was drafted at approximately the same time as Stalin's famous article 'Dizzy with Success', which temporarily halted the drive for all-out collectivisation in the Soviet countryside and demanded a 'fight on two fronts' in the RCP. This slogan was soon to reverberate around the Comintern, claiming 'leftist' victims in Germany, Czechoslovakia, France and elsewhere.[31]

The message was clear, if unstated: communists should temper any inopportune revolutionary ardour in order not to sully Soviet relations with the Western powers, especially Germany. Manuilsky was unusually frank on this score at the Eleventh ECCI Plenum in March 1931:

> Can the perspectives of the People's Revolution in Germany be viewed outside of the whole complicated international tangle and, in the first place, outside the question of the U.S.S.R? Is it possible to imagine for a moment any big revolutionary movement in Central Europe which did not give rise to consequences in the form of a big international struggle?[32]

These were no empty words. The plenum voiced concern over the 'revolutionary impatience' of the communist parties and specifically the KPD's tendency to terroristic violence. Under ECCI pressure, the Central Committee of the KPD issued a resolution in November 1931 condemning 'individual terror' and 'left-sectarian states of mind, directed against the mass-work of the Party'.[33] The Soviet need to preserve stability in Europe was doubtless not the sole determinant behind this and other shifts in communist party policy in the period 1930–3. The patent inapplicability of revolutionary terminology to the actual situations facing the parties and the reluctant realisation that in most countries the communists were too weak to foment insurrection played their part in the subtle adaptations of the Comintern line. But it is difficult to avoid the conclusion that the Stalinist ECCI leaders were fully aware of the Soviet government's requirements and acted accordingly.

Peace was the overriding aim of a rapidly industrialising Soviet Union and this dictated elemental caution in foreign affairs. The Comintern, in process of being demoted to the margins of Soviet policy, likewise had to display restraint and circumspection, but could never formally renounce its revolutionary mission. Stalin's elusive role only added to the atmosphere of indecision and prudence. Herein lie the contradictions and tensions of a 'revolutionary' Third Period that was not revolutionary. But it must be re-emphasised that in the early 1930s the tactics of the Comintern were not exclusively defined by the needs of Soviet foreign policy. National and local conditions impinged on the elaboration of policies on the ground. A certain duality existed, always muted, but none the less real. In this sense the Comintern cannot be called a mere instrument of the Soviet state, if by the word 'Comintern' we mean an international organisation of communist parties as distinct from the Stalinised central apparatus in Moscow. By examining the concept of 'social fascism' we will be able to assess the impact of this duality.

THEORY AND PRACTICE OF SOCIAL FASCISM

It should be evident from the previous chapters that the notion of the degeneration of social democracy into a bourgeois party had a long pedigree in communist thinking. Its origins are to be found well before the Sixth Congress in the summer of 1928. The etymology of the term 'social fascism' can ultimately be traced to such Leninist constructions as 'social patriotism' and 'social chauvinism', both used to denounce the activities of leading socialists in the years after 1914. The American historian, Theodore Draper, has unearthed the first usage of the derogatory label 'social fascist'. In November 1922 the Soviet government newspaper *Izvestiia* published a brief notice in which the words 'social fascists' were coined to describe the nefarious role of the Italian socialists in Mussolini's rise to power.[34] It was an isolated case, but the defeat of the German party in October 1923 lent the term greater credibility. As we have seen, in early 1924, Zinoviev, followed by Stalin, insisted that social democracy had been transformed from a right-wing working-class party into a wing of the bourgeoisie, even into 'a wing of fascism'. Incorporated into the resolutions of the Fifth Congress in July 1924, these dubious formulations foreshadowed the more uncompromising positions of the Sixth Congress.

What emerges clearly is the endemic hostility of the Comintern leadership towards social democracy. This attitude was somewhat tempered under Bukharin, yet anti-social democratic feeling remained just below the surface in the Comintern Executive and in the national parties. For many communists, the social democratic parties and reformist trade unions were the most dangerous enemy precisely because they retained widespread working-class support. It was commonly held that only by overcoming the ideological appeal of reformism, by winning over the majority of organised workers and by defeating social democracy once and for all could communists unite the working class for a revolutionary assault on capitalism. The stakes were very high. Hence the stridency of 'social fascism'.

But why exactly were social democrats turning once again into 'social fascists' by the late 1920s? The answer lies partly in Stalin's political designs as outlined above, but also in the Comintern's evaluation of social democracy's relationship with the capitalist state and in the changing nature of that state. The *Theses on the International Situation and the Tasks of the Communist International*, adopted by the Sixth Congress, affirmed that the contradictions of capitalist stabilisation would result in 'the most severe intensification of the general capitalist crisis', forcing the bourgeoisie to seek new ways of upholding its power. The theses adumbrated two methods of achieving this: the 'co-opting' of social democracy into the existing political structures, and the establishment 'in critical moments' of a fascist regime. The first strategy was characterised by 'the grafting together of the State apparatus and capitalist organisations with the upper stratum of the Labour organisations, led by social democracy'. This 'bourgeoisification' of the 'Labour bureaucracy' signified that social democracy had 'passed from shame-faced defence of capitalism to open support of capitalist construction; from mouthing phrases about the class struggle to the advocacy of "industrial peace" '. The second strategy involved a 'process of fascisation' of the capitalist state in which the bourgeoisie 'utilises the discontent of the petty and middle urban and rural bourgeoisie, and even of certain strata of the declassed proletariat, for the purpose of creating a reactionary mass movement' and an 'open and consistent dictatorship'. Thus, 'a new type of State, openly based on violence, coercion and corruption' was emerging.[35] The expected fusion of these two processes underlay the theory of 'social fascism'.

The congress resolution produced concrete instances of the 'treacherous role' of the social democratic 'upper strata': their 'class-splitting policy' of expelling communists from the trade unions which weakened the workers' resistance to capitalist attacks; their justification of the use of 'terror' against the workers; their support for the armed forces and expansionist strivings of the bourgeois state; and their 'fundamental hostility' to the USSR.[36] The last indictment was by no means the least. The constant fear of the Soviet leaders was the prospect of a Franco-German rapprochement directed against the USSR. The German SPD was committed to a Western-oriented foreign policy and the entry in May 1928 of the social democrats into a coalition government, led by the anti-Soviet socialist Hermann Müller, made this eventuality all the more alarming. The SPD confirmed its pro-Western stance in 1929–30 by firmly supporting the Young Plan, which reduced Germany's reparation payments to the Allies and to which the Soviet government and KPD were vehemently opposed. It seems reasonable to conclude that the international policies of the SPD more than any other single factor contributed to the vitriolic 'social fascist' rhetoric employed by the Comintern in the years 1929–33.

A noteworthy feature of the resolution of the Sixth Congress was the attack on the 'so-called "Left" social-democratic leaders' as 'the most dangerous enemies of Communism'. Under this rubric fell the Austro-Marxists, led by Otto Bauer and Friedrich Adler, the British Independent Labour Party (ILP) and similar trends in Italy, Germany and Norway. The highly suspect assertion that such groups were developing 'reactionary' tendencies was rationalised by reference to their backing of 'imperialist war preparations against the U.S.S.R.' and their subtle devious methods of deceiving the workers. They 'make verbal claims of being in favour of unity but . . . in fact, unreservedly support the criminal splitting tactics of the Second International'. Therefore, 'Communists must resolutely expose the "Left-Wing" social-democratic leaders as the most dangerous channels through which bourgeois politics may penetrate into the working class'.[37] In the late 1980s, Soviet historians argued that this erroneous formulation alienated precisely that wing of the workers' movement closest to the communists with whom a broad anti-fascist united front could have been negotiated.[38] Although this argument is persuasive with the benefit of hindsight, in fact throughout the Third Period Comintern leaders confidently expected that the mass of workers would become disillusioned with the 'labour bureaucrats' and flock to the communist parties under the revolutionary banner. This misguided prognosis precluded the idea of united fronts and broad alliances with both the reformist 'bosses' and the 'left' social democrats.

Given the contentious nature of the Comintern's analysis we need to ask why such conclusions seemed plausible to the majority of communists. First, as noted above, the theory of 'social fascism' represented neither a total break with past practices, nor was it introduced overnight. Communists in 1928–9 were not confronted with a sudden *volte-face* completely altering their conceptions of social democracy. 'Social fascism' evolved over many months, was the subject of much debate, disagreement and probably misunderstanding and became official Comintern doctrine only after the Tenth ECCI Plenum in July 1929 (document 12). Historians have tended to over-emphasise elements of rapid change rather than continuity in the Comintern's Third Period tactics. This is not to say that it was 'business as usual'. Far from it, but perhaps the choices did not appear so immediate or stark to communist activists in the factories and mines.

Secondly, the behaviour of the social democrats themselves played an important role in legitimating 'social fascism'. The expulsion of communists from reformist trade unions in Germany and Britain and the conciliatory stance of the SPD leaders towards capitalist rationalisation provided longer-term evidence of social democracy's 'degeneration'. Short-term catalysts seemed to confirm the point. On May Day 1929 pitched battles were fought between workers and the police in the working-class districts of Berlin after the social democratic police chief, Zörgiebel, had proscribed outdoor rallies, a ban which the KPD leaders decided to challenge. Over thirty people were killed, 194 were injured and 1228 arrested. The violence of the police response had a major impact on the attitude of the Comintern and German communists to social democracy and to the Weimar state. Many party members, and not a few leaders, began to see 'little Zörgiebels' everywhere. The KPD's Twelfth Congress, convened a month after the bloodshed, raised the rallying cry: 'Social Democracy is preparing, as an active and organizing force, the establishment of the fascist dictatorship.' As Eve Rosenhaft has asserted, the 'consequence of the Berlin events for the Party was thus to confirm the political analysis of the "Third Period" '.[39] For the KPD 'conciliators', however, the May Day tragedy was the result of the mistaken policies of the Thälmann leadership which had overestimated the party's strength and irresponsibly called for mass demonstrations without the necessary prior preparation. Such views were given short shrift from a belligerent and self-confident congress.

If the introduction of 'social fascism' in 1929 was partly rationalised in terms of social democratic 'terror', its continued relevance into the 1930s was predicated upon the strategies and tactics employed by the German SPD leaders inside and outside government. One such strategy was known as the 'lesser evil', whereby the opposition SPD tolerated the undemocratic practices and deflationary policies of increasingly right-wing Weimar governments with the aim of keeping Hitler out of office. In line with this policy, the SPD declined to put up a candidate in the Presidential elections of 1932 and voted for the reactionary General Hindenburg. For the communists, the 'lesser evil' represented a betrayal of working-class interests and justified the claim that the social democratic leaders had become the willing instruments of the bourgeoisie.

The theory of 'social fascism' was thus grounded in the rhetoric of the 'bourgeoisification' and 'statisation' of the social democratic upper strata. But what practical effects did this have on communist tactics? First, it marked a far more aggressive stance towards 'bourgeois parliaments', which were to be used solely for propagandistic purposes. This attitude was typified by Klement Gottwald, the new 'Bolshevised' leader of the KSČ, in his inaugural address to the Czechoslovak National Assembly in December 1929. Responding to accusations from non-communist deputies that his party was under the command of Moscow, Gottwald boasted: 'We go to Moscow to learn from the Russian Bolsheviks how to wring your necks. (*Outcry*) And you know that the Russian Bolsheviks are masters at it! (*Uproar*).'[40]

Parliamentary activity, however, had always been secondary for communists. The most decisive changes of the Third Period occurred in the crucial field of trade union and industrial policy. It was here on the shopfloor that the new course was to have its most far-reaching and deleterious impact, sharpening the lines of division between communist and social democratic workers. The broad goal was to break through the 'trade union legalism' of the union leaderships and establish, as James Wickham has argued in relation to the KPD, a communist party:

> doubly independent of reformism: organisationally independent, in that now new 'rank-and-file' organisations were to allow the party to take the initiative outside the official reformist institutions, and socially independent in that these organisations were to be based on layers of the working class – the unorganised and above all the unemployed – which the reformists had ignored.[41]

The Tenth ECCI Plenum, held from 3 to 19 July 1929, marked a new stage in the radicalisation of the Comintern's trade union tactics. Henceforth every strike, every demonstration was to become an integral component of the immediate struggle for the revolution, for socialism. Ever since the previous plenum in February 1928, Lozovsky, head of the Profintern, had been urging communist trade unionists to adopt a more aggressive stance towards the reformist 'bosses' and to lead economic struggles independently of the 'labour bureaucracy'. For Lozovsky, the official trade unions were 'schools of capitalism' which could never be won over for the revolutionary cause. Hence he was prepared to broach the vexed issue of creating separate Red Unions, a highly controversial step that would inevitably deepen the split in the working-class movement. The uncertainties of the Russian inner-party feuds and the consequent hesitations of the Soviet leadership had delayed a definitive mandate for Lozovsky's position, but with the defeat of the 'Bukharinites' these vacillations appear to have abated.

In his address to the Tenth Plenum, Lozovsky emphasised the recent politicisation of economic struggles, conjuring up the vision of a four-stage route to 'class war': economic strike, political strike, revolt and civil war.[42] The plenum resolution, noting the 'incessant and increasing growth of class contradictions' and the 'accelerated rate' of working-class radicalisation in capitalist societies, was slightly more sober, but maintained that 'in the new conditions the economic struggle of the proletariat assumes an ever more sharply expressed political character'. Examples were cited ranging from the Ruhr to Poland, from the USA to India. The vital element in these global struggles was the fact that the unorganised masses, that is the largely unskilled, non-unionised, young and women workers exploited by capitalist rationalisation, were displaying 'ever-growing activity' and striking in ever-growing numbers. The main aim of the communists was thus to seize the revolutionary offensive, gain the leadership of these economic and political strikes and win the majority of the workers by organising the hitherto unorganised. This task required a greater concentration on the 'united front from below' both within and especially outside the reformist unions.[43]

This aim demanded a dual-pronged thrust that in practice proved essentially contradictory: on the one hand a determination to work 'from below' *within* the existing unions and to lead the economic struggles of unionised workers, but on the other a commitment to create so-called 'revolutionary trade union oppositions' *outside* the unions and to organise the non-unionised in various independent strike and 'action' committees under communist direction. Although the Tenth Plenum resolution placed strict conditions on the formation of new Red Unions, it unambiguously asserted that 'Communists cannot be opposed on principle to splitting the trade unions.'[44] In several countries, including Germany and to a lesser extent Britain and America, new communist unions were set up as rivals to the established reformist organisations.

This dichotomy was further compounded by the fact that the Comintern leaders were convinced that the growing army of unemployed represented a revolutionary force. To organise both unemployed and unorganised workers while simultaneously maintaining work in the existing unions proved beyond the capabilities of the communist parties, particularly as their strength in the factories was severely affected by sackings and dismissals. Communist 'trouble-makers' and 'strike-leaders' were the first to be laid off. Invariably, the end result was that communist parties became divorced from the mass of unionised workers and took on the character of 'parties of the unemployed'. This in turn opened up a major theoretical and practical lacuna in the Comintern's overall strategy. How were these parties to lead economic strikes and struggles and convert them into a mass political strike against the capitalist state when the majority of communists were unemployed and no longer carried economic muscle in the factories and unions? The answer from Comintern tacticians, as outlined above, was that parties must create a broad revolutionary united front of employed and unemployed workers. In the increasingly harsh and divisive conditions of the Depression this goal proved unrealisable, despite certain successes such as the National Unemployed Workers' Movement in Britain led by Wal Hannington.

The consequences of the 'independent leadership' of strikes, of 'organising the unorganised' and of forming separate Red Unions can only be described as disastrous. The Comintern leadership crucially failed to adopt a differentiated analysis of national economic, political and cultural conditions. What was good for Germany, where the gulf between social democrats and communists was deepseated and the economy was rapidly deteriorating, was declared equally good for Britain, where the vast majority of workers remained committed to the Labour Party and its affiliated trade unions and the economic situation was less catastrophic. By grossly overestimating the radicalisation of the labour movement and by mistakenly inflating local industrial disputes into mass political struggles, the Comintern hierarchy displayed a chronic misunderstanding of the nature of working-class response to straitened material circumstances. Economic depression and mass unemployment made the calling of unofficial strikes particularly hazardous. Defeat, dismissals and persecution ensued and the jobless were notoriously difficult to organise on a permanent basis. They could just as easily lapse into apathy and introspection as march on town halls demanding redress. The ill-conceived and occasionally adventurist nature of Comintern tactics meant that communist influence in national trade union and labour movements dwindled to insignificance.

Two examples, the first from Czechoslovakia, the second from Britain, illustrate the drastic consequences of the Comintern's insistence on a militant industrial strategy based largely outside the existing trade union structures. In Czechoslovakia, many leading officials of the Red Unions bitterly resisted the turn to the left in 1928–9, accusing the Czechoslovak Stalinists of adopting 'a semi-anarchistic, radical programme designed to split the party, destroy all the traditions of its past and uproot the communist movement from our environmental conditions and relations', thus making 'the party a body alien to the Czechoslovak worker'.[45] The result was an acrimonious split in the Red Unions with almost half the membership eventually rejoining the social democratic organisation. The 80 000 party loyalists who remained in the revamped Red Unions were unable to exert any meaningful impact on the Czechoslovak labour movement during the harsh years of the Great Depression despite constant haranguing from the Comintern and Profintern.

In Britain, the communist party since 1924 had sponsored the National Minority Movement (NMM), an organisation of leftist union opposition groups which agitated within the reformist unions in order to build up support for the revolutionary cause. By 1926 the NMM could claim, with some exaggeration, 950 000 members and considerable influence in the important mining and engineering industries. By the early 1930s it had faded into virtual oblivion as a result of the CPGB's fiercely anti-union stance. The emphasis on creating rank-and-file bodies outside the official trade-union framework and the insistence on leading strike action in opposition to those unions had manifestly backfired. Workers would not consistently support wildcat strikes in economic circumstances that were highly unpropitious. Even more disconcerting, party membership had slumped from 10 800 at the end of 1926 to just 2555 by November 1930. The lesson drawn by General Secretary Pollitt was that a return to work *within* the unions was required, a return to a more practicable 'united front from below'. A change of line in this direction was in fact proclaimed following a bad tempered session of the Profintern's Central Council in December 1931, but progress in trade union work in Britain remained patchy. Pollitt himself detected one reason for the isolation of the communists when he intimated to the Thirteenth ECCI Plenum in December 1933 that the jargon of the Third Period had confounded the average British party member. He said:

> We use certain words here in our resolutions and discussions, and the Party comrades feel that unless they are using the same words they are not communists. 'Re-orientation', 'fascisation', 'orientation', 'social-fascists' – the comrades have developed a psychology where they believe that they are not carrying out the Party line unless these types of words are occurring every other minute. . . . I have noticed many comrades coming to the Lenin School [in Moscow], who in England could talk simply and clearly to the workers – [they] go back speaking a foreign language.[46]

There seems little doubt, then, that in Britain the language of 'social fascism' alienated the mass of working people from the communist movement.

Another country where the policies of the Third Period had significant repercussions was Spain. Hitherto the Comintern had paid scant attention to the tiny and ineffectual Spanish Communist Party (PCE), but the downfall of the monarchy and the declaration of the Second Republic in April 1931 brought the problems of the Iberian peninsula to the fore. The Comintern leaders were caught unawares by the changes, but soon prognosticated a two-stage Spanish revolution – the bourgeois-democratic followed by the proletarian – in line with Leninist theory. This signified that the PCE should under no circumstances defend the Republican government or forge alliances with the socialists, but organise the urban and rural masses for a 'Soviet Spain'. These directives fundamentally misinterpreted the balance of class power in Spain, underestimating the influence of the pre-industrial elites and fuelling the bitter recriminations among communists, socialists and anarchists. Thus, the 'social fascist' rhetoric of the Comintern, combined with socialist governmental repression of PCE activists, formed an inauspicious backdrop to the struggles that lay ahead.[47]

All this does not mean, however, that communist tactics during the Third Period had no rationale, as some historians have claimed. Borkenau, for instance, stresses the communists' 'blind frenzy', their 'hatred' and desire for 'vengeance' like people who 'suddenly start to leap about aimlessly'.[48] In the past decade or so, social historians have attempted to rethink this overly negative interpretation of the Third Period by pointing to the rational motivations behind, and achievements of, the communists' trade union, community and cultural activities in the early years of the Great Depression. For one of these historians, the policies of the Third Period laid the basis of 'a visible revolutionary and oppositional culture' which 'presented a challenge, formally and organizationally, at least both to social democracy and capitalism'.[49] The mushrooming of workers' newspapers and factory broadsheets, the creation of workers' theatres, sports and leisure groups, and the emphasis on women and youth issues marked the communists off, it is argued, from their inactive ideologically supine social democratic rivals. In some coalmining and textile communities of Wales and Scotland, the so-called 'Little Moscows', communists gained a hegemonic role among the population by their hard work and dedication to local causes.[50]

While acknowledging the heavy hand of the Comintern, this line of enquiry focuses more on the national than the international level. A central theme of this work is that the communist parties operated in a specific local context that could not but influence the formulation of tactics and grassroots responses. In this view the Comintern is just one of several sources of policy-making, and not necessarily the most important. An historian of the American party, Fraser M. Ottanelli, has aptly summarised this approach: 'the Party's experience centered around an indigenous quest for policies, organizational forms, language, and overall cultural forms that would adapt the Communists' radicalism to domestic realities and political traditions.' In short, 'the course of the CPUSA was shaped by a homespun search for policies which would make it an integral part of the country's society as well as by directives from the Communist International'.[51]

By shifting the focus away from Moscow to the rich and differentiated pastures of the domestic scene, this methodology provides a valuable corrective to the traditional 'from above' interpretation of the Third Period. It also raises key questions about the nature of the parties' relationship to the central Comintern bodies. There is evidence to suggest that by early 1932 there were rumblings of discontent from below with the Comintern's sectarian policies. Some communists were tentatively adapting the 'social fascist' line to suit local circumstances. In Czechoslovakia, for example, a broader application of the united front tactics during a large miners' strike in Northern Bohemia in April 1932 met with a good measure of success. Social democratic trade union functionaries and workers joined in the struggle as the communists softened their approach to lower and middle-ranking socialist organisations without renouncing their hostility to the 'social fascist' hierarchy. For the first time since 1929 the communists did not insist on their leading role as a precondition of the united front.

Fortified by this salutary experience, certain KSČ leaders, notably Josef Guttmann, concluded that Comintern tactics should be reconsidered. At the Twelfth ECCI Plenum in August–September 1932 Guttmann launched a wide-ranging critique of the KPD's restricted conception of the united front and its equivocal attitude to the Nazi threat, a threat which was not confined solely to Germany. In effect, Guttmann had dared to challenge the Comintern's 'social fascist' line, probably the first communist leader to do so publicly. The crisis in the relationship between the KSČ and Comintern simmered for many months. Party boss Gottwald initially supported Guttmann's analysis, but after considerable pressure from the Comintern Executive Gottwald succumbed and agreed to discipline the unrepentant Guttmann. The sordid affair was finally 'resolved' with the expulsion of the 'Trotskyite' Guttmann in December 1933.[52] Similar doubts about the sectarian nature of the united front from below tactics were expressed by the Central Committee of the Swiss party in the summer of 1932, but its plea for a broader conception was flatly rejected by the ECCI.[53] Clearly not all European communists were convinced of the efficacy of the 'social fascist' theory.

In America, too, communists attempted to modify the line. Otta-nelli argues that the CPUSA, through its regional and local organi-sers, became firmly rooted in the struggles of ordinary American citizens against poverty, unemployment, and racial and sexual dis-crimination. These activists concentrated not on 'revolutionary pos-turing', but on the 'immediate grievances' of the dispossessed. To this extent, local economic disputes and community welfare action had a dynamic of their own and the revolutionary political designs of the Comintern appeared secondary for these party activists. Neverthe-less, successes were limited and the CPUSA remained a tiny sect with little national appeal. Ottanelli concludes that this resulted from the erroneous premise that the Depression would revolutionise the workers and draw them *en masse* into the party. In fact, 'in the United States and elsewhere, economic hardship tended to weaken labor's initiative rather than reinforce the revolutionary movement'.[54] This was indeed the case, but Ottanelli overlooks the fact that the belief in the revolutionising effects of the Depression originated in Moscow, not New York or Chicago. It would seem, then, that one important factor in the failure of the CPUSA to become a mass party was its reliance on Comintern strictures.

If the Comintern line was ill-suited to conditions in America, it proved ultimately disastrous in Germany. The 'orthodox' interpreta-tion of the left's response to the growth of fascism can be summarised as follows: the powerful German labour movement failed to arrest the rise of Nazism primarily because of the divisive 'social fascist' tactics imposed on the KPD by the Comintern, which precluded any chance of a broad anti-fascist front with the social democrats. With the German working class thus split and with the inability of both the KPD and SPD to appreciate the danger of Nazism, the way was left open for Hitler to fill the void in Weimar politics despite the electoral strength of the left-wing parties.

There is no denying the fact that the rift between communists and social democrats proved fatal and that the KPD should take its full share of the responsibility, but it should not obscure other consider-ations. First, not all the blame for the split lies with the communists.

The SPD leadership harboured a deep hostility towards Bolshevism and rarely displayed a willingness to collaborate with Moscow's 'German agents'. Moreover, viewed through contemporary communist eyes, the Comintern's Third Period line, elaborated with Germany in mind, met with no little success. Dick Geary's assertion that 'it is significant that support for the KPD reached its peak precisely when it spoke the language of "social fascism" '[55] may need qualification, but it is true that Party membership rose sharply from 130 000 in 1928 to perhaps as high as 360 000 by the end of 1932. Similarly, the KPD increased its vote from 3 264 793 in May 1928 to 5 980 614 in November 1932, the latter figure representing almost 17 per cent of the poll. Finally, the divisions in the German working-class movement had deeper socio-economic roots and were not simply the product of ideological chicanery in Moscow.

Having said this, the tragic failure of the KPD has its source in the Comintern's theory of fascism which informed communist practice in those crisis years, 1929–33. The Comintern's interpretation of fascism was not static and unchanging. Confusion and eclecticism characterised the communist movement's initial response to what was after all a new, puzzling and ill-defined political phenomenon. In this the communists were not alone. But the early relatively subtle insights into the nature of Italian fascism succumbed after 1928 to the straitjacket of Stalinist orthodoxy with untold consequences. As David Beetham has contended, the Comintern's Third Period analysis involved 'a conscious rejection of a level of understanding of fascism already available'.[56] By this he means that the studied observations of Gramsci, Togliatti, Zetkin and Radek on the complex social composition and class nature of Italian fascism were ignored when interpreting the far more serious threat of Nazism.

The reason for this, according to one school of thought, is to be found in the 'economistic catastrophism' of Comintern theorists, who equated the rise of fascism with the inevitable demise of capitalism.[57] The notion that fascism represented the last fling of a moribund capitalism, the final attempt by the bourgeoisie to retain economic and political power in the face of a working class whose triumph was conditioned by the laws of history, overlooked the mass nature of the fascist movement and underestimated its ability to act independently of, and even against, the interests of the bourgeoisie. Taken to its extreme, this view had perilous implications. For if fascism was the last stage of a dying capitalism, then proletarian revolution would surely follow, and if that were so why should fascism be feared? Furthermore, the Comintern failed to draw a clear distinction between parliamentary democracy which permitted working-class organisation and fascist dictatorship which crushed it unremittingly. Both were regarded as manifestations of bourgeois class rule, different in degree not in essence. Hence the Brüning and von Papen Weimar governments (March 1930–November 1932) were vilified by the Comintern and KPD as regimes 'for the implementation of fascist dictatorships', a formulation that suggested nothing worse could be expected of 'Hitler-fascism'. The crude equation 'social democracy = social fascism' drastically compounded matters in that socialist reformism was seen as the principal force holding back the workers from their true revolutionary tasks, and as such was the main enemy of communism. The result was a crippling underestimation of the *real* fascist danger.

A trenchant and prescient critic of the Comintern's response to German fascism was the exiled Trotsky. In a series of stinging articles and essays penned between 1930 and 1933, he assailed the Stalinist leaders of the Comintern and communist parties for their myopic determination to crush 'social fascism' before Nazism. Fascism, he reiterated again and again, was the chief danger since its victory would be a catastrophe for the German revolution and 'signify an inevitable war against the USSR'. He agreed that social democracy was strategically an enemy of communism, but tactically in the concrete German situation the KPD should renounce the nonsense of 'social fascism' and create a united front with the social democrats against the threat of Nazism.[58] The main practical problem left open by Trotsky's otherwise penetrating critique was how to forge a united front with the social democrats given the deep mutual hostility between the two camps? And even if the daunting obstacles to joint action were overcome, would a united German working class be strong enough to prevent Hitler's *Machtergreifung* without the support of other social groups and political parties? Whatever the answer, the KPD never seriously considered a broad united front with social democracy before January 1933.

Given the theoretical miasma at the heart of the Comintern's analysis of fascism, what tactics did the German Communist Party adopt in the years 1929–33 to achieve its ultimate goal of winning over the majority of the working class, overthrowing Weimar democracy and establishing a 'Soviet Germany'? The 'orthodox' interpre-

tation emphasises the KPD's slavish obedience to Comintern directives, the intellectual bankruptcy of its leadership under Thälmann
and in particular its unchanging hostility to the 'social fascists'. Some
scholars have accused the KPD of collaborating with the Nazis to
destroy the Weimar Republic.[59] Much documentary evidence has
been unearthed to substantiate these claims. A glance at the resolutions of KPD and Comintern gatherings throughout the period
1930–3 does indeed reveal an almost stupefying blindness to the
dangers of Hitler's National Socialist German Workers' Party
(NSDAP) and a consistent emphasis on the social democrats as the
prime enemy. For instance, Thälmann addressing the KPD Central
Committee in February 1932 warned his audience that 'nothing
would be more disastrous than an opportunistic over-estimation of
Hitler-fascism'. While the struggle against Nazism should go on
undiminished, 'our strategy directs its main thrust against Social
Democracy'.[60] The Eleventh ECCI Plenum resolution of April 1931
(document 13) briefly mentioned Hitler for the first time, but devoted
pages to the crimes of international social democracy, 'the principal
social support of the dictatorship of the bourgeoisie' and committed
warmonger against the USSR.[61] Eighteen months later, after the
Nazis' huge electoral gains, the Twelfth ECCI Plenum declared 'only
by directing the main blows against social-democracy . . . will it be
possible to strike at and defeat the chief class enemy of the proletariat
– the bourgeoisie'. Again the National Socialists warranted just one
passing comment.[62] The Thirteenth ECCI Plenum, meeting in
November and December 1933 after the Nazi regime had smashed
the German labour movement, still identified social democracy as
'the main social prop of the bourgeoisie also in the countries of open
fascist dictatorship' and called for a renewed struggle against its
'treacherous leaders'.[63]

Such rhetoric was on occasion translated into joint action with the
Nazis against the social democratic bastions of the Weimar Republic.
Two instances have become notorious: the Prussian referendum of
August 1931 and the Berlin transport workers' strike of November
1932. The former is a fine example of direct intervention from
Moscow in the internal affairs of the KPD and as such deserves
greater attention. For several months the Nazis and other nationalist
right-wing parties had spearheaded a campaign for the dissolution of
the socialist-led Prussian government. The KPD initially refused to
co-operate with the radical right and was supported, it seems, by

Manuilsky and the ECCI. But, as mentioned above, in July 1931 Stalin and Molotov overruled the 'moderates' in the Comintern and KPD leaderships and ordered the communists to participate in the Nazi-sponsored referendum. The 'red–brown plebiscite', as it became known, failed to dislodge the coalition Prussian government and the reputation of the KPD suffered incalculable damage.[64] Trotsky denounced the affair as 'the sheerest adventurism'.[65]

This line of historical enquiry 'from above', though having broad explanatory potency, neglects the nuances and subtleties of what was an extraordinarily complex, confusing and often chaotic situation. Speeches by Thälmann or ECCI resolutions are without doubt important, but how they were applied on the ground is just as relevant. Take the vexed issue of communist relations with the social democrats. The invective showered on the 'social fascist' leaders was crass and lasted well into 1933, but we should not completely overlook the fact that the KPD did begin to reassess its tactics in the light of the changing domestic and international conjuncture. The attempt to forge an 'Anti-Fascist Action' with social democratic workers in the spring of 1932 is a case in point, although it must be acknowledged that the 'Antifa' came too late and elicited only equivocal support from the KPD hierarchy. Nevertheless, much enthusiasm for a united front was displayed at the local level, and the Berlin district party leadership was later severely reprimanded by Thälmann for overstepping the boundaries of the united front from below. It would appear that not all party members and branches were persuaded by the 'social fascist' rhetoric. Acts of local collaboration between communist and social democratic organisations were reported even prior to the 'Anti-Fascist Action'. These examples of KPD–SPD fraternisation should not be exaggerated, but they do give the impression of a divided and uneasy party on the eve of the Nazi seizure of power.

The extent of co-operation between communists and Nazis against the Weimar state should likewise be put into perspective. By the end of 1929 the KPD had already 'identified the NSDAP as a serious challenge, a force to be reckoned with by virtue of its political appeal as well as of its militant violence'.[66] This realisation called for a constant review of KPD policy towards the National Socialists, a policy which ranged awkwardly from violent confrontation to embarrassed flirtation. The latter notwithstanding, in the years 1929–33 it was the communists who bore the brunt of the physical resistance to

Nazi terror. For if we move away from the dizzy heights of top-level tactical manoeuvrings to the knitty-gritty substance of communist responses to the Nazi threat, we find that KPD activists were embroiled in a violent daily struggle with the NSDAP for the hearts and minds of the German working class. Although the Nazis were never able to make significant inroads into KPD and SPD electoral support at the national level, it does appear that in the 'battle for the streets' and taverns of working-class districts the Stormtroopers (*Sturmabteilung* – SA) were able by 1931–2 to recruit fairly widely among an unemployed regarded by the communists as their 'natural' constituency.

The question was: how to combat this Nazi infiltration of 'proletarian territory'? The slogan 'Hit the Fascists wherever you meet them!' adopted in 1929–30 was operable so long as the NSDAP remained a relatively marginal phenomenon. Once this was palpably not the case 'individual terror' was officially renounced by the KPD, to the chagrin of many party activists, and a 'mass ideological struggle' was initiated to win over working-class Nazi supporters. While maintaining the struggle against Nazi intimidation in the streets, the KPD extended the 'united front from below' to include work in bodies such as the SA and the NSBO, the Nazi factory cell organisation. Yet this mutual contact confronted the communists with a painful dichotomy. By agitating within working-class Nazi organisations in order to win over their 'duped' members, the ideological divide between 'proletarian' communists and 'proletarian' Nazis tended to become blurred. Were they, in the words of Conan Fischer, 'class enemies or class brothers'? Fischer has argued controversially that 'the KPD's United Front tactic ... enabled extensive grass-roots links to develop between these two apparently hostile camps ... [and] helped to make Nazism ... an apparent alternative for many ordinary Communists'.[67] The degree of communist–Nazi contact and cross affiliation is a matter of some debate and should be kept in perspective, but it does add a new and disturbing dimension to the left's failure to halt Hitler's drive for power.

It was not, however, the main criterion. Three other crucial factors need to be addressed. First, the German Communist Party was weak and isolated, a state partly self-induced by its obedience to the Comintern's 'social fascist' line, but partly the result of objective circumstances. The KPD may have been the second largest party in the Comintern, its membership and electoral support may have grown steadily since 1930, but it was *the* party of the unemployed par excellence. Even before the Depression a high proportion of members was unemployed and by 1932 approximately 80 per cent was jobless, attracted to the KPD by its outspoken anti-Republic stance. Although the party did meet with some success in organising the unemployed around local welfare issues, the leadership found it hard to control and politicise the movement. What is more, the fact that the KPD was overwhelmingly a party of the unemployed had several vital ramifications: first, the communist 'Revolutionary Trade Union Opposition' (RGO) had precious little industrial muscle, particularly in the social democratic-dominated large enterprises; secondly, the KPD was forced to shift its locus of operations from the factories to the inner-cities and welfare offices where it could never realistically hope to win the 'battle for the streets' because the combined force of the Weimar state agencies and the better equipped and financed SA held the trump cards; thirdly, the party leadership had to face the volatility and resignation of a despairing, overburdened and wildly fluctuating party membership which often bore little resemblance to the image of a communist 'centralised disciplined army', and which in turn posed great difficulties for the consolidation of a stable network of committed activists; and finally the influx of unemployed tended to strengthen the party's insular 'camp mentality' (*Lagermentalität*), itself a product of an oversimplified class evaluation of Weimar society – a crude version of the 'us and them' syndrome. In the final analysis, the unemployed could demonstrate, picket and fight, even vote for the KPD in their millions, but they could neither make a revolution nor 'smash the fascists'.

The second key factor in the tragedy of the German left is the Great Depression itself. Irrespective of Comintern policy, the Depression had torn the heart out of the much-vaunted German labour movement long before January 1933. If the KPD was weak in the early 1930s this was partly a reflection of the weakness of the working class as a whole. Unemployment reached over six million in February 1932, fracturing still further a labour force which had already been atomised by the rationalisation of the mid-1920s. The last vestiges of working-class solidarity became a victim of the economic crisis. In Richard Evans' words, 'Social Democratic unionists protected their jobs at the expense of the Communists; older workers, mostly in the SPD, connived at the dismissal of younger ones, mostly in the KPD. . . . Tensions between those who had jobs and those who had none added to these antagonisms.' Social divisions likewise accentuated the political fissures with the mainly employed skilled social democratic workers living in better-off housing and districts and the jobless unskilled communists confined to the shadier urban quarters.[68] Such conditions were not universal and did not preclude the possibility of collaboration between communist and social democratic workers, but they were hardly auspicious for meaningful joint resistance to fascism.

The third, and critical, factor is the highly problematic one of the role of Stalin in the Nazis' rise to power. Not surprisingly, this question has generated healthy historical debate. The American expert, Robert C. Tucker, has put forward the following interpretation. The essence of Stalin's foreign policy in the 1930s was to broker a deal with Germany as a means of ensuring Soviet survival in a hostile world. Between 1930 and 1933, Stalin accepted, even indirectly aided, the Nazi takeover despite the perceived grave risks entailed in this strategy, including 'the certainty that German Communism would be repressed'. In so doing, he gambled that Hitler's preoccupation with the Western Allies would allow a breathing space for the Soviet Union to construct socialism in peace. Tucker controversially asserts that Stalin also calculated that Hitler's strident anti-Versailles and anti-democratic bellicosity would create great tensions, perhaps a new inter-imperialist war, in the West from which the USSR would remain, at least initially, aloof and ultimately reap the benefit of territorial aggrandisement. The beguiling prospect for Stalin was 'an opening of revolutionary advance' on the Soviet borderlands. Here are the seeds of the Molotov–Ribbentrop pact of August 1939. As for Comintern tactics, Tucker adduces that:

> by forcing upon the KPD a policy of uncompromising belligerence against Social Democracy ('social-fascism'), he [Stalin] abetted the Nazi victory. . . . Insofar as the possibility existed of heading off this event by encouraging a united front of the German Left and other anti-Nazi forces, he was chiefly responsible for its failure to materialize.

Indeed, Zinoviev is reported to have stated in early 1933 that: 'Apart from the German Social Democrats, Stalin bears the main responsibility to history for Hitler's victory.'[69]

Not every historian finds Tucker's scenario persuasive. Another American scholar, Teddy J. Uldricks, argues that Stalin's foreign policy, far from one of 'reckless gambling' on Hitler, was one of 'caution' based on a 'traditional balance of power'. The spectre of German *Lebensraum* in Slavic Eastern Europe, as prophesied in *Mein Kampf*, was scarcely in the strategic interest of the USSR. Uldricks agrees that 'neither Stalin nor the leftist faction of the KPD were apprehensive about the advent of a Nazi regime', but this was because 'they believed that the upheaval which Germany was experiencing would eventually result in a Communist victory'. Stalin did not 'knowingly set the Comintern and German Communist Party on a path which could only lead to the destruction of the KPD'. Moreover, after the Nazi seizure of power 'Moscow's continued attempts to secure bilateral alliances with Paris and London, and the Comintern's "popular front" tactic all testify to the genuine Soviet desire to contain Nazi aggression.' Uldricks concludes that Stalin did not deliberately foster the Nazi menace and that the Soviet–German pact represented 'a bitter alternative forced upon the Russians', not the culmination of Stalin's decade-long diplomatic odyssey.[70]

Whether Stalin aided Nazism's rise to power or not, and he must surely take some measure of responsibility, the crushing of the KPD and the whole German labour movement represented a crisis of major proportions for the Comintern. The theory and practice of 'social fascism' to which the communist parties had adhered since 1929 ended in utter disaster in the concentration camps of the Third Reich. Why? The former Spanish communist, Fernando Claudin, leaves us in no doubt:

The mistakes were in this case the reflection of a deep-going sickness: atrophy of the theoretical faculties, bureaucratization of the organizational structures, sterilizing monolithicity, uncondi-tional subordination to the manoeuvres of Stalin's camarilla, and – as a result of all these factors – widening divorce between the Comintern's policy and the actual situation, internationally and within each country.[71]

Claudin's argument is forceful and succinct. But what these last few pages tell us is that the failure of German communism in the final years of the Weimar Republic cannot be reduced to an essentially monocausal explanation – the degeneration of the Comintern.

Stalin's foreign policy manoeuvrings, the myopia of 'social fascism' and sectarian tendencies in the KPD did indeed disastrously exacerbate the ideological and organisational gulf between communists and social democrats. But economic, social and generational factors were perhaps just as important in consolidating the breach at the level of everyday lived experience.

From a wider perspective, recent socio-historical research on communist party history in the Third Period presents a far more complex and contradictory picture than that offered in the 'orthodox' interpretations. It confirms the idea that however centralised the Comintern apparatus and its decision-making processes, the actual implementation of centrally imposed strategies was influenced by national, regional and local conditions and cultures. Communist party members, though highly disciplined and loyal to the Soviet Union, were not mere automata blindly and irrationally obeying the will of a distant despot. If they had been, the sectarian tactics of the Third Period may have remained unchanged and the Popular Front initiatives may not have evolved in the course of 1934.

It would be misleading, however, to end this chapter on the Third Period by stressing the indigenous determinants of communist policy. The 'view from below' is inherently flawed if it neglects or attenuates the powerful role of the Comintern Executive in Moscow. A shortcoming of the socio-historical approach is precisely this propensity to underestimate the mechanisms of control employed by the Comintern at the international level and by the party leaderships at the national level. Stalinist discipline demanded that members loyally fulfil the party line, deviations were rarely tolerated for long, and space for debate and discussion was severely restricted. While scope for regional, local or individual initiative and adaptation did exist and should be recognised, it must be treated with a fair degree of circumspection. Did it actually mean that on the ground the fundamentals of Comintern tactics were being undermined and distorted? Was policy framed with national circumstances in mind, or was it determined in far-off Moscow in the interests of the USSR? These are, to say the least, moot points and no definitive consensual answer is possible. In our opinion, the juxtaposition of indigenous versus exogenous inputs in communist policy formation and implementation, as discussed in the previous chapter, remains cogent even in the 'Stalinised' Comintern of the 1930s. But in the final analysis it is hard to avoid the conclusion that the strategies of the Third Period were devised in Moscow, were largely incompatible with national conditions and traditions, and displayed an acute misunderstanding of the socio-political consequences of the economic crisis of capitalism. A differentiated approach taking into account national peculiarities was out of the question since it would have undermined Stalin's aim of creating a solid rank of disciplined 'Bolshevik cadres' in the communist parties.

Perhaps the best way of understanding the international communist movement in the early 1930s is to recognise that incipient Stalinism created a stiflingly bureaucratised Comintern apparatus and highly centralised communist parties committed primarily to the defence of the USSR. None the less, it could not totally foreclose all space for national initiative and autonomous activity from below. Indeed, it was a complex combination of Soviet state interests, new thinking in the Comintern hierarchy and communist party responses to national circumstances that explains the belated change of line so agonisingly worked out in 1934–5. The tortuous path of the Popular Front is the main theme of the next chapter.

4. Popular Front and Stalinist Terror, 1934–9

The era of the Popular Front occupies a special place in the historiography of the Communist International and has for many years stimulated a rich controversy. The Comintern's apparently sudden *volte-face* in 1934–5, abandoning the sectarian tactics of the Third Period and embracing broad anti-fascist alliances with socialist and liberal parties, has been seen as the result of Stalin's direct intervention in Comintern affairs and as a temporary tactical shift determined by the needs of Soviet foreign policy. The basic idea common to this interpretation is that the Comintern was a pliant instrument of the Soviet state, its search for anti-fascist unity faithfully mirroring the USSR's quest for collective security agreements with the Western democracies against Nazi aggression. Such a view has a long lineage in Comintern historiography.[1]

This monocausal approach was challenged in the late 1970s and 1980s by scholars who argued that an explanation of the origins of the Popular Front almost exclusively in terms of Soviet diplomatic priorities was an over-simplification. In this analysis the indigenous anti-fascist roots of the Popular Front and the dissensions in the Comintern leadership come to the fore. While acknowledging the importance of developments on the international stage, these historians assert that the decisive impetus for change came from rank-and-file pressure in the national parties and from key figures in the Comintern hierarchy, who were convinced that the tactics of the Third Period had failed to arrest the rise of fascism.[2]

120

In our view, the origins of the Popular Front should be sought in the 'triple interaction'[3] of national factors, internal dynamics in the Comintern leadership and the shifting requirements of Soviet diplomacy. In 1934 these three elements coalesced to shape the transition to the Popular Front. Once inaugurated, the new policy enjoyed rapid success with many communist parties, hitherto marginalised and ineffective, experiencing an unprecedented growth in membership and influence. Popular Front governments were formed in France and Spain in 1936 and in Chile in 1938.[4] In some countries the enthusiasm for anti-fascist unity was such that efforts were made to merge communist and socialist organisations, thus healing the historic split of 1920–1. The period also witnessed innovations in communist and left-wing culture.[5] However, Soviet state interests were never far from the minds of the Comintern leaders. By 1936 the exigencies of collective security and the ferocious attack on 'international Trotskyism' were placing immense strains on the Popular Front alliances. Nowhere was this better illustrated than in the Comintern's activities during the Spanish Civil War.

The first section of this chapter explores the origins of the Popular Front in terms of the 'triple interaction' outlined above. The second examines the contradictory nature of the Popular Front experiments, focusing on the resolutions of the Seventh Congress and the development of the Popular Fronts in France and Spain. The final section discusses the traumatic impact of the Stalinist Terror on the Comintern in light of recent archival discoveries.

ORIGINS OF THE POPULAR FRONT

The year 1933 was a disaster for the Comintern. The Nazi seizure of power and the vicious assault on the German labour movement plunged the International into crisis. Reaction appeared to be on the march. Yet, paralysed by the sectarian postulates of the Third Period, the Comintern leadership in Moscow only very slowly overcame the Stalinist dogma of 'social fascism'. The years of mutual antipathy between communists and social democrats had taken their toll. Neither side was willing to make meaningful concessions, though proposals and counter-proposals were put forward. In mid-February 1933 overtures from the Second International to negotiate a non-aggression pact were ignored. The burning of the Reichstag on

27 February and the subsequent arrest of thousands of communists met with little response in Moscow. The Comintern reply to the appeal of the Second International came only on 5 March, literally hours before the KPD was declared illegal. The ECCI statement called on all communists 'to establish a united fighting front with the social-democratic working masses through the social-democratic parties', but continued to emphasise that 'the chief obstacle . . . remains the policy of class collaboration with the bourgeoisie pursued by the social-democratic parties'.[6] It was a 'half-hearted response to a half-hearted appeal',[7] and it is not surprising that communist approaches for a united front with the social democrats were rebuffed at this time.

Such complacency was not shared by certain national sections of the Comintern. In France and Czechoslovakia, where the parties remained legal and where the threat from Germany was felt most acutely, prominent communists, stunned by the fate of the strong KPD, advocated a broader conception of the united front. On 7 April the General Secretaries of the Czechoslovak and French parties, Klement Gottwald and Maurice Thorez, took the bold and unusual step of telegramming the ECCI urging talks with the Second International. Firsov has shown that it was on Stalin's instructions that the ECCI issued a directive to all parties in the spring of 1933 'to step up the campaign against the Second International and its sections [which] are subverting the struggle against fascism . . . it is necessary to emphasise the flight of social democracy to the fascist camp'.[8] Gottwald's and Thorez's sensible, but premature, recommendation was thus rejected out of hand.

By the end of 1933 the gulf between political reality and Comintern rhetoric could hardly have been wider. The International had reached its nadir. The scale of the crisis was staggering. Of the seventy-two parties represented at the Thirteenth ECCI Plenum in November–December, only sixteen were legal and seven 'semi-legal'. The French and Czechoslovak parties with barely 30 000 members had become, with the exception of the Bolsheviks and the disparate Chinese party, the largest sections of the Comintern. Yet those anticipating a revision of tactics were disappointed. Speakers at the plenum maintained the familiar depressing litany of attacks on social democracy interspersed with ritualistic predictions of imminent revolutionary upheaval. Wilhelm Pieck, reporting on the work of the smashed KPD, pronounced incredibly that 'the present situation in

Germany is characterised by the growth of a new upsurge of the revolutionary mass movement under the leadership of the Communist Party'.[9] Any steps towards a more differentiated analysis of bourgeois democracy and fascism remained strictly limited.

Yet within twelve months a fundamental reorientation had taken place. By the end of 1934 communists were seeking united action against fascism not only with social democratic, but even non-socialist, parties. Exactly when and why did this change occur? The catalyst for the 'turn' can be found in the events in France in February 1934 when socialist and communist workers ignored ideological barriers and united against a common fascist threat. Paris had become the centre of the European anti-fascist movement and the PCF was thrust to the forefront of Comintern attention. On 6 February a demonstration by fascists against the Daladier government erupted into violence, leaving several dead and many injured. Fearing a repetition of the German catastrophe, socialist and communist workers, the latter in advance of the party leadership, voted to support a general strike. The strike of 12 February was a spectacular success in Paris and throughout France, setting in motion a powerful groundswell for rank-and-file unity.[10] Léon Blum, the leader of the French socialists, described this unity from below as 'an electric current' which was to spark left-wing coalition. It was to have an important influence on Comintern and PCF policy. The need for united working-class action against fascism was brought into sharper relief by events in Austria. On the same day as the general strike in France social democratic workers in Vienna and Linz organised armed resistance to the authoritarian Dollfuss regime. This ended in bloody defeat, but made it clear that social democrats in Austria, unlike Germany, were prepared to fight fascism.

However, in the weeks following 12 February the gap between the French party leadership and local communist cells widened. The former clung to the old tactics while many of the latter, blatantly ignoring national party policy, enthusiastically joined socialists in the anti-fascist committees which were springing into existence and issued statements in favour of united action with the socialists. Popular mass rallies repeated the same theme. Why was the PCF executive so keen to bury the spirit of 12 February? The answers are not hard to find. The Comintern had intervened repeatedly in the internal affairs of the French party, propelling Thorez into the General Secretaryship in 1931 under the supervision of the ECCI agent, Evžen Fried (alias Clément). Thorez was hardly likely to change the sectarian line without countenance from Moscow and as yet this was not forthcoming. Indeed, the PCF was criticised by name in *Pravda* on 1 March for concluding alliances with the leaders of social democracy. Thorez's compliance was further reinforced by the rival presence of Jacques Doriot. Doriot's disagreements with the 'class against class' tactics were long-standing and after 12 February he intensified his attacks on the party leadership, openly defying the instruction to disband the local anti-fascist committees. The feud that ensued between Thorez and Doriot can be seen as symbolic of the dual character of communism: the loyal functionary versus the charismatic mayor of the powerful 'red' St Denis region of Paris. The crisis in the PCF smouldered for many weeks, virtually crippling the party. Meanwhile the climate of opinion in Moscow was barely perceptibly shifting in favour of Doriot's position.

The February events in France and Austria made a lasting impression on the Bulgarian communist, Georgi Dimitrov, who was to play a singularly important role in the change of line. Dimitrov had been in charge of the Comintern's West European Bureau, based in Berlin, since 1929 and had witnessed firsthand Hitler's rise to power. He had urged in a letter to Moscow in the autumn of 1932 that the leading role of the communist party should not be made a precondition for 'a common struggle of communist, social-democratic and other masses of workers' against fascism.[11] Dimitrov was also beginning to question the International's hitherto fatalistic understanding of fascism as an inevitable product of a decaying capitalism with social democracy as its covert ally. Dimitrov's less dogmatic attitude towards social democracy was to develop over the next year. Arrested in March 1933 accused of setting fire to the Reichstag, he humiliated the prosecution and its major witness, Hermann Göring, at his trial in Leipzig. This accomplished performance earned Dimitrov an international prestige and influence rarely attained by a non-Russian communist. Offered Soviet citizenship, he was eventually released and given a hero's welcome on his arrival in Moscow in late February 1934.

Stalin must have been impressed. In March and again in early April he summoned Dimitrov for talks. Soon after, apparently dissatisfied with the work of Manuilsky and other ECCI leaders, the 'boss' suggested that Dimitrov should become General Secretary of the Comintern, a post he was to hold until 1943. Stalin also promised him the continuing support of the Soviet Politburo. Regarding Comintern strategy, Stalin remained cautious yet open to new ideas. He was to retain this vacillating position for the rest of 1934. His views on the bourgeoisie and parliamentary democracy had certainly not altered. The former had 'taken the road to fascism' and a struggle for the latter was 'absurd'. However, Stalin appears to have given Dimitrov almost *carte-blanche* to experiment. Indeed, on 2 May Stalin told him: 'You choose yourself where and what to say and write. . . . Select only basic problems.' The one caveat was that Stalin's culpability for the disastrous tactics of the Third Period could in no way be implied or questioned.[12] Emboldened, Dimitrov embarked on a thorough revision of the Comintern line.

One of his first actions as *de facto* head of the International was to deal with the impasse in the French party. On 23 April Thorez and Doriot were summoned to Moscow. Doriot, no doubt expecting to perform a ritualistic recantation, refused to attend. Thorez dutifully made the long journey. Meeting with Thorez on 11 May, Dimitrov insisted that 'the walls between communist and social democratic workers must be broken down'. He added significantly that 'we must prove that the communist party really and truly wants and can wage a joint struggle. The experience of February and recent days shows how successful this has been.'[13] The 'turn' in Comintern policy can thus be dated with some certainty from mid-May 1934. For a time the obtuse Thorez seems to have resisted, but with further prompting from Moscow he finally rallied to the new orientation and championed it at the PCF conference at Ivry, held between 23 and 26 June. A month later the communist and socialist parties signed an anti-fascist 'Pact of Unity of Action'.

This move towards the united front 'from above' met with sharp resistance on the part of some Comintern stalwarts. A protracted and intense struggle had erupted in Moscow pitting the cautious 'innovators' led by Dimitrov, Manuilsky and Kuusinen against the intransigent 'fundamentalists' around Piatnitsky, Kun, Lozovsky and Knorin. Opinion in many communist party leaderships was similarly divided. The persistence of the debates in the international movement suggests that Stalin had yet to commit himself one way or the other. It also demonstrates that Moscow had trouble in imposing the new line. The main battleground was the ECCI commissions preparing the reports for the forthcoming Seventh Congress scheduled for the end of 1934. Dimitrov proposed that the Comintern line should

be 'boldly' reassessed: 'what must be changed must be changed'. On
1 July he submitted an outline memorandum which had far-reaching
implications. Its underlying premise was that in light of Hitler's
triumph the whole experience of the united front tactics should be
critically examined. As for the question of 'social fascism', the report
noted the 'developing differentiation in the ranks of soc[ial] democracy' which in turn necessitated a 'differentiated approach' to social
democratic parties and their leading cadres. Here Dimitrov tacitly
raised the possibility of a 'united front from above'. He also
introduced another novel element, hinting at a change in communist
relations with 'different strata of the petty-bourgeoisie'.[14] These
comments should not, however, be taken out of context. Dimitrov's
re-analysis was forceful yet circumspect. He took pains to emphasise
the 'decisive importance' of the communist party in the anti-fascist
struggle, his prime concern being to extend *working-class* unity against
fascism. It is most doubtful that at this point he envisaged any
extension of the united front into the Popular Front. This was to
come only in the autumn of 1934 and then mainly under French
initiative.

Dimitrov's outline report and an accompanying letter (document
14) was sent to Stalin and the Soviet Politburo. Archival material
shows that Stalin's attitude to Dimitrov's proposals was ambiguous
and that he still retained an acute hostility towards social democracy,
including its left wing. This is exemplified in his comments written
in the margins of Dimitrov's letter. In response to the question: 'is
the blanket characterisation of social democracy as social fascism
correct?', Stalin wrote, 'yes, with regard to the leadership, but not
"blanket" '. And in reply to Dimitrov's query: 'is it correct to
consider social democracy everywhere and under all conditions the
main prop of the bourgeoisie?', Stalin answered unequivocally, 'In
Persia, of course not. In the principal capitalist countries – yes'.[15]
Regardless of Stalin's serious reservations, which were almost certainly communicated to Dimitrov, the process of elaborating an
effective response to fascism continued in the Comintern leadership.
Dimitrov struggled hard to convince Stalin of the need for change.

In late August 1934 Manuilsky, Togliatti and others spoke of the
necessity for communists to enter into negotiations with petty-bourgeois and peasant parties, whose class base was susceptible to fascist
influence. This recommendation was the backdrop to the PCF's
initiatives in October to form a broad cross-class Popular Front

alliance against fascism. On 9 October Thorez, probably supported by Fried, exhorted the PCF–SFIO negotiating committee to extend their co-operation to include 'the middle classes'. The following day in a major speech he appealed to the centre-left Radical party to join a vast *Rassemblement Populaire*. The approach may have been a logical extension of recent thinking in Moscow, but the tempo of change in France caused alarm in the divided Executive Committee. A Comintern delegation, including Gottwald and Togliatti, visited Thorez on the morning of 24 October and tried to dissuade him from giving his planned speech that evening in Nantes, where the Radical party conference was due to open. Thorez was unmoved, possibly because the delegation was not mandated to veto his initiative. He duly delivered his speech which marked the birth of the term 'Popular Front'.[16] If Thorez had been desultory in the first half of 1934 in reading the signals from Moscow, in this instance he seems to have anticipated developments in the Comintern.

During these crucial months Stalin appears to have sustained his indeterminate stance on the emergent line in the Comintern. No source, Russian or otherwise, has so far detailed Stalin's response to the Popular Front experiment in France. Carr states that it was only in December 1934 that Stalin, preoccupied with the Kirov murder, 'was finally persuaded to declare himself' in favour of the new policy. He reportedly congratulated Thorez on the success of the Popular Front campaign.[17] Stalin's 'green-light' was, of course, crucial and at an acrimonious ECCI Presidium session on 9 and 19 December a majority approved the PCF's activities. The following month the Political Secretariat of the Comintern explicitly ratified the Popular Front slogan. The scene was now set for the Seventh Congress.

We have yet to address the controversial third element of the 'triple interaction'; that is, the delicate question of the relationship between Comintern tactics and Soviet foreign policy. As we have indicated, many historians have seen the 'turn' purely as a function of the changing needs of the latter. The equation is neat: the Soviet Union's policy of collective security with the Western democracies, first adumbrated in December 1933, is said to have determined the transition to the Popular Front in the Comintern. Fernando Claudin, for example, has little hesitation in claiming that the explanation for the turn in the Comintern 'lies . . . in Soviet policy, and, more specifically, Soviet foreign policy.' Moreover, it is asserted that Stalin himself gave the signal for the turn as early as May 1934. Subsequently, there is a clear sequence of events in which developments in the Comintern are shaped by the requirements of Soviet diplomacy.[18] Although Claudin is quite correct to point to the importance of Soviet foreign policy, there are certain problems with his analysis. First, the image presented here of a totally compliant and reactive Comintern underestimates the internal dynamics of the communist movement and posits too mechanical a relationship between the Comintern and Narkomindel. European communists, and not just the Soviet government, had to find new methods of combating the fascist threat. Secondly, Soviet international priorities were not as clear-cut and unchanging as Claudin suggests. Although a diplomatic orientation towards the Western powers became the main thrust of Soviet foreign policy, relations with Germany were not severed and collective security agreements were a long time in the making. Thirdly, Claudin exaggerates Stalin's surety of purpose in both Comintern strategy and Soviet diplomacy. Stalin tended to vacillate, keeping his options open and this encouraged rearguard actions by opponents of the Popular Front and collective security.

The year 1934 was one of transition both in the Comintern and Soviet foreign policy. By the end of 1933, it was becoming clear to the Kremlin that Hitler's aggressive ambitions potentially signalled the end of the special Rapallo relationship. Litvinov, supported by the temporarily rehabilitated Radek and Bukharin (who apparently retained some influence over Stalin at this time), now sought to end the USSR's international isolation, seeing France as a natural ally against Nazi expansionism. This hesitant protracted process towards a 'marriage of convenience' was to culminate in the Franco-Soviet Mutual Assistance Pact of May 1935. However, this dénouement was far from inevitable. Soviet diplomacy, like Comintern tactics, remained in flux throughout 1934 and beyond. It is quite possible that a 'pro-German' faction associated with Molotov existed in the Politburo, which resisted rapprochement with France. Just as importantly, there was no automatic correlation between Franco-Soviet détente and changing Comintern attitudes towards social democracy. As Julian Jackson aptly puts it: 'given that in France the advocates of an anti-German foreign policy . . . tended to be on the centre-right . . . any strategy which reinforced the strength of the anti-government left was hardly a necessary consequence of the Soviet Union's new diplomatic priorities'.[19] This is not to say that the latter were uninfluential, but there could be no water-tight guarantee in the spring of 1934 that the new course emerging in the Comintern would complement a Soviet foreign policy, which itself was fluid.

The correlation between Comintern's evolving tactics and Soviet diplomatic goals becomes crystal clear only from late 1934, with Thorez's appeal to the pro-Soviet Radicals and Litvinov's desperate efforts for a pact with Paris. By this time the USSR had joined the League of Nations and Stalin, whose tentative feelers for an 'Eastern Locarno' had been rebuffed by Germany and Poland, finally opted for the 'French alternative'. There can be no doubt that he perceived the complementarity between the Comintern's policy of broad anti-fascist alliances and Narkomindel's search for collective security with the Western democracies against Nazi Germany. In the words of Jonathan Haslam:

> Both the Narkomindel and the Comintern's strategy were a response to the same threat; collective security and Popular Front were twins. But they were difficult and by no means identical twins, always pulling youthfully in different directions; and Stalin was not always there with a firm hold on the harness.[20]

The relationship between the 'turn' in the Comintern and Soviet foreign policy is thus far more complex than many historians have assumed.

We have argued that the origins of the Popular Front should properly be seen in the 'triple interaction': mass action 'from below' in national sections; internal debates and initiatives in the Comintern Executive; and the Soviet Union's quest for security in the face of perceived Nazi aggression. The rise of fascism provoked a profound crisis of theory and practice in the communist movement and threatened the very survival of its leading European parties. It was the Comintern's response to this threat, as much as events on the international stage, which accounts for the shift from the sectarian dead-end of the Third Period to the Popular Front. That Stalin remained the ultimate source of authority is not in dispute, but in the uncertain atmosphere of 1934 Comintern reformers were allowed a conditional freedom to pilot a new line that was not simply the brainchild of the Soviet Politburo and Narkomindel. However, as we shall see, this was to be a shortlived moment in the history of the Stalinist Comintern. From 1935 the ongoing search for indigenous forms of the Popular Front became inextricably interwoven with, and indeed increasingly subservient to, the foreign policy requirements of the Soviet state. This phenomenon was most evident in France and Spain where the Popular Front had its greatest impact.

THE POPULAR FRONT: CONTRADICTIONS AND FAILURE

From 25 July to 21 August 1935, 513 delegates from sixty-five communist parties assembled in Moscow for the Seventh Congress of the Communist International. Dimitrov delivered the main report which formally signalled the break with the sectarian rigidity of the Third Period and ratified for the whole movement the Popular Front policies pioneered by the French party. The decisions of the Seventh Congress have been variously interpreted by historians and political theorists. Many have depicted them as proof of the Comintern's subordination to the state interests of the Soviet Union. The goal of proletarian revolution was, in effect, postponed in favour of broad anti-fascist unity 'with declared enemies of revolution', a policy in concert with the USSR's quest for Western democratic allies.[21] For others, such as Eric Hobsbawm, the Popular Front constituted 'a turning-point in international Communist expectations, because there was no adequate precedent for it in official doctrine'.[22] It was both an inspired search for a strategy to defeat fascism and a reformulation of the Marxist approach to such key questions as class alliances, democracy and the nation, which in sum constituted an implicit rupture with the Bolshevik model of revolution. To this extent, the rethinking is said to presage the striving for 'national roads to socialism' between 1944 and 1947 and the 'Eurocommunist' experiments of the 1970s.[23] For pre-*glasnost* Soviet scholars, the resolutions of the Seventh Congress were imbued with the ideas of Lenin and elaborated a new strategic line for the communist movement which not only addressed the burning anti-fascist and general democratic tasks of the day, but also enhanced the prospects of the Marxist–Leninist conception of revolutionary socialism. In this view the congress was of truly historic significance.[24]

The new course enunciated at the Seventh Congress redefined the character of communist politics by encouraging parties to address the daily interests of the workers, to seek anti-fascist alliances 'from above' as well as 'from below' and by so doing enter the mainstream of national political life. But the break with the past was partial. The close identification of Stalin with the sectarian tactics and theories of the Third Period precluded any far-reaching critical examination of the experience of the previous six years. As such the Popular Front era was marked by an unresolved tension between tradition and innovation, between inherited ideological and organisational structures and the initiatives of communist parties to re-engage with democratic national political cultures. It was, in short, a highly contradictory period in Comintern history.

Nowhere is this tension clearer than in Dimitrov's report to the congress. He defined fascism as a distinct and aberrant state: '*the open terrorist dictatorship of the most reactionary, most chauvinistic and most imperialist elements of finance capital*'.[25] This analysis of the extremely narrow class base of the fascist state, first made at the ECCI plenum in December 1933, facilitated the search for broad cross-class anti-fascist unity. Furthermore, the rise to power of fascism was 'not an *ordinary succession* of one bourgeois government by another, but a *substitution* [of] one State form of class domination – bourgeois democracy – [by] another form – open terrorist dictatorship.' The enormity of the fascist threat now faced the 'toiling masses' with 'the necessity of making a *definite* choice, and of making it to-day, not between proletarian dictatorship and bourgeois democracy, but between bourgeois democracy and fascism'. The struggle for the defence of bourgeois democratic liberties must be secured by 'a *broad people's anti-fascist front*'. At its heart, Dimitrov stressed repeatedly, would be '*the proletarian united front*' of communist and socialist workers, but now strengthened by a 'fighting alliance' with the peasantry and urban petty-bourgeoisie. These were the groups most susceptible to fascist ideology and its nationalistic appeal. Hence, communists must resolutely protect the interests of these strata and present themselves as heir and tribune of democratic freedoms and national independence. As Dimitrov stated:

> proletarian internationalism must, so to speak, 'acclimatise itself' in each country in order to sink deep roots in its native land. *National forms* of the proletarian class struggle . . . in the individual countries are in no contradiction to proletarian internationalism; on the contrary, it is precisely in these forms that the *international interests* of the proletariat can be successfully defended.

Dimitrov even envisaged the possibility, hitherto unprecedented, of communist participation in a coalition Popular Front government. Given the highly controversial nature of the subject, Dimitrov's language was necessarily oblique and ambiguous. He announced that communists would 'declare for the formation of such a government on the basis of a definite anti-fascist platform'. However, he implied that the communist party would actually join a Popular Front government only in a genuinely pre-revolutionary situation of political crisis. In these conditions it might 'prove to be *one* of the most important transitional forms' to the proletarian revolution. Dimitrov was very careful to legitimise this apparent heresy with reference to Lenin's appeal to seek immediate 'forms of *transition* or *approach* to the proletarian revolution'. The whole issue was far from academic. The French party was to be faced with precisely this dilemma in May 1936 when Blum invited the PCF to participate in his newly-elected cabinet.

Dimitrov's tortuous deliberations on the nature and aims of the Popular Front government revealed the limits of the shift in Comintern thinking. It would be a grave error, he insisted, to see an anti-fascist coalition government as 'a special *democratic intermediate stage* lying between the dictatorship of the bourgeoisie and the dictatorship of the proletariat'; that is, as a means to a gradual transition to socialism. At best it was a temporary expedient in the struggle against fascism which would assist 'the revolutionary training of the masses' in exposing the illusory belief that a solution to the problems of capitalism could be found within the bounds of bourgeois democracy. This could only be achieved by an insurrectionary seizure of power and the establishment of the dictatorship of the proletariat. As Dimitrov made palpably clear:

> We state frankly to the masses: *Final salvation* this [Popular Front] government *cannot* bring. . . . Consequently it is necessary *to prepare for the socialist revolution*! Soviet power and *only* Soviet power can bring such salvation!

In essence, Dimitrov was redefining the tactics and not the strategy of the Comintern, and therefore we feel justified in avoiding the term 'strategy' when referring to the Popular Front. Although Dimitrov may have envisaged a new, if ill-defined, perspective for the transition to socialism, there was nothing in his address which openly challenged the universal applicability of the Bolshevik model of revolution. Moreover, the conditions laid down for the 'organic unity' of communists and socialists (document 15) were 'so rigid as to preclude any real progress' and amounted to little more than 'the absorption of Socialists into a Bolshevik Party that viewed the Russian experience and the Russian model as definitive'.[26] This intransigence was quite evident in Thorez's speech at the congress. He told delegates that the PCF was seeking unity with the French socialists on the basis of: 'Preparation for armed insurrection, for the dictatorship of the proletariat, for Soviet power as the form of the workers' government; consistent internationalism; affiliation to a single party of the working class; [and] democratic centralism.'[27] Such Leninist rhetoric was hardly likely to convince potential anti-fascist allies of the sincerity of communist proposals to safeguard democracy.

Hence, the balancing act demanded of communist parties by the Comintern was most delicate. First, they had to persuade extremely wary socialist leaders that after five years of 'social fascist' abuse, the Comintern's hand of friendship should be taken seriously. Secondly, communists were enjoined to retain their distinct revolutionary identity while engaging in an essentially reformist defence of bourgeois democratic liberties. How were they to prepare for 'Soviet power' while simultaneously co-operating in parliament with the socialists and centrists? In the heat of the daily struggle, the thin line between 'leftist adventurism' and 'rightist opportunism' was not always clearly drawn and transgressions to one side or the other were commonplace. Thirdly, party leaders had to cope with conflicting pressures that pulled them in different directions. The all-important signals from Moscow were generally cautious so as not to alarm unduly the non-communist partners in the Popular Front alliance. Moderation was the order of the day. And yet the anti-fascist Popular Front initiatives 'from below' attracted large numbers of radicalised rank-and-file workers who tended to take the parties' revolutionary credentials at face value. This militancy at the base clashed with the circumspection of the leadership. It also presented problems for maintaining Stalinist discipline and centralist control from above. Paradoxically, the very success of the Popular Front could prove a double-edged sword. Finally, divided counsels persisted in the Soviet and Comintern hierarchies on the scope of the Popular Front orientation, some insisting on a narrower, others on a broader, definition of its aims. Dimitrov's long occasionally confused report and the congress resolution on fascism (document 16) gave precious little guidance on these sensitive and intractable issues.

The most important speaker after Dimitrov was Togliatti. His address focused on the crucial question of the international dimension of the Popular Front and the danger which German and Japanese militarism posed to the security of the USSR. Togliatti dutifully intoned: 'the world party of the Bolsheviks and of Stalin is the guarantee of our victory on a world scale. Let us close our ranks, comrades, in the fight against imperialist war, for peace, for the defence of the Soviet Union.' There is no doubt that for Stalin and the Soviet leadership this was the prime task of the Comintern and its national sections. But Togliatti also hinted at the dichotomy between the domestic policies of the parties and their internationalist obligations. If the search for national forms of the class struggle was to be successful, then communist parties required a measure of autonomy in relation to the foreign policy requirements of the Soviet Union. Togliatti necessarily emphasised the 'complete identity of aim between the peace policy of the Soviet Union and the policy of the working class and Communist Parties', but stated that this identification:

> by no means signifies that at every given moment there must be a complete coincidence in all acts and on all questions between the tactics of the proletariat and Communist Parties that are still struggling for power and the concrete tactical measures of the Soviet proletariat and the C.P.S.U.[28]

Togliatti's veiled plea for greater freedom of manoeuvre for the sections should not be over-emphasised, but it was echoed in the congress resolution on the activities of the ECCI, which instructed that body 'as a rule to avoid direct intervention in the internal organisational matters of the Communist parties'.[29] This decentralisation, first broached by Dimitrov in his July 1934 letter to Stalin, was designed to allow parties greater independence in their day-to-day operations. But what did this decentralisation amount to? Did it result in a relocation of power from the centre to the periphery? Again, the overall picture is contradictory. With three notable exceptions (France, Spain and Belgium), the practice of sending ECCI representatives to intervene in the internal affairs of the parties was abolished. It appears that sections were now permitted to elaborate tactical innovations more in tune with local and national conditions. This was consistent with Dimitrov's notion that the form of the Popular Front would vary according to national circumstances.

Parties which remained legal responded enthusiastically to Dimitrov's counsel that 'the masses must be taken as they are, and not as we should like to have them'.[30] In their efforts to sink 'deep roots' into their national soil, the French, British, American and Czechoslovak parties modified their methods of work and identity. Although this process was uneven, recent studies of the everyday life of these parties have revealed that the rejection of a pure 'oppositional' culture and the efforts to work with 'the grain of popular culture' were important factors in the growth of membership and influence. Communists sought policies, language and symbols which reflected the indigenous radical-democratic heritage: Jacobin republicanism, Chartism, Washingtonian idealism, and Hussite egalitarianism. Communist politics acquired new dimensions in the search for left-wing unity in trade unions and at grassroots level. A reform of internal party organisation, which allowed for residential branches alongside the Bolshevik model of factory-based cells, was implemented in some parties.[31] In these areas, communists were successful in effecting a departure from past practices.

However, this reorientation must be put firmly into perspective. The communists' belated attempts to claim a stake in national life and traditions left them open to accusations of opportunism and populism, charges which were not easily rebuffed. The PCF's embarrassment on national defence expenditure is a case in point. In May 1935, after the signing of the Franco-Soviet pact, a joint communiqué was issued which noted Stalin's full approval of the French government's policy of military rearmament. This statement jarred disconcertingly with the PCF's long-standing commitment to anti-militarism and opposition to national defence budgets. How could communists support 'bourgeois rearmament' after the senseless slaugther of World War I? But within twenty four hours of the declaration, the French party was pasting up posters announcing 'Stalin is Right!'.[32] The PCF's anti-militarist principles were not totally reversed overnight, but the lingering impression was that they had been sacrificed on the altar of Stalin's *Realpolitik*. French national defence was justifiable if it was in the interests of the USSR. Such about-turns did little to consolidate the rapprochement with the Socialist party, which possessed a strong pacifist wing, and hence placed the Popular Front in France under strain. Elsewhere, in Britain, the USA and Czechoslovakia, the situation was even less conducive to joint action. Here, no formal Popular Front agreements were secured and, despite a number of successful collaborative ventures, relations between communists and the centre-left remained on the whole cool.

As far as organisational changes are concerned, the tactical flexibility bestowed on the parties by the Comintern should not be misinterpreted as a kind of 'de-Bolshevisation' in which the 'world party of revolution' transmogrified into a federal institution. On the contrary, the latest archival research suggests that the reorganisation of the Comintern's cumbersome bureaucratic structures, rather than inaugurating a move towards decentralisation, actually strengthened the levers of centralised intervention and facilitated Stalin's direct control. Although this may not have been the original intention of the reform, the rationalisation of the Comintern apparatus in Moscow seems to have resulted in a greater concentration of power in fewer hands. The formal channels of debate in the ECCI were restricted, no plenary session of that body being held after August 1935, and the Seventh Congress was to be the last world gathering of communists. Furthermore, all major questions concerning strategy and the composition of party leaderships remained the prerogative of Moscow. Like the postulates of the Third Period, the Popular Front was declared universally applicable regardless of local conditions. Most relevantly, the reorganisation of the Comintern was undertaken at precisely the time when the Soviet system itself was turning into a police state, a transformation which precluded any meaningful democratisation of the International's organisational structures and its relations with the national sections.[33]

The contradictions inherent in the Popular Front are clearly illustrated in the country where it had been born and where it enjoyed the greatest success, France. Following Thorez's appeal for a *Rassemblement Populaire* in October 1934, the PCF continued to be the moving force for a Popular Front, presenting itself as the most vigilant proponent of anti-fascist unity at the base. This close relationship with the popular movement was to reinforce the communists' revolutionary identity and distance them from the other parties in the alliance. At the same time, the PCF executive, mindful of Moscow's diplomatic priorities, continued its *ouverture* to the middle-class Radicals and sought to make the Popular Front an electoral coalition. This was eventually achieved following the Radicals' decision to support the PCF call for a huge demonstration by all anti-fascist organisations on Bastille Day, 14 July 1935. This manifestation of Republican unity paved the way for negotiations which culminated in the signing of the programme of the *Rassemblement Populaire* in January 1936. Another notable success came in March with the reunification of the socialist (CGT) and communist (CGTU) trade unions. Finally, the Popular Front election triumph in May gave France a socialist Prime Minister, Léon Blum, for the first time in its history and marked the crowning moment of the anti-fascist movement.

The communists were the main beneficiaries of these developments in three important respects: party recruitment, trade union influence and electoral success. Party membership soared from 87 000 in 1935 to 326 500 by 1937, out-stripping the Socialists for the first time since the early 1920s. Between May and July 1936 alone, the party attracted over 100 000 new adherents, largely from the working class. Communist influence in the trade union movement also grew impressively. The merger of the CGT and the CGTU encouraged an enormous increase in membership from 786 000 in 1935 to 3 960 000 in 1937, most of the new recruits being younger, previously unorganised, workers. Communist control over key sections, such as the manufacturing industry, was significantly extended. The PCF also gained at the polls, its share of the vote increasing from 8.4 per cent in 1932 to 15.3 per cent in 1936 and its parliamentary representation rising from 12 to 72 seats.

Nevertheless, the election victory and the scenes of jubilation which accompanied it hid a fragile unity and masked deep underlying tensions in the Popular Front alliance. Among the Socialist leaders there persisted profound suspicions about the motives and sincerity of the communists' claim to be a 'national' party committed to the defence of democratic liberties. A cautious champion of the Popular Front, Blum had written shortly before the signing of the Pact of Unity of Action in July 1934 that 'I myself remain convinced . . . that this modification, or transformation [in the PCF], is the result of instructions emanating from Moscow'.[34] These doubts were strengthened in May 1936 when an apparently divided PCF Politburo, acting on the repeated warnings of the ECCI Secretariat,[35] refused

Blum's invitation to participate in government, preferring to support from outside the Popular Front coalition in the capacity of 'a ministry of the masses'. Both the Socialists and the Radicals were distinctly wary of the growing communist influence over the labour movement and of the PCF's electoral showing. More urgently, the wave of strikes and factory occupations that hit France on an unprecedented scale in May and June 1936 inevitably struck fear into the hearts of the middle classes, including the Radicals. During those tense weeks it appeared that the revolutionary threat carried by the PCF was in process of consummation, despite the fact that the party leadership did its level best to reign in the militant strivings of the workers.

And it is precisely here that we detect the ultimate contradiction in the Popular Front orientation of the Comintern and the French party. The PCF pursued a twofold aim: first, to pressurise French governments into active involvement in an international anti-fascist coalition sponsored by the USSR; and, secondly, to establish a powerful mass base in the working-class movement. The election victory and subsequent strike waves brought into sharp relief the incompatibility between these goals. For if the popular movement from below raised the spectre of the 'red menace', then the alarm generated among the Radicals (and Socialists) would weaken the already wavering French commitment to collective security. Therefore, Narkomindel officials in Moscow were as suspicious as the Radicals of the PCF's unexpected triumphs. A revived and seemingly strident communist party could serve to drive the French, and by extension the British, centre-right into an anti-Russian and possibly pro-Nazi stance. In all likelihood the response of the Germans to revolutionary developments in France would be equally hostile, seriously undermining international peace and stability.

Hence, the *événements* of May–June 1936, regardless of Thorez's famous appeal that *'il faut savoir terminer une grève'*, [it is necessary to know how to end a strike], reinforced latent fears and mistrust of the USSR in the world community. The Popular Front in France was doomed. National and international contradictions proved insurmountable. As Deutscher has explained:

> by a curious dialectical process, the Popular Fronts defeated their own purposes. They had set out to reconcile the bourgeois West with Russia; they increased the estrangement. They had intended primarily to press reluctant governments into coalition with Rus-

sia; but as the strength of their pressure grew, it widened the gulf between the would-be allies.[36]

The logic of the Popular Front innovations – insertion into the 'parliamentary game' and appeals to democratic national traditions – threatened Moscow's ideological patrimony over the PCF (and other communist parties). However, the tension thus engendered was invariably resolved in favour of the 'internationalist duty' of foreign communists to defend the interests of the USSR, as mediated by the Comintern leadership. The Spanish Civil War demonstrated this essential truth even more graphically.

The Spanish Communist Party (PCE) had been one of the smallest in Europe, beset by factional struggles and rarely engaging the serious attention of the Comintern. This situation was changing by the mid-1930s. After the bloody suppression of the Asturian miners' uprising in October 1934, the PCE played a minor, yet positive, role in the emerging Spanish Popular Front. This was an extremely fragile political alignment comprising the liberal Republican party, the Socialists (PSOE), the PCE and the quasi-Trotskyist Workers' Party of Marxist Unity (POUM). The Popular Front's narrow election victory in February 1936 and the spontaneous wave of strikes and land seizures that followed provided the pretext for General Franco's military coup in July. A social revolution 'from below' exploded and a brutal internecine conflict ensued which was to last until March 1939. The Spanish Civil War rapidly became a *cause célèbre* for the international left, a symbol of the wider struggle for democracy over fascism.

Franco's coup posed an acute dilemma for the Soviet leadership. Within a week of the uprising, Hitler and Mussolini were providing invaluable military aid to the rebels. Blum, fearful of provoking German aggression, reversed the initial decision of the French Popular Front government to assist the Spanish Republic and together with Britain implemented a policy of non-intervention. This left the USSR as the only major power willing to defend the Republican cause. Yet, as Stalin was well aware, Soviet intervention might place the already delicate alliance with France under intoler- able strain, or even precipitate a full-scale 'imperialist' war for which the Red Army was ill-prepared. On the other hand, victory for Franco would seriously weaken the collective security system, alter the balance of forces in Europe in favour of fascism, and, conceivably, push ultra-conservative circles in Britain and France into the arms of Berlin and Rome. In the end, the hope of expanding the collective security framework seems to have tipped the balance. After weeks of vacillation, Stalin and the Politburo finally decided in late September to send regular shipments of arms to the Republic. It is possible that pressure from the international communist movement contributed to this decision.[37] Intervention demanded the direct and constant involvement of the Comintern as one arm of a vast network of Soviet influence, which included some 2000 military advisers and numerous secret police agents, diplomatic envoys and ECCI supervisors.

From the start, Stalin became heavily embroiled in events on the Iberian peninsula. It has been claimed that 'practically not one document on the Spanish question escaped his attention'. Although on occasion Dimitrov seems to have influenced the 'boss's' thinking, Stalin took all the major decisions.[38] His basic quandary was how best to aid the Republic without antagonising his would-be Western allies, or indeed exacerbating the already strained relations with Nazi Germany. The answer: military supplies should be despatched to the Republic, but no steps should be taken that could be construed as the 'Sovietisation' of Spain. In a famous letter, dated 21 December 1936, to Largo Caballero, the Spanish socialist Prime Minister, Stalin offered the following 'friendly advice'. He suggested firstly that in Spain the 'parliamentary road' could prove more appropriate to revolutionary development than it had in Russia. It was important to appease the rural and urban middle strata and also to associate the Republican party more closely in the exercise of government. Crucially, these measures would 'prevent the enemies of Spain from regarding it as a communist republic'.[39]

Stalin's 'advice' to limit the revolution to its bourgeois-democratic stage was obviously predicated on Soviet foreign policy concerns. But in the Comintern a slightly different theoretical understanding of the Spanish revolution emerged. Togliatti, who was to become the chief ECCI adviser in Spain, suggested in October 1936 that the anti-fascist revolution laid the foundations for a 'new type of democratic republic', an intermediate stage going beyond the bounds of bourgeois parliamentary democracy. Togliatti appeared to hint that the broadly based Popular Front in Spain was developing the necessary conditions for a transition from capitalism to socialism distinct from the Bolshevik model.[40] Although Togliatti's hushed whispers found a sympathetic echo in some communist circles, they were soon silenced by the steady deterioration of the Republican position. The significance of his conception was to become evident only later in the post-war strategy of the Italian communists.

The Comintern's task throughout the Spanish Civil War was to strengthen the unity of the Popular Front in defence of the Republic. This was clearly in line with the demands of Soviet foreign policy and the anti-fascist policies of the Seventh Congress. As early as 23 July, two months before Stalin had decided to send military aid, Dimitrov told a meeting of the ECCI Secretariat that the main objective was the defeat of fascism and that it would be 'a fatal error' at this time to emphasise the creation of soviets or the dictatorship of the proletariat.[41] Therefore the communists, and their Republican and moderate socialist allies, consistently prioritised the centralised war effort over social upheaval. The military question was declared paramount. Revolutionary elements had to be restrained. But the Spanish Trotskyists and anarchists, extremely wary of Soviet hegemony, refused to merge their local workers' militias into a single Republican army increasingly under communist control. They insisted that the best prospects for defeating Franco's insurgents lay in the reality of the 'revolution from below'. The fierce conflict between the adherents of the two perspectives – the primacy of war versus the primacy of revolution – further fragmented and debilitated the anti-fascist resistance.

In his impressive section on the Spanish Civil War, Claudin maintains that 'had the war been nothing but a technico-military enterprise there would be nothing for reproach in the contribution made by the PCE, Comintern and USSR to the Spanish people's struggle against Fascism'.[42] Indeed, Soviet military hardware was absolutely vital, as shown by the defence of Madrid in November 1936. Soviet involvement initially boosted Republican morale. The Comintern played a major role, organising a massive campaign of solidarity and recruiting up to 40 000 volunteers through the International Brigades. Men and women of fifty nationalities fought in the Brigades, most of them communists, many of them refugees from fascist regimes or veterans of anti-fascist struggles. Their contribution to the Republican cause is deservedly legendary.[43]

However, Soviet and Comintern intervention also exacted a mighty toll. Russian military advisers were increasingly dictatorial in their treatment of Spanish personnel, blatantly interfering in the politics of the Republican zone. Comintern cadres, like the Frenchman André Marty, were no better. The most indefensible import from Moscow was Stalin's private vendetta against 'international Trotskyism'. In December 1936 and again in February 1937 the ECCI Presidium warned the PCE that the 'complete and final crushing' of the Trotskyists as traitorous 'agents of fascism' in the workers' ranks was an imperative condition of victory.[44] The outcome was the murderous attack on the POUM and anarchists in Catalonia in May 1937, which demonstrated the awesome ability of Stalin's security organs to spread terror beyond Soviet borders. The culpability of Comintern officials in the bloodletting is beyond reasonable doubt. This 'civil war within the civil war' resulted in acute internal disunity in the Republican camp and facilitated the triumph of Franco's superior military machine.

The contradictory face of Soviet and Comintern involvement in the Spanish Civil War is thus clear. Soviet aid was essential to defend the Republic, but the Stalinist practices that came with it proved disastrous. The argument, common in far left circles, that Stalin sacrificed the Spanish revolution on the altar of collective security is superficially persuasive, but betrays a lack of understanding of the complexities of the domestic and international conjuncture. The primacy of revolution, championed by the Trotskyists and anarchists, was incontrovertibly harmful to Soviet state interests and was therefore forcibly rejected. Equally, the communists' containment of the revolution can be viewed as overly zealous. But their reformist political platform *was* a viable strategy for unifying broad sectors of the centre-left. More importantly, Comintern and PCE insistence on building an efficient unified army capable of defeating the rebels was a logical response to the exigencies of war. The fact that this policy gained the support of the liberals and socialists in the Popular Front government cannot simply be attributed to the omnipotent hand of Stalin. It made military sense. The real tragedy of Spain is that Stalin's declaration of war against Trotskyism shattered any chance of attaining the elusive goal of broad anti-fascist unity. It was also an ominous sign of his personal control over international communism.

COMINTERN AND THE TERROR

It remains one of the great paradoxes that at a time when the International had embraced a more flexible policy of Popular Front alliances against fascism, Stalin unleashed his violent assault on the Comintern. The Moscow Show Trials and the Great Terror that swept Soviet society between 1936 and 1938 had a profound influence on the attitudes of the communists' erstwhile partners in the anti-fascist struggle. Liberals and socialists recoiled from the barbarity of the repressions and relations between them and the communists markedly deteriorated. The impact of the Terror on Comintern officials, foreign communists and political émigrés in the USSR was for many years a taboo subject in Soviet historiography. The authoritative *Outline History of the Communist International*, published in English in 1971, devoted a mere two paragraphs to the 'cult of the Stalin personality', as it was euphemistically called. Thanks to the historical *glasnost* of the Gorbachev period and to post-Soviet researches, this lamentable situation has changed and new light has been shed on the purges in the Comintern as archival material becomes more accessible. The Stalinist terror in its wider sense has also been the focus of detailed study by Western scholars in the last decade or so. Challenging interpretations have been posited to explain the origins and scope of the purges, though naturally no definitive consensus has emerged on such a contentious and highly charged theme. We must await the opening up of all the relevant Russian files to get a clearer picture, but even then controversy will abound. This section on the Comintern and terror should thus be seen as a contribution to an ongoing debate.

To begin with, a few words are in order on methodological and evidential problems. Official Comintern pronouncements on the Terror comprise little more than justifications of the three Moscow Show Trials and propaganda accounts of the activities of the 'Trotskyite spies and murderers'. Hence, they are of limited value. Before the 1960s one of the main sources of information was the work of Soviet émigrés, some of whom claimed close links with the People's Commissariat of Internal Affairs (NKVD), Stalin's secret police. In addition, the memoirs of foreign ex-communists were influential in evoking the atmosphere of the times. These sources, while offering many valuable insights, have to be handled with care partly because of the frailty of human memory and partly because of the sensationalist nature of some of the reporting. With few exceptions, Western literature on the Terror has tended to marginalise the Comintern, concentrating mainly on the decimation of strictly Soviet institutions and society. This is true even of the most recent works.

Unofficial Soviet studies also share this emphasis. Roy Medvedev in his massive *Let History Judge* devotes just six pages to the purges in the Comintern and communist parties. Even the increasingly accessible Russian archives present problems for the researcher. The veracity of materials from institutions such as the NKVD/KGB, which daily engaged in fabrication, disinformation and lies, can hardly be taken for granted. In short, great caution is needed in assessing the various sources of evidence.

Another relevant factor in understanding Stalinist terror is that repression could take different forms: dismissal from official positions, removal from place of residence, expulsion from the party, arrest by the NKVD, internal exile, deportation to the Gulag system of labour camps, and judicial and non-judicial execution. Not all of those repressed were shot. It is also important to distinguish between the periodic bureaucratic party purges and 'verification' campaigns which punctuated the internal life of the Russian party and the Comintern from the late 1920s onwards, and the mass terror of the years 1936–8 when literally no one was safe. The campaigns of the first half of the 1930s inspired great fear and insecurity in party and Comintern ranks. But it can be argued that they did not necessarily form part of a masterplan concocted by Stalin, a kind of gradual build-up to the violent excesses of the later 1930s. Certainly, the idea of a long-standing general plan of action to eliminate all real and potential opponents cannot be discounted, but other factors may have been at work. 'Revisionist' Western studies indicate that centre–periphery tensions, intra-elite institutional rivalries, provincial and local power struggles, and deep-seated class antagonisms all fanned the flames of repression that engulfed Soviet officialdom and society.[45] These theories have aroused highly critical, and occasionally vitriolic, rebuttals from many Western specialists, but they have forced historians to rethink their assumptions on the origins of the Terror.

Having said that, some of the newer explanations for the scope of the Terror in the Soviet system as a whole – centre–periphery conflicts, for example – bear little relation to the repression of foreign communists and political émigrés attached to the Comintern. Can it be, then, that the 'orthodox' fixation with Stalin's pathological fear of opposition, combined with the profound xenophobic tendencies displayed by the Soviet leadership, really does account for the Terror in the Comintern? Received knowledge suggests that Stalin was indeed instrumental in perpetrating and organising the whole process. Writing in the mid-1960s Branko Lazitch concluded that the 'critical element was to be found in. . . . Stalin's personality and his impact on the political system he had been shaping since his accession to total power'. The 'Comintern genocide' becomes comprehensible 'once the paranoid traits of Stalin's personality are taken into account'.[46] More specifically, Medvedev has asserted that Stalin on one occasion signed the death warrant of 300 Comintern operatives.[47] Given the fact that he regularly issued telegrams to regional party functionaries demanding that defendants be shot in short order,[48] Medvedev's claim is quite plausible. At this level, Stalin's responsibility is undeniable. In Tucker's words, he was 'the Terror's director general'.[49]

By early 1937 Stalin had convinced himself, probably on the basis of NKVD 'investigations', that the Comintern was a hotbed of subversion and anti-Soviet espionage. Dimitrov recorded in his diary these ominous words from Stalin, dated 11 February 1937: 'All of you there in the Comintern are working in the hands of the enemy.' Similarly, Nikolai Yezhov, the feared head of the secret police, informed Dimitrov on 26 May 1937 that 'the biggest spies were working in the Communist International'. Six months later Stalin made his point crystal clear: 'We must chase out the Trotskyites, shoot them, destroy them. They are worldwide provocateurs, the most vile agents of fascism.'[50] Incontrovertible proof of Stalin's incitement to terror is his remarkable toast at a private reception in honour of the twentieth anniversary of the Bolshevik Revolution:

anyone who attempts to destroy the unity of the socialist state, who aspires to detach from it ind[ividual] parts and nationalities is an enemy, a sworn enemy of the state, of the peoples of the USSR. And we shall destroy any such enemy, even if he is an old Bolshevik, we shall destroy his whole kith and kin. Anyone who encroaches on the unity of the socialist state in action or in thought, yes, even in thought, will be mercilessly destroyed. To the final destruction of all enemies. . . . ! (Cries of approval: To the Great Stalin!).

Dimitrov records his own comments thus: 'I can add nothing to what comrade Stalin has said regarding the merciless struggle against enemies. . . . I myself will do everything in my power to ensure the

Comintern takes this into account.'[51] Dimitrov, a loyal Stalinist, probably genuinely believed that the Comintern was infiltrated by 'enemies of the people', but he must also have known that many innocents would be sucked into the maelstrom.

It is important to contextualise Stalin's and Dimitrov's comments. In 1937–8 suspicion, xenophobia and fear of foreign interventions were rife in the USSR. Party leaders and the press assured the Soviet people that 'enemies' – Trotskyite–Bukharinite wreckers, double-dealers, foreign agents and spies – were concealing themselves everywhere. As the authoritative French-language weekly *Journal de Moscou* put it in April 1938: 'it would be no exaggeration to say that every Japanese living abroad is a spy. . . . and every German citizen. . . . is a Gestapo agent'.[52] These alien elements, so it was believed, had infiltrated party and state institutions, aided by the lack of 'Bolshevik vigilance' among party officials. In conditions of aggressive capitalist encirclement from East and West, the Soviet leaders' demands for total unity behind the party's general line appeared to many as rational and functional. Any potential 'fifth column' in the event of war had to be eliminated and any organisation that had connections abroad, such as the Comintern and Narkomindel, was a prime and natural suspect.

The roll-call of eminent foreign communists who disappeared in the 'avalanche of repressions' makes disturbing reading. Nearly all parties suffered, but the worst affected were those that were illegal and hence defenceless: the German, Yugoslav, Hungarian, Italian, Austrian, Bulgarian, Finnish and Baltic parties. Targeting the help-less appears to have been one of the principles on which the NKVD operated. Thus relatively few British, American, French, Czechoslo-vak and Scandinavian communists were purged, partly because these parties were legal and mass arrests could have aroused a national outcry. The Chinese communists, isolated in Yenan, were also largely spared. Party leaders or ex-leaders who were arrested and later shot or died in the Gulag include the Germans Eberlein, Neumann, and Remmele, the Swiss Fritz Platten, who was a friend of Lenin and, like Eberlein, had played an important role in the founding congress of the Comintern, virtually the entire elite of the Yugoslav party and literally hundreds of other foreign communist notables. It has been calculated that more members of the pre-1933 KPD Politburo were killed in the Stalinist purges than under Hitler – seven as opposed to five; and of the sixty-eight KPD leaders who fled to the USSR after the Nazi seizure of power, forty-one suffered the same fate.[53]

The most savagely hit was the small, but influential, Polish party (KPP). Stalin harboured a profound distrust of Poles, the origins of which cannot be traced with any degree of certainty. It may go back to his controversial military role in the Russo-Polish War of 1920, or his belief that the KPP was the stronghold of Luxemburgism – 'the Polish "variety of Trotskyism" ',[54] or his characterisation of the Polish state as a semi-fascist and anti-Soviet ally of Germany. Whatever the case, as early as May 1929 the Russian delegation to the ECCI 'with the assistance of Stalin' requested that the Soviet secret police should investigate the affairs of the Polish party in order to 'expose the provocateurs' in its ranks.[55] This is probably the first example of the Soviet security forces expanding their operations into the international communist domain. Although, or perhaps precisely because, Poles established closer ties with the Bolsheviks than any other foreign communists, the decision of May 1929 was no idle threat. Two prominent figures in the KPP were arrested in the early 1930s, and by the summer of 1937 the entire Central Committee suffered the same fate. Those who died at the hands of the NKVD included Lenski, the General Secretary of the party and member of the ECCI Presidium, and Warski, Walecki and Wera Kostrzewa, the 'three Ws' who had crossed swords with Stalin in 1924. Walter Laqueur estimates that approximately five thousand Polish communists were arrested and killed in the spring and summer of 1937.[56] But not only communists perished. It has been claimed that as many as 50 000 Poles living in the USSR were shot before 1939.[57] At this time it was safer for Poles to be languishing in a Warsaw jail than to be 'at liberty' in Moscow.

In late 1937 it was proposed to disband the KPP as a whole on the groundless charge that it had been infiltrated by Polish fascist and Trotskyite–Bukharinite agents. The decision dissolving the party was initially kept secret on Stalin's orders, but became known in Poland by the early summer of 1938 and was formalised by the ECCI Presidium in August of that year. By autumn 1938 all Polish party organisations had ceased to exist, causing untold consternation and confusion among the rank and file. The Soviet chroniclers of these events conclude that 'the facts and documents prove that the mass repression of Polish communists and the dissolution of the KPP were inspired by Stalin and fulfilled on his insistence'.[58] The false accusations levelled against the Polish party were officially retracted only in 1956 after Khrushchev's famous 'secret speech'.

Neither were tens of thousands of ordinary party members, refugees and even non-communist workers resident in the Soviet Union spared the paroxysm of violence. Tucker maintains that 'during the Great Purge, no group was more totally terrorised than foreign Communists who had sought asylum in Russia or simply gone there to work or study'.[59] The total number of non-Soviet victims of the Terror is still a matter of great conjecture. Indeed, the precise figures may never be known. One recent Moscow source asserts that 1422 foreign communists were shot in the entire period 1930–53, most of whom were posthumously rehabilitated.[60] This statistic relates only to judicial executions and ignores non-communist victims. Other observers, while not risking an exact calculation, have implied that the figure was substantially higher. Rather than speculate on those actually shot, commentators have preferred to estimate the numbers arrested or sent to labour camps in Siberia. For example, Arvo Tuominen, General Secretary of the Finnish party and a resident of Moscow until 1938, maintains that 'at least 20,000 Finns' and even more Latvians and Lithuanians fell prey to the Great Terror.[61] A recent source, however, claims that this number is 'probably high'.[62] Several authors have reiterated the following well-documented, but still seemingly approximate figures: around 800 Yugoslavs were repressed, over 120 Italian communists died, hundreds of Hungarians and Bulgarians were arrested, over a thousand German communists had been incarcerated by spring 1938, and many Romanian, Austrian, Greek, Estonian, Swiss, Turkish, Indian, Persian and Korean communists perished.[63] In most cases their wives and associates were also detained, their children placed in NKVD orphanages. Many of the arrested Germans and Austrians were handed over to the Gestapo in early 1940 in an unconscionable deal between the two dictators.

Victims in the Comintern apparatus form a separate category. The highest-ranking sufferers were the long-time Stalinist stalwarts Piatnitsky, Kun and Knorin, who were arrested, imprisoned and later shot.[64] In November 1937 Stalin denounced them to Dimitrov thus: 'Knor[in] is a Polish and German spy. . . . Piatnitsky is a Trotskyite. . . . Kun has acted with the Trotskyites against the party. In all likelihood he is also mixed up in espionage.'[65] Needless to say, these accusations were completely false as witnessed by the posthumous rehabilitations of 1956. The scope of the purges of Soviet and foreign functionaries in the ECCI is very difficult to gauge. The following statistics were culled from the Comintern Archive by Firsov: on 20 January 1936 the Russian party organisation boasted 394 members, but by 1 April 1938 the numbers had shrunk to 171, a drop of 57 per cent.[66] Another Russian scholar has calculated that 113 ECCI workers were arrested in 1937–8, the main sufferers being Soviet (26), Polish (22) and German (16) communists.[67] Regardless of the exact numbers involved and even allowing for natural turnover, this represents a brutal attack on Russian and foreign operatives in the Comintern apparatus.

The baleful atmosphere at Comintern headquarters and at the Hotel Lux, home to the majority of foreign communist activists, is graphically described in a letter sent to Stalin on 28 March 1938 by the Hungarian economist and former ECCI member, Evgeny Varga (document 17). The author expresses his orthodox conviction that in conditions of capitalist encirclement it is better to arrest two inno-cents than allow one spy to go free. Nevertheless, he bemoans the morbid hatred of foreigners fostered by the mass arrest of communist political émigrés, which in turn was creating profound demoralisa-tion. Varga writes: 'This demoralisation is enveloping the majority of Comintern workers and is spreading even to individual members of the ECCI Secretariat.' A 'dangerous atmosphere of panic' was being engendered whereby 'many foreigners gather up their belong-ings every evening in expectation of arrest. Many are half mad and incapable of working as a result of constant fear.'[68] Varga's brave letter produced no immediate effect. The arrests continued, but became more sporadic after late 1938.

The organisational mechanisms through which Stalin and the NKVD unleashed this onslaught on the Comintern and foreign parties remain shrouded in mystery. Yet progress has been made.[69] It appears that two administrative organs formed the backbone of the repressive structures, the Comintern party committee (*partkom*) and the ECCI Cadres Department. The system was complicated, but seems to have worked like this: all the 400 or 500 Soviet and foreign communists in the RCP who were employed in the Comintern apparatus were organised in primary party cells, and it was these cells which conducted the grassroots purging of Comintern opera-tives. The *partkom*, composed of the secretaries and deputies of the various cells, issued instructions and co-ordinated the whole process.

The ECCI Cadres Department provided the biographical and political information necessary not only to adjudicate personnel disputes, but also to implicate 'deviationists' and 'spies'. The dossiers compiled on Soviet and émigré communists, a key component of which were 'autobiographies' and 'autocritiques', proved essential for the 'investigations' carried out by the secret police. Documents prepared by the Cadres Department show that leading British communists, such as Pollitt, were suspected of having contacts with 'enemies of the people'.[70] It appears that in 1937 the NKVD planned a trial at which Pollitt was to be the prime defendant, accused of recruiting Comintern militants to the British Intelligence Service. For reasons still obscure, the trial never took place.[71]

Crucially, by the mid-1930s the Comintern *partkom* and Cadres Department were in direct liaison with the NKVD at a cross-institutional personal level. That is, certain top functionaries in the Comintern bureaucracies either doubled as agents of the Soviet security organs or collaborated closely with them. Shady characters such as Kotelnikov, secretary of the *partkom* in the Comintern, and Alikhanov, chief of the Cadres Department, kept the NKVD informed of the purges in the Comintern and generally fuelled the wheels of repression. Hence we are faced with the important fact that Comintern officials were not only victims of the terror. Some, perhaps many, actively collaborated in the whole bloody process. Several, like Alikhanov, did so to no avail and were themselves shot. They knew too much. We shall return to the question of leadership complicity later.

Concrete indication of the growing authority of the secret police had come at the Seventh Comintern Congress. Mikhail Trilisser (alias Moskvin), head of the NKVD's Foreign Intelligence Service, and Yezhov, soon to become Stalin's henchman *par excellence*, were elected to the ECCI at Stalin's express wish. Historians may have overestimated the significance of this cadre reshuffle, but in light of future events it does appear a sinister development, suggesting that the 'boss' was highly suspicious of the Comintern and its ability to put its own house in order. From this time on the Soviet security organs in the guise of Trilisser, Yezhov and their subordinates were establishing their authority over an impotent, docile and doubtless terrified Comintern hierarchy. In 1937 Trilisser took on the responsibility of ruthlessly purging one of the most important ECCI sections, the Department of International Communication (OMS), before himself falling to the axe. By 1939 at the latest, all major policy directives and personnel issues, including the composition of communist party leaderships, had to be verified in advance by the NKVD.

But it was not simply through this body that Stalin sought to dominate the International. It seems that the General Secretary's personal secret chancellery and the Russian party's clandestine 'Special Section', over which Stalin exercised decisive influence, maintained contacts with, and in all probability controlled, the administrative and cadre departments of the Comintern. We are thus presented with a complex model of parallel institutions and overlapping bureaucratic competencies, the central thread being Stalin's power to appoint 'his' security men as watchdogs. It can thus be surmised that by the mid-1930s Stalin had established an interlocking network of party and NKVD organisational and personal controls over the Comintern's leading representatives and bodies. The Comintern and its national sections were either unable or unwilling to prevent this process, in itself convincing proof of the subordinate position of the once proud 'world army of the proletariat'.

The role of Manuilsky, Dimitrov, Kuusinen and other dignitaries in the Terror is less than glorious. Despite the well-documented fact that Dimitrov attempted to save some of the arrested foreign communists, he and Manuilsky were heavily involved in the purges of the Comintern apparatus. It was Manuilsky who at a session of the ECCI Presidium in June 1937 accused his startled colleague, Béla Kun, of insulting comrade Stalin and maintaining contacts with the Romanian secret police since 1919. Kun, himself no stranger to false denunciations, was soon detained by the secret police and later implicated, together with Piatnitsky and Knorin, in a vast 'plot' that was to be known as the 'Fascist-Spy Organisation of Trotskyites and Rightists in the Comintern'. The planned Show Trial was never held evidently because Piatnitsky defiantly refused, even under sustained torture, to accept the trumped-up charges and testify against himself and others. The accused were shot regardless.[72] Archival documents recently published in Russia illuminate still further the degree of Dimitrov's and Manuilsky's complicity in the Terror. On 10 October 1937 they informed the Central Committee of the RCP that 'a number of CI [Comintern] sections, for example the Polish, have turned out to be entirely in the hands of the enemy'. What is more, key organs in the Comintern, notably the OMS, had been infiltrated by 'enemies of the people'. This department, they wrote, 'should now be totally liquidated and urgently reorganised' by drafting in 'new, carefully selected and verified workers'.[73] We can only presume their request was granted.

How can the attack on devoted Stalinists in the international communist movement be explained? *Why* did it happen? Those psychopathological accounts that place prime emphasis on Stalin's paranoid personality cannot be dismissed out of hand. It is not necessary to inflate 'the mad Georgian's' blood-thirstiness and irrational whims to appreciate his crucial role in the Terror. His craving for total obedience from subordinates did not exclude the Comintern and foreign communist elite. Stalin's need to eliminate all real or potential rivals in the Russian party–state complex could not but spill over into the Comintern apparatus, which in reality was little more than an adjunct of that complex. Indeed, for the Comintern to have escaped the Terror would be totally inexplicable given the onslaught on all other Soviet institutions. As it was, countless loyal Stalinists became bemused and helpless victims at the stroke of a pen. It is surely no coincidence that many were Jews. To what extent this aspect of the purges was a product of Stalin's personal predilections, or rather was fuelled by popular anti-semitic sentiment, is impossible to answer. What can be said is that Jews formed a high percentage of staff in the Comintern and hence were likely to suffer disproportionately.

Historians, however, are rarely satisfied with monocausal explanations, especially for such a multi-variegated phenomenon as the Terror. Several hypotheses have been put forward in an attempt to find a pattern of repression, to fathom why some and not others were targeted. Branko Lazitch has affirmed that one of the 'guiding principles' of the Soviet security organs was to pinpoint old Leninist cadres, many of whom had been activists in the Zimmerwald Left during World War I. He contends, with some exaggeration, that 'all foreign Communists who had followed Lenin or had collaborated with him before October 1917 . . . and during the foundation of the Comintern in 1919, were exterminated'.[74] Stalin, in his urge to crush all resistance, 'had to kill the spirit of old Bolshevism in the first place. The repression was therefore an essentially counter-revolutionary phenomenon.'[75]

Other historians see an inter-relation between repression and policy clashes. One interpretation is that the Terror represented a violent backlash against the advocates of the Popular Front. The Soviet scholar Anatolii Latyshev has argued forcibly that the Comintern was slipping out of Stalin's control by 1934. Threatened by this process, he resisted the emerging alliance between communists and social democrats and, in Latyshev's words, 'arrived at the VII Congress fearful of an explosion of personal criticism. . . . I believe he considered the VII Congress his personal defeat. Therefore from 1937 he inflicted a crushing blow on those communists who had pursued the congress line.'[76] Latyshev's theory is challenging and suggestive, but can be queried on three counts. Although Stalin was a belated and reluctant convert to the Popular Front, he was a convert none the less. From 1935 the Comintern's anti-fascist policy was coterminous with the search for collective security against Nazi Germany and was therefore a useful weapon for Stalin. Secondly, the principal Comintern victims, Piatnitsky, Kun and Knorin, far from being adherents of the Popular Front, were highly sceptical of its implications. Why didn't Dimitrov, Thorez or Togliatti disappear? Finally, in the opinion of one eminent historian, 'the only parties spared by the waves of arrests, trials, summary executions and deportations were those which were actively engaged in the Popular Front policy'.[77]

Jonathan Haslam has offered a rather different, and more convincing, explanation of the origins of the Great Purges in the Comintern. His argument runs as follows. By the summer of 1936 the Stalinist regime was entering a period of crisis in both domestic and foreign policy arenas. Criticism of Stalin's personal abuse of power was growing from the remnants of the old left and right oppositions, and the more radical members of the RCP were dissatisfied with the 'bourgeoisification' of Soviet society and the timid anti-revolutionary foundations of Stalin's Comintern and diplomatic manoeuvres. The impotence of the Popular Front in France during the militant strike wave of June 1936 and the Soviet Union's tardy response to the outbreak of the Spanish Civil War served to strengthen the dissentient voices. 'Stalin', Haslam concludes, 'appeared to be losing his grip in Moscow.' Hence, the threat to his position originated as much from Comintern as domestic policy differences and for this reason it was inevitable that 'Stalin's counter-attack would also be directed against those who stood for revolutionary internationalism as against *raison d'état*.' The deadly assault on the Comintern was the result.[78]

More recent research based on Comintern Archive material appears to corroborate Haslam's conclusions by stressing the interconnections between the 'deviations' of the late 1920s and the mass bloodletting of the period 1936–8. This view does not necessarily imply that Stalin had a long-standing masterplan of action, but it does suggest that these deviations served as 'a "clone" of repression', a 'model infinitely copiable and transferable'.[79] As early as September 1932, Comintern workers were being exhorted to display 'maximum vigilance in the fierce struggle against opportunism . . . and petit-bourgeois conciliation of the counter-revolutionary theory and practice of Trotskyism and the right-wing deviation'. A month later the famous 'Riutin Platform', circulated by a number of middle-ranking Bolsheviks, railed against the 'personal dictatorship of Stalin', which had transformed the Comintern from the 'headquarters of the world proletarian revolution . . . into merely Stalin's office for the affairs of the communist parties'. The 'Platform' was a serious warning to the wary General Secretary and alerted him to the potentiality of a 'left–right bloc'. However, it was Kirov's murder in December 1934 that acted as the spark for the large-scale arrest of ex-oppositionists in the Comintern central organs. Examples include the old Zinovievite Georgi Safarov, who worked in the Eastern Department of the ECCI, and his associate Lajos Magyar. In the second half of 1936, after two ex-members of the Comintern party organisation appeared as defendants in the Zinoviev–Kamenev trial, the ECCI *partkom* recommended in effect a series of round-ups of staff having 'Trotskyite and right-wing vacillations'. Many of the suspects mentioned on the lists were arrested.[80]

In all likelihood, then, Stalin's Terror was far from random. It was directed initially at ex-oppositionists in the ECCI departments and from there engulfed members of the Comintern hierarchy and the party leaderships and rank and file. An important reason for this was the fact that, once begun, the purges gained a dynamic of their own as NKVD interrogations revealed that ever more 'double-dealers' were embroiled in 'enemy plots'. In the Comintern as elsewhere, denunciations and informing were wholesale. Fear, bitterness, conviction, fanaticism, servility and hypocrisy can be included among the psychological inputs behind such behaviour. It has been argued that a form of 'collective psychosis' was generated, making accomplices in crime out of thousands of officials from top to bottom. Certainly, the drive for personal survival must have been compelling and partly accounts for such grim spectacles as long-time colleagues accusing each other of 'vile attacks' on the party line. Careerism, private rivalries and sheer greed are other factors to be borne in mind. We should not forget that some benefited from the upward social mobility engendered by the purges, while others used the opportunity to settle old scores or acquire 'the bigger room next door'. It is likewise almost certain that NKVD operatives often acted on their own initiative without direct sanction from above, becoming a law unto themselves in the desperate quest to fulfil the 'norms'. Clearly, Stalin could not know of, or approve, every arrest.

More specifically, it has been asserted that the fierce attack on the German, Polish and Baltic parties was conditioned mainly by Stalin's fear that their leaders would never agree to his plan to strike a deal with Hitler to partition Poland. In this opinion, Stalin's 'Russian national Bolshevism' and designs for territorial aggrandisement in Eastern Europe were anathema to old-guard communists, both foreign and Soviet.[81] This theory appears logical and, in the continued absence of archival evidence to the contrary, remains a tempting interpretation of the repression of KPD, KPP and Baltic party activists. However, it rests on Stalin's intention in 1937–8 to forge a pact with Nazi Germany, which is debatable. Moreover, as we have seen, many factors influenced the mass arrest of foreign communists. To prioritise just one may be shortsighted.

The impact of the Terror on the Comintern and international communist movement can only be described as calamitous. After 1936–7, the Comintern apparatus in Moscow basically ceased to function in a collective sense. Those ECCI Presidium meetings that were held during the Terror years seem to have been depressing affairs, often convened by the Russians to inform members of yet another NKVD arrest. It has been reported that not even formal votes were taken on these occasions since detention by the security organs was considered 'proof' of guilt. It is possible that from late 1938 organisational procedures normalised somewhat, but surely it is no exaggeration to conclude with Spriano that 'given a holocaust of such proportions, the Communist International could not survive as a political organization with the slightest vitality or internal life'.[82]

Stalin used the Comintern as a kind of ideological screen for his personal dictatorship. After the February–March 1937 plenum of the RCP Central Committee, the liquidation of Trotskyism as a 'fascist agency' became one of the prime tasks of the communist movement.

Not only did ECCI dignitaries repeat the standard formulas on the 'Trotskyite terrorists and bandits', but foreign communist leaders, regardless of any private misgivings, slavishly trumpeted the Stalinist line on the Show Trials, virulently denouncing the accused and demanding increased vigilance in their own ranks. Most party members seem to have believed that the 'traitors' received their just desserts. Such staunch international support was invaluable for Stalin, not least as a propaganda tool for domestic consumption.

More important from a wider perspective, the Terror posed a grave threat to the anti-fascist struggle in Europe. To be sure, the ultimate failure of the Popular Front and collective security as defence mechanisms against fascism cannot simply be explained by the grisly stories emanating from the Lubianka. Haslam has rightly suggested that 'at moments in the historical process even the most ingenious solutions are utterly ineffective'. But the same author also tells us that:

> Across the board, association with Stalin's rule of terror made the position of all European communist parties that much more difficult; it weakened the case for the Popular Front, since it exacerbated suspicions on the left and in the centre that, should the communists attain power, a bloodbath might well engulf them.[83]

Dimitrov's reiteration in late 1937 of Stalin's dictum that 'it is impossible to put an end to capitalism without having put an end to social-democratism in the working-class movement' could only alienate the moderate left and prejudice the quest for anti-fascist alliances.[84]

Notwithstanding the phenomenon of the 'fellow-traveller', opinion in social-democratic, liberal and intellectual circles was understandably hostile to events in the USSR. In August 1936 the prominent German social democrat Rudolf Hilferding wrote to one of his colleagues that 'the Moscow Trial has had a catastrophic effect and has dreadfully compromised the policy of the Popular Front'. Indeed, the purges contributed to the failure of the Preparatory Committee for a Popular Front in Germany, set up in Paris in June 1936.[85] The reaction of many French and British socialists was broadly the same. Léon Blum, plunged into depression by the Bukharin trial, lamented its impact on the cause of unity in France, and Harold Laski, the distinguished British left-wing academic, maintained in November 1937 that 'there is no doubt the mass executions in the Soviet Union in the last two years have greatly injured the prestige of Russia with the rank and file of the Labour Party . . . [and] cost the supporters of the United Front' dear.[86]

From Spain to Romania to Japan, the rise of the extreme right seemed unstoppable, hopelessly compounded by the British and French policy of appeasement. In Europe and in Asia the threat to peace was mounting. The Comintern's response to aggressive fascism – the creation of broad cross-class Popular Front alliances – made political sense. But the great hopes of 1935–6 were shattered by 1937–8. The Popular Front experiment lay in tatters, victim of the Great Terror, its own internal contradictions and limitations, and the Soviet leadership's lukewarm advocacy of a line it probably always regarded as tactical and temporary. Following early successes in France and Spain, the Popular Front was nowhere able to generate effective anti-fascist unity. To this extent, the international movement had proven incapable of protecting the USSR, a lesson not lost on Stalin. From now on the Soviet Union would rely on itself. Responsibility for the failure of the Popular Front does not lie solely with the communists, in particular those thousands of ordinary party members and sympathisers who bravely and honestly struggled against fascist expansion. But Stalin's merciless onslaught on 'Trotskyism' at home and abroad and the Comintern's fierce verbal attacks on social democracy surely go a long way in explaining this failure. The imposition of 'high Stalinism' in the USSR and the resultant atrophy of the internal regime in the Comintern proved a mighty obstacle to united action. After the Munich agreement of September 1938, the Popular Front was dead in all but name. The final nail in its coffin was the rapprochement between Germany and the USSR, culminating in the infamous Nazi–Soviet Pact of August 1939. The Comintern's controversial activities in World War II and its unexpected demise in May–June 1943 will be the subject of our final chapter.

5. Comintern in East Asia, 1919–39

Michael Weiner*

Throughout the existence of the Communist International its influence in East Asia was mediated on the one hand by the context of colonialism and the anti-colonial nationalist movements which emerged during the period, and on the other by the predominance of the rural economy. As a consequence it was the peasantry, rather than the industrial proletariat, which constituted the overwhelming bulk of the regional population. Korea and Taiwan were subject to direct colonial control, while China's semi-colonial status was determined by its relationship with both the metropolitan states of Europe and the United States, and with Japan. The exception to this pattern was Japan, an imperial power in its own right where both capitalism and nationalism were relatively well developed. Although initial Comintern interest focused on Japan, as the only state in the region possessing an industrial proletariat of substance, it was in China where the Comintern had its greatest impact.

While there may be a case for widening the scope of this chapter to include Korea and Japan, there are compelling reasons not to do so. First, it is not possible to comprehend fully the appeal of communism without reference to indigenous nationalism and the national-liberation movements which this gave rise to. Although never an issue in imperial Japan, nationalists in China and Korea

* This chapter is written by Dr Michael Weiner, Director of the East Asia Research Centre, University of Sheffield.

were initially drawn to communism as a vehicle for anti-imperialist struggle. Secondly, the initial Comintern assessment overestimated the size and revolutionary potential of the Japanese working classes. Throughout the inter-war period most Japanese workers were only partially engaged in industrial labour. The same argument could be applied to China, but, unlike its Chinese counterpart, the Japanese Communist Party (JCP) was an illegal organisation almost from its inception in 1922. Although responsible to Moscow, the JCP existed underground, its leaders under constant surveillance by the Special Higher Police (*Tokkô Keisatsu*) and subject to periodic government purges which decimated the party leadership.

In neither Japan nor Korea, moreover, was Comintern presence the decisive factor it was in China. True, the December Theses of 1928 resulted in the integration of the Korean Communist Party (KCP) in the JCP, but there is little to suggest that Korea figured large, if at all, in Comintern councils. Like its Japanese counterpart, the effectiveness of the KCP was constrained by both intense inner-party factional conflict and the coercive instincts of the colonial administration. In comparison to the hundreds of Comintern and Soviet advisers who would be sent to China during the 1920s and 1930s, Comintern influence elsewhere in the region was marginal. It is for the reasons enumerated above, and of course the fact that the Chinese communists ultimately achieved power, that the following discussion is restricted to an analysis of Comintern involvement in China.

COMINTERN AND THE COLONIAL QUESTION

At the First Comintern Congress in March 1919, very little time or discussion was devoted to the 'colonial' question. With the exception of a small number of Chinese and Korean émigrés, Asian representation at the congress was minimal. At this time the Bolshevik leadership was reluctant to acknowledge the impact revolutionary change in the colonial and semi-colonial states of the periphery might have on world revolution. While Lenin accepted that colonial liberation might accompany or come about as a consequence of revolutionary upheaval in the metropolitan states, he was not prepared to contemplate the reverse. Bukharin, too, though acknowledging that national or colonial revolutions were an aspect of the 'great revolutionary world process', remained convinced that they had no direct relation to the developing proletarian revolution. The possibility of establishing a dictatorship of the proletariat in China, India and Ireland, he reasoned, was much reduced by the absence of strong working classes in those countries. Even Zinoviev, in a presentation on the activities of the Comintern made at the Eighth Bolshevik Party Congress in March 1919, excluded all reference to the East.[1]

By 1920, however, despite the confident predictions of the previous year, European revolution had failed to materialise. Instead, mass demonstrations against Japanese colonialism and European imperialism had taken place in Korea and China respectively in the spring of 1919. It had also begun to dawn on the Bolsheviks that anti-imperialist struggles in the East could help stabilise the shaky Soviet regime. Thus, the Second Comintern Congress, held in the summer of 1920, addressed both the 'national' and 'colonial' questions in some depth. The more substantive role of Asian communists at the Second Congress was manifested in the person of the Indian communist, M. N. Roy, who contested Lenin's theses on the 'colonial' question. Even at this early stage, the Lenin–Roy debate threw into sharp focus the issues which would dominate Comintern activities in the Far East throughout its existence. These tensions were posed in a series of inter-related debates: whether, or to what extent, communist parties in colonial regions should be prepared to co-operate with local bourgeois nationalist forces; the form which collaboration of this type should take; and the relative roles of the small, but politically conscious, urban working classes and the far more numerous, but largely inarticulate, peasantry.

Whereas Lenin conceded the possibility of communist movements collaborating with, and even accepting the temporary leadership of, radical nationalist elements, Roy rejected such subordination of the communist movement to the national bourgeoisie. In large part their differences grew out of discussions concerning the mobilisation and role of the colonial peasantry. Lenin's willingness to contemplate Soviet movements which were entirely peasant-based was countered by Roy's insistence that Soviet organisations in colonial regions demanded the participation of an already existing class-conscious working class. Roy's position was also grounded in his assessment of the critical role of revolutions in Asia to the future of the world communist movement. Since, he argued, it was the extraction of super-profits from its colonies which had enabled European capitalism to buy off the labour aristocracy in the metropolitan states, colonial liberation was an essential prerequisite for the overthrow of the capitalist system in Europe.

The wide divergence between the theses of Roy and Lenin was by no means resolved at the Second Congress. Instead both were accepted in a draft decision to encourage collaboration with revolutionary nationalism. The final draft neatly avoided discussion of the likely conflict which would arise between communist movements, committed to both national liberation and proletarian revolution, and nationalist movements whose proletarian commitment and concern with the social demands of urban workers and the rural poor was often in doubt. The *Theses on the National and Colonial Question* (document 3), which resulted from the protracted debate between Lenin and Roy, allowed for the formation of temporary agreements or alliances between communists and nationalist forces in colonial regions. The precise form such alliances might take was not spelled out, but it was assumed that the independent character of the proletarian movement would be preserved.[2]

As would become even more apparent at the First Congress of the Peoples of the East held in Baku in September 1920, the issue of colonial liberation was of far greater complexity than the leaders of the Comintern appreciated. Strongly worded resolutions affirming the revolutionary unity of Russian Bolsheviks and colonial peoples in the anti-imperialist struggle were one thing, but the formulation and implementation of practical strategies to achieve these objectives in countries which lacked an industrial proletariat presented problems of a different order altogether. While the Baku Congress illustrated both the complexities of the colonial situation and some of the ambiguities glossed over by the Second Comintern Congress, it also formalised the Bolshevik commitment to the liberation of colonial peoples. The Baku Congress confirmed the stature of the Comintern as a world organisation. The shift in Comintern attention to the East which Baku marked was best summarised by Zinoviev who, in a radical departure from his position of one year earlier, assessed the proceedings of the Baku meeting as an important supplement to those of the Second Congress.

The initial decision to hold the Baku Congress was taken at a meeting of the ECCI in July 1920. This was followed by an 'Appeal to the Enslaved Masses of Persia, Armenia and Turkey' to attend a congress in Baku scheduled for mid-August. The agreed date was later revised to accommodate delegates from regions further east including, it was hoped, India and China. On the eve of the congress, nearly two thousand delegates representing twenty-nine separate nationalities were addressed by a number of communist luminaries including Karl Radek, Béla Kun and John Reed. At its first session on 1 September Zinoviev, affirming the primary role of the colonial periphery in the struggle between capital and labour, insisted that the greatest potential for revolutionary change now existed in the East, home to the majority of the world's population. The Baku Congress, he observed, provided the greatest opportunity to 'secure the mass representation of the toilers of the whole of the East'. To great applause, Zinoviev concluded with a declaration of 'holy war against English imperialism' followed by a solemn commitment to 'the fraternal alliance of the peoples of the East with the Communist International'. The manifesto adopted by congress demanded the:

> liberation of all humanity from the yoke of capitalist and imperialist slavery. . . . In this holy war all the revolutionary workers and oppressed peasants of the East will stand with you. . . . Long live the unity of all the peasants and workers of the East and West, the unity of all the toilers, all the oppressed and exploited.[3]

Impressive though these declarations seemed at the time, Baku was not the genuine Congress of the Peoples of the East envisaged by the Bolsheviks. Rather it was a heterogeneous gathering of communists, anarchists and radical nationalists. Even Zinoviev, while defending the congress as a revolutionary development, conceded that the ideological and cultural diversity represented at Baku indicated the magnitude of the task ahead. Of great concern, too, was the fact that the delegations from India and China numbered only fourteen and seven respectively. Equally apparent was the Comintern's determination to gloss over or ignore entirely the dissonant views regarding the colonial question which had been expressed at the Second Comintern Congress. Only weeks earlier, for example, in response to Roy's call for colonial liberation in anticipation of socialist revolution in the West, Tom Quelch, a delegate from the British Socialist Party, had warned that most British workers would regard an anti-imperialist uprising in India as an act of treason. A lack of trained interpreters also increased the likelihood that the nuances of Comintern policy,

including the establishment of 'conditional' alliances between communist and bourgeois-democratic elements, were lost on many
delegates. None the less, Zinoviev remained convinced that, as the
revolutionary struggle advanced, the peoples of the East would
discard their ideological and cultural baggage as had the Russian
peasantry.

A crucial aspect of the Baku Congress was its implications for the
security of the Soviet state. It was Radek, for example, who observed
that the struggle against British capitalism would not be restricted to
the metropolitan core, but where it was most vulnerable – in the
colonies. As would become rapidly evident, Moscow was all too
aware of the tactical advantages which could be drawn from Baku in
future negotiations with the British. More starkly, Radek also noted
that colonial revolutions would 'ease the position of the Soviet
republic'.[4] Such concerns were not lost on members of the British
Cabinet, in particular Churchill and Curzon, who regarded the
anti-imperialist commitment of the congress as a direct threat to
British interests. Moreover, the correct relationship between communist and nationalist-bourgeois elements remained unresolved at
Baku. The Comintern policy of limited co-operation or alliance
outlined by Zinoviev at the opening session of the congress, though
pragmatically sound in view of the relative weakness of communist
movements in the East, was open to wide interpretation. Ultimately,
it was the vagueness of Comintern policy which accounted for both
its broad appeal and the difficulties encountered by indigenous
communist parties, initially in Turkey and later in China.

CHINA: THE FIRST UNITED FRONT

Despite the limitations imposed by both the enormous ideological
diversity represented at Baku and the incapacity of the Comintern
to construct a coherent colonial policy, subsequent disappoint-
ments in Europe further enhanced the relative importance of the East
in the international revolutionary movement. As we have seen, initial
Comintern efforts in East Asia were directed at Japan, where the
existence of a sizeable industrial working class appeared to provide a
fertile environment for revolution, but it was in China where the
Comintern would have its greatest impact. The early Chinese
revolutionary movement was comprised of two distinct elements: the

anti-imperialist 'bourgeois-nationalist' Guomindang and the Chinese Communist Party (CCP). One of the first Comintern agents active in China was Lenin's personal emissary, Grigory Voitinsky, whose immediate task was to reorganise and discipline the various Marxist Study Groups with the intention of creating a communist party amenable to Comintern direction. In this, Voitinsky and those who followed were remarkably successful, and by 1925 there were said to be some ten thousand Comintern advisers active in China.

Although increased emphasis on centralised control and party discipline encountered opposition elsewhere in the world communist movement, the Bolshevik model was initially welcomed by Chinese radicals. Indeed, the centralisation of party authority was first proposed by Chen Duxiu, the founder and General Secretary of the CCP, at the First Party Congress in Shanghai in July 1921. Chen saw it as a practical means of drawing together the diverse and deeply fragmented groupings which constituted early party membership. In common with other parties in the region, the infant CCP lacked a mass base and most closely resembled a loose federation of radical urban intellectuals. In the face of opposition from those who sought to limit the CCP to a co-ordinating role, Chen's proposal allowed for central supervision of local party bodies in matters of finance, publications and policy formulation. However, reflecting the commitment of many early members to a social democratic conception of socialist revolution, decision-making remained voluntary and consensual. What is more, the party constitution did not specify democratic centralism as its fundamental organisational principle, while the central leadership of the CCP exercised no control over admission to the party and lacked clear disciplinary authority.[5]

While committed to party unity, Chen was a vigorous opponent of the extreme version of the Bolshevising project introduced by the Comintern. In common with other early party leaders, a devotion to internationalism, individualism and social democracy had preceded his conversion to communism. The CCP thus sought mass support from among socialists and radical nationalists alike; indeed membership was open to all opponents of the existing order. Not surprisingly, Chen's conceptualisation of the party as a broad church wherein elected party leaders would be responsible to the rank and file resulted in conflict with both the Comintern and its representatives in China. In fact, Chen questioned not only the centralising role of the Comintern, but also whether the CCP should affiliate with that organisation.[6] As an independent and unconventional Marxist, Chen challenged the primacy of Moscow in the Comintern and was seldom prepared to accept uncritically the advice of its foreign advisers, whom he held in scant regard.

During his tenure as General Secretary, which lasted until 1927, Chen was also the principal obstacle to bureaucratic centralism. In his view, the revolutionary greatness of men like Lenin was a consequence of their intellectual independence from Marxist orthodoxy and their determination to accommodate the Marxist project to new historical contexts and national circumstances. But, like other founder members of the CCP, Chen's assimilation of Marxist theory was incomplete, at least in comparison to his European counterparts. This was to put Chen at a distinct disadvantage in his dealings with the Comintern, particularly after 1923 when the party entered into the first united front with the Guomindang. Although opposed in principle to this policy, the CCP leadership was unable to generate a sustained ideological challenge to Comintern authority.

Between 1922 and 1927 the Comintern issued a series of directives which were to define the early history of the Chinese Communist Party. In August 1922 the ECCI adopted a resolution which required the CCP to submerge itself within a Guomindang-dominated united front. This decision was reinforced by the terms of the accord of January 1923 signed by Sun Yat-sen, the authoritative leader of the Guomindang, and Adolf Ioffe, the Soviet diplomat. This agreement acknowledged that the current stage of economic and social development in China precluded a rapid socialist revolutionary transition. The most immediate objectives in China, those of national independence and unification, would best be achieved through implementation of the Guomindang programme. Radek insisted that co-operation with Sun's Guomindang would continue until the CCP was capable of independent action. Although Radek's directive at least implied that the Chinese communists would retain a measure of autonomy in the united front, it was clear that the ECCI regarded the Guomindang as the principal source of revolutionary change in China.

The CCP executive initially envisaged the united front with the Guomindang as an alliance of equals, in which the party would preserve its independence as a 'bloc without'. In its *First Manifesto on the Current Situation* issued in June 1922, the CCP emphasised limited co-operation with the Guomindang in a 'united front of democratic revolution'. The temporary nature of the united front was summarised in the manifesto of the Second Congress, held one month later. An alliance with the nationalist bourgeoisie, it was argued, would not only assist in the struggle against feudal elements, but would strengthen the proletariat. Once the anti-imperialist 'democratic revolution' had been accomplished and feudal barriers removed, the socialist transformation would proceed along clearly defined class lines.[7] In other words, tactical independence was to be retained in the united front until the CCP would emerge, as a consequence of the inevitable divisions between proletarian and bourgeois strata in the alliance, as a mass party capable of challenging the Guomindang.

Such a position was unacceptable to Sun Yat-sen, for whom, at most, the assimilation of the CCP *within* the Guomindang was a precondition to the formation of a united front. Although the eventual alignment of the CCP as a 'bloc within' corresponded to both the Comintern's assessment of the situation in China and to Sun's determination to establish the Guomindang as the dominant partner, communist acceptance of the united front was provisional. It appears that the CCP finally acceded to Comintern directives regarding the united front, but with considerable reluctance.[8] Indeed, as late as January 1923, the CCP continued to emphasise cross-party co-ordination of activities rather than amalgamation with the Guomindang.

The misgivings of the early CCP leadership were further exacerbated by the arrogance and at times colonialist contempt expressed by Comintern officials. Although Chen was essential to its activities in the East, the Comintern patronised him and was impatient with what it regarded as his ill-conceived experiment with democratic socialism. Dignitaries such as Radek dismissed opposition to a united front in which the CCP would be subordinate to the Guomindang and instructed the Chinese communists to: 'Get out of your Confucian scholar's rooms of communism and into the masses!'[9] Although later vilified for having surrendered control of the labour movement to the Guomindang at the Third CCP Congress in June 1923, Chen continued to warn against the subordination of labour to capital. Indeed, Chen's controversial proposal that the communist-dominated labour movement be subject to cross-party control came about as a result of Comintern pressure. Although both the Comintern and the CCP would reaffirm their commitment to an 'independent' trade union movement within a matter of two months, the Third Congress formalised the establishment of the united front. Its manifesto acknowledged that: 'The KMT [Guomindang] should be the central force of the national revolution and should assume its leadership', but retained for the CCP the right to engage in 'propagandistic and organizational work among the workers and peasants'.[10] For his own part, Sun Yat-sen conceived of the CCP as a political faction subject to Guomindang control, while for the CCP leadership the united front presented an opportunity to gain control of the Guomindang party apparatus from within. The intentions and relative strength of the CCP in the united front were outlined in the *Bulletin of the Chinese Socialist Youth Corps*, in April 1924:

We who have joined the Kuomintang must give our united attention to effective work in the lower echelons. We must by all means avoid harmful competition for posts in the upper Kuomintang echelons.... All our efforts should go into the city and district party branches.[11]

Indeed, CCP members were extremely successful in obtaining and retaining senior posts in the Guomindang largely because of the superior organisational skills and experience of communist cadres. Despite opposition in the Guomindang, Sun countenanced the appointment of leading communists to head the departments of organisation and peasant affairs. Even the departments of propaganda and labour, while nominally under the direction of Guomindang officials, were actually run by communist appointees, a number of whom had emerged through the Socialist Youth Corps. Throughout the decade following the formal establishment of the CCP, the role and influence of students in the revolutionary movement was of critical importance. The ability of students to mobilise support for the party in urban and rural areas also ensured a rapid rise in the CCP hierarchy for several Youth Corps leaders. In Shanghai, the first trade unions were established under the guidance of students, while in Guangzhou, the seat of Guomindang power, the Socialist Youth Corps successfully penetrated the nationalist-dominated labour movement. Student cadres took the initiative in organising peasant unions throughout the lifetime of the united front. Most importantly, it was through the student movement that the Comintern would seek to exercise control over the party.

Despite the existence of opposition in the Chinese section, the Comintern found it unnecessary to purge cadres during this period. Unlike its counterparts in Europe, the CCP was still a relatively small organisation which suffered from an absolute shortage of experienced party workers. Rather than purge the CCP of dissident elements of the right, centre and finally the left, which was the experience of contemporary European communist parties, the Comintern initially exploited organisational weakness in the party. Although removed from office after the debacle of 1927, for which the Comintern held him responsible, Chen, for example, was not expelled from the CCP as a Trotskyist until 1929. Numerous factors accounted for this, some of which corresponded to changes in the objectives, role and capacities of the Comintern itself. In other words, the Comintern was not yet the monolithic Stalinist creation it would become. Similarly, while clearly interventionist in its relationship with national sections, the Comintern in the early 1920s lacked the authority to impose Moscow's views unchallenged on the world communist movement. One must also bear in mind that the early CCP leaders, for all their opposition to the united front, were not respected Marxist ideologues. In this respect they constituted far less of a threat to Stalin, and by extension the Comintern, than did their European contemporaries. It was not until the internationalisation of the Stalin–Trotsky split that the CCP was ideologically differentiated between left and right.

From the mid-1920s, CCP compliance with Comintern objectives would be ensured through the displacement of the early leadership by a generation of Moscow-trained Chinese cadres, often referred to as the 'Red Compradors'. This practice was initially introduced under the direction of Peng Shuzhi, Qu Qiubai and their Comintern patrons and subsequently refined by Wang Ming. Ultimately, it was through the systematic usurpation of authority in the party between 1927 and 1935 by returnees from the Moscow branch of the CCP that the Comintern was able to impose Bolshevik patterns of party discipline and ideological conformity on the CCP.[12] Indeed, ·a defining characteristic of Comintern involvement in China during this period was the extension of the Bolshevik model to both the CCP and its main nationalist rival, the Guomindang.

During the mid-1920s China would thus be regarded as a testing ground for Stalin's theory of revolution in colonial and semi-colonial regions. It was an approach which assigned a central role to the national bourgeoisie in the anti-imperialist and anti-feudal struggle. As summarised in a series of Comintern directives, the nationalist and bourgeois dominated Guomindang was regarded as a revolutionary consortium, incorporating diverse class interests, but amenable to Bolshevik ideology and organisation. Soviet endorsement and cultivation of the Guomindang took numerous forms, the most important of which was the despatch of thousands of military and political advisers to China. The objective of this largesse was the reorganisation of the Guomindang along Soviet lines. A new Bolshevik inspired constitution for the Guomindang was drafted under Comintern guidance and in late 1923 the party was restructured along democratic centralist lines.

Critical to both the Bolshevisation and initial triumph of the Guomindang in its struggle with the CCP was the Huangpu (Whampao) Military Academy near Guangzhou. Established in 1925, the Academy was modelled on Trotsky's Red Command Schools and emphasised the acquisition of military skills, ideological training and party discipline. All Huangpu cadets were required to join the Guomindang. Training in Bolshevik military techniques was provided by Chinese and Soviet instructors, while political instruction was increasingly left to CCP officials. Under the command of one of Sun Yat-sen's most promising lieutenants, Chiang Kai-shek, the Huangpu Academy functioned as a channel for the transmission of Bolshevik doctrine and organisational theory for the Guomindang and CCP alike.

In common with counterparts in the CCP during the mid-1920s, Chiang Kai-skek's rapid ascent in the Guomindang paradoxically owed much to this 'Moscow connection'. Chiang had supervised a mission to Moscow in 1923 and within two years of attending the First Guomindang Congress in 1924 had removed the senior generation from leadership and established an authoritarian regime which, though anti-communist, drew its organisational sustenance from the Bolshevik model. Contradictory though it may appear, the Bolshevising process in China during the period 1922–7 proved itself to be class neutral, available to both proponents and opponents of proletarian revolution. By the mid-1920s China was home to two semi-Bolshevised political movements, nationalist and communist. Although ideological antagonists, the Guomindang and CCP occupied a common terrain at the organisational level.[13]

Despite the centralising trends in the CCP, the imposition of

Comintern control over the party was far from complete. The notion that the Bolshevik party could serve as a model to be emulated, but that CCP policy should be determined in China remained common-place among early indigenous advocates of Bolshevism. Ideological diversity continued well into the 1920s.[14] Not only had the creation of a united front been fiercely contested by the leadership of the CCP, but the Comintern itself lacked the organisational capacity to manage the activities of either national sections or its own agents. This situation, it is true, gradually changed after the arrival of Mikhail Borodin as the principal Soviet representative in China in the autumn of 1923. A new stage in the Bolshevisation of the CCP was then inaugurated. Borodin's pedigree as a Bolshevik organiser was far more secure than that of his predecessors and he was well integrated into the apparatus of the Comintern. It was Borodin, for example, who chaired the committee responsible for drafting the new constitution which reorganised the Guomindang along Soviet lines. However, it must be stressed that neither Borodin nor Voitinsky were merely mechanical transmitters of Comintern decisions taken in Moscow. They operated largely independently of each other from their respective offices in Guandong and Shanghai and, despite his status, Voitinsky did not exercise authority over Borodin or Karak-han, the Soviet ambassador in Beijing.[15] This fragmentation of Comintern patronage fostered rivalries in the CCP leadership, most notably between the early 'Bolshevisers' Peng Shuzhi, who worked with Voitinsky, and Qu Qiubai, whose mentor was Borodin.

Let us return, though, to the outcomes of the united front policy in China. Initially at least, the CCP was the principal beneficiary of the united front. In terms of numerical strength the party grew from fewer than one thousand members in January 1925 to become a mass-based urban party by mid-1926 with approximately thirty thousand adherents. The catalyst for this transformation was the leading role of CCP members in the May Thirtieth Movement, in which industrial action taken by textile workers in Shanghai resulted in a year-long strike and boycott of foreign concessions in Guangz-hou and Hong Kong. Of the communist leaders involved in the mobilisation of mass support for the strike, Li Lisan, the head of the newly established Shanghai General Labour Union, emerged as the dominant figure.

Communist growth, albeit in the framework of the united front, also served to widen left–right divisions in the Guomindang. Until that time, Guomindang anxieties had been held in check by the commanding presence of Sun Yat-sen. But the latter's death in March 1925, coupled with subsequent communist successes and a resolution adopted by the CCP Central Committee in October 1925 to exercise greater political independence, exacerbated these anxieties. The offending document was seized on by the Guomindang 'right' which immediately proposed the expulsion of communists. By drawing a sharper distinction between itself and the Guomindang, the CCP also found itself increasingly at odds with Stalin and the Comintern. Although encouraged by the initial CCP successes of the previous May, by the end of 1925 Stalin reiterated his support for the Guomindang as a multi-class revolutionary party. In any event, the triumph of the 'left' at the Second Guomindang Congress in January 1926 and the election of Wang Jingwei as its new chairman appeared to confirm the ascendancy of the 'left' in the united front. CCP members remained in effective control of key administrative organs in the Guomindang, while the 'Red General', Chiang Kai-shek, commanded the most disciplined military force in China.

Belief in the ascendancy of the 'left' was a dangerous illusion. In March 1926 Chiang ordered the arrest of all political commissars attached to military units under his command, confined his erstwhile Soviet advisers and disarmed the strike committees formed the previous summer. The communist response reflected both the wide divergence of views in the CCP and, crucially, the unwillingness of the Comintern to act against Chiang. In fact, the Comintern ignored the coup and confidently predicted that: '*The power of the generals as a result of the pressure of the revolutionary movement is beginning to disappear.*'[16] In Guangzhou, however, the local CCP branch advocated immediate action against Chiang, while others called for the dissolution of the united front. Aware that the party lacked the military strength to challenge Chiang, the Central Committee in Shanghai shied away from an irrevocable break with the Guomindang. Yet in a private letter to the Comintern which foreshadowed a shift in CCP policy, Chen recommended a gradual disengagement from the united front.[17]

The Comintern response was equivocal even when, in May 1926, Chiang induced the Guomindang Central Executive to order the expulsion of communists from all senior posts and to reduce the ability of the CCP to retain its independence in the united front.

Borodin, for example, failed to support the decision of the CCP Central Committee in June 1926 to seek greater autonomy within the alliance and refused to permit the arming of communist units with Soviet supplied weapons. To a certain extent the cautious response of Stalin, Bukharin and Borodin was determined by the fact that the Guomindang remained the most reliable instrument for the reunification of China. Undoubtedly, the military offensive launched by the northern warlord, Wu Peifu, reinforced Comintern perceptions. Likewise, the swift release of Russian advisers and Chiang's renewed public backing of Comintern may have persuaded Borodin that preservation of the revolution was inextricably tied to support for the Guomindang.

But even at this critical juncture the Comintern response was fragmented and inconsistent. Voitinsky, now representing the Far Eastern Department of the Comintern, presented an alternative set of proposals to the Soviet Politburo which, while stopping short of a withdrawal from the united front, would have allowed for a greater degree of separation between the CCP and the Guomindang. This position was recast by Zinoviev in the form of a 'transitional formula', which would have permitted at least the consideration of a gradual disengagement from the united front should conditions continue to deteriorate. This tentative criticism of the united front policy and, by implication, of support for the Guomindang clearly placed Zinoviev in opposition to the Stalin–Bukharin duumvirate. Though not so radical a departure from Comintern orthodoxy as Trotsky's explicit opposition to 'entryism', which dates from August 1926, Zinoviev's attempt at compromise not only failed, but seriously weakened his own authority in the Comintern while enhancing that of Stalin.

While there is little doubt that the Comintern reaction was influenced by the availability, or unavailability, of reliable data, it must be placed in the broader context of the deepening power struggle in Moscow for control of both the Comintern and the Russian party. In this sense, the Comintern response to the potential disintegration of the united front in China provided a – perhaps the – forum in which the leadership of the RCP would be contested and ultimately decided. Despite mounting evidence that the Guomindang represented bourgeois nationalist interests alone, and despite the theoretical gymnastics required to sanctify preservation of the united front, the opposition of Trotsky and Zinoviev intensified Stalin's support of Chiang. Stalin and Bukharin had advocated the alliance with the nationalist Guomindang partly because they believed it was the correct Leninist revolutionary strategy, and partly because a cautious policy in China corresponded with the Soviet need for peaceful coexistence with the Western powers and Japan. A non-antagonistic relationship with the Guomindang meant relative stability in war-torn China, which in turn meant a breathing space for the USSR. As elsewhere, the security interests of the Soviet state ultimately took precedence over what were perceived as potentially destabilising policies.

The success of Guomindang armies, which had set out on the Northern Expedition from Guangzhou under the leadership of Chiang in July 1926, introduced a new element to this already tangled situation. Chiang's decision to challenge the northern war-lords had been supported by neither the Comintern nor the Russian Politburo, but even Stalin's initial reservations were swept aside by Guomindang successes in the field. On the face of it, the Nationalists' expansion also provided the CCP with an opportunity not only to regain but extend its own influence in liberated areas. Dissident elements in the CCP, however, remained sceptical of both Guomindang intentions and of Comintern generosity. In some newly liberated areas, particularly in Jiangxi Province, Guomindang suppression of peasant and labour unions led the CCP Central Committee to order the resignation of all communist magistrates.

Almost immediately thereafter, though, the Seventh ECCI Plenum directed CCP members to 'permeate' the Guomindang government apparatus. Stalin rationalised support for the united front on the grounds that the Guomindang did not represent the narrow class interests of the bourgeoisie. On the contrary, the anti-imperialist nationalism of the Guomindang not only appeared to justify a natural alliance with the CCP, but ensured subordination to the Comintern. Stalin's argument ignored not only the assessment of some Chinese communist leaders that the Guomindang government was a military cabal, but those of his own advisers. One of them, Pavel Mif, in a draft rejected by Stalin, had maintained that there was little to distinguish the Guomindang armies from those of the warlord opposition. Repudiating a further proposal made by the CCP that it be authorised to train separate military units, Stalin insisted that Chiang represented the forces of 'armed revolution in China' and recommended that the party:

take every measure to neutralise the anti-peasant elements in the [Guomindang] army, to preserve the army's revolutionary spirit, and to ensure that the army assists the peasants and rouses them to revolution.[18]

How a militarily weak CCP was to accomplish this task, or, as Stalin also advised, 'occupy various leading posts in the revolutionary army', remained to be seen. To the consternation of the CCP leadership, Voitinsky, who had earlier advised against communist participation in a Nationalist government, abruptly reversed his position. The subsequent removal of the left-Guomindang government of Wang Jingwei, of which the CCP was a junior partner, from Guangzhou to Wuhan seemed to confirm Stalin's faith in the united front. The establishment of a rival Nationalist base under Chiang Kai-shek early in 1927 at Nanchang, however, threatened the delicate Guomindang–CCP–Comintern balance of power. Cut off by Chiang's forces from Shanghai, its principal source of revenue, the Wuhan government was compelled to rely on rural taxation to finance its war with the northern warlords. Under these circumstances the peasantry, the very people whom the CCP had been directed to mobilise in the united front, were increasingly exploited by a government of which the CCP had become a member.

There were, moreover, two distinct Guomindang armies in existence: one, under Wang's control, had advanced to Wuhan and later moved north, the other under Chiang, whose objective was the city of Shanghai to the east. In the face of opposition from Borodin and General Galen, head of the Soviet military mission in China, Chiang was persuaded to call a temporary halt to the Shanghai campaign, providing Chiang with an opportunity to reaffirm his status as a faithful Comintern ally. This concession ensured both the continued flow of Soviet war materials and the support of the CCP, which in the final analysis could be relied on to obey Comintern directives. Chiang's tactics proved successful when, as his armies approached the outskirts of Shanghai in February 1927, the communist-dominated General Labour Union called a general strike. Despite CCP appeals that Chiang be prevented from entering the city, the Comintern ordered the strikers to avoid conflict with Guomindang military units and to bury their weapons.[19] As a result, when Chiang's army entered Shanghai in April it encountered no serious military opposition. Chiang's subsequent decision to abandon the united front policy of his mentor Sun Yat-sen and take decisive action against the extensive CCP organisations resulted in the massacre of thousands of communists, either real or suspect. The first united front had proved disastrous.

Chiang's defection from the revolutionary path would not, however, be interpreted in Moscow as a failure of Comintern policy. Only days before the 'liberation' of Shanghai, the Comintern had distributed autographed portraits of Chiang among the Bolshevik leadership, while Stalin, at a meeting of RCP workers in Moscow, had contemptuously asserted that his Chinese protégé would be 'squeezed out like a lemon, and then flung away' once the northern warlords had been brought to heel.[20] To preserve Comintern infallibility, a dialectical explanation for Chiang's defection was sought in the theses of the Seventh ECCI Plenum adopted in December 1926. These had predicted, somewhat ambiguously, the transition of the united front from a revolutionary bloc of 'four classes' (big bourgeoisie, petty bourgeoisie, peasants and workers) to a bloc of 'three classes' (peasants, workers and petty bourgeoisie). This allowed the Comintern and Stalin, despite evidence to the contrary, to interpret Chiang's defection as a 'progressive' step which had purified the Guomindang of big bourgeois elements and ensured its conversion into an 'organ of the revolutionary democratic dictatorship of the proletariat and peasantry'.[21] From this perspective, Chiang's coup of 12 April 1927, now diagnosed as a counter-revolutionary alliance of upper bourgeois and imperialist elements, had merely confirmed the ECCI analysis. The Guomindang government at Wuhan, cleansed of bourgeois-feudal elements, could resume its central role in the revolutionary united front.

In preserving the united front the Comintern had upheld Stalin. But it manifestly failed to address the fundamental contradictions which informed his China policy. Not the least of these was the maintenance of a class-based alliance whose constituent members advocated mutually antagonistic policies. To ensure CCP compliance with the latest ECCI decisions, the Comintern despatched Roy as its delegate to the Fifth CCP Congress in May 1927. Although the ECCI theses were duly adopted by the party, Roy's assessment of the military situation was bitterly opposed by Borodin and Chen. Roy proposed a period of retrenchment, while Borodin and Chen supported a second northern expedition. Initially overruled by his opponents, Roy appealed to his Comintern superiors. In a typically worded directive from Moscow, the Comintern ordered its Chinese section to cooperate with the Wuhan government in the service of agrarian revolution.

As enunciated at its Fifth Congress, the agrarian programme of the CCP was further committed to nationalisation of land and abolition of private property. How this would be achieved while retaining the support of the Wuhan government and its officer corps, which was drawn primarily from among the landlord classes, was unclear. Seeking also to avoid any disruption of the second northern expedition, which had been launched by the Wuhan government in the spring of 1927, the CCP exempted all land held by the families of revolutionary army officers from nationalisation. To this end the All-China Peasants' League was established not to facilitate, but suppress the activities of the revolutionary peasant unions in liberated areas. The hollowness of the CCP 'basic principles' at this juncture was also reflected in the rejection by the Central Committee of a proposed land redistribution scheme contained in the famous *Report on an Investigation of the Peasant Movement in Hunan* drafted by Mao Zedong.[22] For his efforts in mobilising the peasants Mao was removed as director of the peasants' department of the CCP.

The decision to assist in the effective suppression of the peasantry also exposed the limits of central authority in the CCP. In some areas, particularly Hunan where the Communist Youth Corps had been extremely successful in organising peasant opposition to the landlord class, shifts in CCP or Comintern policy were largely ignored. The disruption in party discipline which this reflected had two consequences. On the one hand, the activities of the Youth Corps had greatly enhanced the mass appeal of the CCP among the peasantry. On the other, continued land confiscation in liberated areas threatened to unravel relations with the left Guomindang government at Wuhan. When, on 21 May 1927, the loyalist Guomindang garrison in the Hunan capital of Changsha violently suppressed revolutionary elements in the city, the CCP encountered an all too familiar dilemma: whether to preserve the united front in compliance with Comintern directives, or dissolve its alliance with the Guomindang and thereby invite Comintern censure. At an emergency meeting of the CCP Politburo, Chen, who had little confidence in the Wuhan government's commitment to agrarian revolution, recommended a final break with the Nationalists. Borodin agreed with Chen's assessment, but warned that Moscow would not countenance a dissolution of the united front. Others, notably Zhou Enlai, opposed Chen on the grounds that conflict with the Guomindang would benefit neither peasants nor workers, but would strengthen the position of the Nationalist military.

The CCP response, drafted at the Eighth ECCI Plenum at the end of May, retained the framework of the united front, since to do otherwise would have meant isolating Stalin in the struggle with Trotsky. The excesses of peasant cadres were to be restrained while, at the same time, the Comintern called for a purge of counter-revolutionary elements in the Guomindang military establishment. ECCI reasoning was not difficult to follow. An army under firm Comintern direction would preserve the anti-imperialist united front, isolate the renegade Chiang and facilitate the internal transformation of the Guomindang as a truly revolutionary bloc. The creation of a separate Red Army was, however, to be delayed. Instead, elite military units trained by the CCP under the supervision of Comintern advisers would provide the fulcrum for this conversion. Stalin, citing a Comintern document from May, declared that: 'It is time to act. *The scoundrels must be punished. If the Kuomintangists do not learn to be revolutionary Jacobins they will be lost both to the people and to the revolution.*'[23] In the event, the Comintern misjudged both the capacity of the CCP to manipulate Guomindang civil and military structures and the willingness of the Wuhan government to participate in the process. The CCP and Borodin sought to delay implementation of what they correctly perceived as a misconceived policy, but were overtaken by events.

The catalyst for the dissolution of the united front and the rapprochement between the rival Guomindang regimes was, however, provided by the Comintern itself in the form of its representative, Roy. Unlike Borodin and Chen, whose compliance with Comintern directives was tempered by an appreciation of indigenous conditions, Roy interpreted their failure to implement the decisions of the Eighth Plenum as further evidence of a lack of discipline in the CCP. Roy ill-advisedly informed the Chairman of the Guomindang, Wang, of Comintern policy – even going so far as to make public Stalin's planned reorganisation of the Guomindang, for which he was censured and recalled to Moscow. Rather than relinquish control of the Guomindang to the CCP or its Comintern patrons, Wang intensified the suppression of peasant movements and ordered the expulsion of communists from the Wuhan government. Despite opposition from the Guomindang left and a commitment by the CCP to disarm peasant-worker units, by the end of July a new united front had come into existence; one which pitted the combined forces of the Wuhan government, Chiang Kai-shek and the Christian warlord, Feng Yuxiang, against the CCP.

The Comintern response largely repeated the mistakes of 1924–5. Just as Chiang, two years earlier, had affirmed his allegiance to the Comintern while ordering the suppression of communists, the Wuhan government alleged that it was the CCP and not the Comintern against which it had turned. For its own part the CCP scrupulously avoided confrontation with the Nationalists, but by mid-July even the ECCI was forced to concede that Wang had aligned himself with the 'rightist' menace. This was an important distinction since it permitted Stalin the opportunity to disassociate himself from a disastrous policy of his own creation. In the face of unremitting opposition from Trotsky and Zinoviev, Stalin maintained that leftist 'revolutionary' elements in the Guomindang would subsequently remove the traitor Wang from office. This interpretation of events, which was transmitted through the Comintern to the CCP, was hardly surprising. To accept the alternative view would require Stalin to either reverse course or accept the consequences of Comintern failure. The fiction of a united front had to be maintained to preserve Stalin's infallibility.

While ordering their resignation from the Wuhan government, the ECCI directed Chinese party members to remain in the Guomindang. When informed of a planned insurrection to be carried out by communist-officered Wuhan units, Stalin vetoed the action. But, despite the efforts of Chen to forestall the revolt, units of the Guomindang army in Jiangxi Province, under communist command, rebelled against the Wuhan government on 1 August. The rebel forces were quickly forced to abandon their bases in Jiangxi, retreating south to the port city of Shantou. At a hastily convened meeting of the CCP Central Committee on 7 August, an emergency Politburo was created to direct party affairs. Chen was summarily dismissed as General Secretary and replaced by Qu Qiubai, a Moscow-trained 'Bolsheviser' who had engineered Chen's downfall. Under the guidance of a new team of Comintern advisers led by Stalin's henchmen Heinz Neumann and Besso Lominadze, a new party line was introduced which belatedly recognised the dissolution of the CCP–Wuhan alliance. But, while urging resistance against both the

Nanchang and Wuhan regimes, the Emergency Conference Resolution of 7 August reiterated the directive of the Eighth ECCI Plenum to 'reorganize the KMT [Guomindang] and make it a genuine mass organization of the urban and agrarian toiling masses'.[24] As the situation continued to deteriorate, Stalin finally sanctioned the establishment of Chinese Soviets – the same Trotskyist policy which he had so recently opposed. But the CCP's urban base had been reduced to a single city, Guangzhou. Despite the misgivings of local party leaders, the CCP was ordered to take control of the city in December 1927. The Guangzhou Commune survived only three days, 11–14 December, and with its bloody suppression by Guomindang forces the CCP was effectively cut off from the cities.

Between 1923 and 1927 CCP policy had been shaped by ECCI directives which limited its scope for independent action. Unprepared for the defection of the Guomindang, the CCP had been reduced to political insignificance in a matter of months. Like its predecessor, the 'bloc of three classes' on which the CCP–Wuhan alliance had been constructed disintegrated under the shifting sands of Comintern policy. The debacle of 1927 had come about as a result of a profound failure on the part of the Comintern to appreciate either the nationalist impulses of the Chinese masses or the relative weakness of the urban proletariat. Contrary to Stalin's expectations, the Guomindang and its generals had refused to co-operate in their own demise. The Comintern interpretation of events in China was mediated by numerous factors, not the least of which was the inner-party power struggle between Stalin and Trotsky. It must be borne in mind, however, that the primitive organisational state of the CCP, combined with its concentration in backward rural areas, also help to explain the disasters of 1927.[25] The contours of a new Comintern strategy for China first emerged during the Fifteenth RCP Congress in December 1927, were further refined at the Ninth ECCI Plenum in February 1928 and transmitted to the CCP at the Sixth Comintern Congress in the summer of 1928.

THE RISE OF THE 'RED COMPRADORS'

The Sixth CCP Congress was held in Moscow between July and September 1928 under the watchful gaze of the Comintern, whose Sixth Congress convened during the same period. Both meetings provided an opportunity for the Comintern to supervise a comprehensive review of CCP strategy and to rid not only itself, but also its national sections, of any remaining vestiges of Trotskyist influence.[26] After discussing the events of the previous year, the CCP congress adopted a series of resolutions which confirmed Stalin's doctrinal 'correctness' and assigned responsibility for past failures to the previous party leadership. As expressed in the Political Resolution, reconstruction of the party would require an internal transformation based on the principle of democratic centralism. Chen was denounced as a rightist, who had failed to oppose the Guomindang, while his successor, Qu, was condemned for the 'blind actionism' of the Guangzhou uprising. The events of the previous year had also confirmed that China had not yet passed through the bourgeois-democratic stage of the revolution. The defection of the Guomindang from the united front was interpreted as a realignment of the national bourgeoisie with feudal landowning elements. In line with the Comintern's emergent 'Third Period' sectarianism, congress resolved to seek actively the overthrow of the Guomindang government.

In other respects the revolutionary agenda remained unchanged: national unification, preceded by the expulsion of imperialist elements and followed by rural transformation and the abolition of private property. As confirmed by the *Theses on the Revolutionary Movement in Colonial and Semi-Colonial Countries* (document 11) adopted by the Sixth Comintern Congress in September 1928, the CCP was also to prepare itself for military confrontation with the Guomindang:

> In China, the rising wave of the revolution will once more confront the party with the immediate practical task of preparing for and carrying through armed insurrection as the only way to complete the bourgeois-democratic revolution and overthrow the power of the imperialists, landlords, and national-bourgeoisie – the power of the Kuomintang.[27]

The revolution in China had entered what the ECCI described as a 'trough between two waves'; an interregnum separating the last outburst of mass revolutionary spirit from the next. The next revolutionary upsurge was imminent, but not yet in sight. The Comintern did not, however, indicate how long the current 'trough' would persist and it was left to the CCP leadership to identify the moment when preparation could be successfully translated into direct action.

Although the party congress acknowledged the necessity of peasant mobilisation, the central role of the urban proletariat in the revolutionary process remained an article of faith. Mao Zedong understood this as at least a partial endorsement of his rural-based strategy which had successfully organised millions of peasants in Hunan Province. The 1928 formula of the 'Democratic Dictatorship of Workers and Peasants' certainly implied a larger revolutionary role for the Chinese peasantry, but the centrality of the agrarian problem in the revolution did not displace the primacy of the urban proletariat. Indeed, the mobilisation of the peasantry could only proceed under 'proletarian hegemony', which in turn required the CCP to first re-establish its urban proletarian class base. It was, moreover, the labour leader Li Lisan, who had risen to prominence during the May Thirtieth Movement, to whom the Comintern entrusted responsibility for restoring the fortunes of the CCP.

Though never elected General Secretary, Li's would be the dominant voice in party councils until 1930, responsible for CCP attempts to restore its fragmented urban bases. During the 'white terror' of 1927, for example, the CCP lost 84 per cent of its membership, mostly in the cities. Zhou Enlai would later report that in July 1928 the proletariat constituted a meagre 10 per cent of party members, and fifteen months later that figure had diminished to only 3 per cent.[28] It also fell to Li to realise the co-ordination of peasant and labour movements envisaged by the Sixth Comintern Congress. During the two years which followed, the 'Li Lisan Line' evolved in response to Comintern directives which were often ambiguous and at times even contradictory. It was this, as we shall see, which permitted the Comintern to disassociate itself from Li when his policies failed. Ultimately, it would prove impossible for the party to reconcile Li's urban strategy with that of Mao, who doubted the capacity of the CCP to seize, let alone retain, control of China's cities.

The futile two-year campaign by the CCP to gain control of China's cities, for which Li would be held accountable, proved Mao correct and encouraged further efforts to organise the peasantry. But failure was due only in part to Li's doctrinally sound (at least in terms of Comintern directives), though misplaced urban bias. Not only had the Sixth CCP Congress reiterated the revolutionary primacy of the urban proletariat, but the Ninth ECCI Plenum had imposed an ambiguous strategy on its Chinese section. In the circumstances, it is hardly surprising that Li misinterpreted Guomindang weaknesses as an indication that the next 'revolutionary wave' had finally arrived.

Also at the Sixth CCP Congress the Bolshevisation of the party, first introduced in August 1927, proceeded under Comintern direction. For the first time the existence of an immutable party line, shorn of deviationism of the left or right, became a firmly established aspect of CCP doctrine. Congress also adopted the Stalinist version of self-criticism as a prerequisite to the creation of a 'completely proletarian revolutionary party – a bolshevised party'.[29] The main architect of Bolshevisation during this period was Wang Ming. Wang was a 'Red Comprador' archetype: Moscow trained, fluent in Russian and a committed Stalinist, who rarely visited his homeland and whose rise to power in the CCP was due almost entirely to a network of relationships developed with Comintern officials. Wang's mentor and patron was Pavel Mif, rector of Sun Yat-sen University in Moscow. Until 1927, Mif's association with the CCP had been restricted to several years as an undistinguished member of the Comintern's Far Eastern Secretariat. At Sun Yat-sen University, however, Mif established a reputation as a party loyalist by expanding the Trotskyist purge. It was in his capacity as rector that Mif also came into contact with, and developed the careers of, a number of Russian-speaking Chinese students, the most ambitious of whom was Wang. Mif's primary objective in cultivating the 'twenty-eight Bolsheviks', as they were later to be known, was to ensure the absolute subordination of the CCP to the Comintern.

Unlike his predecessors, Wang ultimately secured power in the CCP by establishing control over the Chinese students at Sun Yat-sen University and the party's Moscow branch. This was achieved by a series of purges of 'dissidents' and 'Trotskyite deviationists'. Mif's former students under Wang's leadership then wrested control of the CCP from Li. The 'Returned Student Group', of which Wang was the dominant figure, retained effective control of the party from 1931, when Wang was elected General Secretary of the CCP, until the Zunyi Conference of January 1935, which heralded Mao Zedong's ascent to party leadership. Wang's influence was particularly evident at the Fourth Central Committee Plenum in January 1931, which endorsed the contents of his pamphlet *The Two Lines* (also referred to as *The Struggle for the CCP's Further Bolshevisation*). In this publication, written under Mif's supervision and guided by Comintern directives, Wang advocated the 'pitiless struggle' against any form of deviationism as the 'basis of all actions and leadership' of the CCP.[30]

From a Comintern perspective, the deepening economic crisis of the capitalist world seemed to augur well for the international revolutionary movement. At the Sixteenth RCP Congress in June 1930 Stalin predicted a rapid transformation of the current economic crisis into revolutionary mass movements. In October 1929, though cautious to avoid setting a timetable, the ECCI had directed the CCP to prepare for the overthrow of the Guomindang government and the establishment of a 'Soviet proletarian–peasant' dictatorship. Despite the party's acknowledged weakness in urban areas, the Comintern directive was formally adopted by the CCP Politburo in January 1930. By March the CCP membership was informed that 'the great historical mission – the seizure of national political power – is about to confront us'.[31] Though prompted by ECCI demands for action, the decision to employ the largely peasant Red Army in an attempt to seize control of major urban centres was designed to enhance Li's credibility in both Moscow and China. While recognising the critical role of peasant uprisings, the party resolution entitled 'The New Revolutionary Rising Tide and Preliminary Successes in One or More Provinces' still assigned primacy to the urban working classes as the revolutionary vanguard. Within a matter of weeks, however, Li repudiated his opposition to a policy of enveloping the cities from the countryside and threw the Red Army into battle.

In a typically ambiguous directive issued on 23 July, the ECCI urged both action and restraint on its Chinese section. While confidently declaring that 'the new upsurge in the Chinese revolutionary movement has become an indisputable fact', the ECCI noted that 'the waves of the labor and peasant movements have not yet been combined' and cautioned against a national uprising. Instead, the CCP should seek to exploit Guomindang weaknesses in 'a few important provinces' and prepare the Red Army for the seizure of industrial and administrative centres.[32] The peasant armies of the CCP would, in effect, be relied upon to set in motion a train of events which would enable urban cadres to assume their leading role in the revolution. This was followed by a communiqué issued under the authority of the party's Revolutionary Military Committee which predicted the imminent collapse of the Guomindang and directed the Red Army to move against Nanchang, Wuhan and Changsha, the capital of Hunan province. The initial assault on Nanchang was unsuccessful, but on 28 July Changsha fell to units of the Fifth Red Army. The anticipated uprising of the urban proletariat, however, failed to materialise. Threatened by both foreign gunboats and Guomindang forces, the Red Army withdrew from Changsha within the week.

The failure of the Red Army to retain control of Changsha and the scale of the disaster effectively sealed Li's fate. Criticism was levelled from outside the party by former General Secretary Chen and from inside by Mif's Moscow-trained student protégés. Qu Qiubai, who had been dismissed by the Comintern only two years earlier, was ordered by Moscow to investigate the situation and orchestrate Li's removal. Control of the party apparatus, however, enabled Li initially to rebut criticism of his policies and the Third Party Plenum held in September 1930 endorsed his leadership. In fact, the Plenum found little to distinguish Li's position from that of the Comintern which he had assiduously attempted to implement. Li may have been guilty of minor tactical errors, but the strategy had been devised by the Comintern. By the time the Fourth Party Plenum met in January 1931, sufficient theoretical justification for Li's removal had been found. Accused of anti-Leninist 'adventurism' and Trotskyist deviation from Comintern policy, Li was summarily recalled in disgrace to Moscow. The ECCI, in an effort to distance itself from yet another failure in China, had already set the wheels in motion. In a letter dated 16 November 1930, it assigned sole responsibility for the most recent debacle to Li. The ECCI was equally contemptuous of Li's quasi-Trotskyist defence that the Comintern did not fully appreciate local conditions in China, observing that: 'He was bold enough to oppose loyalty to the Comintern to loyalty to the Chinese revolution.'[33]

The same ECCI directive also signalled a return to the pre-Changsha urban strategy of the CCP: a strengthening of the urban revolutionary base to complement the rural successes already achieved. The CCP was also instructed to consolidate the various rural Soviets based in Jiangxi province into a centralised Soviet government. Although riven by internal factionalism, the new Politburo, closely supervised by Mif, set about implementing Comintern policy. Under Wang Ming, the 'two-line struggle' against deviationists from the right and the ultra-left became a critical element of CCP theory and practice. The party was subjected to relentless centralisation and a series of debilitating purges whose objective was the elimination of Trotskyist tendencies. The new CCP leadership was comprised of Stalinists like Wang, centralising bureaucrats who had acquired the techniques of political control in Moscow and then abused the authority vested in them by the Soviet state when they returned to China. Their intention was not to assist but to dominate and control the CCP in the interests of the Comintern and, by extension, the Soviet Union. Following his return to Moscow in 1932, Wang continued to direct party affairs by radio until 1934 when contact was lost for a full two years. When Wang finally returned to China in late 1937, his attempts to reassert authority in the CCP were thwarted by Mao.

The period of Wang's ascendancy marked the zenith of direct Comintern intervention in CCP affairs. Mif and Otto Braun were the last Comintern agents sent to manage the affairs of its Chinese section, while the 'Returned Student Group' represented the final occasion on which the CCP would be dominated by Moscow-trained intellectuals. In fact, doubts remain as to the extent of Wang's authority in the party, particularly with regard to the Jiangxi Soviet. The Chinese Soviet Republic at Ruijin in Jiangxi was formally established by the First All-China Soviet Congress in November 1931. A draft constitution was published which identified the Jiangxi Soviet as a transitional 'democratic dictatorship of the proletariat and peasantry' and Mao was elected Chairman of the sixty-one member Central Executive Committee. Although nominally responsible to the party leadership in Shanghai, the Jiangxi Soviet maintained an unprecedented degree of autonomy, relatively free of both Comintern and Central Committee intervention until 1932. In any event, communications between Jiangxi and Moscow were irregular, while the CCP leadership in Shanghai operated under the shadow of the Guomindang's 'white terror'. It was under these conditions that the party leadership was induced to transfer to the capital of the Jiangxi Soviet in the autumn of 1932. With Wang Ming's subsequent departure to Moscow, the authority of the Central Committee was diluted still further by the dispersal of individual Committee members to various areas under CCP control. It is also important to bear in mind that the capacity of the Shanghai party to direct activities in Jiangxi was further limited by constant Guomindang military pressure. Between November 1930 and October 1933, Chiang Kai-shek launched no fewer than five 'encirclement campaigns', the last of which forced the abandonment of the Jiangxi Soviet and resulted in the 'Long March'.

For its part, the Comintern was far more concerned with Japanese military expansion in Manchuria and the potential threat which this posed to the Soviet Union than with bringing Mao to heel. Addressing the Eleventh ECCI Plenum in April 1931, the staunch Stalinist Manuilsky assigned China pride of place among national revolutionary movements in the colonial world. The possibility of anti-Japanese resistance in China was discussed at the Twelfth ECCI Plenum in September 1932 at which the CCP was directed to employ 'widely and consistently' the tactics of the 'united front from below', while retaining its hostility to the 'agent of imperialism', the Guomindang.

A clear opportunity to develop a united front was lost, however, when the CCP failed to make common cause with rebels in Fujian Province in 1933. Although non-communist, the political programme of the Fujian People's Government seemed in some respects to meet the criteria outlined in the September 1932 ECCI directive. At least three factors account for this failure. First, the CCP Central Committee, still dominated by the 'Returned Students', remained committed to a programme of Bolshevising the party and strengthening its 'proletarian' leadership. The observation that the role of the workers had been subordinated to that of the peasants in Soviet areas was both a challenge to the party leadership and an acknowledgement that the Bolshevising project of the Central Committee was far from complete. Second, was the accelerating pace of the Japanese offensive in the north. Third, was the fact that the fifth 'encirclement campaign' launched by Chiang Kai-shek in the late summer of 1933 had proved far more effective than its predecessors.

By January 1934 the capital of the Jiangxi Soviet was under threat and at the Second Congress of Chinese Soviets Mao urged an immediate expansion of the Red Army. In the months which followed, the Guomindang policy of encirclement not only forced the Red Army to abandon its previously effective guerilla tactics, but reduced communications between Jiangxi and Moscow to a trickle. Following the decision to abandon the Jiangxi Soviet in the autumn of 1934, contact with the Comintern was temporarily lost. During this first phase of the Long March Mao and disaffected members of the 'Returned Student Group' successfully challenged Wang's leadership at the Zunyi Conference in January 1935. Based on contemporary and later accounts, the Wang Ming faction stood accused of failing the party in four respects. It had misjudged the domestic consequences of the Japanese invasion of Manchuria, ignored a potential alliance with the Fujian rebels against the Guomindang in 1933, dogmatically pursued a 'pure proletarian line' in the cities (which had of course been Comintern policy), and employed improper military tactics in the defence of Soviet areas.

In the summer of 1935 the Seventh Comintern Congress adopted the Popular Front policy and by December the CCP had largely conformed to the new line. The party's Wayaobao Conference in that month resolved to seek an All-China united front, which would include the Guomindang provided its military operations against the Red Army ceased. This change does not necessarily imply the total subordination of CCP policy to that of either the Comintern or Wang Ming. Prior to the Seventh Congress, Wang had opposed any form of collaboration with the Guomindang, persuading some to argue that his conversion was 'assisted' by the Comintern in Moscow.[34] In any event, Wang's ability to influence CCP policy had diminished significantly by this time. As indicated earlier, the very qualities which had made him such a useful tool of the Comintern now earnt him the label of untrustworthy 'Red Comprador'. A more likely explanation is that the CCP for its own reasons had slowly edged closer to the position now advocated by the Comintern. The establishment of a second CCP–Guomindang united front in 1937 owed at least as much to anti-Japanese nationalism as it did to the Popular Front policy formulated at the Seventh Congress.[35]

The congress resolution called for the creation of a 'national-revolutionary struggle of the armed people against the imperialist enslavers, in the first place against Japanese imperialism and its Chinese servitors'.[36] From the Comintern perspective, the focal point of the anti-Japanese struggle would be the Chinese Soviets, but an alliance with Chiang had clearly not been ruled out. The Second United Front with the Guomindang was finally achieved after the Xian Incident of December 1936 and in the spring of 1937 the journal *Bolshevik* carried a piece by Wang Ming acceding to the terms which Chiang had set out as preconditions for the establishment of a united front. These included the dissolution of both the Soviet Republic and the Red Army, the integration of the latter under Guomindang control and suspension of the class struggle and communist propaganda.[37] This in itself was not surprising since the USSR had already entered into negotiations with the Guomindang government resulting in a Non-Aggression Treaty in August. Though hailed by *Izvestiia* as entirely in accord with the 'character of Soviet–China relations', the terms of this treaty effectively committed the USSR to a policy of support for the Guomindang government. Thereafter, and until 1945, the central Guomindang government would be the principal beneficiary of Soviet military assistance. The possibility of Soviet aid actually reaching the Red Army during the anti-Japanese struggle which followed was made even more remote by the Soviet–Japanese Declaration of April 1941.

A formal response by the CCP to the ECCI initiative did not take place until September 1937 – two months after the Marco Polo Bridge Incident which marked the outbreak of full-scale war between Japan and China. A National Salvation Conference had been scheduled to meet in the autumn, but planning was interrupted by the Japanese offensive. In mid-August, the CCP proposed national mobilisation, the creation of a National Assembly and the conclusion of mutual assistance pacts with countries opposed to Japanese aggression. On 22 September the CCP published a ten-point manifesto which laid the groundwork for a united front with the Guomindang, and identified Sun Yat-sen's 'Three People's Principles' as 'the paramount need of China today.' In some respects, the manifesto reiterated the contents of Wang's earlier article. In Mao's view, however, the search for an alliance with the Guomindang did not signify that the party had abandoned 'the historically determined principles of national revolution and democratic revolution'. 'Communism', he wrote, 'is to be implemented in a future stage of revolutionary development.'[38] In other words, a united front with the nationalist bourgeoisie, though desirable and even necessary in strategic terms, was transitional. This also confirmed the contents of an earlier address to the party in April 1937 in which Mao argued that the fundamental aims of the CCP remained unchanged. Whatever the outcome of negotiations with the Guomindang, the party would retain independent programmes and policies.

The struggle between Mao and his opponents over this issue came to a head at the Luochuan Conference in August 1937. The Comintern appears to have played no role in resolving the dispute. Recognising the inevitablility of Mao's triumph, and perhaps no longer in a position to affect the outcome, the Comintern subsequently endorsed Mao's denunciation of more conciliatory approaches to the united front. It is equally true to say that by 1937–8 CCP confidence in the Comintern and its plenipotentiaries had largely evaporated. Previous attempts at compliance with the twists and turns in Comintern policy had achieved little but a series of disastrous defeats. Likewise, Stalin's support for Wang and his predecessors had in any event been conditional on unquestioning adherence to Comintern policy. Ideological purity, though, was no substitute for success, particularly as measured in a contemporary context which found the USSR increasingly isolated and in need of allies, however heterodox their views might be. In contrast to the collective failures which had gone before, Mao's pragmatic alternative, dependent though it was on the mobilisation of rural peasant rather than urban worker, offered a period of stability in the East. Mao Zedong, whose peasant instincts had by turn been ignored or criticised by the Comintern, was confirmed by Moscow as new party leader. In recognising Mao's ascendancy, Stalin would also reassure himself that the Comintern had always acknowledged the need to adapt Marxist–Leninist ideology to conditions in China.

Between 1919 and 1939, the basic contours of Comintern policy in China were determined by three factors. First, the assumption that world revolution was a unitary process; secondly, the belief that the Bolshevik model of 'successful' revolution was universally applicable; and, thirdly, the fact that Comintern activities were increasingly subordinated to the shifting foreign policy requirements of the Soviet state. The sense of urgency which characterised Comintern activities in China after 1923 was itself a consequence of the gradual convergence of Soviet diplomatic interests with those of the Comintern. As a result, throughout the 1920s the Comintern alliance with the Guomindang was given precedence over the potential for a CCP sponsored peasant revolution. In applying the Bolshevik concept of revolution to the anti-colonial struggle in China, the Comintern failed to come to terms with the fundamental processes underlying revolutionary developments in China. In contrast to the framework provided by the Russian Revolution, the revolutionary movement in China was determined by the forces of nationalism and anti-colonial struggle, the agrarian question and the peasant movement, and the relationship between the CCP and its ideological antagonist, the Guomindang.

Ironically, it was initial Comintern success in reorganising the Guomindang along democratic centralist lines and constructing a united front with the CCP which exposed the contradictions of Comintern policy. It was a policy flawed from the outset, which presupposed a unilinear alignment of proletarian, peasant and national-bourgeoisie interests. Given the disintegration of the united front in 1927, the failure of Comintern tactics ultimately called into question the basic tenets of Lenin's model of colonial revolution as supplementary to revolution in the metropolitan capitalist states. Despite the overwhelmingly agrarian basis of economic relations in China and the relative weakness of the urban proletariat, the Comintern line remained wedded to the notion of unitary class struggle based largely on the revolutionary pre-eminence of the urban worker. It was not until the collapse of the Jiangxi Soviet and the Long March that the CCP, partially freed from Comintern restraints, was able to pursue successfully a path which combined peasant-based revolution with national liberation.

6. From War to Dissolution, 1939–43

The period August 1939 to June 1943 is universally regarded as marking the apogee of the Comintern's subordination to the dictates of Stalin's foreign policy. The dramatic 'about turn' of September 1939 in the wake of the Nazi–Soviet Pact, the *volte-face* of June 1941 after the German invasion of the USSR and the dissolution of the Comintern in May 1943 are eloquent testimony to this view. Newly discovered documents confirm that Dimitrov and the ECCI Secretariat on many occasions acted in total compliance with Stalin's wishes. This material should in no way be underestimated. However, recent research on the experience of individual parties has suggested a slightly more nuanced understanding. In this interpretation, strict Stalinist discipline and devotion to the Soviet cause co-existed ambivalently with limited autonomous responses to diverse national and local situations. In extremely difficult war-time conditions, the retreat of the Comintern as a fully functioning directing centre created space for a tentative groping towards what became known after 1945 as 'different roads to socialism'. The dichotomy of 'Muscovite centralisation' versus 'national specificity' traced throughout this book is evident, albeit in necessarily veiled guise, right up to the dissolution of the Comintern. Indeed, one of the explanations put forward by the ECCI Presidium for this significant act implied the tension between the 'organisational form' of the Comintern and the 'independence of its sections'.

This final chapter will address these issues by examining two key moments: first, the impact of the Nazi–Soviet Pact and Stalin's 'imperialist' characterisation of the war in the period September 1939 – June 1941; and secondly, the 'death' of the International in the spring of 1943. How far were the responses of the communist parties determined by Moscow fiat? Why did the vast majority of communist leaders and members alike support the stark vicissitudes of Comintern policy at this time? To what extent, if at all, were the parties able to adapt Comintern strategy to suit local conditions? Did the war years mark the complete Stalinisation of the international communist movement?

NAZI–SOVIET PACT AND 'IMPERIALIST' WAR

No single event in the history of the international communist movement has given rise to such fierce polemic as the Nazi–Soviet Non-Aggression Pact. Claudin has objected that 'of all the "turns" made by the Comintern, none was more contrary to the interests of the working-class movement or more prejudicial to the Comintern itself than the one that resulted from the Soviet–German pact of August 1939'.[1] It is not our job here to discuss the diplomatic background to the agreement or to fathom Stalin's motives. Reams have been written on these subjects ever since the ink was dry on Molotov's and von Ribbentrop's signatures. Our task is narrower, but no less fascinating. We aim to evaluate the reactions of the Comintern leaders and the main communist parties to the *volte-face* and to assess the Pact's impact in the light of the immediately preceding experience of the Comintern. The powerful emotions raised by the Nazi–Soviet rapprochement cannot be fully understood without taking on board the centrality of the anti-fascist struggles of the mid-to-late 1930s.

First, however, a narrative account of those dramatic days of late August and September 1939 is in order. On 22 August, the eve of the signing of the Pact, the ECCI Secretariat decided that the prospect of a Soviet–German understanding would 'not exclude the possibility and the necessity of agreement between Britain, France and the USSR'. What is more, it urged communist parties 'to continue even more energetically the struggle against the aggressors, especially German fascism'.[2] Comintern pronouncements, in effect, still recommended the anti-fascist line of the Seventh Congress and still drew a distinction between 'peaceful' bourgeois democratic and 'war-like' fascist regimes. Clearly, the ECCI Secretariat did not foresee all the consequences of the Pact, which suggests that Dimitrov and Manuilsky were not in close contact with Stalin at this crucial time or that the Soviet leaders themselves were engaged in hectic *ad hoc* manoeuvres with little thought for theoretical niceties. On the basis of the resolution of 22 August and subsequent ECCI statements in early September, Soviet historians concluded that 'in the first days of the Second World War . . . the Comintern leaders continued to regard German fascism as the main danger, as the aggressor. . . . In essence it was recognised that the Polish nation was defending its independence in this war.'[3]

This interpretation of the conflict was soon to change drastically, and we now know that Stalin was the architect of this turn. On 5 September Dimitrov wrote to Central Committee secretary Andrei Zhdanov informing him that, given the new international climate, the ECCI was encountering 'exceptional difficulties' in elaborating the tasks of the communist parties. Stalin's 'direct assistance' was required more than ever before. Two days later, on 7 September, Dimitrov had a personal interview with Stalin in the presence of Molotov and Zhdanov, a meeting which was to have fateful repercussions for the international communist movement. According to Dimitrov's diary entries, Stalin characterised the war as a fight between two groups of capitalist states for a re-carving of the world. Thus, 'the division of capitalist countries into fascist and democratic has lost its former sense'. He demanded that the Popular Front slogan be renounced, and, referring to the hapless Poland, he cynically commented that 'the destruction of this state in present conditions would mean one less bourgeois fascist state'. Even more tellingly in light of future developments, Stalin observed: 'Would it be bad if we spread the socialist system to new territories and populations as a result of the crushing of Poland?' Finally, he proposed that the ECCI Presidium should publish theses decisively denouncing the war and its perpetrators.[4]

Stalin's words were incorporated, literally it seems, into the pivotal 'short thesis' issued by the ECCI Secretariat to the communist parties following its meeting on 9 September (document 18). These directives proclaimed that nowhere could the working class or communists lend support to the war. On the contrary, the parties in the belligerent states must actively oppose the unjust war, exposing its imperialist, rather than anti-fascist, essence. More specifically, the thesis insisted that 'the communist parties, particularly in France, Britain, Belgium and the USA, which have taken up positions at variance with this standpoint, must immediately correct their political line'. The parties were also instructed to launch a decisive offensive against the 'treacherous policy of social democracy', a tactic strongly reminiscent of the sectarian Third Period.[5] For largely unexplained reasons, the directives took varying lengths of time to reach their destinations, delays which partly account for the confusion in the ranks of the communist parties.

The historic import of this change of line is clear. The Comintern and its member sections were to eschew open anti-fascist propaganda, draw no ideological distinction between capitalist countries and renounce any support for the belligerent bourgeois governments. As a consequence, the term 'fascist' to describe Germany disappeared from Comintern publications and the special danger of Anglo-French imperialism came to the fore in communist propaganda. Instead of the previous Popular Front tactics of anti-fascist alliance both 'from above' and 'from below', the new policy advocated anti-war unity solely 'from below' in stark opposition to the bourgeoisie and their socialist 'lackeys'. The most fervent adherents of the new line postulated that the war would summon forth revolutionary struggles and transformations. Although this was construed as a return to the Leninist principles of 'revolutionary defeatism', this slogan in fact never became official Comintern policy. The 'turn' did, however, amount to nothing less than a fundamental revision of the anti-fascist strategy employed by the International since 1934–5. It also served to isolate communists from their erstwhile partners in the socialist and trade union movements.

The cynical nature of the Pact and particularly the Comintern's characterisation of the war as 'imperialist' and 'unjust' on both sides raised tentative, yet nagging, uncertainties in the heads of loyal communists. The most audacious even began to question the Soviets' commitment to 'proletarian internationalism'. In some parties bitter internal dissensions were the result, the tense dispute in the British party being a prime example. The caustic recriminations that raged throughout the CPGB hierarchy in September and October 1939 are now well documented thanks to the return of relevant archival material from Moscow in the late 1980s.[6]

The CPGB, like all communist parties, was deeply shaken and surprised by the Nazi–Soviet Pact, but approved it as an astute diplomatic move by the Soviet government. However, the party's Central Committee continued to uphold the need to 'resist fascism whether it comes from abroad or at home'. This 'struggle on two fronts', militarily against Nazi Germany and politically against the Chamberlain government, necessarily entailed support for the war effort of the British people. This was to remain the party's official position until early October, a position profoundly at odds with the new anti-war Comintern line. It is interesting to note that on 14 September Harry Pollitt, the chief exponent of the 'fight on two fronts', actually suppressed a Soviet press telegram in which responsibility for the war was laid at 'the hands of two imperialist groups of powers'. Such action was unprecedented by a leading foreign communist, but did not prevent divisions appearing for the first time in the hitherto united CPGB Political Bureau.

These divisions were rapidly accentuated after the arrival in London of Dave Springhall, the CPGB representative in Moscow. On 25 September he informed the Party Central Committee of the Comintern Secretariat's 'short thesis'. Thereafter, two opposed camps emerged, one around Pollitt, Gallacher and Campbell who strongly resisted the new line, the other around Dutt, Rust and Springhall who equally vehemently backed Moscow's directives. The other members tended to waver. At a vindictive session of the Central Committee on 2–3 October, the battle was played out to its conclusion. Dutt, demanding 'absolute identity on the international line', uttered the remarkable words that 'the duty of a Communist is not to disagree but to accept', while Pollitt's deepest conviction was to 'Smash the fascist bastards once and for all.' He insisted that the main enemy was fascism and the war was essentially a just one. In so doing, he displayed a patriotic inclination, referring to the need 'to look after the national honour of our country' and 'defend the British people'. Coupled with his doubts on the new Comintern line, this bordered on the heretical. With the full authority of Dimitrov and Stalin behind them, Dutt and his companions won over the majority of the Central Committee, the vote being sixteen to two (Pollitt and Campbell) in favour of the 'short thesis'. Despite his subsequent public espousal of the new line and self-criticism, Pollitt was effectively replaced as General Secretary by the 'cold intellectual', Dutt.

Why did British communists go against their instinctive anti-fascism and back the Comintern line? The explanations for this strike at the heart of the communist experience in the inter-war years. For some, like Dutt and Rust, the cogency of the ECCI Secretariat's 'short thesis' was beyond dispute. Dutt, couching his argument in all kinds of theoretical casuistries, fiercely asserted that with the failure of Britain and France to form a Peace Front with the USSR the whole international situation had changed. An historical leap had occurred and, thus, the party line had to accommodate this fact: the war was predatory and unjust and Anglo-French imperialism was its prime motivator. Besides, for Dutt the broader perspectives of the 'centralised world party' necessarily outweighed any narrower national considerations.

Dutt's inner conviction of the correctness of the Comintern line was not readily shared by many other Central Committee members. Several acknowledged that their 'political somersaults' stemmed from a blind faith in the Comintern and the USSR, not from any real empathy with the views expressed in the 'short thesis'. As Maurice Cornforth explained at the crucial October meeting, 'I believe that if one loses anything of that faith in the Soviet Union one is done for as a Communist and Socialist.' Perhaps the most revealing words are those of John Campbell, who many years later reflected: 'If you didn't live through that time you can't understand what the pressures were to convince ourselves that the line of the International and Soviet Union was right, as we had done previously over the Moscow Trials.'[7] Another factor was undoubtedly the need to preserve party unity at this supremely testing moment. The leadership was concerned that the party rank and file should be rallied behind a united Central Committee and not sink into fractious squabbling. In short, deep-seated loyalty to the party and the Comintern combined with a granite-like trust in Stalin and the Soviet Union appear to have been the dominant sentiments in determining British communists' reactions to the change of line.

But according to Kevin Morgan, 'it would be wrong to regard the transition to the new line as simply an exercise in Bolshevik discipline'. For the party as a whole, the overriding feeling was one of confusion. Diverse responses to a complicated and rapidly evolving situation were natural. For many members, the preceding experience of anti-fascist activity in Britain and Spain deeply coloured attitudes and the 'war on two fronts' policy was welcomed as an opportunity to 'have a go at the Nazis', while retaining a hostile stance towards the Chamberlain government. For others, the horrors of the Great War and a hatred of aggressive British imperialism had inculcated a profound pacifism. The anti-war line came as a relief to such communists.[8]

Elsewhere, the Nazi–Soviet Pact and 'short thesis' elicited reactions of varying intensity and perplexity. In all parties, however, the eventual outcome was total identification with the Moscow line. In France, the situation was in many ways even more traumatic than in Britain: 'The disillusionment and confusion of French Communists were profound, and militants left the party in droves. One-third of the party's parliamentary delegation resigned.'[9] The PCF's initial support for a defensive war effort against the 'Nazi aggressors' was overturned under Comintern pressure, and on 21 September the party's Central Committee called for peace, declaring that the war was no longer anti-fascist. The PCF was then outlawed, its press banned, thousands of members, including parliamentary deputies, were arrested and many leaders fled into exile. With this the party was plunged temporarily into organisational disarray, in no position to manoeuvre for an autonomous response to the demands of war. The initial reaction of the small Belgian party was similar to the CPGB's and PCF's: 'If Hitler attacks Belgium, the Communists will stand in the front ranks defending its independence and the freedom of its populace arms in hand.' But, as Spriano notes, the positions adopted by the Western communist parties 'had no real effect and amounted to a catalogue of intentions more than anything else'.[10]

More broadly, the 'turn to the left' inherent in the Comintern's imperialist characterisation of the war has been interpreted as a temporary victory for the 'sectarian' tendencies over the 'democratic' elements in the international communist movement. In this view, the bitter experience of the Spanish Civil War had divided the International between 'revolutionaries', associated with leading figures in the Spanish Party and later Josip Tito, who demanded a more independent and offensive role for the communist parties, and 'moderates' around Togliatti who were committed to a wider definition of the Popular Front and transitional parliamentary paths to socialism. These two tendencies, it is argued, continued to compete over strategy throughout the period 1938–48 with Stalin supporting first one side then the other according to the changing international situation. The point is that Spanish communists, deeply antagonistic towards the 'democratic' powers, found it easier to adapt to the consequences of the Nazi–Soviet Pact than their British and French comrades. Some openly welcomed the left turn.[11] Talk of a blanket imposition by Moscow of the new line is thus something of an over-simplification in that it ignores the existence of indigenous 'leftist' communists for whom the war offered revolutionary opportunities.

Indeed, it is important not to overlook aspects of continuity in Soviet and Comintern policy in explaining the divergent responses of foreign communists. Collective security with Britain and France and the Popular Front experience had far from overcome the deeply ingrained suspicions of 'so-called bourgeois democracy'. Stalin's long-standing and profound mistrust of British intentions towards the USSR struck powerful chords with many rank-and-file communists. It is reasonable to suggest that for these militants the Nazi–Soviet Pact and the invective against Anglo-French imperialism did not represent such a sharp break with past practices. To this extent, the 'about turn' of September–October 1939 was not a universally dislocating event, but reflected the perceptions and convictions of perhaps a substantial minority of party activists.

This said, the story of the Comintern and the Nazi–Soviet Pact is a sordid one. No amount of theoretical sophistry could hide the fact that the Comintern had jumped to the discordant tune of Soviet foreign policy. Stalin had shown his disdain for the international movement and his total control over the Comintern leadership in Moscow. The change of line embodied in the ECCI 'short thesis' emanated not from a careful assessment of the needs of the communist parties, but from Stalin's immediate concern not to antagonise his new German ally and provide Hitler with a pretext to violate the Pact. Hence, in rapidly taming the Comintern's anti-fascist predilections Stalin unwittingly laid bare two hitherto implicit, but vitally important, inter-related processes: first, the interests of the international working class were subordinate to the immediate diplomatic interests of the Soviet Union; and, secondly, the vanguard of that working class, that is the Comintern and communist parties, were ideologically and politically dependent on the Stalinist leadership of the USSR. To this extent, the Comintern had become a mere appendage of the Soviet state. The 'about turn' of September 1939 marked the explicit consummation of the 'Stalinisation' process begun a decade earlier.

Controversies nevertheless remain: did Stalin's undoubted control of the ECCI Secretariat preclude all debate over attitudes to the war? Was this control replicated in the wider relationship between the Comintern and its member sections? That is, to what extent were Moscow's directives actually implemented by the parties on the ground? Indeed, in conditions of war-time dislocation how far was the Comintern able to influence the national parties? To address these issues we must turn to the activities of the Comintern and the main communist parties in the period October 1939–June 1941.

What did the Comintern actually *do* during the war years? The question is not as odd as it may seem. Many aspects of the Comintern war-time experience remain underexplored. For instance, we cannot be sure what issues divided the leaders or how regularly Dimitrov and Manuilsky consorted with Stalin. We do not know exactly how directives and instructions were disseminated from Moscow to the parties. We do know that the war seriously disrupted established lines of communications and that Comintern journals and proclamations were issued with far less frequency. The principal form of contact with the national sections was by radio. The Comintern leadership took great pains to develop secret radio links with European communists and much energy was expended in training the necessary cadres. Nevertheless, coded messages to the occupied countries did not always reach their rightful destination and the sending of couriers was an even riskier business. We also know that the Comintern headquarters were temporarily transferred to Ufa in the Urals in the autumn of 1941 as the *Wehrmacht* reached the gates of Moscow. The main task there was to beam propaganda to Nazi-controlled Europe. Finally, we can say with some certitude that Stalin considered dissolving the Comintern in 1940 and again in 1941, but was dissuaded by the changing international situation. We shall return to this question in the next section of the chapter.

The standard periodisation of Comintern history between autumn 1939 and spring 1943 is divided neatly in two by Operation Barbarossa, the Nazi invasion of the USSR launched on 22 June 1941. The first period was essentially one of stark opposition to the 'imperialist' war, which for parties such as the French bordered on collaboration with the German occupiers;[12] the second represents yet another *volte-face* in Comintern strategy engineered by the anxious Stalinist leadership. Communist indifference to the war now gave way overnight to a life-and-death struggle against the Nazi forces of darkness. Everything was to be sacrificed to aid the Soviet Union. Communists were to give unstinting support to the Allied governments in their anti-fascist efforts. Broad national fronts and resistance movements were the order of the day and all careless talk of a revolutionary socialist outcome to the war was to cease in order to assuage the 'democratic bourgeoisie'. In both phases, it is said, communists unerringly carried out the Kremlin line.

There is a good deal of truth in this interpretation. The evidence does indeed suggest that the Comintern hierarchy in Moscow unquestioningly supported the dictates of Stalin and Molotov. Any scope for internal debate in the ECCI Secretariat on strategic issues appears to have been strictly limited. However, this approach does not do full justice to the complexities of the situation. First, by denying any degree of confusion or vacillation at the top in what was, after all, an extremely fraught and ever-changing international climate, it imposes an artificial order and overall sense of direction beyond the capacities of even the Stalinist leadership. More important, an undifferentiated view 'from above', on the leading actors, tends to overlook the multi-dimensional responses of lower-level communists operating in diverse local contexts and places too much emphasis on a monolithic Bolshevik unity that, probably, rarely existed. Finally, it overestimates the degree of continuing control the Comintern was able to exercise over hard-pressed parties in war-torn Europe.

It cannot be denied, however, that official Comintern directives during the war obediently mirrored the changing priorities of Soviet foreign policy: from September 1939 to 22 June 1941 a policy of neutrality in the 'inter-imperialist' conflict, and thereafter a desperate quest for broad anti-fascist struggles. One example will suffice. After the German–Soviet Boundary and Friendship Treaty signed on 28 September 1939, special stress was placed on the nefarious role of Anglo-French imperialism, bent, so it was absurdly asserted, on continuing the war in disregard of Hitler's peace offers. Naked Nazi aggression was cynically misrepresented and in late October Molotov scoffed at the concept of an 'ideological war', arguing that:

> In Britain, as in France, the partisans of war have declared an ideological war against Germany. . . . No war of this kind would be justifiable today for any reason. Hitlerite ideology, like any other, can be accepted or rejected: this is a matter of personal

political ideas. But anyone can see that an ideology cannot be destroyed by force. It is therefore not only senseless, but downright criminal, to portray this war as a struggle to destroy Hitlerism, under the false banner of a battle for democracy.[13]

Dutifully, the Comintern played the same repugnant tune. In his important article on the war, published in November 1939 after Stalin had personally corrected the original draft, Dimitrov wrote: 'the imperialists of Britain and France have passed over to the offensive, have hurled their peoples into war against Germany . . . it is [they] who now come forward as the most zealous supporters of the continuation and further incitement of war'.[14] Stalin's fear of Germany's intentions, combined with an ideologically constructed deep mistrust of Britain, were the prime determinants of Soviet, and in turn Comintern, policy. The 'imperialist' characterisation of the conflict remained essentially intact throughout 1940 and early 1941.

But, interestingly, Soviet historians have claimed that the rapid collapse of France in the summer of 1940, which sent urgent warning signals to the Kremlin, heralded the first tentative signs of a rethinking of Comintern positions. Comintern leaders now began to raise crucial questions with Stalin regarding communist participation in the emerging anti-Nazi resistance movements in the occupied territories. On 19 June the ECCI Secretariat, after consulting Stalin and Zhdanov, issued a declaration in the name of the PCF stating that: 'We, French communists . . . will fight decisively and fiercely against the enslavement of our nation by foreign imperialists.' Under the impact of this statement, the British party, at least temporarily, adopted a more 'defencist' posture, emphasising the necessity of war production and the arming of the workers in the factories. This painfully slow process of overcoming 'Stalinist dogmas' in 1940-1 has been compared to the similar process of 1933-4.[15]

There may have existed, then, a certain space, albeit highly proscribed, for Dimitrov and Manuilsky to influence the framing of Comintern policy. Stalin did not decide everything in a vacuum. That Dimitrov was not entirely happy with the pro-German orientation of Molotov has been implied by Ernst Fischer, a high-ranking Austrian Comintern propagandist. Already in the spring of 1940 he had asked Dimitrov whether the Comintern could 'responsibly continue to call on the French and British workers to combat the war', and whether the communists should rather become 'a resolute and consistent war party'. Dimitrov replied: 'You must write that down! Be very careful how you phrase it, just making it clear enough for the penny to drop but not so plainly as to raise the alarm in Berlin. I agree with you, but it's a complex situation and something I can't decide off my own bat.'[16]

In the spring of 1940 Dimitrov was evidently unable, or unwilling, to push too hard for a less dogmatic stance, but a further opening came after the German invasion of Yugoslavia and Greece in April 1941. Stalin now agreed that the struggle of the Yugoslavs and Greeks against Nazi aggression was justified. As the theatre of operations moved towards the Soviet sphere of influence, so resistance activities against the Germans could be cautiously sanctioned. Yet the overall conception of the war and the role of the combatants remained unaltered. This changed only on 22 June 1941.

The final theme for discussion is how the Comintern line was actually implemented on the ground by the communist parties most affected by the war. Here brief surveys of the relations between the Comintern and the British and Yugoslav parties will demonstrate the complexities of the situation. Borkenau, whose damning assessment of the role of the CPGB in the war has gained popular currency, wrote that the party 'was transformed, like other Comintern parties, into an outright instrument of the Kremlin . . . and assumed a coherently traitorous attitude to its own country, never again to be abandoned. . . . British communists followed a line, not only of defeatist propaganda but also of defeatist actions.' These actions included the organisation of strikes, the spreading of panic and the casting of doubt on the British government's intentions of fighting fascism. The party's essentially pro-German stance was 'assigned to it by Moscow' and resulted in a serious loss of standing with British workers.[17]

However, as Kevin Morgan has shown in his detailed study of the CPGB in the years 1935–41, the relationship between Moscow and British communists was somewhat more complicated than the Borkenau thesis would permit. While agreeing that 'Soviet professions of eternal friendship with Germany were reflected in the willingness of the CP almost to absolve Hitler of any responsibility for the war', Morgan asserts that Comintern pressure was only one among many factors which informed communist politics before 22 June 1941. He identifies strains of 'economism', 'pacifism' and good old British commonsense in the CPGB's response to Moscow's imperialist conception of the war. Indeed, such attitudes were apparent not only among the rank and file, but also at the leadership level, regardless of Dutt's revolutionary ramblings. Hence, in the factories and mines many communist-unionists were loth to risk the hard won achievements of the Popular Front period by propagating a massively unpopular anti-war campaign. Union activists such as Central Committee member Arthur Horner downplayed the party's official position on the war and continued to campaign for miners' unity and rights. A picture is thus drawn of a fragmented communist party, on the one hand willingly complying with the Comintern's disastrous strictures against the war, often to the point of absurdity, but on the other modifying them to suit local moods and attitudes. Morgan concludes that the failure of British communists even to attempt to politicise economic struggles, as demanded of them by Moscow, 'revealed the huge divide between the extravagant formulae which the Party photocopied [sic] from Comintern pronouncements and the down-to-earth political analysis which guided, if only implicitly, its day-to-day activities'.[18]

The situation in the Balkans was different again. Here the tension was between an essentially sectarian and revolutionary Yugoslav party and a more cautious Comintern leadership concerned with balancing local social transformations with the requirements of Soviet foreign policy. By 1940 the Yugoslav Communist Party (KPJ) had become one of the models held up by the Comintern for emulation, mainly because of its success in combining legal and illegal work to rouse working-class unrest. A sign of Moscow's approbation was the fact that in June of that year the Comintern decided to locate its secret radio transmitter in Zagreb through which it communicated with the parties of central and south-eastern Europe. Partly as a result of this official recognition, Tito, who had been formally appointed party leader in early 1939, grew sufficiently confident to challenge the Comintern's prudent assessment of the prospects for revolutionary change in Yugoslavia.

It is not our intention to bolster the 'Tito myth' by over-estimating the depth and consistency of the disagreement between the KPJ and Moscow. Clearly, Tito's scope for manoeuvre and 'dissent' was circumscribed and on many occasions he was wise enough to compromise and backtrack. In short, we must not view the Soviet–Yugoslav split of 1948 as an inevitable consequence of war-time confrontations. Nevertheless, already by 1939 Tito, in the words of

Geoffrey Swain, 'had got the measure of the Comintern'. He came to realise that on issues relating to international affairs and Soviet security Comintern directives had to be obeyed. Yet he 'chose to ignore instructions on domestic matters with which he fundamentally disagreed'. For instance, in the autumn and winter of 1940–1 Tito and the KPJ leadership insisted on an imminent revolutionary perspective in Yugoslavia based on the slogan of a 'genuine people's government'. The Comintern, however, viewed this as an untimely appeal for the dictatorship of the proletariat which might provoke foreign intervention in an area of vital concern to the USSR. Disregarding Moscow's advice, the Yugoslav communists upheld the offending slogan at their Fifth Party Conference in October 1940 and again in their new year communiqué for 1941. Swain has interpreted this as 'in essence a snub to the Comintern'. Thus, Tito's undoubted internationalist fidelity to the Soviet Union co-existed uneasily with a commitment to policies that he perceived were in the national interests of the Yugoslav people. By 1948 the latter sentiment had gained the upper hand.[19]

DISSOLUTION OF THE COMINTERN

Historical controversy attends the Comintern to the very moment of its dissolution in the spring of 1943. Why was this decision taken, when, and by whom? Was it not ultimate proof of the bankruptcy of the Soviet commitment to world revolution and of the Comintern's complete subordination to Stalin's manipulative *Realpolitik*? Did the dissolution represent the actual organisational break-up of the Comintern and its links with the parties, or did the apparatus and mechanisms of Soviet control remain intact only to re-emerge after the war in the shape of the Communist Information Bureau (Cominform)?

The official ECCI Presidium resolution (document 19) recommending the Comintern's dissolution, dated 15 May 1943, must be placed firmly in its historical context. At that time the tide of war was turning. The Red Army had won the battle for Stalingrad, resistance movements in Nazi-occupied territories were expanding their operations and the Soviet leadership was urgently demanding a second military front in north-western Europe. It was in these conditions that Stalin decided to dissolve the Comintern. The precise sequence of events is still not completely clear, but recent Russian research confirms Stalin's determining voice in the death of the Comintern.

The ECCI resolution of May 1943 came as yet another shock for many communist activists, even those resident in Moscow.[20] Only the Yugoslav party appears to have been cursorily consulted on the proposed dissolution. The resolution offered the following explanations for the disbanding of the Comintern: 'long before the war it became more and more clear that, with the increasing complications in the internal and international relations of the various countries, any sort of international centre would encounter insuperable obstacles in solving the problems facing the movement in each separate country'. Hence, 'the organisational form of uniting the workers chosen by the first congress of the Communist International . . . has even become a drag on the further strengthening of the national working-class parties'. Moreover, the World War had 'sharpened the differences in the situation of the separate countries'. The unstated, but implicit conclusion was that communist parties required greater independence and freedom of manoeuvre to carry out the anti-fascist struggle. Given these developments, and because 'some sections have raised the question of the dissolution of the Communist International', the ECCI Presidium decided to seek ratification from the parties for the disbandment. Within four weeks agreement was forthcoming from thirty-one of the Comintern's sixty-five affiliated sections. With this shaky mandate, the Presidium formally announced that from 10 June 1943 the ECCI, its Presidium and Secretariat and the International Control Commission would be dissolved. A committee including Dimitrov, Manuilsky and Togliatti was formed 'to carry out the actual winding up of the affairs of the organs, apparatus, and property of the Communist International'.[21]

In a rare interview on 28 May, Stalin, inferring that the dissolution was a *fait accompli*, adduced other explanations for the Comintern's demise. He believed the dissolution to be 'perfectly timely' because 'it exposes the lie of the Hitlerites to the effect that "Moscow" allegedly intends to intervene in the life of other nations and to "Bolshevise" them'. Furthermore, 'it exposes the calumny of the adversaries of Communism within the Labour movement to the effect that Communist Parties in various countries are allegedly acting not in the interests of their people but on orders from outside'. Finally, the end of the Comintern 'facilitates the work of patriots of all countries for uniting all freedom-loving peoples into a single international camp for the fight against the menace of world domination by Hitlerism'.[22]

Let us now examine the various Soviet and Western interpretations of the dissolution of the Comintern. The official version, outlined above, remained standard orthodoxy in Soviet historiography until the advent of *glasnost* in the mid-1980s. No mention was made of Stalin's pivotal role in the dissolution, the impetus, it was said, coming from the ECCI Presidium only in the spring of 1943.[23] But according to Soviet accounts of the Gorbachev era, this is a caricature of the true story. As noted above, it has been claimed that 'Stalin had expressed himself generally in favour of the dissolution of the Comintern in April 1941', his motive being 'to preserve friendly relations with Hitlerite Germany'.[24] Operation Barbarossa put paid to these plans. Immediately, on 22 June 1941, Stalin summoned Dimitrov to the Kremlin and told him that the task of the Comintern and communist parties was now to defend the USSR and defeat fascism, not to propagate ideas of socialist revolution.[25] These instructions formed the basis of Comintern activity until May 1943.

Things moved fast in that month. Using Dimitrov's diaries as evidence, Firsov has pieced together the course of events. On 8 May Molotov sent for Dimitrov and Manuilsky and it was decided to draw up a document on the dissolution of the now superfluous International. Three days later Dimitrov despatched a draft resolution to Stalin. That same evening, at a meeting in Stalin's office it was agreed that the ECCI Presidium would consider the draft, propose it to the member sections, request their assent and, once received, the resolution would be published. Stalin apparently was in no great hurry. A gathering on 19 May decided to publish the text in ten days. But on the very next day an agitated General Secretary phoned Dimitrov: 'Is it not possible to put the Presidium's resolution to press today? We should hurry up with publication.' Firsov attributes Stalin's impatience to his foreign policy calculations – on 20 May he met the American diplomat, Joseph Davies, whose official mission was to seek the dissolution of the Comintern. The following day the Russian party Politburo unanimously ratified the resolution and on 22 May it appeared in *Pravda*. Firsov concludes that 'Stalin was the initiator' of the Comintern's demise, motivated not only by the interests of the communist parties, but also by the diplomatic requirements of the USSR to strengthen relations with its Allies in the anti-Hitler coalition.[26] This view of Stalin's determinant role in the Comintern's dissolution has recently been substantiated by Boris Ponomarev, a long-time leading official in the RCP and in 1943 a close collaborator of Dimitrov in the ECCI apparatus.[27]

Aleksandr Vatlin sees other factors at work between 1941 and 1943. He asserts that 'the real dissolution of the centralised Comintern apparatus had already occurred at the start of the Great Patriotic War'. There gradually set in an 'easing of the brakes' whereby communist parties no longer had to look over their shoulders to Moscow for guidance. Vatlin suggests that just as the war had squeezed concessions from the Soviet leadership at home, so 'under threat of destruction from without the Stalinist system was forced to emancipate the communist movement' abroad. But by this time the Comintern scarcely mattered to Stalin. If the final goal remained 'world revolution', the Red Army was better equipped than the Comintern, which in essence had become a mere 'friendship society' uniting the workers of the world with the USSR. Vatlin also makes the interesting point that for Stalin, in his quest for territorial expansion, the ideology of Pan-Slavism may have appeared more attractive than proletarian internationalism. It was surely no coincidence that a Congress of Slavic Peoples opened in Moscow precisely in May 1943. In Vatlin's opinion, the dissolution of the Comintern can be better explained by these considerations than Stalin's concern to appease the British and Americans.[28]

Vatlin's emphasis is somewhat different to that of most Western observers, be they communist or non-communist. A consensus has emerged which sees the dissolution of the International as essentially an expedient of Stalin's foreign policy. Contemporary commentators, communist memoirists and latter-day historians have interpreted it, like Firsov, as Stalin's attempt to improve relations with his Western Allies in the common struggle against Nazi Germany. Perhaps the most striking example of this school of thought is the work of Claudin, the Spanish dissident communist, who has produced what is probably the most critical analysis of the events of May–June 1943. He argues passionately that the immediate cause of the dissolution was Stalin's *raison d'état*, not objective circumstances affecting the Comintern and parties themselves. The decision to disband the Comintern formed an integral part of Stalin's effort to forge a compromise with the Western Allies: the concessionary act of removing the Comintern, that scourge of the bourgeoisie, would provide a concrete demonstration of the Soviet disavowal of the ideology of world revolution, specifically in Western Europe, in return for which the Americans and British would recognise a Soviet 'sphere of influence' in post-war Eastern Europe. This, Claudin says, was the irony of history: 'Born with a programme of world revolution in the near future, it died twenty-five years later postulating a prospect of brotherly collaboration between the Soviet state and the capitalist states.'

But the death of the International signified more than this, according to Claudin. It represented 'an admission of bankruptcy' and 'gave expression . . . to the historical crisis of the Comintern'. By explicitly recognising the incompatibility of a single directing centre with the 'deep differences of the historic paths of development of various countries', the ECCI resolution was in effect admitting that for 'the greater part of the history of the Comintern, the latter was not the type of international organization that the working-class movement needed to have'. The International, with 'its draconic subordination of the periphery to the centre', had become 'ship-wrecked on the fact of nationality', victim of a theoretical, political and organisational crisis that had its origins in Lenin's conception of world revolution 'as a sort of tremendous civil war on the international scale'. The contradiction between the Comintern's ultra-centralised structure and the 'real needs of the working-class movement' lay at the heart of the failure of the International to secure a single revolutionary victory despite the economic crisis of capitalism and the traumas of World War II.[29]

This reading of the dissolution and its historic significance has been expanded upon by Spriano. While acknowledging that the Comintern's demise 'makes sense only in connection with Moscow's general view of the prospects for post-war peaceful co-existence', Spriano insists that the dissolution 'was not just a consequence of Stalin's assumption that it would be useful in negotiations with the Allies'. The ultimate decision was no doubt Stalin's, but perhaps the motivations were more varied than Claudin and others would have it. Spriano suggests there was an 'endogenous' input, arguing that 'the national outlook of each Communist party, the fact that they were virtually buried in patriotic coalitions' was an important factor in the dissolution. Moreover, the death of the Comintern 'widened the freedom of manoeuvre of the various CPs and enhanced their

ability to sink roots in their respective national realities; to some
extent, it also encouraged them to apply independent policies'.[30]

There are indications that the concerns of the national communist
parties may have had some impact in Moscow. Stalin himself at the
RCP Politburo session of 21 May 1943, called to discuss the
proposed disbandment of the Comintern, displayed an awareness of
the parties' need for greater autonomy. In responding to a suggestion
that the headquarters of the Comintern could be moved to London,
the 'boss' said revealingly:

> Experience has shown that even in Marx's time, even in Lenin's
> time, and also nowadays it is impossible to lead the international
> workers' movement from one centre. Especially today, in condi-
> tions of war, when the communist parties of Germany, Italy and
> ot[her] countries are aiming to overthrow their governments and
> carry out the tactics of defeatism, and the communist parties of the
> USSR, England, America and ot[hers], on the contrary, are
> aiming to support their governments in every possible way for the
> speediest destruction of the enemy. We overestimated our strength
> when we created the CI and thought that we would be able to lead
> the movement in all countries. This was our mistake.... The
> proposed step will undoubtedly reinforce the communist parties as
> nat[ional] workers' parties and at the same time will strengthen
> the internationalism of the popular masses, the base of which is
> the Soviet Union.[31]

Regardless of this apparent sensitivity to the strivings for national
autonomy, we must conclude that Stalin's overriding preoccupation
was with Soviet security, and here the Comintern had outlived its
purpose. Indeed, it was a positive hindrance to the successful
prosecution of the war and to Soviet post-war prospects. Crucially,
its dissolution would represent no real weakening of Moscow's
control of the international communist movement, since the prestige
of the USSR and of Stalin, the great war-time Generalissimo, was
now of such mythical proportions that communists worldwide would
adhere to the Soviet line even without a Comintern to enforce it. For
Spriano, the 'real novelty' lies in the fact that 'an even more rigid
and hierarchical relationship' between Moscow and the parties was
the post-war result.[32] In short, Stalinist discipline and orthodoxy
were so deeply entrenched, particularly at the leadership level, that

it would take the cataclysms of 1956, 1968 and 1980–1 for this profound faith to be slowly and painfully undermined.

This brings us conveniently to the final point: was the Comintern really dissolved? Historians have known for many years that despite the formal declaration of June 1943, an organisational framework remained in existence in Moscow. An apparatus as unwieldy as the Comintern's could hardly be removed overnight and it does seem that Dimitrov, Togliatti and other ECCI officials continued to function as supervisors of the major parties. Borkenau, writing in the early 1950s, went too far when he insisted that: 'The Comintern exists to this day.'[33] But a Russian scholar more recently has asserted that 'an acquaintance with the documents supports [the] idea that in reality Comintern was not dismissed'.[34] This argument is based on the creation in 1943 of a special group of Comintern cadres, headed by Dimitrov and attached to the RCP Central Committee apparatus. On the instruction of the Politburo, this sector was formally reorganised in July 1944 into the Department of International Information of the Central Committee. Dimitrov retained his position as chief of the Department. In addition, three 'special institutes' were established soon after the dissolution. These secret institutes, mysteriously numbered 99, 100 and 205, were staffed largely by former Soviet and foreign cadres of the Comintern's Executive Committee, were often located in the same premises and carried out similar organisational and technical activities to those undertaken by ECCI departments.[35]

'Institute 99' worked with German, Italian, Hungarian and Romanian prisoners of war with the aim of training ideologically sound cadres, some of whom were sent home after 1945 at the disposal of the local communist parties. 'Institute 100' appears to have taken over many of the tasks of the ECCI Department of International Communication (OMS), maintaining radio links and other underground lines of contact with European communist parties. Thus, directives and recommendations from Moscow were beamed abroad and information from the parties found its way back to headquarters. 'Institute 205' was created from the Comintern's Press Department and acted as an information filter for the Soviet leaders, keeping them up to date on developments in the communist and working-class movements abroad. It also maintained a vast card index on foreign state and party leaders.[36]

The evidence suggests, then, that although the executive bodies of the Comintern were dissolved in 1943, Stalin was anxious to retain a mechanism of control over the international movement, especially in the soon-to-be liberated countries of Central and Eastern Europe. Indeed, with the elimination of the ECCI and its replacement by organs attached to the RCP Central Committee, it would appear that the lines of Soviet influence became even more direct. The dissolution of the Comintern may have been interpreted by some foreign communists as an emancipating gesture, but it was never intended to inaugurate an era of real autonomy for the communist parties. As the Italian party leader, Luigi Longo, later reflected: 'The CP of the USSR remained the reference point, the "hierarchy" that had to be respected under the new dynamic of the workers' movement. From this point of view, the logic of the Third International survived . . . and determined the behaviour of all, or almost all, the Communist parties.'[37] The road to 'polycentrism' in the international communist movement was to be long and hard.

Legacy of the Comintern

From the perspective of the mid-1990s the legacy of the 'Soviet experiment' seems self-evident: failure. The communist party–state structures in the USSR and Eastern Europe have collapsed in disgrace, the Marxist–Leninist project has imploded and at least one influential observer has declared that the near universal triumph of liberal democracy and the free market signifies the 'End of History'.[1] For some scholars the whole communist enterprise was fundamentally 'wrong' from its very inception in October 1917, 'a world-historical fraud'.[2] Such views are no longer restricted to unsympathetic Western specialists. The tendency to dismiss the last seventy-five years of the Russian past is, understandably, strong among many academics and the general public in the former Soviet Union. The logical corollary is that the legacy of the Communist International, like that of the USSR, is one of failure from beginning to end, an historic mistake of major proportions. To what extent is this an accurate assessment of the Comintern's troubled existence? Is there really nothing positive in the balance sheet of Lenin's 'world party of the revolution'? Indeed, is it possible to evaluate the Comintern dispassionately?

Among Western Comintern experts there is no consensus on this question, for the simple reason that in a pluralistic environment there never was a single orthodox 'line'. Even at the height of the Cold War E. H. Carr and others declined to pay homage to the dominant 'totalitarian paradigm'. But without too much exaggeration we can say that most non- or ex-communist writers have appraised the history of the Comintern in an almost exclusively negative light. A brief selection of quotations will illustrate the point: 'the Comintern as a whole is a failure';[3] 'the Third International failed in its central mission – to revolutionize the world – and in the process became the sorry tool of Stalin's foreign policy';[4] 'the Comintern lost all significance of its own and was merely a channel for the transmission of the Kremlin's orders to other parties'.[5] Claudin's exhaustive account is more benign, but even he concludes that the experience of the International 'demonstrated . . . the failure of the Comintern form, the failure of an external form imposed on the international proletariat and subordinated to the needs of a national state'.[6]

With the consolidation of *glasnost* in the USSR in the late 1980s, a certain convergence of view between East and West became apparent. Soviet historians began to draw similar pejorative conclusions about the 'lessons' of the Comintern in stark contrast to the rosy portraits of the Brezhnevite 'era of stagnation'. In 1989 one author asserted that:

'the substitution of the capitalist world economy by a world system of communism', proclaimed as the ultimate goal of the Comintern, was not, and could not be achieved. This aim, like the conception of world revolution, was based on an underestimation of the potential of capitalism, on an undialectical treatment of its contradictions, and on a revolutionary-romantic overestimation of the strength of social and national liberation movements.[7]

This assessment was a remarkable indictment of the Comintern and a bold critique of the utopian visions of its Bolshevik founders. It is also a fine example of how far Soviet historians had travelled under the impulse of the 'Gorbachev revolution'.

Measured by its original *raison d'être* the Comintern can hardly be considered a success. We would readily agree with its detractors on this score. The twin goals of the creators of the International, announced repeatedly and vociferously, were to smash an historically redundant capitalism by means of a worldwide socialist revolution and to liberate subject colonial peoples from the yoke of imperialism. Both tasks the Comintern had conspicuously failed to achieve by the time of its dissolution in 1943. There *was* no world revolution. Born in Moscow in euphoric days when victory seemed assured, the International was gradually transformed from an idealistic relatively pluralist body of enthusiastic revolutionaries into a stiflingly bureaucratised mouthpiece for the Soviet state. In the absence of revolutions in Central and Western Europe, the concept of proletarian internationalism became identified with devotion to the cause of the USSR and with the duty to protect the first socialist 'motherland'. Faith in the 'revolutionary epoch' could not be foresworn, but few believed in the imminence of world revolution.

The tension felt by foreign communists attempting to balance fealty to Moscow with responsiveness to indigenous realities was invariably resolved in favour of the former. 'Iron discipline', intolerance of political rivals, the ossification and regimentation of Marxist thought and the inability to countenance a differentiated approach to the problems of socialist revolution prohibited the search for alternative strategic and tactical orientations more applicable to European conditions. Those who resisted the process of 'Bolshevisation' and subsequent 'Stalinisation' were demoted, expelled and later purged. By the late 1930s the International had indeed become a pliant instrument of the Stalinist state. The Comintern Executive legitimated the absurdities of 'social fascism'; justified the unjustifiable: the Terror, the mass repression of loyal communists and Stalin's tyranny in the USSR; supported the reprehensible Nazi–Soviet Pact, compelling national parties to abandon the anti-fascist struggle; and offered no resistance to Stalin's dissolution of the organisation. There is precious little glory in these acts.

It should be clear to readers of this volume, however, that the explanations for this transformation are multiple and complex. Stalin's victory in the Soviet power struggles of the 1920s is clearly of enormous significance. As long as the USSR remained the sole outpost of socialism, the Bolsheviks were bound to have the determinant voice in Comintern policy-making and to that extent the consolidation of Stalin's rule was crucial. More than any of his rivals Stalin dismissed the Comintern as an effective revolutionary organisation. It is hard to imagine that Trotsky, Zinoviev or even Bukharin would have been quite as assiduous as he in imposing Soviet state interests on the international movement, in reducing the Comintern to total dependence on the Russian party. What is more, the 'boss' undoubtedly stamped his ugly personality on the International, particularly during and after the years of the Great Terror. This fact cannot be over-emphasised.

But as we have taken pains to show, Stalin could scarcely control the entire international movement from his Kremlin office. Even in the formidably bureaucratised Comintern of the 1930s there was a dynamic interplay between the 'centre' and 'periphery', between the Executive Committee in Moscow and the national sections operating in diverse political and socio-economic conditions. To be sure, scope for local adaptation and initiative had narrowed drastically since 1928–9, but ECCI directives still had to be interpreted and implemented on the ground. Communist party leaders could even exert influence over the central decision-making processes, as in 1934–5 with the shift to the Popular Front. Future research may reveal that those parties that retained their legality and worked within democratic parliamentary structures were more susceptible to the counter-veiling pressures of national political life than those that were persecuted and outlawed and thus far more dependent on the Comintern.

Furthermore, external circumstances beyond the influence of the mightiest despot also played a major role in the degeneration of the Comintern. The demise of its commitment to revolutionary change cannot be understood solely in terms of Stalin's theory of 'socialism in one country' or his 'betrayal' of the original aims of the Bolshevik Revolution. Stalin's Great Russian nationalist predilections, his disdain for foreign communists and his dismissive attitude to the idea of European revolution after the abortive 'German October' of 1923 are all well documented. Yet two things must be remembered. First, for the best part of the inter-war period most communist parties remained weak minority organisations incapable of seriously challenging the established socio-political order. The historic split in the international labour movement, inherent in the 'Twenty-one Conditions', did not result in the expected influx of proletarians into the ranks of the communist parties. Many workers remained committed to reformist social democratic ideals; most had their time cut out finding the next loaf of bread. Secondly, from the early 1920s bourgeois Europe was being 'recast' after the unprecedented strains of the Great War. Capitalist stabilisation in the industrially advanced countries of Europe and North America rendered the situation essentially non-revolutionary. In Italy and large areas of Eastern Europe, right-wing authoritarian regimes mercilessly crushed all manifestations of socialist activity. Hence disciplined consolidation, organisation and preparation inevitably became the watchwords of the communist movement. This state of affairs hardly improved in the 1930s, despite the worst economic depression in the history of

capitalism. Indeed, the position of many communist parties deteriorated as fascist repression became more widespread and ruthless.
With the exceptions of Spain and China, there was little likelihood
of revolutionary convulsions.

The Comintern would have had to adapt to this totally unforeseen
outcome regardless of who donned Lenin's mantle. Trotsky, granted,
was far more alive than Stalin to the revolutionary prospects
attendant upon the 'crisis of capitalism' and may well have adopted
more aggressive tactics in specific circumstances, such as the massive
strike wave in France in 1936 and the Spanish Civil War. It could
further be objected that the cautious policies of the Stalinised
Comintern helped to cement the 'non-revolutionary' situation, not
merely reflect it. The Popular Front tactics spring to mind here. But
even if communists had encouraged social upheaval, what were the
chances of survival in a Europe of aggressive fascists, unreconciled
bourgeois and appeasing democrats? In these cases hard-headed
realism should not be confused with 'Stalinist betrayal'. It seems
fanciful to conclude that Trotsky, when confronted by the rise of a
murderously counter-revolutionary fascism, would have translated
this defensive scenario into a triumph of proletarian revolution under
the auspices of the Comintern. The task of protecting the only
'socialist bastion', the USSR, appeared far more logical and pressing
to foreign communists than stoking the unpredictable fires of revolution 'from below'.

We would argue, however, that gauging the success of the Comintern should not be reduced to the single issue of world revolution.
Such categorical imperatives as total 'success' or outright 'failure' are
not the stuff of historical analysis. The Comintern's legacy is surely
deeply ambiguous. There *are* positive features among the many
negative phenomena. In the 1920s the International nurtured an
impressive range of theoretical responses to the problems of the day:
the threat of fascism, the transition to socialism, the relationship of
the state to society, the attitudes to be adopted towards the social
democrats, petty-bourgeoisie and peasantry. Trotsky, Bukharin and
Gramsci, to name but three, offered diverse solutions to these
problems and inspired various sections of the left well into the 1970s
and 1980s. In short, the communist movement's theoretical legacy is
far richer than the Stalinist straitjacket would suggest. Communists
strove to defend the daily interests of working-class people in local
communities – the 'Little Moscows' of Wales and Scotland, for

example – and encouraged indigenous radical cultural trends. It is also possible that the threat of communism was a not inconsiderable factor in persuading capitalist governments to undertake social reform in the hope of assimilating labour movements. In concrete terms, during the Popular Front era and the years 1941–5, communists were among the most active anti-fascists, fighting in Spain and organising the resistance to Nazism in many occupied territories. The unprincipled zigzags of Soviet and Comintern policy should not blind us to these accomplishments.

After World War II, communism enjoyed a massive expansion as a result of the heroic Soviet war effort, the sinister presence of the Red Army (eastern Germany, Poland and Romania) and the partisan and liberation movements (Yugoslavia, Albania, China, Vietnam). Growth was also discernible in France, Italy and Greece. From the Soviet perspective the Comintern had helped lay the foundations of this expansion by consolidating disciplined communist parties led by an efficient, highly trained and fiercely loyal band of Stalinist cadres capable of administering the new 'People's Democracies'. The creation of the Communist Information Bureau (Cominform) in September 1947 represented an attempt to reincarnate the Comintern, though only the East European parties plus the Italian and French were invited to attend the founding meeting. The Cominform was designed to institutionalise Muscovite control over these parties at a time of increasing Cold War tension. Immediately after its establishment, the Sovietisation of Eastern Europe was stepped up. The Czechoslovak and Hungarian communists seized power and throughout the region one-party political systems and bureaucratic command economies were imposed. Stalinist repression of both 'heretical' communists and non-communists in the years 1949–54 assumed awesome proportions. It appeared that the international communist movement was as monolithic as ever, dominated by the god-like figure of Stalin.

However, even before the 'Great Leader's' death in March 1953 there were ominous signs of disunity in the ranks. The acrimonious Soviet–Yugoslav rift of 1948 was the first cataclysmic shock, revealing as it did that determined nationally inclined communists such as Tito could successfully stand up to the Russian bear. Thereafter, Moscow's 'leading role' wavered. De-Stalinisation set in. The list of challenges to Soviet ideological and political hegemony is long: the Hungarian and Polish crises of 1956, the Sino-Soviet disputes of the early 1960s, the 'Prague Spring' of 1968, the advent of 'Eurocommunism' in the 1970s, the rise of Solidarity in 1980–1 and the final collapse of the Soviet bloc in 1989. The multiple reasons for the demise of Russian control over the international communist movement and for the shift from 'monocentrism' to 'polycentrism' to ultimate decline are the subject of another book. But one factor deserves attention here: the Leninist heritage.

The single constant feature of the international communist movement from the days of the Comintern through to the 1980s was its commitment to the Leninist model of the party. The concepts of 'democratic centralism', the 'vanguard role of the party' and the 'dictatorship of the proletariat' increasingly failed to make sense in a rapidly changing post-war world. And yet communist parties found it almost impossible to reject or even adapt these concepts. They were never able to escape the constraints of the essentially undemocratic Bolshevik party structure, a structure set in stone by the Comintern under Lenin's successors. The universalisation and dogmatisation of Marxist–Leninist principles meant that parties were slow to modernise to keep pace with national and international socio-economic and cultural transformations. The search for more democratic practices, most evident in the Italian party after 1956, was further hindered by old-guard leaders steeped in ideological orthodoxy. Arguably the underlying dilemma was one of self-identity: what would distinguish communists from social democrats if they renounced their commitment to Marxist–Leninist revolutionary goals and forms of organisation? Boundaries and defining characteristics would become blurred, raising the danger that communism could be subsumed within the hegemonic reformist trends. The need to cling on to old self-affirmative certainties remained strong.

Neither were communists able to develop a genuine sense of national identity. Marx and, to a lesser extent, Lenin did not systematically address the issue of nationalism. The fundamental belief that nationalism was a 'building block' of moribund capitalism and therefore destined for the rubbish bin of history predisposed communists to underestimate the attractions of the modern nation-state to large sections of the working classes. Although communist parties were influenced by national traditions and cultures, their internationalist obligations and deeply ingrained loyalty to a foreign country – 'the ties that bind'[8] – greatly impeded their attempts to sink roots into indigenous soils. The label 'agents of Moscow' stuck all too readily. During the Comintern period only Gramsci from his isolated prison cell in Fascist Italy began to theorise a strategy for revolution attuned to Western conditions.

It is in these Marxist–Leninist lacunae that the legacy of the Communist International lies. The early Comintern leaders began a process of universalising a Bolshevik model that was specific to Russian political, social and cultural contexts. This model was then subject to Stalinist hyper-centralisation and bureaucratisation, which, combined with the Terror, inflicted incalculable damage on the socialist ideal. This Stalinist outcome was not historically pre-ordained. Pre-revolutionary Bolshevism was a relatively broad church and there were decisive turning-points – 1923–4, 1928–9 and 1934–5 – when alternative paths could have been taken. But given the collapse of European communism, it is hard to avoid the conclusion that the seeds of the demise of the communist ideal should, ultimately, be sought in the original Leninist prescriptions.

Documents

1. LETTER OF INVITATION TO THE FIRST CONGRESS OF THE COMMUNIST INTERNATIONAL, 24 JANUARY 1919 (*extracts*)

[The letter was signed by Lenin, Trotsky and seven foreign Moscow-based revolutionaries. It aptly summarises the Bolsheviks' conception of proletarian democracy, their profound antipathy towards the socialist 'betrayers' of the working class and the necessity of an 'organizational break' with the Second International. The text identified thirty-nine parties and groups to be represented at the forthcoming congress.]

I. Goals and Tactics

1. The present period is one of the disintegration and collapse of the entire world capitalist system, which will also entail the collapse of European civilization as a whole if capitalism itself, with its insurmountable contradictions, is not eliminated.

2. The task of the proletariat today is to seize state power quickly. Taking state power consists in destroying the bourgeois state apparatus and organizing a new apparatus of proletarian power.

3. ... Not a false, bourgeois democracy – that hypocritical form of rule by the financial oligarchy – with its purely formal equality, but a proletarian democracy, which can realize freedom for the toiling masses; not parliamentarism but self-administration of these

masses through their elected bodies; not capitalist bureaucracy but administrative bodies created by the masses themselves with their real participation in managing the country and in socialist construction. Such must be the form of the proletarian state. Its concrete expression is the power of the soviets. . . .

7. The basic method of struggle is mass actions of the proletariat, up to and including open armed conflict with the state power of capital.

II. Relations with the Socialist Parties

8. The old 'International' split into three basic groups: the open social chauvinists, who, throughout the imperialist war of 1914–18, supported their own bourgeoisies and reduced the working class to the role of executioner of world revolution; the 'center,' whose leading theoretician is Kautsky and which is a conglomerate of eternal vacillators, incapable of following any definite course of action and at times acting as outright traitors; and finally the revolutionary left wing.

9. Toward the social chauvinists who appear everywhere and at the most critical moments take up arms against the proletariat, merciless struggle is the only conceivable response. Toward the 'center,' our tactic is to break away from it the most revolutionary forces, while ruthlessly criticizing and exposing its leaders. At a certain stage of development an organizational separation from the centrists is absolutely necessary. . . .

III. The Question of Organization and the Party's Name

13. The creation of the Third International has been made possible by the formation in different parts of Europe of groups and organizations of cothinkers who stand on a common platform and generally use the same tactical methods. These are first of all the Spartacists in Germany and the Communist parties in many other countries.

14. The congress must propose an overall fighting body, the center of the Communist International, that has permanent relations with the movement and gives it systematic leadership, subordinating the interests of the movement in each country to the common interests of the revolution on an international scale. . . .

15. The congress must take the name 'First Congress of the Communist International,' while the various parties become its sections. . . .

In view of the above, we propose that all fraternal parties and organizations place on the order of the day consideration of the convening of an international Communist congress. . . .

Source: J. Riddell (ed.), *The German Revolution and the Debate on Soviet Power. Documents: 1918-1919. Preparing the Founding Congress* (New York: Pathfinder Press, 1986) pp. 447–52.

2. MANIFESTO OF THE COMMUNIST INTERNATIONAL TO THE PROLETARIAT OF THE ENTIRE WORLD, ADOPTED BY THE FIRST CONGRESS, 6 MARCH 1919
(*extracts*)

[Drawn up by Trotsky, the Manifesto was clearly intended to emphasise the line of continuity between the First and Third Internationals and to stake out the latter's claim to be the legitimate heir of Marx and Engels. Its affirmation of Soviet democracy is noteworthy – a Russian concept suitable for 'honest workers in every country'. Also there is no mention of the leading role of the party.]

Seventy-two years have passed since the Communist Party proclaimed its program to the world in a manifesto written by Karl Marx and Frederick Engels, the proletarian revolution's greatest educators. . . . We Communists, the representatives of the revolutionary proletariat of the different countries of Europe, America, and Asia who have gathered in Soviet Moscow, consider ourselves the heirs and executors of the cause whose program was proclaimed seventy-two years ago. Our task is to generalize the revolutionary experience of the working class, cleanse the movement of the corroding influence of opportunism and social patriotism, and rally the forces of all truly revolutionary parties of the world proletariat. Thus we will facilitate and hasten the victory of the communist revolution in the entire world. . . .

The entire bourgeois world accuses the Communists of destroying freedom and political democracy. That is not true. Once in power, the proletariat does no more than reveal the complete impossibility of applying bourgeois democratic methods. It then creates the conditions and forms of the new and higher workers' democracy. . .

[T]he proletariat must create its own instrument in order above all to weld the working class together and ensure it the opportunity of revolutionary intervention into humanity's future development. That instrument is the workers' councils [Soviets]. . . . This irreplaceable organization of working-class self-rule. . . stands as the proletariat's greatest conquest and most powerful weapon in our time.

In every country where the masses' thinking has awakened, workers', soldiers', and peasants' councils will continue to be built. The main task facing class-conscious, honest workers in every country today is to consolidate the councils, increase their authority, and counterpose them to the bourgeois state apparatus. . . . Through the councils, the working class will take power most surely and easily . . . [and] having taken power, will govern all aspects of economic and cultural life, as it is already doing in Russia. . . .

If the First International foresaw the road that lay ahead and indicated its direction; if the Second International assembled and organized millions of proletarians; then the Third International is the International of open mass action, the International of revolutionary realization, the International of the deed.

Socialist criticism has sufficiently denounced the bourgeois world order. The task of the international Communist party is to overthrow this system and construct in its place the socialist order. . . .

Under the banner of workers' councils and the revolutionary struggle for power and the dictatorship of the proletariat, under the banner of the Third International – workers of the world, unite!

Source: J. Riddell (ed.), *Founding the Communist International. Proceedings and Documents of the First Congress: March 1919* (New York: Pathfinder Press, 1987) pp. 222–32.

3.   THESES ON THE NATIONAL AND COLONIAL QUESTIONS, ADOPTED BY THE SECOND CONGRESS, 28 JULY 1920 (*extracts*)

[After much debate and disagreement, Lenin's original theses were accepted, albeit with important amendments. The key notion is that

communists should lend conditional support to 'revolutionary liberation movements' in the colonies. In effect, this meant cooperating
with national bourgeois-democratic movements, such as Sun Yat-
sen's Guomindang in China.]

... 4. [T]he entire policy of the Communist International on the
national and colonial questions must be based primarily upon uniting
the proletarians and toiling masses of all nations and countries in
common revolutionary struggle to overthrow the landowners and the
bourgeoisie. Only such a unification will guarantee victory over
capitalism, without which it is impossible to abolish national oppression and inequality. ...

11. With respect to the states and nations that have a more
backward, predominantly feudal, patriarchal, or patriarchal-peasant
character, the following points in particular must be kept in mind:

a. All Communist parties must support with deeds the revolutionary liberation movement in these countries. ...

d. It is especially necessary to support the peasant movement in
the backward countries against the landowners and all forms and
vestiges of feudalism. We must particularly strive to give the peasant
movement the most revolutionary character possible, organizing the
peasants and all the exploited into soviets where feasible. ...

e. A resolute struggle is necessary against the attempt to portray
as communist the revolutionary liberation movements in the backward countries that are not truly communist. The Communist
International has the duty to support the revolutionary movements
in the colonies ... only on condition that the components are
gathered in all backward countries for future proletarian parties –
communist in fact and not only in name. ... The Communist
International should arrive at temporary agreements and, yes, even
establish an alliance with the revolutionary movement in the colonies. ...But it cannot merge with this movement. Instead it absolutely must maintain the independent character of the proletarian
movement, even in its embryonic stage. ...

12. ... The class-conscious Communist proletariat of all countries
... has a responsibility to give particular care and attention to the
survivals of national feelings in the long-enslaved countries and
peoples. ... The victory over capitalism cannot be successfully accomplished without the proletariat and with it all working people of

all countries and the nations of the entire world voluntarily coming together in a unified alliance.

Source: J. Riddell (ed.), *Workers of the World and Oppressed Peoples, Unite! Proceedings and Documents of the Second Congress, 1920,* vol. 1 (New York: Pathfinder Press, 1991) pp. 283–90.

4. STATUTES OF THE COMMUNIST INTERNATIONAL, ADOPTED BY THE SECOND CONGRESS, 4 AUGUST 1920
(extracts)

[The Statutes were drafted by Zinoviev to provide the hitherto rather loosely structured Comintern with a more centralised organisational framework. Points 8 and 9 are particularly relevant, presaging Russian dominance of the Executive Committee and binding member sections to the decisions of that body.]

. . . [T]he Communist International adopts as its statutes the following points:

1. The new international working men's association was founded to organize the common activity of the proletarians of different countries who strive for one single goal: overthrowing capitalism and establishing the dictatorship of the proletariat and an international soviet republic to completely abolish classes and realize socialism, the first stage of the communist society. . . .

4. The highest authority of the Communist International is the world congress of all parties and organizations belonging to it. The world congress meets regularly once a year. . . . The world congress shall discuss and decide the most important questions of program and policy affecting the work of the Communist International. . . .

5. The world congress elects the Executive Committee of the Communist International, the governing body of the Communist International between world congresses. The Executive Committee is responsible only to the world congress. . . .

8. The party of the country where, by decision of the world congress, the Executive Committee is located bears the main burden of the Executive Committee's work. The party of that country appoints five representatives with decisive vote to the Executive

Committee. In addition, the ten to thirteen most important Communist parties . . . shall each send one representative with decisive vote to the Executive Committee. Other organizations and parties accepted into the Communist International have the right to appoint one representative apiece with consultative vote to the Executive Committee.

9. The Executive Committee directs all the activities of the Communist International from one congress to the next . . . and issues directives binding on all organizations and parties belonging to the Communist International. The Executive Committee of the Communist International has the authority to demand of its member parties the expulsion of groups or individuals that breach international discipline, as well as the authority to expel from the Communist International any party that contravenes the resolutions of the world congress. . . .

Source: J. Riddell (ed.), *Workers of the World and Oppressed Peoples, Unite! Proceedings and Documents of the Second Congress, 1920,* vol. 2 (New York: Pathfinder Press, 1991) pp. 694–9.

5.   THESES ON THE CONDITIONS FOR ADMISSION TO THE COMMUNIST INTERNATIONAL, ADOPTED BY THE SECOND CONGRESS, 6 AUGUST 1920 (*extracts*)

[Perhaps the most reproduced of all Comintern documents, the 'Twenty-one Conditions' have generated intense historical debate. The Conditions were drafted by Zinoviev ('but, to the last detail, inspired by Lenin') and were intended to create a strictly centralised, highly disciplined and ideologically pure International. For this reason many historians have detected a close affinity between these Leninist prescriptions and the subsequent Stalinist degeneration of the Comintern.]

. . . . The Second Congress of the Communist International establishes the following conditions of membership in the Communist International:

1. *All propaganda* and *agitation* must have a truly communist character and correspond to the program and resolutions of the Communist International. . . .

Periodical and nonperiodical publications as well as all party publishing houses must be completely subordinate to the party executive committee. . . . It is impermissible for the publishing houses to misuse their autonomy to pursue policies that do not correspond entirely to those of the party. . . .

2. Every organization wishing to join the Communist International must consistently and systematically remove reformists and centrists from all positions of any responsibility in the workers' movement . . . and replace them with reliable Communists. . . .

3. In almost every country of Europe and America the class struggle is entering the phase of civil war. Under such conditions the Communists can place no faith in bourgeois legality. . . . In all countries where a state of siege or emergency laws make it impossible for Communists to carry out all their work legally, it is absolutely necessary that legal and illegal activity be combined.

4. The duty to disseminate communist ideas carries with it a special obligation to conduct vigorous and systematic propaganda in the army. . . .

5. Systematic and consistent agitation is necessary in the countryside. The working class cannot be victorious unless it has the support of the rural proletariat and at least a part of the poorest peasants. . . .

6. Every party that wishes to belong to the Communist International is duty-bound to expose not only overt social patriotism but also the duplicity and hypocrisy of social pacifism. . . .

7. Parties wishing to belong to the Communist International are duty-bound to recognize the need for a complete break with reformism and the policies of the Center and must conduct propaganda for this among the broadest layers of the party membership. Without this, no consistent communist policy is possible.

The Communist International demands unconditionally and as an ultimatum that this break be carried out at the earliest possible date. The Communist International cannot accept that notorious opportunists as, for example, Turati, Modigliani, Kautsky. . . . and MacDonald should have the right to consider themselves members of the Communist International. . . .

9. Every party wishing to belong to the Communist International must carry out systematic and persistent activity in the trade unions . . . and other mass workers' organizations. In these organizations it is necessary to organize Communist cells that win the unions . . . to the cause of communism through persistent and unremitting work. . . .

10. Every party that belongs to the Communist International has the obligation to wage a tenacious struggle against the Amsterdam 'International' of Yellow trade unions. It must conduct forceful propaganda among workers organized in unions on the need to break with the Yellow Amsterdam International. . . .

12. Parties belonging to the Communist International must be organized on the basis of the principle of democratic *centralism*. In the present epoch of intensified civil war, the Communist Party will be able to fulfil its duty only if it is organized in the most centralized way possible and governed by iron discipline, and if its central leadership, sustained by the confidence of the party membership, is strong, authoritative, and endowed with the fullest powers.

13. Communist parties of those countries in which the Communists pursue their work legally must from time to time carry out purges (re-registrations) of the party membership in order to systematically cleanse the party of the petty-bourgeois elements that worm their way into it.

14. Every Party that wishes to belong to the Communist International is obligated to render unconditional assistance to every soviet republic struggling against the forces of counterrevolution. . . .

16. All decisions by congresses of the Communist International as well as decisions by its Executive Committee are binding on all parties. . . . The Communist International, working under conditions of most acute civil war, must be organized in a far more centralized way than was the Second International. At the same time, of course, in all their activity the Communist International and its Executive Committee must take into account the diverse conditions under which each party has to struggle and work, adopting universally binding decisions only on questions in which such decisions are possible.

17. Taking all this into consideration, all parties that wish to belong to the Communist International must change their name . . . [to] *Communist* Party of such and such country (Section of the Communist International). . . .

21. Party members who reject on principle the conditions and theses laid down by the Communist International must be expelled from the party. . . .

Source: J. Riddell (ed.), *Workers of the World and Oppressed Peoples, Unite!*, *Proceedings and Documents of the Second Congress, 1920*, vol. 2 (New York: Pathfinder Press, 1991) pp. 765–71.

6. DIRECTIVES ON THE UNITED WORKERS' FRONT, ADOPTED BY THE ECCI, 18 DECEMBER 1921

(extracts)

[An admission of strategic defeat or a temporary tactical retreat? The united front tactics, like NEP in the Soviet Union, have been variously interpreted. The move towards limited co-operation with social democrats marked a reluctant recognition that capitalism was not about to collapse and that communists would have to pursue longer-term goals. It also provoked a storm of controversy in the Comintern.]

1. The international labour movement is passing at present through a peculiar transition stage, which presents both the Communist International as a whole and its individual sections with new and important tactical problems.

The chief characteristics of this stage are: The world economic crisis is growing more acute. Unemployment is increasing. In practically every country international capital has gone over to a systematic offensive against the workers, as shown primarily in the fairly open efforts of the capitalists to reduce wages and to lower the workers' entire standard of life. The bankruptcy of the Versailles peace has become ever more apparent to the broadest strata of the workers. . . .

2. . . . under the influence of the mounting capitalist attack there has awakened among the workers a spontaneous *striving toward unity* which literally cannot be restrained, and which goes hand in hand with a gradual growth in the confidence placed by the broad working masses in the communists.

3. . . . Considerable sections belonging to the old social-democratic parties also are no longer content with the campaign of the social-democrats and centrists against the communist vanguard, and are beginning to demand an understanding with the communists. But at the same time they have *not yet* lost their belief in the reformists, and considerable masses still support the parties of the Second and the Amsterdam Internationals. These working masses do not formulate their plans and aspirations clearly enough, but by and large the new mood can be attributed to the desire

to establish the united front and to attempt to bring about joint action by the parties and unions of the Second and Amsterdam Internationals with the communists against the capitalist attack. To that extent this mood is progressive. In essentials the belief in reformism has been undermined. . . . The communist vanguard can only gain if new sections of workers are convinced by their own experience of the illusory character of reformism and compromise. . . .

7. Confronted by this situation, the ECCI is of the opinion that the slogan of the third world congress of the Communist International 'To the Masses', and the interests of the communist movement generally, require the communist parties and the Communist International as a whole to *support the slogan of the united front of the workers* and to take the initiative in this matter. The tactics of each communist party must of course be worked out concretely in relation to the conditions in each country. . . .

17. The principal conditions which are equally categorical for communist parties in all countries are, in the view of the ECCI. . . . the absolute independence of every communist party which enters into an agreement with the parties of the Second and the Two-and-a-half Internationals, its freedom to put forward its own views and to criticize the opponents of communism. . . .

18. The ECCI considers it useful to remind all brother parties of the experiences of the Russian Bolsheviks, that party which up to now is the only one that has succeeded in winning victory over the bourgeoisie and taking power into its hands. During the fifteen years (1903–1917) which elapsed between the birth of bolshevism and its triumph over the bourgeoisie, it did not cease to wage a tireless struggle against reformism or, what is the same thing, menshevism. But at the same time the Bolsheviks often came to an understanding with the mensheviks during those fifteen years. . . .

22. The united front of the workers means the united front of all workers who want to fight against capitalism, which includes those who still follow the anarchists, syndicalists, etc. . . .

24. The ECCI will follow carefully every practical step taken in the field under discussion. . . .

Source: J. Degras (ed.), *The Communist International, 1919–1943. Documents*, vol. 1 (London: Frank Cass, 1971) pp. 309–16.

7. THESES ON TACTICS, ADOPTED BY THE FIFTH CONGRESS, JULY 1924 (*extracts*)

[In the aftermath of the disastrous 'German October' and the inner-party struggles in the USSR, the decisions of the Fifth Congress heralded a shift to the left. The theses on tactics, written by Zinoviev, emphasised the united front 'from below' and introduced the notion of the 'Bolshevisation' of communist parties.]

VIII. The United Front Tactics

Despite serious opportunist errors and the distortion of united front tactics by the right – which in many cases might have meant the outright ruin of the communist parties – the application of united front tactics between the fourth and fifth congresses was, by and large, of undoubted use to us, and furthered the development of a number of Comintern sections into mass parties. . . .

United front tactics are only a method of agitation and of revolutionary mobilization of the masses over a period. . . .

1. The tactics of the united front *from below* are necessary always and everywhere. . . .

2. Unity *from below* and at the same time negotiations with leaders. This method must frequently be employed in countries where social-democracy is still a significant force. . . .

3. United front only *from above*. This method is categorically rejected by the Communist International.

The tactics of the united front from below are the most important, that is, a united front under communist party leadership covering communist, social-democratic and non-party workers. . . .

United front tactics were and remain a method of revolution, not of peaceful evolution. They are the tactics of a revolutionary strategic manoeuvre of the communist vanguard, surrounded by enemies, in its struggle against the treacherous leaders of counter-revolutionary social-democracy. . . . United front tactics were and are a means of gradually drawing over to our side the social-democratic and the best non-party workers; they should in no circumstances be degraded to the tactics of lowering our ideals to the level of understanding reached by these workers. . . .

In the present period the most important task of the CI is the Bolshevization of its sections. . . . The basic features of a genuine Bolshevik party are:

1. The party must be a real mass party, that is, it must be able, both when legal and illegal, to maintain the closest and strongest contacts with the working masses and express their needs and aspirations.

2. It must be capable of manoeuvre, that is, its tactics should not be sectarian and dogmatic. . . .

3. It must be revolutionary, Marxist in nature, working undeviatingly towards its goal. . . .

4. It must be a centralized party, permitting no fractions, tendencies, or groups; it must be fused in one mould.

5. It must carry out systematic and persistent propaganda and agitation in bourgeois armies.

Bolshevization of the parties means that our sections take over for themselves everything in Russian Bolshevism that has international significance.

Only to the extent that the decisive sections of the CI really become Bolshevik parties will the Comintern become, not in words but in fact, a homogeneous Bolshevik world party permeated with the ideas of Leninism.

Source: J. Degras (ed.), *The Communist International, 1919–1943. Documents*, vol. 2 (London: Frank Cass, 1971) pp. 144–56.

8. THESES ON THE BOLSHEVISATION OF COMMUNIST PARTIES, ADOPTED BY THE FIFTH ECCI PLENUM, APRIL 1925 (*extracts*)

[Officially, the Bolshevisation of the communist parties was not envisaged as a mechanical copying of the Russian model. The theses aimed to strengthen the organisational structures of the parties, particularly in the industrial sphere. However, politically Bolshevisation came to mean the unquestioning acceptance of the policies of the Soviet and Comintern leaderships.]

. . . . The slogan of bolshevization arose in the struggle against the right danger. . . . The correct slogan of the third world congress, 'To the masses', was so wrongly applied in a number of countries over the past two years that there was a real danger of independent communist tactics being replaced by a policy of communist 'coalition' with the counter-revolutionary social-democracy. . . .

Bolshevization of the Comintern sections means studying and applying in practice the experience of the RCP in the three Russian revolutions, and of course the experience of other sections which have serious struggles behind them. . . . But it would be the greatest mistake to transfer Russia's experience mechanically to other countries, a mistake against which Lenin uttered a warning. There is much in the experience of the Russian revolution which Lenin considered of general significance for other countries. . . .

Bolshevization is the application of the general principles of Leninism to the concrete situation of the given country. . . . It is a permanent and continuing process which has only just started in the best European parties of the Comintern. The work still to be done in this direction is tremendous, and will require a number of years to accomplish. . . .

Iron proletarian discipline is one of the most important pre-conditions of bolshevization. Parties which carry on their banner 'Dictatorship of the Proletariat' must realize that there can be no talk of a victorious proletarian dictatorship without iron party discipline, acquired in the course of years and decades.

. . . Bolshevization is incompatible with separatist and federalist tendencies. The world party of Leninism must be strongly fused, not by mechanical discipline, but by unity of will and action. . . .

Source: J. Degras (ed.), *The Communist International, 1919–1943. Documents*, vol. 2 (London: Frank Cass, 1971) pp. 188–200.

9. DECLARATION OF BRITISH DELEGATION ON THE
THESES ON THE COLONIAL QUESTION, SIXTH
CONGRESS, 22 AUGUST 1928 (*extracts*)

[This angry statement exemplifies the nature of 'bureaucratic centralism' evolving in the Comintern in the late 1920s. It is a rare instance of public dissent at a time when conformity and 'iron discipline' were being promoted as a backdrop to the forthcoming struggles against the 'right-wing deviation'.]

... We wish to enter our emphatic protest against the tone and method of polemics introduced by Comrade Kuusinen and certain other comrades, which, if persisted in, can only have the effect of killing healthy discussions. The only possible method of discussion for the Communist International, in our opinion, is to debate questions upon their merits, with full freedom and encouragement for all Sections and individual comrades to state their point of view freely, frankly and fearlessly. The method of hurrying to tie labels on comrades who hold different opinions, before a final decision has been reached, can only result in destroying independent thought and in robbing Comintern discussions of much of their value.

This particularly applies when the comrades who stick labels are those who should be the last to adopt this course. . . . We did not consider this method possible for ourselves, and we demand that the E.C.C.I. shall prevent such methods spreading for the future.

Source: International Press Correspondence, vol. 8 (27 December 1928) pp. 1743–4.

10. THESIS ON THE INTERNATIONAL SITUATION AND THE TASKS OF THE COMMUNIST INTERNATIONAL, ADOPTED BY THE SIXTH CONGRESS, 29 AUGUST 1928
(extracts)

[This extract is a succinct account of the Comintern's periodisation of capitalist development since 1918. The onset of the 'Third Period', it was believed, would mark a radicalisation of the working class, intensify class struggles and signal a further round of imperialist wars and interventions. Note the accent on Soviet achievements.]

1. After the first world imperialist war the international Labour movement passed through a series of historical phases of development, expressing various phases of the general crisis of capitalism.

The *first* period was the period of extremely acute crisis of the capitalist system, and of direct revolutionary action on the part of the proletariat. This period reached its apex of development in 1921, and culminated, on the one hand, with the victory of the U.S.S.R. over the forces of foreign intervention and internal counter-revolution and with the consolidation of the Communist International. On the other hand, it ended with a series of severe defeats for the Western European proletariat and the beginning of the general capitalist offensive. The final link in the chain of events in this period was the defeat of the German proletariat in 1923. This defeat marked the starting point of the *second* period, a period of gradual and partial stabilisation of the capitalist system, of the restoration of capitalist economy, of the development and expansion of the capitalist offensive and of the continuation of the defensive battles fought by the proletarian army weakened by severe defeats. On the other hand, this was a period of rapid restoration in the U.S.S.R., of extremely important successes in the work of building up socialism, and also of the growth of the political influence of the Communist Parties over the broad masses of the proletariat. Finally came the *third* period, which, in the main, is the period in which [the] capitalist economy is exceeding the pre-war level, and in which the economy of the U.S.S.R. is also almost simultaneously exceeding the pre-war level. . . . For the capitalist system this is the period of rapid development of technique and accelerated growth of cartels and trusts, and in which tendencies of development towards State capitalism are observed. At the same time, it is a period of intense development of the contradictions of world capitalism. . . . This third period, in which the contradiction between the growth of the productive forces and the contraction of markets become particularly accentuated, is inevitably giving rise to a fresh series of imperialist wars: among the imperialist States themselves, wars of the imperialist States against the U.S.S.R. . . . and to gigantic class battles.

Source: *Communism and the International Situation* (New York: Workers' Library Publishers, 1929) pp. 5–6.

11. THESES ON THE REVOLUTIONARY MOVEMENT IN COLONIAL AND SEMI-COLONIAL COUNTRIES, ADOPTED BY THE SIXTH CONGRESS, 1 SEPTEMBER 1928 (*extracts*)

[The theses, drawn up by Otto Kuusinen, reflected the emergent 'turn to the left' in the Comintern. After the disasters in China, the leading role of the proletariat and communist parties in the struggle against imperialism was emphasised; the revolutionary role of the 'national bourgeoisie' was attenuated.]

. . . If the communists do not succeed at this stage in shaking the faith of the masses in the bourgeois national-reformist leadership of the national movement, then in the next advance of the revolutionary wave this leadership will represent an enormous danger for the revolution. . . . It is necessary to expose the half-heartedness and vacillation of these leaders in the national struggle, their bargainings and attempts to reach a compromise with British imperialism, their previous capitulations and counter-revolutionary advances, their reactionary resistance to the class demands of the proletariat and peasantry, their empty nationalist phraseology. . . .

The formation of any kind of bloc between the communist party and the national-reformist opposition must be rejected; this does not exclude temporary agreements and the co-ordination of activitites in particular imperialist actions. . . . Of course, in this work the communists must at the same time carry on the most relentless ideological and political struggle against bourgeois nationalism and against the slightest signs of its influence inside the labour movement. . . .

An incorrect understanding of the basic character of the party of the big national bourgeoisie gives rise to the danger of an incorrect appraisal of the character and role of the petty-bourgeois parties. The development of these parties, as a general rule, follows a course from the national-revolutionary to the national-reformist position. Even such movements as Sun Yat-senism in China, [and] Gandhism in India. . . . were originally in their ideology radical petty-bourgeois movements which, however, were later converted by service to the big bourgeoisie into bourgeois national-reformist movements. . . .

It is absolutely essential that the communist parties in these countries should from the very outset demarcate themselves in the most clear-cut fashion, both politically and organizationally, from all petty-bourgeois groups and parties. . . .

The communist parties in the colonial and semi-colonial countries must make every effort to create a cadre of party functionaries from the ranks of the working class itself. . . . [They] must also become genuinely communist parties in their social composition. . . . [they] must give their chief attention to strengthening the party organization in the factories and mines, among transport workers. . . .

Communists must everywhere attempt to give a revolutionary character to the existing peasant movement. . . .

In China, the rising wave of the revolution will once more confront the party with the immediate practical task of preparing for and carrying through armed insurrection as the only way to complete the bourgeois-democratic revolution and overthrow the power of the imperialists, landlords, and national-bourgeoisie – the power of the Kuomintang.

Source: J. Degras (ed.), *The Communist International, 1919–1943. Documents,* vol. 2 (London: Frank Cass, 1971) pp. 530–48.

12. THESES ON THE INTERNATIONAL SITUATION AND THE IMMEDIATE TASKS OF THE COMMUNIST INTERNATIONAL, ADOPTED BY THE TENTH ECCI PLENUM, JULY 1929 *(extracts)*

[This plenum formally expounded the theory of 'social fascism' and branded the 'left' social democrats as a particularly dangerous enemy. With the attack on the Bukharinists already adversely affecting the Comintern, the aim was to identify the 'right-wing opportunists' with the despised social democrats.]

. . . . The correctness of the estimation made by the Sixth Congress of the present third period of post-war capitalism is being ever more obviously demonstrated as a period of the increasing growth of the general crisis of capitalism and of the accelerated accentuation of the fundamental external and internal contradictions of imperialism leading inevitably to imperialist wars, to great class conflicts, to an era of development of a new upward swing of the revolutionary movement in the principal capitalist countries, and to great anti-imperialist revolutions in colonial countries.

1. . . . All these preparations for new imperialist wars are being carried out with the active co-operation and full participation of the 'Socialist Parties,' the 'Left' wing of which play the most despicable part of screening these preparations with pacifist phrases.

3. . . . In this situation of growing imperialist contradictions and sharpening of the class struggle, Fascism becomes more and more

the dominant method of bourgeois rule. In countries where there are strong Social-Democratic parties, Fascism assumes the particular form of Social-Fascism, which to an ever-increasing extent serves the bourgeoisie as an instrument for the paralysing of the activity of the masses in the struggle against the regime of Fascist dictatorship.

5. . . . The Plenum of the E.C.C.I. imposes on all Sections of the Communist International the obligation to intensify their fight against international Social Democracy, which is the chief support of capitalism.

The Plenum of the E.C.C.I. instructs all Sections of the C.I. to pay special attention to an energetic struggle against the 'Left' wing of Social Democracy which retards the process of the disintegration of Social Democracy by creating the illusion that it – the 'Left' wing – represents an opposition to the policy of the leading Social-Demo-cratic bodies, whereas as a matter of fact, it whole-heartedly supports the policy of Social-Fascism.

8. . . . In this connection the central task of the Comintern in the sphere of inner-Party policy has become the fight against opportunism which is a channel for bourgeois influences among the working class and for Social-Democratic tendencies in the Communist movement.

9. . . . The lamentations of the Right-wing renegades about the alleged disintegration of the Comintern . . . merely prove how ur-gently necessary it was to purge the ranks of the Communist movement in order to prevent the disintegrating work of the oppor-tunist elements and secure the genuine Bolshevisation of the Com-munist Parties. . . .

Source: The World Situation & Economic Struggle. Theses of the Tenth Plenum E.C.C.I. (London: CPGB, n.d.) pp. 3–21.

13. THESES ON THE TASKS OF THE SECTIONS OF THE COMMUNIST INTERNATIONAL, ADOPTED BY THE ELEVENTH ECCI PLENUM, APRIL 1931 *(extracts)*

[The remarkable aspect of this extract is the forthright rejection of social democracy's distinction between parliamentary democracy and fascism. During the 'Third Period' the ECCI regarded both as forms of the 'dictatorship of the bourgeoisie' – one 'masked', the other 'open' – with no essential differences between the two.]

... 1. The further intensification of all the fundamental contradictions of capitalism as a result of the economic crisis which affects primarily the weakest links of the capitalist system, the gathering discontent of the broad masses of the people, the spread of Communism and the growing prestige of the land of the Proletarian Dictatorship, give rise, on the one hand, to the ever more open utilisation by the bourgeoisie of the apparatus of violence of its dictatorship, and, on the other hand, to the growth of the revolutionary upsurge and to the increase in a number of countries of the pre-requisites of a revolutionary crisis.

Growing organically out of so-called bourgeois democracy – which is the masked form of the dictatorship of the bourgeoisie – Fascism, which is the naked form of the bourgeois dictatorship, sharpens all the methods of suppressing and enslaving the toilers peculiar to the capitalist system. ...

The recent growth of Fascism has been possible only because of the support given to it by international Social Democracy throughout the whole post-war period of the dictatorship of the bourgeoisie, irrespective of the form the latter has assumed. By drawing a contrast between the 'democratic' forms of the dictatorship of the bourgeoisie and Fascism, Social Democracy lulls the vigilance of the masses in the fight against the growing political reaction and Fascism, conceals the counter-revolutionary character of bourgeois democracy as a form of the dictatorship of the bourgeoisie, and thus serves as an active factor and channel for the fascisation of the capitalist State.

The successful struggle against Fascism demands that the Communist Parties shall mobilise the masses on the basis of a united front from below against all forms of the bourgeois dictatorship, against all the reactionary measures it adopts to pave the way to the open Fascist dictatorship. The struggle demands the speedy and determined correction of the mistakes that have been committed which, in the main, consist of drawing, after the Liberal fashion, a contrast between Fascism and bourgeois democracy and between the parliamentary form of the dictatorship of the bourgeoisie and its open Fascist forms. These mistakes represent a reflection of the Social Democratic influences in the Communist ranks. ...

Source: XIth Plenum of the Executive Committee of the Communist International:

Theses, Resolutions and Decisions (New York: Workers' Library Publishers, n.d.) pp. 8–9.

14. LETTER FROM G. DIMITROV TO THE POLITBURO OF THE RCP, 1 JULY 1934 (*extracts*)

[Dimitrov's letter is a pivotal reassessment of the Comintern's 'social fascist' line and united front 'from below' tactics. In casting doubt on the applicability of these 'Third Period' shibboleths, he cautiously opened the way to an approach 'from above' to the socialist leaders, and ultimately to the Popular Front.]

I. On Social Democracy

1. Is the blanket characterisation of Social Democracy as Social Fascism correct? Through this position we have often blocked the way for ourselves towards Social Democratic workers.
2. Is it correct to treat Social Democracy everywhere and under all conditions as the main social support of the bourgeoisie?
3. Is it correct to treat all left S-D groupings under all conditions as the main danger?
4. Is the blanket treatment of all the leading cadres of S-D parties and reformist trade unions as conscious traitors of the working class correct? Can one expect that together with S-D workers in the process of struggle, quite a number of the currently responsible functionaries of S-D parties and reformist trade unions will change over to the revolutionary path? . . .
6. The question of uniting the revolutionary and reformist trade unions without putting forward in the form of a preliminary condition the recognition of the Communist party's hegemony.

II. On the United Front

1. In connection with the changed situation, the need to change also our tactic of the united front.
2. The need to do away with the position that the united front can only be brought about from below, and to cease viewing every communication to the S-D leadership simultaneously as opportunism.

3. The need to develop the fighting initiative of the masses, without petty tutoring by the Communist party concerning the organs of the united front. . . .

4. The need to change at root our approach to S-D and non-party workers through all our mass work, agitation and propaganda. . . .

III. On the Leadership of the Comintern

The need to change the methods of work and leadership of the Comintern, taking into account that it is impossible operationally, to lead from Moscow on all questions, all 65 sections of the Comintern, situated under the most varied conditions. . . .

The need to concentrate attention on the general political leadership of the Communist movement, on aid to Communist parties on basic policy and tactical questions, on the creation of a tough Bolshevik leadership of Communist parties on the spot and the strengthening of party workers at the cost of cutting back on the cumbersome bureaucratic apparatus of the executive committee of the Comintern.

The need to further development of Bolshevik self-criticism; as a consequence of the fear of which, big political problems still remain unsolved. . . .

A change in the methods of leadership and work of the Comintern is impossible to achieve without a partial revitalisation of the Comintern's cadres.

Especially necessary is close contact between the leadership of the Comintern and the Politburo of the All-Union Communist party (Bolsheviks).

Source: J. Haslam, 'The Comintern and the Origins of the Popular Front 1934–1935', *Historical Journal*, vol. 22 (1979) pp. 682–4. [In Russian in *Voprosy istorii KPSS*, no. 7 (1965) pp. 83–5.]

15. G. DIMITROV'S REPORT, 'THE FASCIST OFFENSIVE AND THE TASKS OF THE COMMUNIST INTERNATIONAL', SEVENTH CONGRESS, 2 AUGUST 1935 (*extracts*)

[Dimitrov's reflections on the role and nature of social democracy, though innovative, were necessarily limited. These extracts illustrate the strict conditions placed on 'organic unity' with the socialist parties, conditions which effectively precluded any possibility of unification.]

. . . Comrades, the development of the united front of joint struggle of the Communist and Social-Democratic workers against fascism and the offensive of capital . . . brings to the fore the question of *political unity, of a single political mass party of the working class*. The Social-Democratic workers are becoming more and more convinced by experience that the struggle against the class enemy demands unity of political leadership, in as much as *duality in leadership* impedes the further development and reinforcement of the joint struggle of the working class.

. . . The cause of amalgamating the forces of the working class in a single revolutionary proletarian party, at the time when the international labour movement is entering the period of closing the split in its ranks, is *our cause*, is the cause of the Communist International.

But . . . the achievement of political unity is possible only on the basis of a number of definite conditions involving principles.

This unification is possible only:

First, on condition of *complete independence from the bourgeoisie and complete rupture of the bloc of Social-Democracy with the bourgeoisie*;

Second, on condition that unity of action be first brought about;

Third, on condition that the necessity of the *revolutionary overthrow of the rule of the bourgeoisie* and the establishment of the *dictatorship of the proletariat in the form of Soviets* be recognised;

Fourth, on condition that support of one's own bourgeoisie *in imperialist war* be rejected;

Fifth, on condition that the party be constructed on the basis of *democratic centralism*, which ensures unity of will and action, and which has been tested by *the experience of the Russian Bolsheviks*.

. . . Being of the opinion that unity of action is a pressing necessity and the truest road to the establishment of the political unity of the proletariat as well, we declare that the Communist International and its Sections are ready to enter into negotiations with the Second International and its Sections for the establishment of unity of the working class in the struggle against the offensive of capital, against fascism and the menace of imperialist war.

Source: G. Dimitrov, *The Working Class against Fascism* (London: Martin Lawrence, 1935) pp. 78–81.

16. RESOLUTION ON FASCISM, WORKING-CLASS UNITY, AND THE TASKS OF THE COMINTERN, ADOPTED BY THE SEVENTH CONGRESS, 20 AUGUST 1935 *(extracts)*

[The Seventh Congress formally ratified the Popular Front as an extension of the united workers' front. The stated aim was to protect 'all toilers' from the threat of fascism and war. But did it also represent a strategic reassessment of the transition to socialism via bourgeois parliamentary forms?]

II. The United Front of the Working Class against Fascism

In face of the towering menace of fascism to the working class and all the gains it has made, to all toilers and their elementary rights, to the peace and liberty of the peoples, the Seventh Congress of the Communist International declares that at the present historic stage it is the main and immediate task of the international labour movement to establish the united fighting front of the working class. For a successful struggle against the offensive of capital, against the reactionary measures of the bourgeoisie, against fascism, the bitterest enemy of all the toilers, who, without distinction of political views, have been deprived of all rights and liberties, it is imperative that unity of action be established between all sections of the working class, irrespective of what organization they belong to, even before the majority of the working class unites on a common fighting platform for the overthrow of capitalism and the victory of the proletarian revolution. But it is precisely for this very reason that this task makes it the duty of the communist parties to take into consideration the changed circumstances and to apply the united front tactics in a new manner, by seeking to reach agreements with the organizations of the toilers of various political trends for joint action on a factory, local, district, national and international scale.

With this as its point of departure, the Seventh Congress of the Communist International enjoins the communist parties to be guided by the following instructions when carrying out the united front tactics:

1. The defence of the immediate economic and political interests of the working class, the defence of the latter against fascism, must be the starting point and form the main content of the workers' united front in all capitalist countries. . . .

5. Joint action with the social-democratic parties and organizations not only does not preclude, but, on the contrary, renders still more necessary the serious and well-founded criticism of reformism, of social-democracy as the ideology and practice of class collaboration with the bourgeoisie. . . .

7. In striving to unite, under the leadership of the proletariat, the struggle of the toiling peasants, the urban petty bourgeoisie and the toiling masses of the oppressed nationalities, the communists must seek to bring about the establishment of a wide anti-fascist people's [popular] front on the basis of the proletarian united front, supporting all those specific demands of these sections of the toilers which are in line with the fundamental interests of the proletariat. . . .

8. In the circumstances of a political crisis . . . the communists must advance fundamental revolutionary slogans. . . . If with such an upsurge of the mass movement it will prove possible, and necessary in the interests of the proletariat, to create a proletarian united front government, or an anti-fascist people's front government . . . the communist party must see to it that such a government is formed.

. . . The participation of the communists in a united front government will be decided separately in each particular case, as the concrete situation may warrant.

Source: J. Degras (ed.), *The Communist International, 1919–1943. Documents*, vol. 3 (London: Frank Cass, 1971) pp. 359–70.

17. LETTER FROM E. VARGA TO J. V. STALIN, 28 MARCH 1938 (*extracts*)

[In this brave letter Varga provides a fascinating insight into the torments of foreign communists and Comintern officials during the Great Terror. While perforce declaring his orthodoxy, Varga demonstrates the disastrous effects of mass arrests at a time of mounting fascist threat. The letter also proves that Stalin was made fully aware of the consequences of his murderous actions.]

Strictly Confidential

To: Comrade Stalin

Copies to: Cdes Dimitrov, Yezhov

THE CADRES PROBLEM IN ILLEGAL PARTIES AND THE MASS ARRESTS

Dear Comrade,

. . . One-sided, narrow nationalism is increasingly gaining ground at the expense of the correct combination of Soviet patriotism and internationalism. Hatred for foreigners is rampant. Foreigners are indiscriminately considered spies; foreign children are called fascists at school. . . .

This growing xenophobia has been triggered off by the mass arrests of foreigners. . . .

To avoid any misunderstanding, I would like to stress that in the present situation I think it absolutely correct to arrest two innocents rather than let one spy get away! . . . But I am concerned primarily about one political issue: the process of the rapid depletion and demoralisation of those cadres of the communist parties in fascist countries, who would have a very prominent role to play in the forthcoming war!

This process is moving along the following lines:

. . . b) an increasing number of former cadres are being arrested in the Soviet Union;

c) the cadres living freely in the Soviet Union are profoundly demoralised and confused by the mass arrests. This demoralisation is enveloping the majority of Comintern workers and is spreading even to individual members of the ECCI Secretariat.

The main cause of this demoralisation is a sense of utter helplessness with regard to arrests of political émigrés. In some cases scoundrels are exploiting the general mistrust of foreigners and the ignorance of the history of fraternal communist parties on the part of many new NKVD officers and making false denunciations in order to have honest revolutionaries from underground parties arrested. . . . Since people do not know what evidence is used to arrest and sentence their countrymen, a dangerous atmosphere of panic is growing among foreigners in the Soviet Union. . . . Many foreigners gather up their belongings every evening in expectation of arrest. Many are half mad and incapable of work as a result of constant fear. . . .

Clearly, people in such a mood cannot be cadres in the grim trials of the forthcoming war. . . .

What can be done to stop the depletion and demoralisation of the underground party cadres?

Of course, sparing conscious enemies is out of the question! But the following steps could be taken:

1) A thorough and unhurried examination of all the cases involving the arrests of foreigners who could be useful cadres for underground parties. The Comintern and those few foreign comrades who are absolutely above suspicion ought to be given an opportunity to help the NKVD in this work by providing explanations.

2) Somehow informing foreign comrades in the Soviet Union and in fascist countries about this examination in order to counter pessimism and panic. . . .

Evgeny Varga
Moscow, 28 March 1938

Source: Printed in 'Muzhestvo protiv bezzakoniia', *Problemy mira i sotsializma*, no. 7 (1989) pp. 89–91. [English translation in *World Marxist Review*, no. 7 (1989) pp. 83–4.]

18. THE ECCI SECRETARIAT 'SHORT THESIS' ON THE SECOND WORLD WAR, 9 SEPTEMBER 1939 (AS DICTATED BY PALME DUTT TO CPGB CENTRAL COMMITTEE, 2 OCTOBER 1939)

[This 'thesis', taken literally from the mouth of 'The Great Leader', was not published until the advent of *glasnost*. The ECCI Secretariat reversed the CPGB's policy of the 'fight on two fronts' and imposed a blanket characterisation of the war as 'imperialist' and 'unjust'. The new line caused an unprecedented split in the party leadership and isolated British communists in the labour movement.]

The present war is an imperialist and unjust war for which the bourgeoisie of all the belligerent states bear equal responsibility. In no country can the working class or the Communist Parties support the war. The bourgeoisie is not conducting war against fascism as Chamberlain and the leaders of the Labour Party pretend. War is carried on between two groups of imperialist countries for world domination. The international working class may under no conditions defend Fascist Poland which has refused the aid of the Soviet Union and repressed other nationalities. The division of States into fascist and democratic states has now lost its former sense.

From this point of view the tactics must be changed. The tactic of the Communist Parties in the belligerent countries in this first stage of the war is to operate against the war, to unmask its imperialist character. The Communist Parties have fought against the supporters of Munich because these have prevented a real anti-fascist front, with the participation of the Soviet Union, in order to be able to carry on a robber war. The war has fundamentally changed the situation. Where Communist Parties have representatives in Parliament these must vote against the war credits. It must be made clear to the masses that war will bring them nothing but new troubles and misery.

In the neutral states we must unmask the governments which maintain the neutrality of their own countries but support the war of other countries and operate on their profits, as for example the Government of the United States has done with regard to the war between Japan and China. The Communist Parties have to take on everywhere the offensive struggle against the treacherous policy of Social Democracy. The Communist Parties which acted contrary to these tactics must now immediately correct their policy.

Source: F. King and G. Matthews (eds), *About Turn. The British Communist Party and the Second World War* (London: Lawrence & Wishart, 1990) pp. 69–70.

19. RESOLUTION OF THE ECCI PRESIDIUM RECOMMENDING THE DISSOLUTION OF THE COMMUNIST INTERNATIONAL, 15 MAY 1943
(*extracts*)

[The final act. Cunningly avoiding the original offensive revolutionary mission of the Comintern, the resolution fails to mention the
decisive factors behind the dissolution. Yet the idea of a centralised
organisation out of step with national developments and specificities
is curiously apt. The demise of the Comintern did not, however, end
Stalin's firm grip over the communist movement.]

The historic role of the Communist International, which was
founded in 1919 as a result of the political union of the great
majority of old, pre-war working-class parties, consisted in upholding
the principles of Marxism from vulgarization and distortion by the
opportunist elements in the working-class movement, in helping to
promote the consolidation in a number of countries of the vanguard
of the foremost workers in real working-class parties, and in helping
them to mobilize the workers for the defence of their economic and
political interests and for the struggle against fascism and the war the
latter was preparing and for support of the Soviet Union as the chief
bulwark against fascism. . . .

But long before the war it became more and more clear that, with
the increasing complications in the internal and international relations of the various countries, any sort of international centre would
encounter insuperable obstacles in solving the problems facing the
movement in each separate country. The deep differences of the
historic paths of development of various countries, the differences in
their character and even contradictions in their social orders, the
differences in the level and tempo of their economic and political
development, the differences, finally, in the degree of consciousness
and organization of the workers, conditioned the different problems
facing the working class of the various countries.

The whole development of events in the last quarter of a century,
and the experience accumulated by the Communist International
convincingly showed that the organizational form of uniting the
workers chosen by the first congress of the Communist International

answered the conditions of the first stages of the working-class movement but has been outgrown by the growth of this movement and by the complications of its problems in separate countries, and has even become a drag on the further strengthening of the national working-class parties.

The World War that the Hitlerites have let loose has still further sharpened the differences in the situation of the separate countries, and has placed a sharp dividing line between those countries which fell under the Hitlerite tyranny and those freedom-loving peoples who have united in a powerful anti-Hitlerite coalition. . . .

Already the seventh congress of the Communist International . . . emphasized the necessity for the Executive Committee of the Communist International, in deciding all questions of the working-class movement arising from the concrete conditions and peculiarities of each country, to make a rule of avoiding interference in the internal organizational affairs of the communist parties. . . .

Guided by the judgment of the founders of Marxism–Leninism, communists have never been supporters of the conservation of organizational forms that have outlived themselves. . . .

In consideration of the above, and taking into account the growth and political maturity of the communist parties and their leading cadres in the separate countries, and also having in view the fact that during the present war some sections have raised the question of the dissolution of the Communist International as the directing centre of the international working-class movement,

The Presidium of the Executive Committee of the Communist International . . . puts forward the following proposal for ratification by the sections of the Communist International.

The Communist International . . . is to be dissolved, thus freeing the sections . . . from their obligations arising from the statutes and resolutions of the congresses of the Communist International. . . .

[Signed by twelve members of the Presidium of the Executive Committee of the Communist International and five representatives of communist parties.]

Source: J. Degras (ed.), *The Communist International, 1919–1943. Documents*, vol. 3 (London: Frank Cass, 1971) pp. 477–9. [Originally in *World News and Views*, vol. 23 (29 May 1943) pp. 169–70.]

Notes

INTRODUCTION

1. M. M. Drachkovitch and B. Lazitch, 'The Communist International', in M. M. Drachkovitch (ed.), *The Revolutionary Internationals, 1864–1943* (Stanford, 1966) pp. 196–7. Access to the Comintern Archive in the Russian Centre for the Preservation and Study of Contemporary Historical Documents (hereafter RCPSCHD – the former Central Party Archive) has improved markedly since the late 1980s. The holdings of the Comintern Archive are vast – some 237 000 files, which according to one analyst represents approximately 55 million pages.

2. A major new multi-volume series is being published by Yale University Press entitled *Documents of Communism*, the first volume of which is H. Klehr, J. E. Haynes and F. I. Firsov (eds), *The Secret World of American Communism* (New Haven and London, 1995).

3. For more detailed documentary texts, see J. Degras (ed.), *The Communist International, 1919–1943: Documents*, 3 vols (London, 1971); J. Riddell (ed.), *The Communist International in Lenin's Time*, 5 vols (New York, 1984–93); A. Adler (ed.), *Theses, Resolutions and Manifestos of the First Four Congresses of the Third International* (London, 1983); H. Gruber (ed.), *International Communism in the Era of Lenin. A Documentary History* (New York, 1972); and H. Gruber (ed.), *Soviet Russia Masters the Comintern: International Communism in the Era of Stalin's Ascendancy* (New York, 1974).

4. K. Marx and F. Engels, *The Communist Manifesto* (Harmondsworth, 1973) pp. 92, 102.

5. For a discussion of these problems, see E. J. Hobsbawm, 'Working-class Internationalism', in F. van Holthoon and M. van der Linden (eds), *Internationalism in the Labour Movement, 1830–1940*, vol. 1 (Leiden, 1988) pp. 3–16.

6. V. I. Lenin, *Collected Works*, 4th edn, 45 vols (Moscow, 1960–70) vol. 21, pp. 15–19, 40.

7. E. Hobsbawm, *Age of Extremes: The Short Twentieth Century, 1914–1991* (London, 1994) pp. 54–84.

8. A. Dallin, 'Domestic Factors Influencing Soviet Foreign Policy', in M. Confino and S. Shamir (eds), *The U.S.S.R. and the Middle East* (Jerusalem, 1973) p. 38.

9. M. van der Linden, 'Comintern Research Problems: A Note on the Period 1919–1933', unpublished manuscript, p. 1.

10. F. Borkenau, *World Communism: A History of the Communist International*, reprint edn (Ann Arbor, 1971). This text was first published in 1938.

11. L. Trotsky, *The First Five Years of the Communist International*, 2 vols (New York, 1972); *The Third International after Lenin* (New York, 1970); *The Struggle against Fascism in Germany* (New York, 1971); and *The Revolution Betrayed* (New York, 1970).

12. I. Deutscher, *The Prophet Unarmed. Trotsky: 1921–1929* (Oxford and London, 1970); *The Prophet Outcast. Trotsky: 1929–1940* (Oxford and London, 1963); *Stalin: A Political Biography*, rev. edn (Harmondsworth, 1976); and 'The Comintern Betrayed', in F. Mount (ed.), *Communism* (London, 1992) pp. 107–14.

13. D. Hallas, *The Comintern* (London, 1985).

14. E. H. Carr, *The Twilight of Comintern, 1930–1935* (London, 1982); and *The Comintern and the Spanish Civil War* (London, 1984).

15. F. Claudin, *The Communist Movement: From Comintern to Cominform* (Harmondsworth, 1975).

16. A. I. Sobolev *et al.*, *Outline History of the Communist International* (Moscow, 1971).

1. COMINTERN IN THE ERA OF LENIN, 1919–23

1. R. Service, *Lenin: A Political Life*, vol. 1 (Basingstoke, 1985) p. 8.

2. Lenin, *Collected Works*, vol. 5, pp. 375, 383–5.

3. Cited in I. Deutscher, *The Prophet Armed. Trotsky: 1879–1921* (Oxford, 1954) p. 90.

4. M. Waller, *Democratic Centralism: An Historical Commentary* (Manchester, 1981) pp. 21–30.

5. The following two paragraphs are based on N. Harding, *Lenin's Political Thought*, vol. 2 (London, 1981) pp. 16–70.

6. Cited in R. C. Nation, *War on War: Lenin, the Zimmerwald Left, and the Origins of Communist Internationalism* (Durham and London, 1989) p. 78.

7. For an iconoclastic interpretation of the impact of Kautsky's Marxism on Lenin, see M. Donald, *Marxism and Revolution: Karl Kautsky and the Russian Marxists 1900–1924* (New Haven and London, 1993).

8. K. Kautsky, *The Dictatorship of the Proletariat* (Manchester, n. d.) pp. 1, 4, 6, 12, 45, 91, 148.

9. Lenin, *Collected Works*, vol. 28, pp. 232, 241–2, 247–8, 292–3 (emphasis in the original).

10. These points are forcibly argued in Claudin, *The Communist Movement*, pp. 56–62.

11. Lenin, *Collected Works*, vol. 27, p. 99.

12. R. K. Debo, *Revolution and Survival: The Foreign Policy of Soviet Russia 1917–18* (Liverpool, 1979) p. 420.

13. E. H. Carr, *The Bolshevik Revolution 1917–1923*, vol. 3 (Harmondsworth, 1966) pp. 67, 68.

14. B. Lazitch and M. M. Drachkovitch, *Lenin and the Comintern*, vol. 1 (Stanford, 1972) pp. 32–3, 43–4; J. D. White, 'National Communism and World Revolution: The Political Consequences of German Military Withdrawal from the Baltic Area in 1918–19', *Europe–Asia Studies*, vol. 46 (1994) pp. 1349–69.

15. Cited in J. Riddell (ed.), *Founding the Communist International. Proceedings and Documents of the First Congress: March 1919* (New York, 1987) pp. 19, 20.

16. Riddell (ed.), *Founding the Communist International*, pp. 113, 114, 169.

17. I. Deutscher, 'Record of a Discussion with Heinrich Brandler', *New Left Review*, no. 105 (September–October 1977) p. 49.

18. For five contradictory versions of Steinhardt's impact, see Lazitch and Drachkovitch, *Lenin and the Comintern*, pp. 80–4.

19. Lenin, *Collected Works*, vol. 29, p. 169.

20. Lenin, *Collected Works*, vol. 31, pp. 21, 24.

21. J. Riddell (ed.), *Workers of the World and Oppressed Peoples, Unite! Proceedings and Documents of the Second Congress, 1920*, vol. 2 (New York, 1991) pp. 765–71.

22. Claudin, *The Communist Movement*, 107–9.

23. Riddell (ed.), *Workers of the World and Oppressed Peoples, Unite!*, vol. 1, pp. 296, 299–300, 406.

24. A. S. Lindemann, *The 'Red Years': European Socialism versus Bolshevism, 1919–1921* (Berkeley, 1974) pp. 174–216.

25. Riddell (ed.), *Workers of the World and Oppressed Peoples, Unite!*, vol. 1, p. 8.

26. For the troubled relationship between the Communist Youth International and the Comintern, see R. Cornell, *Revolutionary Vanguard: The Early Years of the Communist Youth International, 1914–1924* (Toronto, 1982).

27. D. Geary, *European Labour Protest 1848–1939* (London, 1984) pp. 149–55; D. Geary, *European Labour Politics from 1900 to the Depression* (Basingstoke, 1991) pp. 59–64.

28. F. Firsov, 'Lenin's Concept of a World Communist Party and the Development of the Comintern', unpublished manuscript, pp. 8–12; for further details see D. Volkogonov, *Lenin: Life and Legacy* (London: 1995) pp. 50, 391–403.

29. F. Beckett, *Enemy Within: The Rise and Fall of the British Communist Party* (London, 1995) p. 12.

30. RCPSCHD, *fond* (collection) 495, *opis* (inventory) 18, *delo* (file) 136, *list* (folio) 4.

31. B. Lazitch, 'La formation de la section des liaisons internationales du Komintern (OMS) 1921–1923', *Communisme*, no. 4 (1983) pp. 65–80; N. E. Rosenfeldt, *Stalin's Secret Chancellery and the Comintern* (Copenhagen, 1991).

32. Cited by F. I. Firsov, 'Komintern: mekhanizm funktsionirovaniia', *Novaia i noveishaia istoriia*, no. 2 (1991) p. 36.

33. *Izvestiia TsK KPSS*, no. 4 (1990) pp. 181–2.

34. For details, see F. Svátek, 'The Governing Organs of the Communist International: Their Growth and Composition, 1919–1943', *History of*

Socialism Yearbook 1968 (Prague, 1969) pp. 179–266; P. Huber, 'Les organes dirigeants du Komintern: un chantier permanent', unpublished manuscript.

35. Lenin, *Collected Works*, vol. 33, p. 431.

36. For the relevant resolutions of the Third and Fourth Congresses, see Degras (ed.), *The Communist International*, vol. 1, pp. 256–73, 436–42.

37. A. Agosti, 'World Revolution and the "World Party for the Revolution" ', unpublished manuscript, p. 11.

38. Cited in Carr, *The Bolshevik Revolution*, vol. 3, p. 444.

39. Firsov, 'Komintern: mekhanizm funktsionirovaniia', p. 35.

40. F. Firsov, 'Partiia i Komintern', *Kommunist*, no. 7 (1991) p. 93.

41. Gruber (ed.), *International Communism in the Era of Lenin*, pp. 267–95; Lindemann, *The 'Red Years'*, pp. 274–86.

42. See A. A. Galkin's contribution to the roundtable discussion, 'Nekotorye voprosy istorii Kominterna', *Novaia i noveishaia istoriia*, no. 2 (1989) p. 83.

43. Firsov, 'Partiia i Komintern', p. 93.

44. Cited in Claudin, *The Communist Movement*, p. 63.

45. Lenin, *Collected Works*, vol. 32, p. 470.

46. Carr, *The Bolshevik Revolution*, vol. 3, p. 275.

47. E. H. Carr, *The Interregnum, 1923–1924* (Harmondsworth, 1969) p. 222.

48. Carr, *The Bolshevik Revolution*, vol. 3, pp. 393, 414.

49. J. Degras, 'United Front Tactics in the Comintern 1921–1928', in D. Footman (ed.), *International Communism* (London, 1960) p. 9.

50. A. D'Agostino, *Soviet Succession Struggles: Kremlinology and the Russian Question from Lenin to Gorbachev* (London, 1989) p. 49.

51. Degras (ed.), *The Communist International*, vol. 1, p. 313.

52. The organisations represented in Berlin were the Second and Third Internationals and the Vienna Union, the so-called Two-and-a-Half International, which subsequently merged with the Second to form the Labour and Socialist International (LSI).

53. *The Second and Third Internationals and the Vienna Union. Official Report of the Conference between the Executives* (London, 1922) pp. 23, 24.

54. A. Iu. Vatlin, *Komintern: pervye desiat let* (Moscow, 1993) pp. 49–50.

55. G. Swain, 'Was the Profintern Really Necessary?', *European History Quarterly*, vol. 17 (1987) pp. 57–77.

56. K. McDermott, *The Czech Red Unions, 1918–1929: A Study of their Relations with the Communist Party and the Moscow Internationals* (Boulder/New York, 1988); R. Wohl, *French Communism in the Making, 1914–1924* (Stanford, 1966).

57. *International Press Correspondence (Inprecorr)*, vol. 2 (2 December 1922) p. 859.

58. For details, see W. T. Angress, *The Stillborn Revolution: The Communist Bid for Power in Germany, 1921–1923* (Princeton, 1963) pp. 332–50.

59. A. Vatlin, 'Test Ground of World Revolution: Comintern in Germany in the 1920s', unpublished manuscript, p. 10.

60. For details, see Angress, *The Stillborn Revolution*, pp. 378–457; for a recent Russian account based on archival material, see L. G. Babichenko,

'Politbiuro TsK RKP(b), Komintern i sobytiia v Germanii v 1923 g. Novye arkhivnye materialy', *Novaia i noveishaia istoriia*, no. 2 (1994) pp. 125–57.

2. BOLSHEVISING THE COMINTERN, 1924–8

1. Vatlin, *Komintern: pervye desiat let*, pp. 119–41.
2. F. I. Firsov, 'The VKP(b) and the Communist International', unpublished manuscript, n.p.
3. E. H. Carr, *Foundations of a Planned Economy, 1926–1929*, vol. 3, part I (London, 1976) p. 140.
4. Degras (ed.), *The Communist International*, vol. 2, p. 190.
5. Degras (ed.), *The Communist International*, vol. 2, pp. 122, 154.
6. Degras (ed.), *The Communist International*, vol. 2, p. 154.
7. E. H. Carr, *Socialism in One Country, 1924–1926*, vol. 3 (Harmondsworth, 1972) p. 311.
8. Degras (ed.), *The Communist International*, vol. 2, pp. 107, 119.
9. See 'Maria Koszutska: "Spineless People are Dangerous"', *World Marxist Review*, no. 8 (1989) pp. 82–5.
10. Degras (ed.), *The Communist International*, vol. 2, pp. 151–2.
11. Carr, *Socialism in One Country*, vol. 3, pp. 95, 315–18; Gruber, *Soviet Russia Masters the Comintern*, pp. 6–8.
12. Carr, *Socialism in One Country*, vol. 3, pp. 317–18.
13. F. I. Firsov, 'Stalin i Komintern', part 1, *Voprosy istorii*, no. 8 (1989) p. 5.
14. F. I. Firsov, 'K voprosu o taktike edinogo fronta v 1921–1924 gg.', *Voprosy istorii KPSS*, no. 10 (1987) p. 125.
15. Deutscher, *The Prophet Unarmed*, pp. 146, 149.
16. In June 1923 the Bulgarian leftist peasant government of Stamboliski was overthrown by right-wing forces. To the anger of the Comintern, the Bulgarian communists declared neutrality in the conflict. In September the party, under pressure from Moscow, launched a totally ill-prepared uprising and suffered harsh persecution as a result. In Poland the communists proved unable to influence the strikes and demonstrations that rocked the country in the autumn of 1923.
17. J. V. Stalin, *Works*, 13 vols (Moscow, 1952–5) vol. 6, pp. 386–7, 391.
18. Stalin, *Works*, vol. 6, p. 392.
19. Stalin, *Works*, vol. 7, pp. 290–2.
20. Degras (ed.), *The Communist International*, vol. 2, p. 192.
21. Stalin, *Works*, vol. 8, p. 195.
22. A. Iu. Vatlin, *Trotsky i Komintern* (Moscow, 1991) p. 15.
23. E. D. Weitz, 'Bukharin and "Bukharinism" in the Comintern, 1919–29', in N. N. Kozlov and E. D. Weitz (eds), *Nikolai Ivanovich Bukharin: A Centenary Appraisal* (New York, 1990) pp. 59–91.
24. Quoted in R. C. Tucker, *Stalin as Revolutionary 1879–1929: A Study in History and Personality* (New York, 1974) p. 384 (emphasis in the original).
25. D. Volkogonov, *Trotsky*, vol. 2 (Moscow, 1992) p. 73.
26. Trotsky, *The Revolution Betrayed*, pp. 90, 97.

27. R. Palme Dutt, 'Rough Draft on Some Experiences of the Communist International and the Period of Stalin's Leading Role', Archive of the Communist Party of Great Britain (National Museum of Labour History, Manchester), Dutt Papers CP/IND/DUTT/01/01.

28. *Communist Papers. Documents Selected from Those Obtained on the Arrest of Communist Leaders on 14 and 21 October 1925* (London, 1926) pp. 57, 62.

29. Archive of the CPGB, Microfilm, Original reel 4.

30. J. Humbert-Droz, *De Lénine à Staline. Dix ans au service de l'Internationale communiste, 1921–1931* (Neuchâtel, 1971) p. 28.

31. Firsov, 'Stalin i Komintern', part 1, p. 10.

32. On the 'extraordinary confusion' in the PCF, see S. Bahne (ed.), *Archives de Jules Humbert-Droz I: Origines et débuts des partis communistes des pays latins, 1919–1923* (Dordrecht, 1970) pp. 182–3.

33. Carr, *Socialism in One Country*, vol. 3, p. 313.

34. Deutscher, *The Prophet Unarmed*, p. 148.

35. Deutscher, *Stalin*, p. 391.

36. E. J. Hobsbawm, *Revolutionaries: Contemporary Essays* (London, 1982) pp. 3–5.

37. Firsov, 'Stalin i Komintern', part 1, pp. 16–17.

38. See A. Gramsci, *Selections from Political Writings 1921–1926*, trans. and ed. by Q. Hoare, (London, 1978) pp. 426–40.

39. Hobsbawm, *Revolutionaries*, p. 5.

40. Hobsbawm, *Revolutionaries*, p. 47.

41. E. D. Weitz, 'State Power, Class Fragmentation, and the Shaping of German Communist Politics, 1890–1933', *Journal of Modern History*, vol. 62 (1990) p. 294.

42. Weitz, 'State Power', pp. 257, 295.

43. Weitz, 'State Power', pp. 279–86; also the seminal article by J. Wickham, 'Social Fascism and the Division of the Working Class Movement: Workers and Political Parties in the Frankfurt Area 1929/1930', *Capital & Class*, no. 7 (1979) pp. 1–34.

44. *Inprecorr*, vol. 5 (17 April 1925) p. 454 and (24 April 1925) p. 503.

45. Carr, *Socialism in One Country*, vol. 3, pp. 385–7.

46. McDermott, *The Czech Red Unions*, pp. 167–77.

47. Carr, *Socialism in One Country*, vol. 3, p. 951.

48. *Inprecorr*, vol. 5 (28 March 1925) p. 318. 'Internal resistance' and 'great difficulties in all Communist Parties' were also noted in a report of the ECCI Organisational Bureau, dated 7 May 1928. See RCPSCHD, f. 493, op. 1, d. 14, l. 88, 91.

49. E. H. Carr, *Foundations of a Planned Economy 1926–1929*, vol. 3, part II (London, 1976) pp. 636.

50. Stalin, *Works*, vol. 10, pp. 53–4.

51. *Inprecorr*, vol. 6 (20 December 1926) p. 1510.

52. N. N. Kozlov and E. D. Weitz, 'Reflections on the Origins of the "Third Period": Bukharin, the Comintern, and the Political Economy of Weimar Germany', *Journal of Contemporary History*, vol. 24 (1989) pp. 394–9.

53. Degras (ed.), *The Communist International*, vol. 2, pp. 321, 325.

54. Degras (ed.), *The Communist International*, vol. 2, pp. 375–7.

55. Stalin, *Works*, vol. 9, p. 318.

56. Carr, *Foundations of a Planned Economy*, vol. 3, part I, p. 149.

57. Carr, *The Twilight of Comintern*, p. 7.

58. L. Peterson, 'From Social Democracy to Communism: Recent Contributions to the History of the German Workers' Movement, 1914–1945', *International Labor and Working-Class History*, no. 20 (1981) p. 23.

59. Sobolev *et al.*, *Outline History*, p. 269.

60. RCPSCHD, f. 495, op. 3, d. 43, l. 173–4.

61. Archive of the CPGB, Klugmann Papers CP/IND/KLUG/04/01.

62. RCPSCHD, f. 495, op. 6, d. 8, l. 20–3.

63. RCPSCHD, f. 495, op. 3, d. 49, l. 127.

64. RCPSCHD, f. 495, op. 18, d. 569, l. 170–1 (English copy of Russian original).

65. A. Iu. Vatlin, 'Goriachaia osen dvadtsat vosmogo. (K voprosu o stalinizatsii Kominterna)', in *Oni ne molchali* (Moscow, 1991) p. 103.

66. T. Draper, 'The Strange Case of the Comintern', *Survey*, vol. 28 (1972) p. 135.

67. N. I. Bukharin, *Problemy teorii i praktiki sotsializma* (Moscow, 1989) pp. 298–9 (emphasis in the original). 'Koba' was one of Stalin's pseudonyms.

68. *Inprecorr*, vol. 8 (4 September 1928) p. 1039.

69. F. I. Firsov, 'N. I. Bukharin v Kominterne', in *Bukharin: chelovek, politik, uchenyi* (Moscow, 1990) p. 189.

70. *Inprecorr*, vol. 8 (23 August 1928) p. 941.

71. Firsov, 'N. I. Bukharin v Kominterne', p. 190.

72. RCPSCHD, f. 493, op. 1, d. 415, l. 100.

73. Firsov, 'N. I. Bukharin v Kominterne', p. 196.

74. RCPSCHD, f. 508, op. 1, d. 18, n.p.

75. Carr, *Foundations of a Planned Economy*, vol. 3, part I, p. 122.

3. STALIN AND THE THIRD PERIOD, 1928–33

1. Carr, *Foundations of a Planned Economy*, vol. 3, part II, p. 445.

2. RCPSCHD, f. 558, op. 1, d. 2881, l. 7–9; Stalin, *Works*, vol. 11, pp. 307–24.

3. F. I. Firsov, 'Chistka apparata Kominterna', unpublished manuscript pp. 5–9.

4. RCPSCHD, f. 495, op. 2, d. 111, l. 137–9, 149.

5. Humbert-Droz, *De Lénine à Staline*, pp. 353, 356.

6. Cited in Degras (ed.), *The Communist International*, vol. 2, p. 566.

7. Carr, *Foundations of a Planned Economy*, vol. 3, part II, p. 554.

8. F. I. Firsov, 'Stalin i Komintern', part 2, *Voprosy istorii*, no. 9 (1989) p. 5, citing *Annali Feltrinelli*, VIII (1968) p. 670.

9. S. Bahne *et al.* (eds), *Archives de Jules Humbert-Droz III: Les partis communistes et l'Internationale communiste dans les années 1928–1932* (Dordrecht, 1988) p. 165.

10. *Inprecorr*, vol. 8 (13 August 1928) p. 874.

11. F. de Felice, *Fascismo, Democrazia, Fronte Popolare* (Bari, 1973) p. 210.

12. T. Draper, *American Communism and Soviet Russia. The Formative Period* (New York, 1986) pp. 409, 414, 419, 422.

13. It has been suggested that Stalin's 'revolution from above' may just as accurately be seen as a 'revolution from below'. See S. Fitzpatrick (ed.), *Cultural Revolution in Russia, 1928–1931* (Bloomington, 1978).

14. Borkenau, *World Communism*, pp. 351–2.

15. Carr, *The Twilight of Comintern*, pp. 5, 6.

16. Firsov, 'The VKP(b) and the Communist International', n.p.

17. Firsov, 'Stalin i Komintern', part 2, pp. 10–11, citing the former Central Party Archive.

18. *Theses and Decisions: Thirteenth Plenum of the E.C.C.I.* (New York, 1934) pp. 3, 5, 19.

19. Firsov, 'Stalin i Komintern', part 2, pp. 7–12.

20. The quotation is from J. Haslam's review of Carr's work in *Historical Journal*, vol. 26 (1983) p. 1026.

21. See for example, G. Gill, *Stalinism* (Basingstoke, 1990).

22. Deutscher, *Stalin*, p. 400.

23. S. Fitzpatrick, *The Cultural Front: Power and Culture in Revolutionary Russia* (Ithaca, 1992) pp. 113–14.

24. M. Hájek, *Jednotná fronta. K politické orientaci Komunistické internacionály v letech 1921–1935* (Prague, 1969) p. 162.

25. Borkenau, *World Communism*, p. 389.

26. For details, see T. J. Uldricks, *Diplomacy and Ideology: The Origins of Soviet Foreign Relations, 1917–1930* (London and Beverly Hills, 1979), and J. Jacobson, *When the Soviet Union Entered World Politics* (Berkeley and London, 1994).

27. V. V. Sokolov, 'Neizvestnyi G. V. Chicherin. Iz rassekrechennykh arkhivov MID RF', *Novaia i noveishaia istoriia*, no. 2 (1994) pp. 13–14.

28. Carr, *The Twilight of Comintern*, p. 122.

29. B. Kun (ed.), *Kommunisticheskii internatsional v dokumentakh* (Moscow, 1933) p. 920.

30. *Inprecorr*, vol. 10 (8 May 1930) pp. 407–9 and (15 May 1930) pp. 426–7.

31. Carr, *The Twilight of Comintern*, pp. 9–12.

32. D. Z. Manuilsky, *The Communist Parties and the Crisis of Capitalism* (London, n.d.) p. 99.

33. E. Rosenhaft, *Beating the Fascists? The German Communists and Political Violence 1929–1933* (Cambridge, 1983) pp. 76–9.

34. Draper, 'The Strange Case of the Comintern', p. 119.

35. *Communism and the International Situation* (New York, 1929) pp. 6, 16–20.

36. *Communism and the International Situation*, pp. 17–18.

37. *Communism and the International Situation*, pp. 18–19.

38. I. N. Undasynov, 'Ot taktiki edinogo rabochego fronta k taktike "klass protiv klassa" ', *Rabochii klass i sovremennyi mir*, no. 2 (1989) p. 176.

39. Rosenhaft, *Beating the Fascists?*, pp. 33–5.

40. K. Gottwald, *Spisy*, vol. 1 (Prague, 1951) p. 322.

41. Wickham, 'Social Fascism and the Division of the Working Class Movement', p. 17.

42. *Inprecorr*, vol. 9 (4 October 1929) p. 1190.

43. *The World Situation & Economic Struggle. Theses of the Tenth Plenum E.C.C.I.* (London, n.d.) pp. 22–7.

44. *The World Situation & Economic Struggle*, p. 44.

45. McDermott, *The Czech Red Unions*, pp. 234–5.

46. RCPSCHD, f. 495, op. 171, d. 287, l. 104.

47. For details, see P. Preston, *The Coming of the Spanish Civil War* (London, 1983).

48. Borkenau, *World Communism*, pp. 342–3.

49. A. Howkins, 'Class against Class: The Political Culture of the Communist Party of Great Britain, 1930–35', in F. Gloversmith (ed.), *Class, Culture and Social Change: A New View of the 1930s* (Brighton, 1980) pp. 245, 254.

50. S. Macintyre, *Little Moscows: Communism and Working-class Militancy in Inter-war Britain* (London, 1980).

51. F. M. Ottanelli, *The Communist Party of the United States: From the Depression to World War II* (New Brunswick, 1991) pp. 4–5.

52. For the 'Guttmann Affair', see J. Rupnik, *Histoire du Parti communiste tchécoslovaque: des origines à la prise du pouvoir* (Paris, 1981) pp. 95–104.

53. For details, see Bahne *et al.* (eds), *Archives de Jules Humbert-Droz III*, pp. 322–3.

54. Ottanelli, *The Communist Party of the United States*, pp. 17–48.

55. Geary, *European Labour Politics*, p. 69.

56. D. Beetham, *Marxists in Face of Fascism* (Manchester, 1983) p. 2.

57. The classic exposition of this point of view is N. Poulantzas, *Fascism and Dictatorship* (London, 1979); also Claudin, *The Communist Movement*, pp. 604–10.

58. Trotsky's major writings on fascism from the years 1930–4 are reprinted in *The Struggle against Fascism in Germany*. The quotation here is from p. 126.

59. See Borkenau, *World Communism*, pp. 342–3; and S. T. Possony, 'The Comintern as an Instrument of Soviet Strategy', in Drachkovitch (ed.), *The Revolutionary Internationals*, pp. 213–18.

60. Cited in Beetham, *Marxists in Face of Fascism*, pp. 162–5.

61. *XIth Plenum of the Executive Committee of the Communist International: Theses, Resolutions and Decisions* (New York, n.d.) p. 8 (Hitler), pp. 13–16, 23–7 (social democracy).

62. *XII Plenum of the Executive Committee of the Communist International: Theses and Resolutions* (Moscow, 1933) pp. 9–10.

63. *Theses and Decisions: Thirteenth Plenum of the E.C.C.I.*, pp. 5, 14.

64. Firsov has confirmed that the decision to participate in the referendum 'was taken under direct pressure from Stalin and Molotov.' See his 'Stalin i Komintern', part 2, p. 9.

65. Trotsky, *The Struggle against Fascism in Germany*, p. 96.

66. Rosenhaft, *Beating the Fascists?*, p. 66.

67. C. Fischer, 'Class Enemies or Class Brothers? Communist–Nazi Relations in Germany 1929–33', *European History Quarterly*, vol. 15 (1985) p. 273; for a critique of Fischer's article, see D. Geary's 'Response' in *European History Quarterly*, vol. 15 (1985) pp. 453–64; for details, see

C. Fischer, *The German Communists and the Rise of Nazism* (London, 1991) pp. 102–88.

68. On the political and social consequences of mass unemployment, see R. J. Evans, 'Introduction: The Experience of Unemployment in the Weimar Republic', and D. Geary, 'Unemployment and Working-class Solidarity: The German Experience 1929–33', in R. J. Evans and D. Geary (eds), *The German Unemployed* (London, 1987) pp. 15–19, 261–80.

69. R. C. Tucker, *Stalin in Power: The Revolution from Above, 1928–1941* (New York and London, 1992) pp. 225–32; also R. C. Tucker, 'The Emergence of Stalin's Foreign Policy', *Slavic Review*, vol. 36 (1977) pp. 563–89.

70. T. J. Uldricks, 'Stalin and Nazi Germany', *Slavic Review*, vol. 36 (1977) pp. 599–603.

71. Claudin, *The Communist Movement*, p. 166.

4. POPULAR FRONT AND STALINIST TERROR, 1934–9

1. Claudin, *The Communist Movement*, pp. 171–82; Possony, 'The Comintern as an Instrument of Soviet Strategy', 218–22; C. and A. Vassart, 'The Moscow Origin of the French "Popular Front" ', in M. M. Drachkovitch and B. Lazitch (eds), *The Comintern: Historical Highlights. Essays, Recollections, Documents* (New York, 1966) pp. 234–52.

2. J. Santore, 'The Comintern's United Front Initiative of May 1934: French or Soviet Inspiration?', *Canadian Journal of History*, vol. 16 (1981) pp. 405–21; J. Frieden, 'The Internal Politics of European Communism in the Stalin Era', *Studies in Comparative Communism*, vol. 14 (1981) pp. 45–69.

3. The term is taken from J. Jackson, *The Popular Front in France: Defending Democracy, 1934–1938* (Cambridge, 1988) p. 35.

4. For developments in South America, see M. Caballero, *Latin America and the Comintern, 1919–1943* (Cambridge, 1986).

5. For Britain, see G. Andrews, N. Fishman and K. Morgan (eds), *Opening the Books: Essays on the Social and Cultural History of the British Communist Party* (London, 1995).

6. Degras (ed.), *The Communist International*, vol. 3, pp. 252–3; *Inprecorr*, vol. 13 (9 March 1933) pp. 261–2.

7. Carr, *The Twilight of Comintern*, p. 85.

8. Firsov, 'Stalin i Komintern', part 2, p. 10.

9. *Inprecorr*, vol. 14 (30 January 1934) p. 116.

10. On events in France, see Jackson, *The Popular Front*, pp. 28–30; D. R. Brower, *The New Jacobins: The French Communist Party and the Popular Front* (Ithaca, 1968) pp. 31–42.

11. Carr, *The Twilight of Comintern*, p. 125.

12. K. Denchev and M. T. Meshcheriakov, 'Dnevnikovye zapisi G. Dimitrova', *Novaia i noveishaia istoriia*, no. 4 (1991) pp. 68–72.

13. B. M. Leibzon and K. K. Shirinia, *Povorot v politike Kominterna* (Moscow, 1975) p. 93, citing the Bulgarian Party Archive.

14. 'Dokumenty G. M. Dimitrova k VII kongressu Kommunisticheskogo internatsionala', *Voprosy istorii*, no. 7 (1965) pp. 85–8.

15. Firsov, 'Stalin i Komintern', part 2, p. 12. For an English translation of the letter, see J. Haslam, 'The Comintern and the Origins of the Popular Front, 1934–1935', *Historical Journal*, vol. 22 (1979) pp. 682–4.

16. Jackson, *The Popular Front*, p. 37; Carr, *The Twilight of Comintern*, p. 199.

17. Carr, *The Twilight of Comintern*, p. 145.

18. Claudin, *The Communist Movement*, pp. 174–82.

19. Jackson, *The Popular Front*, p. 34.

20. Haslam, *The Soviet Union and the Struggle for Collective Security in Europe, 1933–39* (London, 1984) p. 59.

21. See Carr, *The Twilight of Comintern*, pp. 425–7; P. Frank, *Histoire de l'Internationale communiste, 1919–1943*, vol. 2 (Paris, 1979) pp. 708–10.

22. E. J. Hobsbawm, 'The "Moscow Line" and International Communist Policy, 1933–47', in C. Wrigley (ed.), *Warfare, Diplomacy and Politics. Essays in Honour of A. J. P. Taylor* (London, 1986) p. 172.

23. E. Laclau, *Politics and Ideology in Marxist Theory* (London, 1977) pp. 135–42; Frieden, 'The Internal Politics of European Communism', pp. 46, 68–9.

24. Sobolev *et al.*, *Outline History*, pp. 399–400.

25. All references to Dimitrov's report and reply to the discussion are taken from G. Dimitrov, *The Working Class against Fascism* (London, 1935) pp. 10–11, 35, 63, 67–8, 71, 77–8, 99 (emphasis in the original).

26. P. Spriano, *Stalin and the European Communists* (London, 1985) p. 30.

27. Thorez's speech in *Report of the Seventh World Congress of the Communist International* (London, 1936) p. 36.

28. *Inprecorr*, vol. 15 (1 October 1935) pp. 1243–4, 1250.

29. *Inprecorr*, vol. 15 (19 September 1935) p. 1176.

30. Dimitrov, *The Working Class against Fascism*, p. 23.

31. K. Morgan, *Against Fascism and War. Ruptures and Continuities in British Communist Politics, 1935–41* (Manchester, 1989) pp. 33–55; Ottanelli, *The Communist Party of the United States*, pp. 107–36.

32. D. A. L. Levy, 'The French Popular Front, 1936–37', in H. Graham and P. Preston (eds), *The Popular Front in Europe* (Basingstoke, 1987) pp. 62–3.

33. B. Studer, 'La réorganisation du Comité Executif de l'IC en octobre 1935', *International Newsletter of Historical Studies on Comintern, Communism and Stalinism*, vol. 1 (1993–94) pp. 25–30.

34. Beetham, *Marxists in Face of Fascism*, p. 177.

35. S. Wolikow, 'La question française dans l'Internationale communiste', in S. Wolikow and M. Cordillot (eds), *Prolétaires de tous les pays, unissez-vous? Les difficiles chemins de l'Internationalisme, 1848–1956* (Dijon, 1993) p. 124.

36. Deutscher, *Stalin*, pp. 414–15.

37. For a judicious assessment of Moscow's dilemma, see Haslam, *The Soviet Union and the Struggle for Collective Security*, pp. 107–15.

38. M. T. Meshcheriakov, 'SSSR i grazhdanskaia voina v Ispanii', *Otechestvennaia istoriia*, no. 3 (1993) pp. 87, 93.

39. Cited in Carr, *The Comintern and the Spanish Civil War*, pp. 86–7.

40. *Inprecorr*, vol. 16 (24 October 1936) pp. 1292–6.

41. A. Elorza, 'Stalinisme et internationalisme en Espagne, 1931–1939', in Wolikow and Cordillot (eds), *Prolétaires de tous les pays, unissez-vous?*, p. 198, citing the Comintern Archive.

42. Claudin, *The Communist Movement*, p. 231.

43. For British involvement, see H. Francis, *Miners against Fascism: Wales and the Spanish Civil War* (London, 1984).

44. *Communist International*, vol. 14 (1937) p. 865.

45. See J. A. Getty, *Origins of the Great Purges: The Soviet Communist Party Reconsidered, 1933–1938* (Cambridge, 1985).

46. B. Lazitch, 'Stalin's Massacre of the Foreign Communist Leaders', in Lazitch and Drachkovitch (eds), *The Comintern: Historical Highlights*, p. 172.

47. Cited in R. Conquest, *The Great Terror*, rev. edn (Harmondsworth, 1971) p. 586.

48. Documents from Stalin's Archive printed in *Izvestiia*, 10 June 1992.

49. Tucker, *Stalin in Power*, p. 444.

50. Firsov, 'Chistka apparata Kominterna', pp. 30, 36.

51. A. G. Latyshev, 'Riadom so Stalinym', *Sovershenno sekretno*, no. 12 (1990) p. 19.

52. Cited in *Istoricheskii arkhiv*, no. 1 (1992) p. 119.

53. H. Weber, *'Weisse Flecken' in der Geschichte Die KPD – Opfer der Stalinischen Säuberungen und ihre Rehabilitierung* (Frankfurt a. M., 1989) pp. 19–20, 24.

54. I. Deutscher, *Marxism in Our Time* (London, 1972) pp. 156–7.

55. Firsov, 'Partiia i Komintern', p. 95.

56. W. Laqueur, *Stalin: The Glasnost Revelations* (London, 1990) p. 108.

57. Ex-Insider, 'The Party that Vanished', *Soviet Survey*, no. 33 (1960) p. 105.

58. F. I. Firsov and I. S. Iazhborovskaia, 'Komintern i Kommunisticheskaia Partiia Polshi' (part 2), *Voprosy istorii KPSS*, no. 12 (1988) p. 55.

59. Tucker, *Stalin in Power*, p. 506.

60. N. Gevorkyan, 'What's Behind the KGB's Figures', *Moscow News*, nos 8–9 (1990) p. 31.

61. A. Tuominen, *The Bells of the Kremlin* (Hanover and London, 1983) p. 234.

62. M. Gelb, ' "Karelian Fever": The Finnish Immigrant Community during Stalin's Purges', *Europe–Asia Studies*, vol. 45 (1993) p. 1102.

63. G. Polegaev, 'Yugoslavy i Komintern', in *Arkhivy raskryvaiut tainy . . .* (Moscow, 1991) p. 349; R. Medvedev, *Let History Judge: The Origins and Consequences of Stalinism*, rev. edn (New York and Oxford, 1989); Tucker, *Stalin in Power*; R. Conquest, *The Great Terror: A Reassessment* (London, 1992); Laqueur, *Stalin*.

64. At the time of their arrest Piatnitsky and Knorin were no longer Comintern functionaries, having been transferred to other work in 1935.

65. Latyshev, 'Riadom so Stalinym', p. 19.

66. Firsov, 'Chistka apparata Kominterna', p. 36.

67. M. Panteleiev, 'La terreur stalinienne au Komintern en 1937–1938: les chiffres et les causes', *Communisme*, nos 40–1 (1995) pp. 38, 40. The figure of 113, however, excludes those arrested in certain ECCI departments, such as the OMS.

68. 'Muzhestvo protiv bezzakoniia', *Problemy mira i sotsializma*, no. 7 (1989) pp. 89–91.

69. See P. Huber and B. H. Bayerlein, 'Première esquisse des structures répressives du Komintern. Le cas des communistes suisses à Moscou', *Communisme*, nos 32–34 (1993) pp. 147–76; Firsov, 'Chistka apparata Kominterna'; Rosenfeldt, *Stalin's Secret Chancellery and the Comintern*.

70. RCPSCHD, f. 495, op. 74, d. 41, l. 4–8.

71. A. Vaksberg, *Hôtel Lux: Les partis frères au service de l'Internationale communiste* (Paris, 1993) pp. 228–32.

72. B. A. Starkov, 'The Trial that Was Not Held', *Europe–Asia Studies*, vol. 46 (1994) pp. 1297–1315.

73. 'Riad sektsii Kominterna . . . okazalis tselikom v rukakh vraga', *Istoricheskii arkhiv*, no. 1 (1993) pp. 220–1.

74. Lazitch, 'Stalin's Massacre', pp. 141–6.

75. Spriano, *Stalin and the European Communists*, p. 46.

76. A. G. Latyshev, 'O novykh podkhodakh k izucheniiu istorii Kominterna', in *Komintern: opyt, traditsii, uroki* (Moscow, 1989) pp. 149–50.

77. Spriano, *Stalin and the European Communists*, p. 38.

78. J. Haslam, 'The Soviet Union, the Comintern and the Demise of the Popular Front 1936–39', in Graham and Preston (eds), *The Popular Front in Europe*, 152–60.

79. Huber and Bayerlein, 'Première esquisse', pp. 148–9.

80. Firsov, 'Chistka apparata Kominterna', pp. 1, 12, 16–19, 26, 28–9.

81. See for instance Tuominen, *The Bells of the Kremlin*, pp. 229–30; Tucker, *Stalin in Power*, p. 512.

82. Spriano, *Stalin and the European Communists*, p. 51.

83. Haslam, 'The Soviet Union', pp. 158, 160.

84. *Communist International*, vol. 14 (1937) p. 1173.

85. L. I. Gintsberg, 'Moskovskie protsessy 1936–1938 gg: pozitsiia deiatelei mezhdunarodnogo kommunisticheskogo dvizheniia', *Novaia i noveishaia istoriia*, no. 6 (1991) pp. 10, 14, 18–23.

86. Cited in B. Pearce, 'The British Stalinists and the Moscow Trials', in M. Woodhouse and B. Pearce, *Essays on the History of British Communism* (London, 1975) p. 235.

5. COMINTERN IN EAST ASIA, 1919–39

1. S. White, 'Communism and the East: The Baku Congress, 1920', *Slavic Review*, vol. 33 (1974) pp. 495–6.

2. For the debate and theses, see Riddell (ed.), *Workers of the World and Oppressed Peoples, Unite!*, vol. 1, pp. 211–90.

3. J. Riddell (ed.), *To See the Dawn: Baku 1920 – First Congress of the Peoples of the East* (New York, 1993) pp. 45–52, 231–2.

4. White, 'Communism and the East', p. 503.

5. M. Y. L. Luk, *The Origins of Chinese Bolshevism: An Ideology in the Making, 1920–1928* (Oxford, 1990) pp. 218–20.

6. T. Saich, *The Origins of the First United Front in China: The Role of Sneevliet (Alias Maring)*, vol. 1 (Leiden, 1991) p. 67.

7. C. Brandt, B. Schwartz and J. K. Fairbank (eds), *A Documentary History of Chinese Communism* (New York, 1967) pp. 54–65.

8. R. C. North, *Moscow and Chinese Communists* (Stanford, 1963) pp. 64–5.

9. Cited in Gruber (ed.), *Soviet Russia Masters the Comintern*, p. 389.

10. Brandt *et al.*, *A Documentary History*, pp. 71–2.

11. Cited in C. Brandt, *Stalin's Failure in China* (New York, 1966), pp. 44–5.

12. For details, see G. Benton, *China's Urban Revolutionaries: Explorations in the History of Chinese Trotskyism, 1921–1952* (New Jersey, 1995).

13. G. Benton, 'Bolshevising China: From Lenin to Stalin to Mao, 1921–1944', *Leeds East Asia Papers*, no. 22 (1994) pp. 22–4.

14. H. J. van den Ven, *From Friend to Comrade: The Founding of the Chinese Communist Party, 1920–1927* (Berkeley, 1991) pp. 126–7.

15. C. M. Wilbur and J. L. How, *Missionaries of Revolution: Soviet Advisers and Nationalist China, 1920–1927* (Cambridge, Mass, 1989) pp. 6–7.

16. Cited in North, *Moscow and Chinese Communists*, p. 87 (emphasis in original).

17. Brandt, *Stalin's Failure*, p. 72.

18. Stalin, *Works*, vol. 8, pp. 387–8.

19. For details, see C. M. Wilbur, 'The Nationalist Revolution: From Canton to Nanking, 1923–28', in J. K. Fairbank (ed.), *Cambridge History of China. Volume 12: Republican China, 1912–1949*, part 1, (Cambridge, 1983) pp. 611–25.

20. Cited in H. R. Isaacs, *The Tragedy of the Chinese Revolution* (Stanford, 1951) p. 162.

21. Brandt *et al.*, *A Documentary History*, p. 91.

22. Brandt *et al.*, *A Documentary History*, pp. 80–9.

23. J. V. Stalin, *Marxism and the National and Colonial Question* (London, 1941) p. 249 (emphasis in the original).

24. Brandt *et al.*, *A Documentary History*, p. 122.

25. M. Seldon, *The Yenan Way in Revolutionary China* (Cambridge, MA, 1971) pp. 36–7.

26. W. Kuo, *Analytical History of the Chinese Communist Party*, vol. 2 (Taibei, 1968) p. 47.

27. Degras (ed.), *The Communist International*, vol. 2, p. 543.

28. Y. M. Kau, 'Urban and Rural Strategies in the Chinese Communist Revolution', in J. W. Lewis (ed.), *Peasant Rebellion and Communist Revolution in Asia* (Stanford, 1974) p. 264.

29. Luk, *The Origins of Chinese Bolshevism*, pp. 216–7.

30. Kuo, *Analytical History*, pp. 245–8.

31. North, *Moscow and Chinese Communists*, pp. 131–3.

32. North, *Moscow and Chinese Communists*, p. 137.

33. Cited in Degras (ed.), *The Communist International*, vol. 3, p. 141.

34. J. Garver, 'The Origins of the Second United Front: The Comintern and the Chinese Communist Party', *China Quarterly*, no. 113 (1988) p. 32.

35. G. Benton, 'The "Second Wang Ming Line" (1935–38)', *China Quarterly*, no. 61 (1975) p. 67.

36. *VII Congress of the Communist International: Abridged Stenographic Report of Proceedings* (Moscow, 1939) p. 583.

37. On the origins of the Second United Front, see Shum Kui-Kwong, *The Chinese Communists' Road to Power: The Anti-Japanese National United Front, 1935–1945* (Oxford, 1988); for a critique of this work, see M. M. Sheng, 'Mao, Stalin, and the Formation of the Anti-Japanese United Front: 1935–37', *China Quarterly*, no. 129 (1992) pp. 149–70.

38. Brandt *et al.*, *A Documentary History*, pp. 246, 253.

6. FROM WAR TO DISSOLUTION, 1939–43

1. Claudin, *The Communist Movement*, p. 294.

2. Cited from the Comintern Archive by M. Johnstone, 'Introduction', in F. King and G. Matthews (eds), *About Turn: The British Communist Party and the Second World War* (London, 1990) p. 19.

3. 'Komintern i sovetsko-germanskii dogovor o nenapadenii', *Izvestiia TsK KPSS*, no. 12 (1989) p. 206.

4. F. I. Firsov, 'Komintern: opyt, traditsii, uroki – nereshennye zadachi issledovaniia', in *Komintern: opyt, traditsii, uroki*, pp. 21–2; K. Shirinia, 'The Time of Hard Decisions (On the Soviet–German Pact, the Beginning of World War II and the Comintern Policy)', Novosti Press Agency, (31 July 1989) pp. 9–10.

5. 'Komintern i sovetsko-germanskii dogovor', p. 207; Johnstone, 'Introduction', in King and Matthews (eds), *About Turn*, p. 21. The Russian version of the 'short thesis', held in the former Central Party Archive, was published in full for the first time in N. S. Lebedeva and M. M. Narinskii (eds), *Komintern i vtoraia mirovaia voina* (Moscow, 1994) pp. 88–9.

6. The passages on the CPGB are based on Johnstone's 'Introduction' to King and Matthews (eds), *About Turn*, pp. 13–49 and the speeches of Dutt and Pollitt, pp. 67–87 and 197–210; see also K. Morgan, *Harry Pollitt* (Manchester, 1993) pp. 107–13.

7. King and Matthews (eds), *About Turn*, pp. 40, 131.

8. Morgan, *Against Fascism and War*, pp. 91–102.

9. L. Taylor, 'The Parti Communiste Français and the French Resistance in the Second World War', in T. Judt (ed.), *Resistance and Revolution in Mediterranean Europe, 1939–1948* (London, 1989) p. 53.

10. Spriano, *Stalin and the European Communists*, p. 109.

11. G. Swain, 'The Comintern and Southern Europe, 1938–43', in Judt (ed.), *Resistance and Revolution*, pp. 29–34; also S. Carrillo, *Dialogue on Spain* (London, 1976) p. 71.

12. D. W. Pike, 'Between the Junes: The French Communists from the Collapse of France to the Invasion of Russia', *Journal of Contemporary History*, vol. 28 (1993) pp. 465–85.

13. Cited in Spriano, *Stalin and the European Communists*, p. 119.

14. *World News and Views*, vol. 19 (11 November 1939) pp. 1079–80.

15. 'Komintern i sovetsko-germanskii dogovor', p. 214. On the British party, see M. Johnstone, 'The CPGB, the Comintern and the War 1939–1941: Filling in the Blank Spots', *Science and Society* (forthcoming).

16. E. Fischer, *An Opposing Man* (London, 1974) pp. 354–5.

17. F. Borkenau, *European Communism* (London, 1953) pp. 244–5.

18. Morgan, *Against Fascism and War*, pp. 105–64. Quotations on pp. 117, 152.

19. For details on Tito and the Comintern, see G. Swain, 'Tito: The Formation of a Disloyal Bolshevik', *International Review of Social History*, vol. 34 (1989) pp. 248–71; M. Wheeler, 'Pariahs to Partisans to Power: the Communist Party of Yugoslavia', in Judt (ed.), *Resistance and Revolution*, pp. 110–56; and M. M. Drachkovitch, 'The Comintern and the Insurrectional Activity of the Communist Party of Yugoslavia in 1941–1942', in Drachkovitch and Lazitch (eds), *The Comintern: Historical Highlights*, pp. 184–213.

20. W. Leonhard, *Child of the Revolution* (London, 1957) pp. 217–24; J. Humbert-Droz, *Le couronnement d'une vie de combat, 1941–1971* (Neuchâtel, 1973) p. 155; and A. Kriegel, 'La Dissolution du "Komintern"', *Revue d'histoire de la deuxième guerre mondiale*, (October 1967) p. 37.

21. *World News and Views*, vol. 23 (29 May 1943) pp. 169–70 and (19 June 1943) p. 197.

22. Degras (ed.), *The Communist International*, vol. 3, pp. 476–7.

23. Sobolev *et al.*, *Outline History*, pp. 511–13.

24. Firsov, 'Komintern: mekhanizm funktsionirovaniia', p. 46. The Yugoslav communist, Milovan Djilas, recalls that Dimitrov told him the idea of dissolving the Comintern arose as early as the summer of 1940. See M. Djilas, *Conversations with Stalin* (Harmondsworth, 1969) p. 31.

25. Firsov, 'Partiia i Komintern', pp. 95–6. All indications point to the fact that Firsov had access to Dimitrov's diaries as the source for this meeting.

26. Firsov, 'Partiia i Komintern', pp. 96–7; see also G. M. Adibekov, *Kominform i poslevoennaia Evropa, 1947–1956 gg.* (Moscow, 1994) pp. 6–10.

27. L. Ia. Gibianskii, 'Kak voznik Kominform. Po novym arkhivnym materialam', *Novaia i noveishaia istoriia*, no. 4 (1993) p. 136, note 22.

28. A. Iu. Vatlin, 'Smert Kominterna', *Rodina*, nos 6–7 (1991) p. 84.

29. Claudin, *The Communist Movement*, pp. 20–1, 31–7 (emphasis in original).

30. Spriano, *Stalin and the European Communists*, pp. 194–5, 199, 201–3.

31. Cited in Firsov, 'Partiia i Komintern', p. 96. Stalin repeated a similar argument to Djilas in June 1944. See the latter's *Conversations with Stalin*, p. 67.

32. Spriano, *Stalin and the European Communists*, p. 201.

33. Borkenau, *European Communism*, p. 283.

34. S. Kudriashov, 'The Central Committee of the All-Union Communist Party and Eastern Europe 1945–1953: New Documents', unpublished manuscript p. 10.

35. For a first-hand account of the work of Institutes 99 and 205, see Leonhard, *Child of the Revolution*, pp. 242, 245–50.

36. Kudriashov, 'The Central Committee and Eastern Europe', pp. 10–15; also Adibekov, *Kominform*, pp. 10–21; and L. Ia. Gibianskii, 'Nekotorye neizuchennye problemy istorii Kominterna', in *Komintern: opyt, traditsii, uroki*, p. 164.

37. Cited in Spriano, *Stalin and the European Communists*, p. 202.

LEGACY OF THE COMINTERN

1. For this view, see F. Fukuyama, *The End of History and the Last Man* (Harmondsworth, 1992).

2. M. Malia, 'The Hunt for the True October', *Commentary*, no. 92 (1991) pp. 21–8.

3. Borkenau, *World Communism*, p. 12.

4. M. M. Drachkovitch, 'Introduction' to Drachkovitch (ed.), *The Revolutionary Internationals*, p. xv.

5. L. Kolakowski, *Main Currents of Marxism*, vol. 3 (Oxford, 1978) p. 111.

6. Claudin, *The Communist Movement*, pp. 640–1.

7. I. M. Krivoguz, 'Komintern o mirovoi sotsialisticheskoi revoliutsii', in *Komintern: opyt, traditsii, uroki*, p. 52.

8. J. Barth Urban, 'The Ties that Bind: West European Communism and the Communist States of East Europe', in W. E. Griffith (ed.), *The European Left: Italy, France, and Spain* (Lexington, Mass., 1979) pp. 203–37.

Select Biographical Glossary

Bukharin, Nikolai (1888–1938). Leading Bolshevik activist and theoretician. Played a prominent role in the Comintern from its foundation and was its *de facto* chief from 1926 to 1928. Expelled by Stalin from the Russian party and Comintern in 1929 as a so-called 'right-wing deviationist'. Returned to party life in the mid-1930s, but was executed in March 1938 as an 'enemy of the people'. Rehabilitated by Gorbachev in 1988.

Dimitrov, Georgi (1882–1949). Bulgarian communist who held important posts in the Comintern in the 1920s. With Stalin's backing he became General Secretary of the International in spring 1934, remaining in that post until June 1943. Prime advocate of the anti-fascist Popular Front strategy, he also presided over the Stalinist terror in the Comintern. Leader of communist Bulgaria after World War II.

Gottwald, Klement (1896–1953). The leading 'Bolsheviser' of the Czechoslovak Communist Party after 1929 and influential member of the ECCI Presidium and Secretariat in the 1930s and early 1940s. President of Czechoslovakia from 1948 until his death.

Gramsci, Antonio (1891–1937). Important Marxist intellectual and a leading member of the Italian Communist Party. Worked abroad for the Comintern between 1922 and 1924. Incarcerated by

Mussolini in 1926, he died in captivity eleven years later. Opponent of the Third Period line, his theories on the capitalist state and hegemony, as developed in the *Prison Notebooks*, informed the 'Eurocommunist' movement of the 1970s and 1980s.

Humbert-Droz, Jules (1891–1971). Founder member of the Swiss Communist Party. Held high Comintern office throughout the 1920s and also acted as secret Comintern emissary to several west European parties. Identified as a 'Bukharinite' in 1928–9, he was demoted, but subsequently regained influential positions in the Swiss party. His memoirs and personal archives are a key source for Comintern historians.

Kautsky, Karl (1854–1938). Leading Marxist theoretician of the German Social Democratic Party and Second International before 1914. Founder member of the 'centrist' USPD in 1917. Firm adherent of the democratic road to socialism and fierce adversary of the Bolshevik Revolution and Lenin's interpretation of the 'dictatorship of the proletariat'. Opposed the USPD's entry into the Comintern and rejoined the SPD in 1922.

Kun, Béla (1886–1938). Best known as the leader of the shortlived Hungarian Soviet Republic, 1919. Carried out important functions in the Comintern hierarchy for most of the 1920s and 1930s. Staunch supporter of the 'social fascist' line, 1929–34. Arrested in 1937 as a 'spy' and executed the following year.

Kuusinen, Otto (1881–1964). Finnish communist with close links to the Bolshevik party. Held highly influential positions in the Comintern's Secretariat and Presidium throughout the period 1921–43. Loyal Stalinist, he avoided repression in the terror. Member of the Central Committee of the Soviet party from 1941 until his death.

Lenin (Ulianov), Vladimir Ilich (1870–1924). Russian revolutionary Marxist, leader of the Bolshevik Revolution of October 1917 and main inspiration behind the creation of the Comintern in March 1919. Though he held few official posts in the Comintern, Lenin was its strategic and tactical mentor until his debilitating illness in 1922. His commitment to a strictly centralised organisational model facilitated the subsequent 'Stalinisation' of the International.

Levi, Paul (1883–1930). Socialist lawyer and founder member of the German Communist Party, becoming leader after the murder of Rosa Luxemburg in early 1919. Denounced the party's disastrous 'March Action' of 1921 as a *putsch* and was expelled from the KPD. Joined the German Social Democrats soon after. Committed suicide in 1930.

Manuilsky, Dmitri (1883–1959). Ukrainian revolutionary and member of Bolshevik party from August 1917. Elected to the Comintern's Executive Committee and Presidium in 1924, positions he held until the dissolution of the Comintern in 1943. Loyal adherent of the Stalinist faction and *de facto* head of Comintern, 1929–34. Survived the Terror and after 1945 became a leading member of the Ukrainian government.

Mao Zedong (1893–1976). Founder member of the Chinese Communist Party in 1921. From the late 1920s he argued that peasants, not industrial workers, would form the backbone of the Chinese revolution. Became head of the party during the Long March, 1934–6, and subsequently led the campaigns against the Japanese occupiers in alliance with the nationalist Guomindang. Elected to ECCI *in absentia* in 1935. From 1949 President of the People's Republic of China.

Piatnitsky, Osip (1882–1938). Russian party member since 1898 and close collaborator of Lenin. Long-standing top functionary in the Comintern, responsible for organisational affairs. Supported Stalinist faction in late 1920s and 1930s, but in 1937 opposed the Great Purges and was arrested. Refused to recant and was shot in 1938.

Pollitt, Harry (1890–1960). British communist and trade unionist. Assumed leadership of the CPGB in 1929 as a supporter of the 'left turn', remaining in that position until his forced resignation in October 1939. Returned as General Secretary in 1941. Member of ECCI Presidium from 1931.

Radek, Karl (1885–1939). Revolutionary journalist and propagandist of Polish extraction. Played a significant role in the Comintern from its inception, serving as Moscow's specialist on German affairs. Removed from Comintern leadership in 1924 as a supporter of Trotsky. Recanted and acted as Stalin's adviser on foreign policy in mid-1930s. Arrested in 1937, sentenced to ten years imprisonment and died in the Gulag.

Stalin (Djugashvili), Josef Vissarionovich (1879–1953). Georgian Marxist and long-time member of Bolshevik party. General Secretary of Russian Communist Party from 1922 until his death. In defeating his rivals for power in the RCP, 1923–9, he assumed tight behind-the-scenes control over the Comintern. Developed the concept of 'socialism in one country' and oversaw the subordination of the Comintern to the interests of the Soviet state. Launched murderous attack on Comintern hierarchy and foreign communists in the period 1936–8.

Thälmann, Ernst (1886–1944). German communist and trade unionist. A loyal supporter of the Stalinist faction, he became head of the KPD in 1925. Presided over the disastrous 'social fascist' line which facilitated the Nazi rise to power. Member of Comintern's Presidium, 1924–33. Arrested by the Nazis in 1933, he died in a concentration camp.

Thorez, Maurice (1900–64). Leader of the French Communist Party from 1930 to his death. Faithful adherent of the Stalinist faction, he was a member of the Comintern's Executive Committee from 1928 to 1943. In 1934 he was the first communist to advocate a broad cross-class Popular Front alliance against the threat of fascism.

Togliatti, Palmiro (1893–1964). Founder member of the Italian Communist Party and high-level Comintern functionary, 1924–43. A rather reluctant follower of the Stalinist line in 1928–9, he was nevertheless responsible for purging the 'rightists' from the Italian party. After 1934 was a keen adherent of the Popular Front and implemented this policy during the Spanish Civil War in his capacity as Comintern agent. Leader of the PCI until his death in 1964.

Trotsky (Bronshtein), Lev Davidovich (1879–1940). Famed Russian revolutionary and foremost enemy of the Stalinist regime.

Joined the Bolshevik party in 1917 and organised the seizure of power in Petrograd. Co-founder of the Comintern with Lenin and a leading figure in the ECCI until 1924. Defeated by Stalin in the struggle for Lenin's mantle, he was banished from the USSR in 1929. He maintained a highly critical, and often foresightful, attitude to Comintern tactics during the Third Period. Branded a 'fascist spy' by the Stalinists, he was assassinated by an NKVD agent in Mexico City in 1940.

Zetkin, Clara (1857–1933). Long-standing German social democrat and in 1918 founder member of KPD. Respected figure in the international labour movement both before and after World War I, she occupied leading posts in the Comintern hierarchy from 1921 to 1933. A moderating influence on the 'right wing' of the International, she occasionally clashed with the Stalinists.

Zinoviev, Grigory (1883–1936). Close colleague of Lenin in exile before 1917, becoming the first President of the Comintern in 1919. Generally adopted a 'leftist' standpoint and was partly responsible for inciting the failed revolutionary attempts in Germany in 1921 and 1923. Like Stalin he advocated a firm anti-social democratic stance in the mid-1920s. Removed from his official Comintern positions in 1926 by Stalin and Bukharin, he played no further direct part in the international communist movement. Tried and executed in 1936 after fake Show Trial.

Select Bibliography

In this bibliography we include mainly English language sources. The most relevant Russian works are cited in the notes.

ARCHIVES

Russian Centre for the Preservation and Study of Contemporary Historical Documents, Moscow (formerly the Central Party Archive)

Select material:
fond (collection) 493
opis (inventory) 1 and 2, Sixth Comintern Congress (1928).

fond 495
opis 2,   ECCI Presidium (1919–41).
opis 3,   ECCI Political Secretariat (1926–35).
opis 6,   ECCI Small Commission (1926–33).
opis 18,   ECCI Secretariat (1919–43).
opis 74,   Correspondence between G. Dimitrov and communist party leaders (1934–44).
opis 171,   Thirteenth ECCI Plenum (1933).

fond 508
opis 1,   Minutes of the Meetings of the RCP(B) Delegation in the ECCI (1923–33).

fond 558
opis 1,   Personal fond of Stalin.

Archive of the Communist Party of Great Britain, National Museum of Labour History, Manchester

We consulted microfilmed material returned from the Comintern Archive, including the minutes of Central Committee and Politburo meetings and the minutes of ECCI sessions on the situation in the CPGB; and parts of the Dutt and Klugmann Papers.

COMMUNIST INTERNATIONAL – PRIMARY SOURCES

Fourth Congress of the Communist International. Abridged Report of Meetings held at Petrograd and Moscow, Nov. 7 to Dec. 3, 1922 (London, n.d.).

Resolutions and Theses of the Fourth Congress of the Communist International held in Moscow, Nov. 7 to Dec. 3, 1922 (London, n.d.).

From the Fourth to the Fifth World Congress. Report of the Executive Committee of the Communist International (London, 1924).

Fifth Congress of the Communist International. Abridged Report of Meetings held at Moscow, June 17th to July 8th, 1924 (London, n.d.).

Bolshevising the Communist International. Report of the Enlarged Executive of the Communist International, March 21st to April 14th, 1925 (London, n.d.).

Report on the Activities of the Executive Committee of the Communist International, March–November 1926 (Moscow, 1926).

Communism and the International Situation (New York, 1929).

The World Situation & Economic Struggle. Theses of the Tenth Plenum E.C.C.I. (London, n.d.).

Class against Class. The General Election Programme of the Communist Party of Great Britain 1929 (London, n.d.).

XIth Plenum of the Executive Committee of the Communist International. Theses, Resolutions and Decisions (New York, n.d.).

XII Plenum of the Executive Committee of the Communist International. Theses and Resolutions (Moscow, 1933).

Theses and Decisions. Thirteenth Plenum of the E.C.C.I. (New York, 1934).

VII Congress of the Communist International. Abridged Stenographic Report of Proceedings (Moscow, 1939).

The Second and Third Internationals and the Vienna Union (London, 1922).

Communist Papers. Documents Selected from Those Obtained on the Arrest of Communist Leaders on 14 and 21 October 1925 (London, 1926).

COMMUNIST INTERNATIONAL – JOURNALS

Communist International.
International Press Correspondence (Inprecorr).
World News and Views.

PUBLISHED DOCUMENTARY SOURCES

Adler, A. (ed.), *Theses, Resolutions and Manifestos of the First Four Congresses of the Third International* (London, 1983).

Bahne, S. (ed.), *Archives de Jules Humbert-Droz: Origines et débuts des partis communistes des pays latins, 1919–1923* (Dordrecht, 1970).

Bahne, S. (ed.), *Archives de Jules Humbert-Droz II: Les partis communistes des pays latins et l'Internationale communiste dans les années 1923–1927* (Dordrecht, 1983).

Bahne, S. *et al.* (eds), *Archives de Jules Humbert-Droz III: Les partis communistes et l'Internationale communiste dans les années 1928–1932* (Dordrecht, 1988).

Brandt, C., Schwartz, B. and Fairbank, J. K. (eds), *A Documentary History of Chinese Communism* (New York, 1967).

Daniels, R. V. (ed.), *A Documentary History of Communism*, vol. 2 (London, 1987).

'Defending the Innocent', *World Marxist Review*, no. 7 (1989) pp. 83–6.

Degras, J. (ed.), *The Communist International, 1919–1943. Documents*, 3 vols (London, 1971).

Dimitrov, G., *The Working Class against Fascism* (London, 1935).

Dimitrov, G., *Selected Articles and Speeches* (London, 1951).

Eudin, X. J. and Slusser, R. M. (eds), *Soviet Foreign Policy, 1928–1934: Documents and Materials*, 2 vols (University Park and London, 1967).

Gramsci, A., *Selections from Political Writings 1921–1926*, trans. and ed. by Q. Hoare (London, 1978).

Gruber, H. (ed.), *International Communism in the Era of Lenin. A Documentary History* (New York, 1972).

Gruber, H. (ed.), *Soviet Russia Masters the Comintern: International Communism in the Era of Stalin's Ascendancy* (New York, 1974).

King, F. and Matthews, G. (eds), *About Turn: The British Communist Party and the Second World War* (London, 1990).

Klehr, H., Haynes, J. E. and Firsov, F. I. (eds), *The Secret World of American Communism* (New Haven and London, 1995).

Kun, B. (ed.), *Kommunisticheskii internatsional v dokumentakh* (Moscow, 1933).

Lenin, V. I., *Collected Works*, 4th edn, 45 vols (Moscow, 1960–70).

Lenin, V. I., *Speeches at Congresses of the Communist International* (Moscow, 1972).

Lih, L. T., Naumov, O. V. and Khlevniuk, O. V. (eds), *Stalin's Letters to Molotov, 1925–1936* (New Haven and London, 1995).

Riddell, J. (ed.), *Lenin's Struggle for a Revolutionary International. Documents, 1907–1916: The Preparatory Years* (New York, 1984).

Riddell, J. (ed.), *The German Revolution and the Debate on Soviet Power. Documents: 1918–1919. Preparing the Founding Congress* (New York, 1986).

Riddell, J. (ed.), *Founding the Communist International. Proceedings and Documents of the First Congress: March 1919* (New York, 1987).

Riddell, J. (ed.), *Workers of the World and Oppressed Peoples, Unite! Proceedings and Documents of the Second Congress, 1920*, 2 vols (New York, 1991).

Riddell, J. (ed.), *To See the Dawn. Baku, 1920. First Congress of the Peoples of the East* (New York, 1993).

Stalin, J. V., *Works*, 13 vols (Moscow, 1952–5).

SECONDARY SOURCES

Agnew, J. and McDermott, K., 'Stalin, the Comintern and European Communism, 1934–39', *Modern History Review*, no. 3 (February, 1996) pp. 28–30.

Agosti, A., 'L'historiographie de la Troisième Internationale', *Cahiers d'histoire de l'Institut de recherches marxistes*, no. 2 (1980) pp. 7–59.

Agosti, A., 'World Revolution and the "World Party for the Revolution" ', unpublished manuscript.

Alexander, M. and Graham, H. (eds), *The French and Spanish Popular Fronts: Comparative Perspectives* (Cambridge, 1989).

Anderson, P., *Considerations on Western Marxism* (London, 1976).

Anderson, P., 'Communist Party History', in R. Samuel (ed.), *People's History and Socialist Theory* (London, 1981) pp. 145–56.

Andrews, G., Fishman, N. and Morgan, K. (eds), *Opening the Books: Essays on the Social and Cultural History of the British Communist Party* (London, 1995).

Angress, W. T., *Stillborn Revolution: The Communist Bid for Power in Germany, 1921–1923* (Princeton, 1963).

Banac, I. (ed.), *The Effects of World War I: The Class War after the Great War: The Rise of Communist Parties in East Central Europe, 1918–1921* (New York, 1983).

Beckett, F., *Enemy Within: The Rise and Fall of the British Communist Party* (London, 1995).

Beetham, D., *Marxists in Face of Fascism* (Manchester, 1983).

Benton, G., 'The "Second Wang Ming Line" (1935–38)', *China Quarterly*, no. 61 (1975) pp. 61–94.

Benton, G., 'Two Purged Leaders of Early Chinese Communism', *China Quarterly*, no. 102 (1985) pp. 317–28.

Benton, G., 'Bolshevising China, From Lenin to Stalin to Mao', *Leeds East Asia Papers*, no. 22 (1994) pp. 1–34.

Benton, G., *China's Urban Revolutionaries: Explorations in the History of Chinese Trotskyism, 1921–1952* (New Jersey, 1995).

Bertrand, C. L. (ed.), *Revolutionary Situations in Europe, 1917–1922: Germany, Italy, Austria–Hungary* (Montreal, 1977).

Body, M., 'Reminiscences of the Third International', *Studies on the Soviet Union*, no. 1 (1969) pp. 26–30.

Borkenau, F., *European Communism* (London, 1953).

Borkenau, F., *World Communism. A History of the Communist International*, reprinted edn (Ann Arbor, 1971).

Brandt, C., *Stalin's Failure in China* (New York, 1966).

Branson, N., *History of the Communist Party of Great Britain 1927–1941* (London, 1985).

Braun, O., *A Comintern Agent in China, 1932–1939* (London, 1982).

Braunthal, J., *History of the International, 1914–1943*, vol. 2 (London, 1967).

Buber-Neumann, M., *Under Two Dictators* (London, 1949).

Buber-Neumann, M., *La révolution mondiale* (Tournai, 1971).

Caballero, M., *Latin America and the Comintern, 1919–1943* (Cambridge, 1988).

Calhoun, D. F., *The United Front: The TUC and the Russians, 1923–1928* (Cambridge, 1976).

Cammett, J. M., 'Communist Theories of Fascism, 1920–1935', *Science and Society*, no. 2 (1967) pp. 149–63.

Carr, E. H., *The Bolshevik Revolution, 1917–1923*, vol. 3 (Harmondsworth, 1973).

Carr, E. H., *The Interregnum, 1923–1924* (Harmondsworth, 1969).

Carr, E. H., *Socialism in One Country, 1924–1926*, vol. 3 (Harmondsworth, 1972).

Carr, E. H., *Foundations of a Planned Economy, 1926–1929*, vol. 3, parts I–III (London, 1976–8).

Carr, E. H., *The Twilight of Comintern, 1930–1935* (London, 1982).

Carr, E. H., *The Comintern and the Spanish Civil War* (London, 1984).

Carsten, F. L., *Revolution in Central Europe, 1918–1919* (London, 1972).

Claudin, F., *The Communist Movement: From Comintern to Cominform* (Harmondsworth, 1975).

Claudin, F., 'The October Revolution and the International Communist Movement', *Critique*, nos 10–11 (1978–9) pp. 5–14.

Cohen, S. F., *Bukharin and the Bolshevik Revolution: A Political Biography, 1888–1938* (New York, 1975).

'Comintern Reminiscences: Interview with an Ex-Insider', *Soviet Survey*, no. 32 (1960) pp. 109–15.

Conquest, R., *The Great Terror: A Reassessment* (London, 1992).

Cornell, R., *Revolutionary Vanguard: The Early Years of the Communist Youth International 1914–1924* (Toronto, 1982).

Crossman, R. (ed.), *The God that Failed* (New York, 1965).

D'Agostino, A., *Soviet Succession Struggles: Kremlinology and the Russian Question from Lenin to Gorbachev* (London, 1989).

Davidson, A., *The Theory and Practice of Italian Communism* (London, 1982).

Debo, R. K., *Revolution and Survival: The Foreign Policy of Soviet Russia, 1917–18* (Liverpool, 1979).

Degras, J., 'Revisiting the Comintern', *Soviet Survey*, no. 33 (1960) pp. 38–47.

Degras, J., 'United Front Tactics in the Comintern, 1921–1928', in D. Footman (ed.), *International Communism*, St Antony's Papers, no. 9 (London, 1960) pp. 9–22.

Deutscher, I., *The Prophet Unarmed. Trotsky: 1921–1929* (Oxford and London, 1970).

Deutscher, I., *The Prophet Outcast. Trotsky: 1929–1940* (Oxford and London, 1963).

Deutscher, I., *Marxism in Our Time* (London, 1972).

Deutscher, I., *Stalin: A Political Biography*, rev. edn (Harmondsworth, 1976).

Djilas, M., *Conversations with Stalin* (Harmondsworth, 1969).

Djilas, M., *Memoirs of a Revolutionary* (New York, 1973).

Donald, M., *Marxism and Revolution. Karl Kautsky and the Russian Marxists 1900–1924* (New Haven and London, 1993).

Drachkovitch, M. M. (ed.), *The Revolutionary Internationals, 1864–1943* (Stanford, 1966).

Drachkovitch, M. M. and Lazitch, B. (eds), *The Comintern: Historical Highlights. Essays, Recollections, Documents* (New York, 1966).

Draper, T., *The Roots of American Communism* (New York, 1966).

Draper, T., *American Communism and Soviet Russia* (New York, 1986).

Draper, T., 'The Ghost of Social-Fascism', *Commentary*, no. 2 (1969) pp. 29–42.

Draper, T., 'The Strange Case of the Comintern', *Survey*, no. 3 (1972) pp. 91–137.

Eley, G., 'International Communism in the Heyday of Stalin', *New Left Review*, no. 157 (1986) pp. 90–100.

Esenwein, G. and Shubert, A., *Spain at War: The Spanish Civil War in Context, 1931–1939* (London, 1995).

Ex-Insider, 'The Party that Vanished', *Soviet Survey*, no. 33 (1960) pp. 100–6.

Fainsod, M., *International Socialism and the World War* (New York, 1969).

Firsov, F. I., 'What the Comintern's Archives Will Reveal', *World Marxist Review*, no. 1 (1989) pp. 52–7.

Firsov, F. I., 'The VKP(b) and the Communist International', unpublished manuscript.

Firsov, F., 'Lenin's Concept of a World Communist Party and the Development of the Comintern', unpublished manuscript.

Fischer, C., *The German Communists and the Rise of Nazism* (London, 1991).

Fischer, C., 'Class Enemies or Class Brothers? Communist–Nazi Relations in Germany 1929–33', *European History Quarterly*, no. 3 (1985) pp. 259–79.

Fischer, E., *An Opposing Man* (London, 1974).

Fischer, R., *Stalin and German Communism* (Cambridge, MA, 1948).

Fishman, N., *The British Communist Party and the Trade Unions, 1933–1945* (London, 1995).

Fitzpatrick, S., 'The Foreign Threat during the First Five-Year Plan', *Soviet Union/Union Soviétique*, no. 1 (1978) pp. 26–35.

Fowkes, B., *Communism in Germany under the Weimar Republic* (London, 1984).

Fowkes, B., 'The Origins of Czechoslovak Communism', *European Studies Review*, no. 3 (1971) pp. 249–74.

Francis, H., *Miners against Fascism: Wales and the Spanish Civil War* (London, 1984).

Frank, P., *Histoire de l'Internationale communiste, 1919–1943*, 2 vols (Paris, 1979).

Freymond, J. (ed.), *Contributions à l'histoire du Comintern* (Geneva, 1965).

Frieden, J., 'The International Politics of European Communism in the Stalin Era, 1934–39', *Studies in Comparative Communism*, no. 1 (1981) pp. 45–69.

Gankin, O., 'The Bolsheviks and the Founding of the Third International', *Slavonic and East European Review*, vol. 20 (1941) pp. 88–101.

Gankin, O. and Fisher, H., *The Bolsheviks and the World War: The Origins of the Third International* (Stanford, 1940).

Garver, J., 'The Origins of the Second United Front: The Comintern and the Chinese Communist Party', *China Quarterly*, no. 113 (1988) pp. 29–59.

Geary, D., *European Labour Protest 1848–1939* (London, 1984).

Geary, D., *European Labour Politics from 1900 to the Depression* (Basingstoke, 1991).

Gelb, M., ' "Karelian Fever": The Finnish Immigrant Community during Stalin's Purges', *Europe–Asia Studies*, no. 6 (1993) pp. 1091–116.

Getty, J. A. and Manning, R. T. (eds), *Stalinist Terror: New Perspectives* (Cambridge, 1993).

Graham, H. and Preston, P. (eds), *The Popular Front in Europe* (Basingstoke, 1987).

Gruber, H., *Léon Blum, French Socialism, and the Popular Front: A Case of Internal Contradictions* (Ithaca, 1986).

Hájek, M., *Jednotná fronta. K politické orientaci Komunistické internacionály v letech 1921–1935* (Prague, 1969).

Harding, N., *Lenin's Political Thought*, 2 vols (Basingstoke, 1977 and 1981).

Haslam, J., *Soviet Foreign Policy, 1930–1933. The Impact of the Great Depression* (London, 1983).

Haslam, J., *The Soviet Union and the Struggle for Collective Security in Europe, 1933–1939* (London, 1984).

Haslam, J., 'The Comintern and the Origins of the Popular Front 1934–1935', *Historical Journal*, no. 3 (1979) pp. 673–91.

Haslam, J., 'Political Opposition to Stalin and the Origins of the Terror in Russia, 1932–1936', *Historical Journal*, no. 2 (1986) pp. 395–418.

Hobsbawm, E. J., *Revolutionaries: Contemporary Essays* (London, 1982).

Hobsbawm, E. J., 'The "Moscow Line" and International Communist Policy, 1933–47', in C. Wrigley (ed.), *Warfare, Diplomacy and Politics. Essays in Honour of A. J. P. Taylor* (London, 1986) pp. 163–88.

Hobsbawm, E. J., 'Working-class Internationalism', in F. van Holthoon and M. van der Linden (eds), *Internationalism and the Labour Movement, 1830–1940*, vol. 1 (Leiden, 1988) pp. 3–16.

Hobsbawm, E., *Age of Extremes. The Short Twentieth Century, 1914–1991* (London, 1994).

Hochman, J., *The Soviet Union and the Failure of Collective Security, 1934–1938* (Ithaca and London, 1984).

Hoisington, W. A., 'Class against Class: The French Communist Party and the Comintern', *International Review of Social History*, no. 1 (1970) pp. 19–42.

Howkins, A., 'Class against Class: The Political Culture of the Communist Party of Great Britain, 1930–35', in F. Gloversmith (ed.), *Class, Culture and Social Change: A New View of the 1930s* (Brighton, 1980) pp. 240–57.

Huber, P., 'L'appareil du Komintern 1926–1935: premier aperçu', *Communisme*, nos 40–1 (1995) pp. 9–35.

Huber, P. and Bayerlein, B. H., 'Première esquisse des structures répressives du Komintern. Le cas des communistes suisses à Moscou', *Communisme*, nos 32–34 (1993) pp. 147–76.

Hulse, J. W., *The Forming of the Communist International* (Stanford, 1964).

Humbert-Droz, J., *De Lénine à Staline: Dix ans au service de l'Internationale communiste, 1921–1931* (Neuchâtel, 1971).

Humbert-Droz, J., *Dix ans de lutte anti-fasciste, 1931–1941* (Neuchâtel, 1972).

Humbert-Droz, J., *Le couronnement d'une vie de combat, 1941–1971* (Neuchâtel, 1973).

Hung-yok Ip, 'The Origins of Chinese Communism: A New Interpretation', *Modern China*, no. 1 (1994) pp. 34–63.

Jackson, G., *Comintern and Peasant in East Europe, 1919–1930* (New York, 1966).

Jackson, J., *The Popular Front in France. Defending Democracy, 1934–1938* (Cambridge, 1988).

Jacobson, J., *When the Soviet Union Entered World Politics* (Berkeley and London, 1994).

James, C. L. R., *World Revolution, 1917–36: The Rise and Fall of the Communist International* (London, 1937).

Johnstone, M., 'Introduction', in F. King and G. Matthews (eds), *About Turn: The British Communist Party and the Second World War* (London, 1990) pp. 13–49.

Johnstone, M., 'The CPGB, the Comintern and the War 1939–1941: Filling in the Blank Spots', *Science and Society* (forthcoming winter-97).

Judt, T. (ed.), *Resistance and Revolution in Mediterranean Europe 1939–1948* (London, 1989).

Kahan, V. (ed.), *Bibliography of the Communist International (1919–1979)*, vol. 1 (Leiden, 1990).

Kahan, V., 'The Communist International, 1919–43: The Personnel of its Highest Bodies', *International Review of Social History*, no. 2 (1976) pp. 151–85.

Kahan, V., 'A Contribution to the Identification of the Pseudonyms used in the Minutes and Reports of the Communist International', *International Review of Social History*, no. 2 (1978) pp. 177–92.

Kemp-Welch, A. (ed.), *The Ideas of Nikolai Bukharin* (Oxford, 1992).

Kirby, D., *War, Peace and Revolution: International Socialism at the Crossroads, 1914–1918* (New York, 1986).

Kitchen, M., *Fascism* (London, 1976).

Klehr, H., *The Heyday of American Communism. The Depression Decade* (New York, 1984).

Kolakowski, L., *Main Currents of Marxism*, vol. 3 (Oxford, 1981).

Kozlov, N. N. and Weitz, E. D., 'Reflections on the Origins of the "Third Period": Bukharin, the Comintern and the Political Economy of Weimar Germany', *Journal of Contemporary History*, no. 3 (1989) pp. 387–410.

Kozlov, N. N. and Weitz, E. D. (eds), *Nikolai Ivanovich Bukharin: A Centenary Appraisal* (New York, 1990).

Kriegel, A., 'La dissolution du "Komintern" ', *Revue d'histoire de la deuxième guerre mondiale*, (October, 1967) pp. 33–43.

Krivitsky, W. G., *I Was Stalin's Agent* (London, 1939).

Kudriashov, S., 'The Central Committee of the All-Union Communist Party and Eastern Europe, 1945–1953', unpublished manuscript.

Kuo, W., *Analytical History of the Chinese Communist Party*, 4 vols (Taibei, 1968–71).

Kuusinen, A., *Before and After Stalin* (London, 1974).

Laqueur, W., *Stalin: The Glasnost Revelations* (London, 1990).

Lazitch, B., 'La formation de la section des liaisons internationales du Komintern (OMS) 1921–1923', *Communisme*, no. 4 (1983) pp. 65–80.

Lazitch, B., 'The Founding of the Comintern: Letters from Souvarine to Zinoviev', *Survey*, no. 4 (1989) pp. 175–88.

Lazitch, B. and Drachkovitch, M. M., *Lenin and the Comintern*, vol. 1 (Stanford, 1972).

Lazitch, B. and Drachkovitch, M. M., *Biographical Dictionary of the Comintern: New, Revised and Expanded Edition* (Stanford, 1986).

Leonhard, W., *Child of the Revolution* (London, 1957).

Liebman, M., *Leninism under Lenin* (London, 1980).

Lindemann, A. S., *The "Red Years": European Socialism versus Bolshevism, 1919–1921* (Berkeley, 1974).

Lowenthal, R., 'The Rise and Decline of International Communism', *Problems of Communism*, no. 2 (1963) pp. 19–31.

Luk, M. Y. L., *The Origins of Chinese Bolshevism: An Ideology in the Making, 1920–1928* (Oxford, 1990).

Macintyre, S., *Little Moscows: Communism and Working-class Militancy in Interwar Britain* (London, 1980).

Martin, R., *Communism and the British Trade Unions 1924–1933* (Oxford, 1969).

McDermott, K., *The Czech Red Unions, 1918–1929: A Study of their Relations with the Communist Party and the Moscow Internationals* (Boulder/New York, 1988).

McDermott, K., 'Rethinking the Comintern: Soviet Historiography, 1987–1991', *Labour History Review*, no. 3 (1992) pp. 37–58.

McDermott, K., 'Stalinist Terror in the Comintern: New Perspectives', *Journal of Contemporary History*, no. 1 (1995) pp. 111–30.

McDermott, K., 'Stalin and the Comintern during the "Third Period", 1928–33', *European History Quarterly*, no. 3 (1995) pp. 409–29.

McKenzie, K., *The Comintern and World Revolution, 1928–1943* (New York, 1963).

Medvedev, R., *Leninism and Western Socialism* (London, 1981).

Medvedev, R., *Let History Judge*, rev. edn (New York and Oxford, 1989).

Melograni, P., *Lenin and the Myth of World Revolution* (Atlantic Highlands, 1989).

Molnár, M., *From Béla Kun to János Kádár: Seventy Years of Hungarian Communism* (New York and Oxford, 1990).

Morgan, K., *Against Fascism and War: Ruptures and Continuities in British Communist Politics, 1935–41* (Manchester, 1989).

Morgan, K., *Harry Pollitt* (Manchester, 1993).

Mortimer, E., *The Rise of the French Communist Party, 1920–1947* (London, 1984).

Nation, R. C., *War on War: Lenin, the Zimmerwald Left, and the Origins of Communist Internationalism* (Durham and London, 1989).

Nollau, G., *International Communism and World Revolution* (London, 1961).

North, R. C., *Moscow and Chinese Communists* (Stanford, 1963).

Ottanelli, F. M., *The Communist Party of the United States: From the Depression to World War II* (New Brunswick, 1991).

Pantéleiev, M., 'Les "Purges" staliniennes au sein du Komintern en 1937–1938: quelques repères sociologiques', *Matériaux pour l'histoire de notre temps*, no. 34 (1994) pp. 24–5.

Panteleiev, M., 'La terreur stalinienne au Komintern en 1937–1938: les chiffres et les causes', *Communisme*, nos 40–1 (1995) pp. 37–52.

Peterson, L., 'From Social Democracy to Communism', *International Labor and Working-Class History*, no. 20 (1981). pp. 7–30.

Phillips, H. D., *Between the Revolution and the West: A Political Biography of Maxim M. Litvinov* (Boulder, 1992).

Pike, D. W., 'Between the Junes: The French Communists from the Collapse of France to the Invasion of Russia', *Journal of Contemporary History*, no. 3 (1993) pp. 465–85.

Poulantzas, N., *Fascism and Dictatorship. The Third International and the Problem of Fascism* (London, 1974).

Roberts, G., *The Soviet Union and the Origins of the Second World War* (Basingstoke, 1995).

Robrieux, P., *Histoire intérieur du parti communiste, 1920–1945* (Paris, 1980).

Rosenfeldt, N. E., *Stalin's Secret Chancellery and the Comintern* (Copenhagen, 1991).

Rosenhaft, E., *Beating the Fascists? The German Communists and Political Violence, 1929–1933* (Cambridge, 1983).

Rosenhaft, E., 'Communisms and Communities: Britain and Germany between the Wars', *Historical Journal*, no. 1 (1983) pp. 221–36.

Rosmer, A., *Moscow under Lenin* (New York and London, 1971).

Rupnik, J., *Histoire du Parti communiste tchécoslovaque: des origines à la prise du pouvoir* (Paris, 1981).

Saich, T., *The Origins of the First United Front in China: The Role of Sneevliet (Alias Maring)*, 2 vols (Leiden, 1991).

Santore, J. F., 'The Comintern's United Front Initiative of May 1934: French or Soviet Inspiration?' *Canadian Journal of History*, no. 3 (1981) pp. 405–21.

Schwarzmantel, J., *Socialism and the Idea of the Nation* (London, 1991).

Serge, V., *Memoirs of a Revolutionary, 1901–1941* (Oxford, 1967).

Service, R., *Lenin: A Political Life*, 2 vols (Basingstoke, 1985 and 1991).

Shirinia, K., 'The Time of Hard Decisions', Novosti Press Agency (London, 1989).

Shum, K., *The Chinese Communists' Road to Power: The Anti-Japanese National United Front, 1935–1945* (Oxford, 1988).

Sirkov, D., 'On the Policy of the Communist International on the Eve and at the Beginning of World War II', *Jahrbuch für Historische Kommunismusforschung* (Berlin, 1995) pp. 52–62.

Sobolev, A. I. *et al.*, *Outline History of the Communist International* (Moscow, 1971).

Spriano, P., *Stalin and the European Communists* (London, 1985).

Starkov, B. A., 'The Trial that Was Not Held', *Europe–Asia Studies*, no. 8 (1994) pp. 1297–315.

Stern, G., *The Rise and Decline of International Communism* (Aldershot, 1990).

Studer, B., 'La réorganisation du CE de l'IC en octobre 1935', *International Newsletter of Historical Studies on Comintern, Communism and Stalinism*, nos 3–4 (1993–4) pp. 25–30.

Studer, B., *Un parti sous influence: Le Parti communiste suisse, une section du Komintern 1931 à 1939* (Lausanne, 1994).

Sturmthal, A., *The Tragedy of European Labour, 1918–1939* (London, 1944).

Suda, Z., *Zealots and Rebels: A History of the Ruling Communist Party of Czechoslovakia* (Stanford, 1980).

Svátek, F., 'The Governing Organs of the Communist International: Their Growth and Composition, 1919–1943', *History of Socialism Yearbook 1968* (Prague, 1969) pp. 179–266.

Sworakowski, W. S., *The Communist International and its Front Organizations* (Stanford, 1965).

Sylvers, M., 'American Communists in the Popular Front Period: Reorganization or Disorganization?', *Journal of American Studies*, no. 3 (1989) pp. 375–93.

Thompson, W., *The Good Old Cause: British Communism 1920–1991* (London, 1992).

Tiersky, R., *French Communism, 1920–1972* (New York and London, 1974).

Togliatti, P., 'History of the Communist International – Some Problems', *World Marxist Review*, no. 11 (1959) pp. 41–51.

Tomita, T., 'Comintern Reconsidered under Perestroika', unpublished paper.

Trotsky, L., *The First Five Years of the Communist International*, 2 vols (New York, 1972).

Trotsky, L., *The Third International After Lenin* (New York, 1970).

Trotsky, L., *The Struggle against Fascism in Germany* (New York, 1971).

Trotsky, L., *The Revolution Betrayed* (New York, 1970).

Tucker, R. C., *Stalin as Revolutionary 1879–1929* (New York, 1974).

Tucker, R. C., *Stalin in Power: The Revolution from Above, 1928–1941* (New York, 1990).

Tucker, R. C., 'The Emergence of Stalin's Foreign Policy', *Slavic Review*, no. 4 (1977) pp. 563–89.

Tuominen, A., *The Bells of the Kremlin* (Hanover and London, 1983).

Uldricks, T. J., *Diplomacy and Ideology: The Origins of Soviet Foreign Relations, 1917–1930* (London and Beverly Hills, 1979).

Uldricks, T. J., 'Stalin and Nazi Germany', *Slavic Review*, no. 4 (1977) pp. 599–603.

Urban, J. B., *Moscow and the Italian Communist Party* (London, 1986).

Vaksberg, A., *Hôtel Lux: Les partis frères au service de l'internationale communiste* (Paris, 1993).

Valtin, J., *Out of the Night* (London, 1988).

van de Ven, H. J., *From Friend to Comrade: The Founding of the Chinese Communist Party, 1920–1927* (Berkeley, 1991).

Vatlin, A., 'On the Verge of the Break: Trotsky and the Comintern in 1928', in T. Brotherstone and P. Dukes (eds), *The Trotsky Reappraisal* (Edinburgh, 1992) pp. 53–69.

Vatlin, A., 'Test Ground of World Revolution: Comintern in Germany in the 1920s', unpublished manuscript.

Volkogonov, D., *Stalin: Triumph and Tragedy* (London, 1991).

Volkogonov, D., *Lenin: Life and Legacy* (London, 1995).

Waller, M., *Democratic Centralism: An Historical Commentary* (Manchester, 1981).

Waters, E., 'In the Shadow of the Comintern: The Communist Women's Movement, 1920–43', in S. Kruks *et al.* (eds), *Promissory Notes: Women in the Transition to Socialism* (New York, 1989) pp. 29–56.

Weitz, E. D., 'State Power, Class Fragmentation, and the Shaping of German Communist Politics, 1890–1933', *Journal of Modern History*, no. 2 (1990) pp. 253–97.

Westoby, A., *The Evolution of Communism* (Oxford, 1989).

White, J. D., 'National Communism and World Revolution: The Political Consequences of German Military Withdrawal from the Baltic Area in 1918–19', *Europe–Asia Studies*, no. 8 (1994) pp. 1349–69.

White, S., 'Communism and the East: The Baku Congress, 1920', *Slavic Review*, no. 2 (1974) pp. 492–514.

Wickham, J., 'Social Fascism and the Division of the Working Class Movement: Workers and Political Parties in the Frankfurt Area 1929/1930', *Capital and Class*, no. 7 (1979) pp. 1–34.

Wickham, J., 'Working-class Movement and Working-class Life: Frankfurt am Main during the Weimar Republic', *Social History*, no. 4 (1983) pp. 315–43.

Wilbur, C. M. and How, J. L., *Missionaries of Revolution: Soviet Advisers and Nationalist China, 1920–1927* (Cambridge, MA, 1989).

Wohl, R., *French Communism in the Making, 1914–1924* (Stanford, 1966).

Wolikow, S. and Cordillot, M. (eds), *Prolétaires de tous les pays, unissez-vous? Les difficiles chemins de l'internationalisme, 1848–1956,* (Dijon, 1993).

Woodhouse, M. and Pearce, B., *Essays on the History of Communism in Britain* (London, 1975).

Wrigley, C. (ed.), *Challenges of Labour: Central and Western Europe, 1917–1920* (London, 1993).

Index

labour movement crushed, 81,
112, 117, 121
'March Action' (1921), 25, 28, 30
Nazi repression in, 68
'November Revolution' (1918),
1, 11
October revolution (1923), 37–8,
41, 44–5, 215, 231
peace terms with USSR
(1918–18), 9–10
reparations reduced, 100
social democracy condemned in,
71
and united front, 34
working class divisions, 109–10
see also Weimar Republic
Girault (of French CP), 57
Gitlow, B., 88
glasnost, 43, 143, 213
Gorbachev, Mikhail, 43, 213
Göring, Hermann, 124
Gottwald, Klement, 72, 102, 108,
122, 127, 250
Gramsci, Antonio, 20, 60, 110,
216, 219, 250–1
Great Depression, 96, 105, 107,
109, 115
Great Patriotic War *see* Second
World War
Great Terror *see* Terror
Great War (1914–18)
effects, 215
outbreak, 5
Greece: invaded by Germans, 202
Gruber, H., 48
Guangdong, 170
Guangzhou, 167, 170–1, 173–4,
179
Gulag system (labour camps), 144
Guomindang (China)
and agrarian revolution, 176
authority and government
(Wuhan), 172, 175–6, 178–9
CCP seeks overthrow of, 183–4
Comintern urges purge of, 177
communists expelled from, 171,
177
divisions in, 170–1, 178

ECCI hostility to, 183, 186
ends united front with
communists, 175, 180
First Congress (1924), 169
Li misinterprets, 182
military conflict with CCP, 180
military successes, 173–4, 185–6
nature of, 164
recognised by ECCI, 179
and revolution, 169, 182, 237
Second Congress (1926), 171
and Soviet advisers and support,
169, 172–4
Soviet alliance with, 55, 70
united fronts with Chinese
Communist Party, 165–8,
169, 171–4, 177–9, 187–8,
190, 224
'white terror', 185
Guttmann, Josef, 108

Hájek, Miloš, 93
Hallas, Duncan, xxii
Halle Congress (KPD; 1920), 19
Hannington, Wal, 104
Haslam, Jonathan, 129, 153–4, 156
Hilferding, Rudolf, 156
Hindenburg, General Paul, 102
Hitler, Adolf
aggressive ambitions, 128
aids Franco, 139
anti-democratic bellicosity, 116
invades Poland, 155
and Nazi–Soviet Pact, 198
peace offers, 200
rise to power, 82, 92, 109, 111,
114, 124
Soviet tolerance of, 202
SPD opposes, 102
Hobsbawm, Eric, 59–61, 130
Holland: communist party
founded, 11
Hong Kong, 170
Horner, Arthur, 203
Huangpu (Whampao) Military
Academy, 169
Humbert-Droz, Jules
acts for Comintern, 56